D1807667

State and Society in Early Modern Austria

State and Society in

Early Modern Austria

edited by

Charles W. Ingrao

Purdue University Press

West Lafayette, Indiana

Copyright ©1994 by Purdue Research Foundation. All rights reserved.

98   97   96   95   94   5   4   3   2   1

The paper used in this book meets the minimum requirements of American National Standard for Information Sciences—Permanence of Paper for Printed Library Materials, ANSI Z39.48-1984.

Printed in the United States of America
Design by Anita Noble

Library of Congress Cataloging-in-Publication Data
    State and society in early modern Austria / edited by Charles W. Ingrao.
      p. cm.
    Includes bibliographical references and index.
    ISBN 1-55753-048-3 (alk. paper)
      1. Austria—Politics and government—16th century. 2. Austria—
Politics and government—17th century. 3. Habsburg, House of. 4. Holy Roman Empire—History—1517–1648. 5. Holy Roman Empire—History—1648–1804. I. Ingrao, Charles W.
    DB65.5.S73 1994
    943.6'03—dc20   93-33879
                                                      CIP

In memoriam

Volker Press
(1939–1993)

Our friend and colleague Volker Press died of a heart attack on 18 October 1993 at the age of fifty-four. The great number of people who knew him mourn the passing not only of an eminent scholar but of a wonderful human being. While we are saddened by his death, we greet the opportunity to dedicate this volume to his memory.

Born on 28 March 1939 in Erding bei München, Press was educated at the University of Munich. After teaching at Kiel and Frankfurt (1967–71), he was named to the chair in modern history at Gießen in 1971 at the unusually early age of thirty-two. Nine years later, he succeeded to the chair for medieval and early modern history at Tübingen, a position that he held until his death.

While Volker Press had many interests, he was best known as a leading authority on the Holy Roman Empire. He contributed greatly to our understanding of the multilayered political relationships of the empire, ranging from local corporate elites, to the innumerable territorial states, to the German dominions and emperors of the house of Habsburg. His first monograph, *Calvinismus und Territorialstaat: Regierung und Zentralbehörden der Kurpfalz 1559–1619* (1970) was such a tour de force of archival scholarship that it prompted his appointment at Gießen, even before the completion his masterful *Habilitationsschrift* on the imperial knights. After moving to Tübingen in 1981, Press attracted a school of young scholars who undertook a long series of important research projects on the empire's history. Some of their contributions appeared in a half-dozen collections that he edited, as well as in his own *Kriege und Krisen: Deutschland 1600–1715* (1991). Over the past decade, he also played a vital role in helping us to organize two international colloquia on the Holy Roman Empire, in Chicago (1984) and Mainz (1986), as well as the third meeting, in Minneapolis (1991), which is represented in this volume.

Press had other scholarly interests as well. Throughout his life, he stayed close to his birthplace, writing numerous articles on the history of Erding and of his native Bavaria. He also devoted himself to examining the history of that last vestige of the old *Reich,* the principality of Liechtenstein; among the fruits of his labor were his *Liechtenstein: Fürstliches Haus und Staatliche Ordnung* (1988), his admission to the principality's Liechtenstein Institute, and his personal friendship with its ruling family.

In addition to several books, Volker Press has left behind well over two hundred articles that also bear witness to his tremendous energy and enthusiasm for the pursuit of historical knowledge, especially archival research. His favorite workplace was the Vienna State Archives, the destination of lengthy *Archivreisen* that he undertook virtually every summer over the past two decades. Yet his research took him to repositories all over Central Europe. Nobody knew more about the history, the archives, or the princely residences of the empire's *Kleinstaaterei.* And nobody was more in demand for contributions to scholarly conferences and collections.

Press was no less indefatigable as a friend and colleague. Thanks to his Bavarian temperament, his ready appreciation of the joys of life, and his talent for friendship, his fierce commitment to scholarship never cut him off from the personal contacts he loved so much. Numerous appointments attest to the faith that his colleagues had in his discretion, judgment, and collegiality. He served as *Dekan* of the history faculty at both Gießen (1975–76) and Tübingen (1983–85). He was named to countless historical commissions, journals, and academic institutions all over Central Europe. Among those he helped most were graduate students and younger scholars, for whom he worked doggedly to find positions in a finite and fiercely competitive academic job market.

In 1993 he had been named director of the Institute for European History in Mainz (Abteilung Universalgeschichte). The institute would have served as an ideal vehicle for a man of his creative energies. Alas, before he had formally accepted the position, death took the pen from his hand.

Karl Otmar, Freiherr von Aretin

Charles W. Ingrao

Contents

xii **Map: The Habsburg Monarchy, 1740**

xv **Preface**

1 **Introduction**
State and Society in Early Modern Austria
R. J. W. Evans

Part 1
Religion in the Counter-Reformation

27 **Introduction**
Paula Sutter Fichtner

36 **Confessional Absolutism in the
Habsburg Lands in the Seventeenth Century**
Robert Bireley, S.J.

54 **Delayed Confessionalization**
Retarding Factors and
Religious Minorities in the Territories of
the Holy Roman Empire, 1555–1648
Anton Schindling

71 **The Jews and the Emperors**
R. Po-chia Hsia

Part 2
Government and Culture during the Baroque

83 **Introduction**
Nicolette Mout

93　**The Imperial Hofburg**
　　The Theory and Practice of Architectural
　　Representation in Baroque Vienna
　　　Hellmut Lorenz

110　**Status as Commodity**
　　The Habsburg Economy of Privilege
　　　John P. Spielman

119　**Public Opinion and the Phenomenon of**
　　Sozialdisziplinierung **in the Habsburg Monarchy**
　　　Karl Vocelka

Part 3
Government and Economy

141　**Introduction**
　　　Herman Freudenberger

154　**Between East and West**
　　Lower Austria's Noble *Grundherrschaft,* 1550–1750
　　　Herbert Knittler

181　**Between Mercantilism and Physiocracy**
　　Stages, Modes, and Functions of Economic Theory in
　　the Habsburg Monarchy, 1748–63
　　　Grete Klingenstein

215　**Austria and European Economic Development**
　　What Has Been Learned?
　　　John Komlos

Part 4
Government and the People during the *Aufklärung*

229　**Introduction**
　　　James Van Horn Melton

238　**Poverty and Poor Relief in**
　　the Eighteenth Century
　　　Paul P. Bernard

252   **"Libertas commerciorum" or "Moral Economy"?**
The Austrian *Vorlande* in the Famine of the 1770s
  Georg Schmidt

Part 5
Foreign Policy

275   **Introduction**
  Charles W. Ingrao

286   **International Relations,**
the Law of Nations, and the Germanies
Structures and Changes in
the Second Half of the Seventeenth Century
  Heinz Duchhardt

298   **Austria and the Rise of Brandenburg-Prussia**
  Volker Press

312   **Reform and Diplomacy in the**
Eighteenth-Century Habsburg Monarchy
  Karl A. Roider, Jr.

325   **Contributors**

329   **Index**

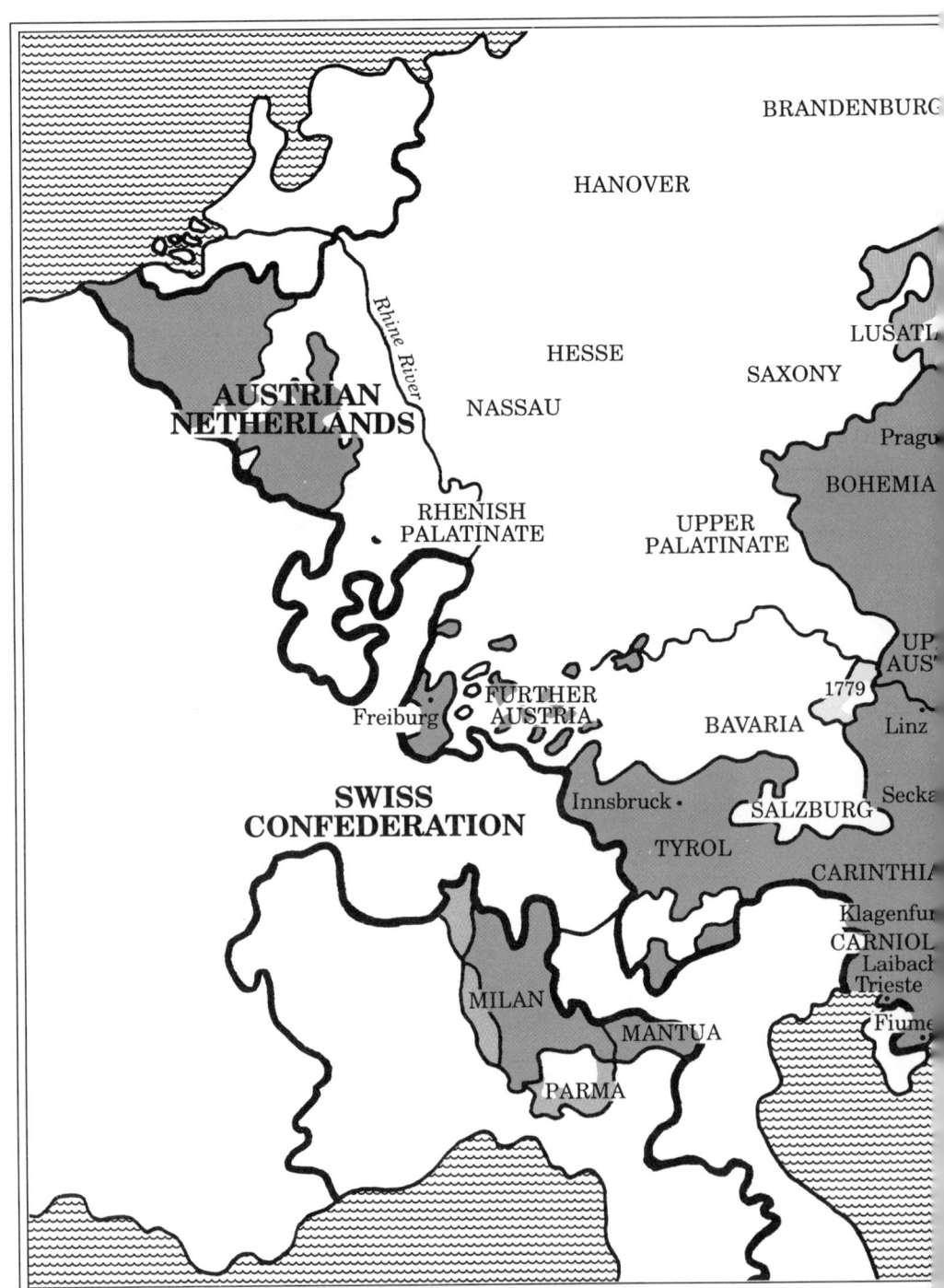

Map   xiii

The Habsburg Monarchy, 1740

━━━ Holy Roman Empire

Losses before 1740

Gains after 1740

POLAND

Breslau

SILESIA

Troppau

Olmütz

MORAVIA

Brno

LOWER
AUSTRIA

Vienna

Bruck

Graz

TYRIA

Danube River

Ofen

Pest

GALICIA
1772

Tisza River

BUKOVINA
1775

HUNGARY

Maros River

TRANSYLVANIA

BACHKA

Temesvár

BANAT

CROATIA

VOJVODINA

WALLACHIA

Belgrade

BOSNIA

SERBIA

OTTOMAN EMPIRE

Preface

The articles published in this volume stem from an international colloquium of historians of early modern Central Europe hosted by the Minneapolis campus of the University of Minnesota on 3–5 October 1991 and jointly sponsored by the centers for Austrian Studies and Early Modern History. It represented the third in an ongoing series of meetings that has brought together some of the Atlantic community's leading authorities of early modern Central Europe. The previous two colloquia, at the University of Chicago in April 1984 and at the Institut für Europäische Geschichte in Mainz in September 1986, focused on the lands and peoples of the Holy Roman Empire. As planners for the third colloquium, my colleague Karl Otmar Freiherr von Aretin and I decided to indulge our interests in the Austrian Habsburg Monarchy.

There were several justifications for our decision. Whereas the resurgence of scholarly interest in the Holy Roman Empire is of relatively recent origin, the Habsburg Monarchy has attracted the attention of numerous historians throughout this century. With the end of the Cold War and the resulting turmoil in East Central Europe, that interest is likely to intensify as Western observers try to understand the region's complex cultural heritage. Of course, in the first half century after the monarchy's demise, historians tended to concentrate on its political and diplomatic history. By contrast, a new generation of American and European historians is now exploring the monarchy's economic, social, and cultural history. The colloquium and especially this volume reflect these developments. Although the role of the Habsburg regime is still evident in the essays that appear in this volume, they now stress the interplay between government and society rather than between that government and its principal political protagonists, foreign or domestic.

Editing a scholarly collection inevitably calls to mind the adage about a chain being only as strong as its weakest link. I am thankful that this volume's contributors were as good as they were at keeping the publication process on course by meeting the numerous schedule deadlines. We are all grateful to David Good and the University of Minnesota's Center for Austrian Studies for providing such a marvelous platform for the original colloquium. The Austrian Cultural Institute was most generous in funding a significant portion of the publication costs. I appreciate the assistance of the authors of the first four introductory essays—Paula Sutter Fichtner, Nicolette Mout, Herman Freudenberger, and James Van Horn Melton—each of whom made valuable editorial suggestions for their respective sections of the book. Certainly I am more fortunate than most Central European historians in having an editor, Margaret Hunt, whose doctorate in German and certifiably Germanic attention to detail rendered my own work both much easier and better. Her achievements in developing the Purdue University Press's series in Balkan and Danubian studies have served far more Habsburg historians than the twenty whose work appears in this volume.

Introduction

State and Society in Early Modern Austria

R. J. W. Evans

The terms in our title are deceptively straightforward. In order to relate the notion of "Austria" to either "state" or "society" in Central Europe between the sixteenth and the eighteenth centuries, the historian must enter the realm of the ineffable. "Austria" was a house, or dynasty; in its territorial sense, it connoted either a limited tract of land along the Danube, where that dynasty had ruled since the High Middle Ages, or else a much broader and miscellaneous assemblage of lands that recognized the sovereignty of the dynasty, but whose inhabitants did not necessarily think of themselves as in any sense "Austrian," even after 1804, when the house of Habsburg assumed the title of "emperors of Austria." Until 1806 some of these lands lay within and some without the Holy Roman Empire, over the whole of which the Habsburgs also possessed certain attributes of sovereignty. The empire, or *Reich,* was a slightly clearer entity than "Austria," but only marginally so. It, too, was amenable to a style of rule that throve on territorial and constitutional imprecision, for a degree of vagueness might suit imperial pretensions, and mitigate objections to them.

In these circumstances, neither state nor society could stand in an unequivocal relationship to the ruler, or to each other. In speaking of the state at all, we risk anachronism. The Habsburg *Staat* was for a long time essentially the *Hofstaat,* the court administration, and that formed a composite authority. Whereas it might come to

operate on a single site, it involved both superimposed and inter-
locking instances, some imperial and some nonimperial, each formally separate and jealously guarding its rights. Rule over, or
rather through, such a state also involved endless bargaining with
local vested interests inside or outside explicitly constitutional
structures.[1]

Society, the object of government, was still more obviously dis-
parate. It consisted of an agglomeration of distinct dominions that
were in one sense equidistant from the source of political authority
but in other respects proved tractable in very different degrees. The
shape and character of the social pyramid might exhibit close similarities from one kingdom or province to the next, but the historical
points of departure were in most cases quite diverse, and the degree
of convergence very modest. Perceptions of mutual foreignness and
suspicion continued to dominate. The greater deference of most of
the Alpine territories was counterbalanced by the extent of subdivi-
sion within them; much of Hungary had barely been subordinated at
all until near the end of the period. Between these extremes, the
comparatively coherent Bohemian lands furnished first the greatest
challenge to Habsburg consolidation and then the greatest opportunity for it.[2]

This book examines some case studies in the evolving relation
between state and society over the area directly ruled by the Austrian Habsburgs. It is inevitably highly selective, and the almost
complete absence of discussion of the situation in Bohemia and Hungary reflects the constraints of institutional financing rather than
any estimate of scholarly significance. But the collection does have a
broad theme: the nature and extent of control exercised by government, especially in light of the rising needs and ambitions of rulers
and their advisers. Such perspectives correspond to a wider program
of current academic inquiry into the origins of the modern state.[3]
Whatever the theoretical limits of rulership in Austria and the practical intricacies of its operation, the Habsburgs met the day-to-day
challenge of sustaining and defending an orderly administration
with many of the same weapons wielded by monarchs whose sovereign powers and pretensions could be formulated much more clearly.
By the same token, the contributors help to indicate some of the ap-

proaches and areas of study actually favored by recent scholarship, at least in German-speaking Europe and in the United States. In what follows, I shall try to gloss their arguments and hint at other relevant findings.[4]

The true starting point—unfortunately, often neglected[5]—must be Ferdinand I, who ruled the Austrian patrimony from the 1520s until his death in 1564. Ferdinand's achievement was fortuitous in two ways. On the one hand, by marriage and through the chance death in battle of his brother-in-law, he was able to lay claim to the crowns of Bohemia and Hungary, whose acquisition raised the Habsburg Danubian *Hausmacht* to European significance. On the other hand, since he remained subordinate elsewhere to his brother, Charles V, this energetic and well-organized prince was encouraged to concentrate his attentions on a prospective "Austrian" polity. He created or modified institutions accordingly, from the upper level of Chancery, Chamber (*Hofkammer*), and War Council down to the local executives which circulated the numerous and detailed public regulations (*Polizeiordnungen*) discussed by Karl Vocelka. It is hardly an accident that no subsequent Austrian ruler until Maria Theresa—with the partial exception of the young Archduke Ferdinand of Styria— worked so unremittingly to strengthen such bodies; all were first and foremost emperors.

Ferdinand I himself became emperor in the end after fierce struggles within the family.[6] Translating his institutions into the context of the *Reich* and subdividing his Austrian inheritance among his sons, he weakened the thrust of his own centralizing initiatives. Nor did his immediate successors—the tolerant and cultivated Maximilian II, the moody and reclusive Rudolph, and the inconstant and superficial Matthias—do anything to confirm them. Artistic and intellectual patronage, military and diplomatic efforts against the Turks, attempts at political and confessional mediation within their own lands and beyond, all sustained sovereign authority in an essentially courtly mode but meant little in terms of administration or of a wider impact on society.[7]

By 1618 the stage was set, either for a radical check to Habsburg power ambitions or for a major advance in them. The threat and the opportunity both owed much to Archduke Ferdinand, and the crucial issue was religion. Since the reign of Ferdinand I, Catholicism—the faith of the dynasty and of a mere residue among the population of its realms—faced a Protestantism that buttressed, and was buttressed by, the political demands of the provincial estates. Uneasy coexistence began to break down around the year 1600, not least because Archduke Ferdinand proceeded actively to persecute Lutherans in Styria, and coreligionists elsewhere moved to a more aggressive defense of their own position. Egged on by Ferdinand, other branches of Habsburg government espoused an open counterreformationary stance, and the resulting bitter conflict culminated in the Defenestration of Prague and the Bohemian revolt.[8]

Victory at the White Mountain allowed Ferdinand II, now head of the house and recently elected emperor, to implement what Robert Bireley here describes as "confessional absolutism." The Catholic faith was single-mindedly reimposed as far as possible throughout the Austrian dominions. That proved to be a slow and incomplete process, but it was a step so significant that Bireley has recently bestowed upon Ferdinand the epithet of "founder" of the Habsburg Monarchy.[9] Such confessionalization involved more than mere doctrine or church attendance or even the particular spiritual and ethical values of Catholicism. As is argued by Anton Schindling, who builds on some impressive new scholarly conclusions for Germany as a whole, it formed part of a policy of state building through patterns of intervention and by the inculcation of new habits of discipline and conformity that was common to all the post-Reformation church establishments, once "cuius regio eius religio" could be made to stick as a principle of rule. A panoply of pressures and restraints might be used to secure uniform and officially acceptable behavior and thought throughout the community.[10]

Yet the proposition that a rampantly counterreformationary priesthood, many of whose members were regular clergy, and which was stretched to restore the rudiments of parish organization, might decisively have advanced the cause of state control invites a skeptical response. The myth of unfettered "absolutism" has by now largely been erased from the historiography of seventeenth-century Europe. Even as a serious goal of monarchs—the early Stuart rulers of Great Britain, for example—its role has been exaggerated.[11] In the case of Ferdinand, three considerations speak against its having been at all consistently resorted to as a weapon of domestic policy. In the first place, Catholic restoration was conceived as a mission to the whole empire, where its visionary character speedily became apparent; its success in Ferdinand's own lands was a by-product, albeit a grandiose one. Secondly, the emperor intended no real subordination of church to state. Devoted to the Roman Catholic hierarchy (if not to individual dignitaries within it) and to its strategies, he neither coveted its assets nor seriously curtailed its autonomy. His pledges would only be redeemed, with accrued interest, by Ferdinand's distant successors.

In the third place, and most importantly, Ferdinand pursued no larger program for the centralization of authority. His claim to be a scrupulous arbiter of the just rights and privileges of the estates may ring hollow to us, but it was—as Bireley suggests—seriously meant. Hence the emperor's encouragement for a suitably Catholic and loyal noble order: grants of money and titles confirmed the aristocracy as the holders of most senior official positions and as the essential mediators between the court and the regions. Little administrative expansion took place at any point during the seventeenth century. On the highest level, an Austrian Chancery was established, but its functions—despite the name—remained substantially imperial; lower down, any conscious consolidation or *Verdichtung* came about primarily through the agency of the lords themselves, the owners of those largely self-regulating *Grundherrschaften* that Herbert Knittler examines. The lords may well have had the greatest share in the content and implementation of *Polizeiordnungen* in the localities, though it is not clear, in the present state of our knowledge, why the vocabulary and emphasis of such regulations should have shifted with time, or how far people actually obeyed them. Perhaps it was true of Austria, as Thomasius wittily observed for north Germany in 1717, that "they are upheld by no one, except by the church doors and other places where they are affixed and secured for purposes of publication."[12]

Thus were set in place the two chief pillars of support for the edifice of sovereignty in the Habsburg lands over the century and more after 1620: the church, especially its religious orders, old and new; and the nobility, especially the high nobles who profited from the eclipse of many knights and gentlemen in Protestant exile or through the economic unviability of small estates.[13] Linking the two there emerged a dominant culture of Catholic baroque, proclaimed above all by zealous and deferential intellectuals from the Society of Jesus, who ran most of the larger educational institutions. This culture did not by any means penetrate uniformly or swiftly: besides massive and effective resistance in parts of Hungary and Silesia, the missionary programs of clergy and their secular helpers took many decades to reach fruition. Yet in some ways the outcome represented a genuinely popular achievement, which arguably embodied more creativity and inspiration from below, in art, architecture, and music, than did other stylistic periods before and after it. Ironically—though logically enough—the deepest, and ultimately the most subversive, reservations about it were nourished within the social elites: among ecclesiastical opponents of the Jesuits, or among free-thinking aristocrats like Count Sporck.[14]

Two essays examine important ways in which this system of rule was sustained during the seventeenth and early eighteenth centuries. The ostentatious propagation of its values was most evident in the grandiose buildings commissioned by churchmen and aristocrats. By comparison, as Hellmut Lorenz shows, the dynasty itself eschewed such magnificence. This was partly a counsel of necessity, dictated by inadequate funding, which stemmed from overall administrative inefficiency and from reluctance or inability to tap the sources of greatest wealth; partly, too, the dynasty indulged an enthusiasm for music and theater, which could sustain imperial pretensions in subtler ways. But its relatively simple tastes also reflected a deliberate decision in favor of traditional values and devotional ideals. In the *pietas Austriaca,* the Habsburgs recognized an intrinsic part of the ethos of their sovereignty.[15]

Austrian rulers could also deploy weapons of social policy. John P. Spielman indicates some of the elements of their distinctive court patronage. While avoiding the profitable but problematical expedient of sale of office (though the device of *Expektanz* might open the back door to it), the dynasty could draw upon reserves available only to the emperor. Besides, at one extreme, the unique feudal cachet of a knighthood of the Golden Fleece, and, at the other, minor trappings such as recognition as a *poeta laureatus,* there was a range of senior noble titles to be bestowed throughout the *Reich.* Moreover, the combination of power over an imperial clientele with influence upon social establishments in Bohemia and Hungary, as well as with significant leverage in church appointments, gave scope for considerable finesse. Evidently, such gratifications did not altogether replace more material reward: grants of monopoly, for example, would hardly be attractive without reasonably flourishing conditions of trade. Yet conferral of status could certainly eke out strained fiscal resources, in the case both of government and of individual—the latter might find supplies of credit opened up to him thereby. The resultant ever more intricate web of social distinctions demonstrated the range of options generated by human vanity, even as it suggested the possibility of diminishing returns.[16]

In fact, the structure gained a further lease on life from the 1680s, thanks to successful confrontation with the Ottomans and the French. The emperors were able to exploit their enhanced role in the *Reich* and in Europe as a whole, while acquiring fresh opportunities for patronage toward the southeast. Italian ambitions could be revived, even Spanish visions nurtured; an older dream of universal empire could be temporarily resuscitated. Charles VI undertook a belated program of conspicuous public works at the Hofburg and Klosterneuburg. Yet the Austrian government was by now dangerously overextended, and things soon turned sour. On the international front, the disastrous Turkish campaign of the later 1730s led directly to a crisis of the whole Habsburg inheritance in the first years of Maria Theresa's rule. At home, awareness of public shortcomings grew apace: criticism of the priorities of the Counter-Reformation, even of its supposed attainments, fed on a rediscovery of Protestant survival in several provinces and on mounting evidence that rival polities, especially Protestant ones, had gained a clear lead in military and economic terms. "Soft" absolutism, which rested on religious and ecclesiastical sanctions alone, seemed to stand in need of radical toughening measures.

The 1740s stand conventionally as the prelude to a higher, or intenser, stage of Austrian state organization in the early modern

period. Beginning with the loss, sealed by later treaties, of most of
the dynasty's Silesian possessions, they ended with the first steps
toward administrative reform, and thereby toward the more rational and efficient management of economy and society. This
periodization has to some extent persisted by default, given historians' neglect of the reign of Charles VI and their tendency to associate it with a purely conservative cast of mind. In fact, mercantilist
ideas were certainly gaining ground before 1740, and trade and industry showed some practical advances: if *oeconomia non facit
saltum,* as Herman Freudenberger's and John Komlos's contributions suggest, these phenomena deserve more attention. The first
cracks in the baroque intellectual and pedagogical edifice had already become manifest—though the metaphor of a single coherent
structure is misleading, anyway. Moreover, new initiatives in the
field of welfare had been undertaken, for example by the provision of
large new poorhouses, particularly for the war wounded, and by
steps toward protection of peasant interests.[17]

Yet the 1740s were crucial, both for perceptions of Austria and
for its reality. The perceived threat to the whole patrimony of a ruler
who—like Ferdinand I for most of his reign and the younger
Ferdinand II—possessed no imperial dignity intensified the sense of
its distinctiveness. Whereas the Pragmatic Sanction, which en-
shrined that distinctiveness, notoriously proved a dead letter at the
other courts of Europe, it thus took on a special significance within
the Habsburg lands, especially in terms of the relationship with
Hungary. The subsequent elevation of Maria Theresa's husband to
headship of the *Reich* hardly affected the new situation at home. As
for the reality, this was an Austria lent extra coherence by a third
pillar of government: the beginnings of a modern bureaucratic ma-
chine. A considerable, though unquantifiable, increase in personnel
resulted from the union of the two most important chanceries; the
creation of a State Council; the expansion of other court depart-
ments (*Hofstellen*); the revamped provincial governments (*Guber-
nia*), together with the extension of circle (*kraj* or *Kreis*) organization
at the local level; the proliferation of committees, both at the center
(*Hofkommissionen*) and in the regions (thirty of them in Bohemia by

1780); and the reform of judicial procedures. At the same time, norms of administrative practice were tentatively introduced, along with regular salary scales, recognizable career paths, some pension expectations (if not rights), elements of training for the public service, and a new *esprit de corps*.[18]

The ethos of Austrian officialdom proved squarely interventionist and regulatory. It directed its activities toward creating a more uniform and productive society. Several aspects of this have attracted notable recent work, for example the expansion of education and the associated attack on superstition.[19] The contributions in this volume concentrate on two areas: economic management and welfare. The performance of the agrarian sector lay at the heart of Maria Theresa and Joseph's concerns, and their genuine involvement with rural life is revealed in a mass of decrees. The stagnant levels of output from both noble and peasant holdings over the previous two hundred years are revealed by Knittler, even for the comparatively advanced province of Lower Austria, with its ready access to the large Viennese market. Against this background, all efforts of the authorities yielded only modest results, not merely because the conservatism of the peasants was vastly underestimated by their rulers but also because the whole issue became entwined with the political contest between Joseph II and vested-interest groups in the regions.[20]

Industrial achievements were more conspicuous: the researches of Freudenberger and others are now confirmed by Komlos's favorable view of Austrian growth in comparative European terms.[21] The organization and levels of textile production appear especially impressive. Yet industrial development cannot disguise—indeed, it may well have exacerbated—a growing existential threat to both surplus peasantry and marginal manufactory workers. Dearth was felt in widely separated parts of the Habsburg lands in those years, particularly during the 1770s. Georg Schmidt shows how powerless the authorities in the *Vorlande* continued to be in the face of elemental challenges. Paul Bernard provides a pioneering investigation of poor-relief in the central areas of the monarchy. Local bodies found themselves unable to carry the weight of ever more serious levels of immiseration, a phenomenon familiar across the continent, from Ireland to the Ukraine. Official initiatives proved paltry and underfunded.[22]

For all its limitations, the pursuit of state power under Maria Theresa and her son, a movement somewhat misleadingly and confusingly, but conveniently, described as "Josephinism," introduced absolute rule in a new key. It has by convention come to be described as "enlightened" absolutism, an exercise of authority motivated by fresh ideas about citizenship and harnessing of resources for the general good, about the mutual duties of governors and governed. At the same time, the circumstances of reform in Austria, as a response to international pressure, must always be borne in mind; and an alternative, skeptical interpretation emphasizes the Habsburgs' goal of military preparedness and their more ruthless exploitation of traditional methods of *Staatsbildung.* Substantial points can be made on both sides. The humane statements of Maria Theresa, in contexts innocent of any propagandist implication; Joseph's vocabulary of state service; the notions of *Polizei* elaborated by cameralist theorists like Sonnenfels, who were patronized by both rulers and exercised considerable public influence; the more private meliorative activities of a Van Swieten: all these must be set against the circumscribed educational and intellectual horizons of the two monarchs, and their obvious primary concern with the army as the vehicle for recovery, and if possible for the expansion, of territory and privilege. Indeed, a coherent, permanent, and much enlarged Austrian military force under tighter central control forms the fourth pillar of the Habsburg polity by the second half of the eighteenth century.[23]

The "humanitarian" versus "militarist" debate is hoary and ultimately sterile. Historians now place different emphases in their approaches to the problem of governmental motivation. The subsistence crisis, reflecting a still-incompletely explained demographic explosion of the mid-eighteenth century, seems to have fueled anxieties both about social disorder and also—so Komlos, in particular, has recently argued elsewhere—about the quality of recruits to the army. The vulnerability of the traditional moral order may likewise have been a root cause of changing attitudes toward pedagogy.[24] Meanwhile, whatever the status of this apparently Malthusian debate *avant la lettre,* the truly innovative ideas under discussion at the highest level in Vienna can be seen to have come specifically from Western Europe. Grete Klingenstein examines the impact of French and British notions of physiocracy and free trade upon key representatives of enlightened court culture in Austria. Her fascinating detective work in the papers of the Zinzendorf brothers yields the remarkable conclusion that François Véron de Forbonnais, one of the less-remembered of the French *économistes,* may thus have influenced Austrian public policy more than the acknowledged local experts, particularly Sonnenfels, who were held at arm's length from the arcana of state.[25] Yet the practical difficulties encountered by reform on such lines were formidable: Schmidt illustrates the perils of removing the very visible hand of state regulation. This experience of the Swabian authorities at the beginning of the 1770s clearly foreshadows the travails of the French government a few years later, beset by accusations of a *pacte de famine.*

Fundamental new elements thus took their place in underpinning the authority of the Habsburg government. And Josephinists were correspondingly severe in their criticism of its previous material and ideological supports. They assaulted the major social and political privileges of the nobility, and they condemned the useless baroque ostentation of the church. Yet these two pillars of confessional absolutism remained indispensable to the new order of things, and reformers sought to subsume rather than to replace them. The chief protagonists of innovation under Maria Theresa were, in fact, aristocrats. If the credentials of Haugwitz, whose family had risen to the dignity of count only during the 1730s, be thought suspect, then consider his successors Kaunitz and the Zinzendorf brothers, who adopted liberal economic theory, or the magnates of largely Bohemian background—Choteks, Kolowrats, Kinskys, and the rest— who presided over wholesale bureaucratic and fiscal restructuring at the center, as well as taking private initiatives toward a degree of serf emancipation and relief of distress. As Bernard shows, it was Count Buquoi, on his estates at Gratzen (Nové Hrady) in southern Bohemia, who founded the system of poor-relief later espoused by Joseph II. Such figures often led the way in acquiring the latest books and journals from abroad and dominated the mildly progressive freemasonic salons of the day.[26]

The church likewise, deeply split by the mid-eighteenth century, had its own reformist wing, whose ideals corresponded closely to the purposes of Austrian rulers. After decades of rather desultory controversy over the issue, it seems clear today that Catholic reform stood at the heart of Josephinism, a program that was impelled by the threat from crypto-Protestants at home and the achievements of Protestant culture abroad to seek to accommodate the church to new circumstances and thereby to renew its popular mission.[27] Even Joseph's move beyond the still-conventional piety and inherited prejudices of his mother to far-reaching measures of tolerance can be construed in terms of a progression identified by some writers in this volume as the final push toward a state church able to reconcile earlier divisions and to realize full confessionalization of the population under loose Catholic aegis. Not for nothing did Maria Theresa, in her last years, and then Joseph at last grasp the nettle of diocesan and parish reorganization.[28] That, in its turn, was of course intimately linked with fresh solutions to problems of the welfare and supervision (*Polizei*) of individual citizens.

It was these attempts to reconstruct the existing edifice, rather than the addition of new wings to it, that provoked stiff domestic resistance to the Habsburg state at the time. Opposition to the bureaucracy and the army lay largely in the future: these were classic nineteenth-century bogies. The campaign to incorporate the nobility within a new civil command system, however, involved a belated assault upon the whole estates tradition. Though by no means unsuccessful in its own terms, it left festering provincial resentments that could gradually turn into dangerous kinds of local patriotism. The abolition of all constitutional dialogue left the regime perilously exposed to future calls for participation from new groups of subjects as well as old ones.[29] The contest over the church arguably proved still more detrimental, at least in the short run. That campaign was likewise by no means unsuccessful, yet the Josephinist ecclesiastical cadres failed to deliver either the spiritual values or the material resources that had been expected of them. More seriously, baroque attitudes could not be so abruptly redirected, both because all manner of political and sectional advantages attached to them, and because they had only just penetrated fully to society as a whole. It is a great irony of later eighteenth-century Austria that the ultimate effectiveness of the protracted and stormy process of the Counter-Reformation, now officially superseded, engendered deep antagonism toward further change among many of those who might otherwise have been expected to back it.

Habsburg government could ill afford to neglect the search for more supporters. If its overtures to nonnoble society remained half-hearted and freighted with the meliorist assumptions of the Enlightenment, its offer to Protestants—a poisoned chalice, as it were—and to Orthodox Christians left tolerance conditional upon their acceptance of bureaucratic intervention and residual Catholic ascendancy. One further group was of growing importance to the Austrian state, as its members had long been significant subjects of the emperor: the Jews. R. Po-chia Hsia points out that Jews long fared better in the *Reich* at large, where they were treated essentially as a privileged corporation like many other intermediate imperial bodies, than they did inside the lands of direct Habsburg rule. From the 1620s, confessional absolutism rendered their position within Austria still more tenuous, despite the relative philosemitism of Ferdinand II himself (a revealing facet of his character), and even Maria Theresa (no less revealingly) showed them no favor.[30]

But during the eighteenth century, the utility of Jews to the authorities became more and more manifest. They were bankers and purveyors to court and army; they took an active part in trade, both at the international level, especially through Trieste, and in the provinces, especially Moravia and parts of Hungary. Within Galicia, acquired by the monarchy in 1773, they formed a substantial proportion of the total population.[31] Joseph II's measure of Jewish emancipation was typically radical, indeed unprecedented, but also typically grudging and conditional. In return for freeing them from many disabilities and restrictions, he expected the rapid assimilation of Jews into Christian society and their ready service to the state in a primarily economic capacity: a kind of mercantilist confessionalization at a stroke. It did not quite work that way; yet the Jewish case illustrates how evolving Habsburg authority, from a loose quasi-imperial embrace, through ecclesiastical, to bureaucratic control, could work to the advantage of one very special community. In the nineteenth century, Jews, greatly expanding in numbers and unmatched in commercial expertise and intellectual flair, would become the fifth and final pillar of Austrian government; or, in view of the backlash that they unleashed, perhaps rather its fifth column.

The last group of essays in this collection is concerned with the international situation of the monarchy. They begin with Charles W. Ingrao's ringing declaration that "foreign policy was the first concern of the Austrian Habsburgs." The priorities of much current scholarship would appear to belie that statement. Heavily domestic in their orientation, many historians have largely abstained from issues of power politics, displaying more interest, for example, in perceptions of the Ottoman threat than in its reality, in recruitment to the Habsburg armies than in their deployment. Such approaches have considerable justification: after all, earlier generations of historians plotted the course of diplomacy and warfare in often numbing detail. Yet large questions about the making of an "Austrian" state and the character of "Austrian" society remain thereby largely unaddressed.

A wider union of Central European lands under Habsburg aegis was called into being in order to meet the challenge to the region from the Ottoman Porte. Its subsequent defense of Christianity against the infidel proved, of course, broadly successful, and the impact of the rhetoric that surrounded it should not be underestimated. But did the long confrontation with a common enemy actually cement those territories together? That appears implausible, given the scope for political and interconfessional strife—between crown and estates, province and province, soldiers and civilians—to which it gave rise, and the absence of any consistent response from government to the larger constitutional implications that it posed. Moreover, the whole ideology of crusade against the Turks was closely and consciously associated with the imperial office, while the resources made available were at least as much German as Austrian.

The unity and integrity of the *Reich* long remained the central Habsburg preoccupation. Over most of the period, the bulk of the dynasty's possessions still lay within it, and whatever tactical advantages might accrue to a given member from acting as *Landesfürst* within Austria, the strategy of the house continued to focus on its imperial role. It was shifts in the German balance that induced political innovation: during the 1620s, in the throes of the Thirty Years' War; during the 1740s, in the next struggle for hegemony. Halfway between those two portentous episodes lie the 1680s, when a far more lasting and complete Austrian triumph yielded no major structural consequences at home at all. Even in conquered Hungary, the regime, having toyed with some centralist plans so extreme and procrustean that they would have been totally unworkable,[32] relapsed into administrative arrangements of a largely medieval kind. Yet in a longer perspective, the events of the 1680s, with the resultant control over the middle Danubian basin and the seeds of an eastern orientation—now offensive rather than defensive—would prove uniquely determinative of Habsburg destinies.

Austrian responses to this changing international situation continue to be variously judged by historians. For Heinz Duchhardt, investigating the attempts of middling German states to confirm their enhanced European status after the Peace of Westphalia, the inflated ambitions of the house of Habsburg now cast it in the role of a *bête noire:* "The simple fact was that great-power pretensions and emperorship were fundamentally incompatible." Ingrao, however, stresses the essential conservatism of imperial policy during the eighteenth century, and support for that verdict has recently been voiced even in the case of Joseph II, often represented as the most expansionist of Austrian rulers.[33] The contributions of Karl Roider and Volker Press bear directly on the same issue. Roider points to official recognition—especially by an irritated Joseph—that Austrian policy in the monarchy's newly acquired Balkan hinterland was futile. Press reminds us how the rise to international prominence of Brandenburg-Prussia, as it "finally filled the vacuum that had been created by the emperor's remoteness from northern Germany," interlinked with the diplomatic options of the Habsburgs.

We should not assume that contemporaries simplified those options into any set of clear alternatives. Cooperation between *Kaiser* and *Reich* was rarely as harmonious as during the wars on two fronts, against Turks and French, at the end of the seventeenth century.[34] Yet the fierce internecine struggles of the 1740s soon revealed the depths of potential antagonism. Unprovoked aggression in southeastern Europe was rarely a Habsburg expedient. Yet the fruits of conquest there were recognized by Austrian governments at least as often as were its pitfalls: witness the continuing utility for imperial armies into the nineteenth century of troops from the *Grenze,* or Military Frontier; the privileges long accorded to prosperous Serbian and Greek merchants in Habsburg towns; and the protracted campaigns waged among local people for proselytes to Roman Catholic and, later, to Enlightenment values.[35] If we seek the symbolic date for an underlying change of direction, the best candidate remains the traditional one, the year of deliverance from the infidel in 1683.

Sovereignty over all the territories of St. Stephen's Crown constituted the first and most important step toward Habsburg disengagement from Germany. Despite much received opinion, the Thirty Years' War had hardly weakened the position of the emperor in the *Reich:* the Westphalian settlement merely altered its character.[36] But in the eighteenth century, the view from Vienna began to change. Maria Theresa, whose highest personal title was that of queen—some said king—of Hungary, and who had no formal authority over imperial institutions, consciously promoted Austrian bodies and Austrian identity. So did Joseph II, whose confrontational politics in the *Reich* were widely interpreted and resisted as serving Austrian self-interest.[37] The loss of most of Silesia and the successive acquisitions of Galicia (1773), Bukovina (1775), and new West Galicia (1795) gave the monarchy far more territory outside the empire than within it, even if the Southern Netherlands be reckoned part of the latter. The bewildering transfers of land in Italy, which left the dynasty in possession of the Milanese, confirmed this development; Venice, too, would fall to it in 1797. Francis II set no better example in defense of the imperial constitution when Napoleon called it in question than did the princes who had solemnly elected him in 1792. His highly unlawful proclamation of himself as Kaiser von Österreich in 1804 condemned what remained of the *Reich* to internal contradiction.

Things could easily have been different. Without Hungary, the Alpine provinces and the kingdom of Bohemia might have been welded together by absolutist endeavor into a coherent realm that would have remained committed more effectively to Austria's continuing mission inside the empire (even while it reflected internally the social and economic predominance of Bohemia). The assertion of the dynasty's rights in northern Italy and the Low Countries amounted to a revival of traditional imperial claims. Maria Theresa was obsessed with *revanche* in Germany against her Prussian rival; and Joseph, having in the 1760s attempted measures of institutional reform within the empire, which might conceivably have harnessed the rising tide of *Reichspatriotismus* for the Habsburg cause, spent the rest of his career pursuing a swap of Bavaria for the Southern Netherlands, which certainly did not appear chimerical to contemporaries. A core bloc of contiguous south German, Austrian, and Bohemian lands might well have sufficed to reduce both the existing constitutional separatism of the Hungarians and the subsequent national separatism of the Czechs—those very factors which combined to render the monarchy unworkable in the end.

These are heady, but by no means idle speculations. They are thoroughly relevant to the present context, for no analysis of the Austrian Monarchy in the early modern centuries can afford to neglect the fluidity of the territorial arrangements upon which the institutions of state and the coherence of society rested. By the same token, to return to our starting point, Austria was uniquely a realm whose identity depended on its eponymous dynasty. Yet even here, much remained more or less deliberately indistinct, partly from the Habsburgs' long bout of schizophrenia about the nature of their imperial mission, partly from the lack of any consistent alternative ideology of dynastic rule. We look in vain for an Austrian equivalent to the cults of *le roi soleil* or of Gloriana, or—it appears—for firm theoretical statements, even in the heyday of Josephinism, about the rationale of personal sovereignty. Thus effective management of the Habsburg patrimony depended still more thoroughly than elsewhere in absolutist Europe upon the practice of individual rulers: their vision, or lack of it; their patronage—a wasting asset by the mid-eighteenth century; their administrative efficiency—usually a strong suit; their endurance. The elusiveness of the relationship in Austria between "society" and "state," between a collectivity bound by no clear territorial or national allegiance and an authority marked by its personal and contingent character, presents a continuing challenge to historians. This volume suggests some of the ways in which that challenge is now being answered.

Notes

1. For some historical reflections on this issue, see R. J. W. Evans, "Historians and the State in the Habsburg Lands," in *Visions sur le développement des etats européens* (Actes du Colloque de Rome, 28–31 mars 1990) (Rome: Ecole Française, in press).

2. So, at least, I have sought to argue in "The Habsburg Monarchy and Bohemia, 1526–1848," in *Conquest and Coalescence: The Shaping of the State in Early Modern Europe,* ed. Mark Greengrass (London: Arnold, 1991), 134–54.

3. The most important project is a massive undertaking under the aegis of the European Science Foundation, The Origins of the Modern State in Europe, whose first volume is indicated in note 1 above.

4. The notes to this Introduction include merely a selection of relevant recent titles, most of them not cited elsewhere in the book. For useful introductions to individual Habsburg rulers, with current bibliography, see *Die Kaiser der Neuzeit, 1519–1918,* ed. Anton Schindling and Walter Ziegler (Munich: Beck, 1990).

5. An exception is Paula Sutter Fichtner's useful introduction in her *Ferdinand I of Austria* (Boulder/New York: East European Monographs, 1982). Current interpretations of Ferdinand stand in the shadow of the major ongoing edition of his correspondence, most recently *Die Korrespondenz Ferdinands I.,* vol. 3: *Familienkorrespondenz 1531 und 1532,* parts 1–3, ed. Herwig Wolfram and Christiane Thomas (Vienna: Holzhausen, 1973–84).

6. Mia Rodríguez-Salgado, *The Changing Face of Empire: Charles V, Philip II and Habsburg Authority* (Cambridge: Cambridge University Press, 1988), casts much fresh light from a mainly Spanish perspective on the 1550s, a crucial decade for the organization of Habsburg power in Europe.

7. The latest work on Ferdinand's son, *Kaiser Maximilian II: Kultur und Politik im 16. Jahrhundert,* ed. Friedrich Edelmayer and Alfred Kohler, Wiener Beiträge zur Geschichte der Neuzeit, vol. 19 (Vienna: Verlag für Geschichte und Politik, 1992), does not alter this overall judgment. Nor does Josef Janáček's *Rudolf II a jeho doba* (Prague: Svoboda, 1987), though his approach is welcome in redirecting attention to Rudolph's political program. The more narrowly administrative history of the period remains obscure. The most important fresh work on this pe-

riod in any part of the Habsburg lands has been carried in recent years by the Czech periodical *Folia Historica Bohemica*.

8. There are significant contributions to this theme in *Crown, Church and Estates: Central European Politics in the Sixteenth and Seventeenth Centuries,* ed. R. J. W. Evans and Trevor V. Thomas (London: Macmillan, 1991), especially from the standpoint of the viability of estates' government as an alternative to Habsburg authority.

9. Ibid., 226–44.

10. See the accessible surveys by Wolfgang Reinhard, "Reformation, Counter-Reformation and the Early Modern State: A Reassessment," *Catholic Historical Review* 75 (1989): 383–404; and by R. Po-Chia Hsia, *Social Discipline in the Reformation: Central Europe, 1550–1750* (London: Routledge, 1989).

11. See Glenn Burgess, "The Divine Right of Kings Reconsidered," *English Historical Review* 107 (1992): 837–61.

12. Quoted by Thomas Winkelbauer in his important article "Sozialdisziplinierung und Konfessionalisierung durch Grundherren in den österreichischen und böhmischen Ländern im 16. und 17. Jahrhundert," *Zeitschrift für historische Forschung* 19 (1992): 317–39, at 324; see also idem, "'Und sollten sich die Parteien gütlich miteinander vertragen': Zur Behandlung von Streitigkeiten und von 'Injurien' vor den Patrimonialgerichten in Ober- und Niederösterreich in der frühen Neuzeit," *Zeitschrift für Rechtsgeschichte* 122 (1992): 129–58.

13. The main literature on these themes is surveyed in my *Making of the Habsburg Monarchy, 1550–1700: An Interpretation* (1979; reprint with new bibliographical preface, Oxford: Oxford University Press, 1991). There are important new contributions to analysis of the decline of the (Protestant) lesser nobility in Karin J. MacHardy, "The Rise of Absolutism and Noble Rebellion in Early Modern Habsburg Austria, 1570–1620," *Comparative Studies in Society and History* 34 (1992): 407–38; and Thomas Winkelbauer, "Krise der Aristokratie? Zum Strukturwandel des Adels in den böhmischen und niederösterreichischen Ländern im 16. und 17. Jahrhundert," *Mitteilungen des Instituts für Österreichische Geschichtsforschung* 100 (1992): 328–53.

14. The important case of Prague University is surveyed anew by Ivana Čornejová, *Kapitoly z dějin pražské university, 1622–54* [sic, though the book actually covers the period 1622–1773] (Prague: Univerzita Karlova, 1992); see, in general, Evans, *Habsburg Monarchy;* and idem, "Die Universität im geistigen Milieu der habsburgischen Länder, 17.–18. Jahrhundert," in *Die Universität in Alteuropa,* ed. Alexander Patschovsky and Horst Rabe (Constance: Universitätsverlag, 1994), 179–200.

15. One of the ceremonial manifestations of that *pietas* is examined, unfortunately in a very amateur fashion, by Magdalena Hawlik-van de Water, *Der schöne Tod: Zeremonialstrukturen des Wiener Hofes bei Tod und Begräbnis zwischen 1640 und 1740* (Vienna: Herder, 1989). See, for the context, Elisabeth Kovács,

"Kirchliches Zeremoniell am Wiener Hof des 18. Jahrhunderts im Wandel von Mentalität und Gesellschaft," *Mitteilungen des Österreichischen Staatsarchivs* 32 (1979): 109–42.

16. This whole subject is addressed broadly in *Klientelsysteme im Europa der frühen Neuzeit,* ed. Antoni Mączak (Munich: Oldenbourg, 1988), and in Mączak's *Rządzący i rządzeni: władza i społeczeństwo w Europie wczesnonowożytnej* (Warsaw: Państwowy Instytut Wydawniczy, 1986), esp. 140–50 and passim.

17. On welfare provision, see Hannes Stekl, *Österreichs Zucht- und Arbeitshäuser, 1617–1920* (Vienna: Verlag für Geschichte und Politik, 1984); Helfried Valentinitsch, "Das Grazer Zucht- und Arbeitshaus, 1734–83," in *Festschrift für Hermann Baltl,* ed. K. Ebert (Innsbruck: Universitätsverlag, 1978), 495–514; Valentinitsch, "Armenfürsorge im Herzogtum Steiermark im 18. Jahrhundert," *Zeitschrift des Historischen Vereines für Steiermark* 73 (1982): 93–115; idem, "Fremd und arm im Zeitalter des Barock," in *Lust und Leid: Barocke Kunst, barocker Alltag* (Graz: Verlag für Sammler, 1992), 275–82. I have put together some thoughts about intellectual changes in "Über die Ursprünge der Aufklärung in den habsburgischen Ländern," *Das achtzehnte Jahrhundert und Österreich* 2 (1985): 9–31.

18. There is now a magisterial survey of the workings of administrative reform, in the provinces as well as at the center, in P. G. M. Dickson, *Finance and Government under Maria Theresia, 1740–1780,* 2 vols. (Oxford: Oxford University Press, 1987), vol. 1, esp. chaps. 9–10. The earlier sections of Waltraud Heindl, *Gehorsame Rebellen: Bürokratie und Beamte in Österreich, 1780–1848* (Vienna: Böhlau, 1991), are also relevant.

19. See, for example, James van Horn Melton, *Absolutism and the Eighteenth-Century Origins of Compulsory Schooling in Prussia and Austria* (Cambridge: Cambridge University Press, 1988); Gábor Klaniczay, "Gerard van Swieten und die Anfänge des Kampfes gegen Aberglauben in der Habsburgermonarchie," *Acta Historica Academiae Scientiarum Hungariae* 34 (1988): 225–47.

20. See Roman Sandgruber, *Die Anfänge der Konsumgesellschaft: Konsum-güterverbrauch, Lebensstandard und Alltagskultur in Österreich im 18. und 19. Jahrhundert* (Vienna: Verlag für Geschichte und Politik, 1982); and idem, "Einkommensentwicklung und Einkommensverteilung in der zweiten Hälfte des 18. Jahrhunderts: Einige Quellen und Anhaltspunkte," in *Österreich im Europa der Aufklärung,* ed. Richard G. Plaschka and Grete Klingenstein (Vienna: Österreichische Akademie der Wissenschaften, 1985), 1:251–63. Analysis of the agrarian balance-sheet for reformist Habsburg government in this period is still hampered by failure to incorporate conclusions reached for non-German regions of the monarchy, especially Hungary. The latest survey of the rich research there is by Imre Wellmann in *Magyarország története,* vol. 4: *1686–1789,* ed. Győző Ember and Gusztáv Heckenast, 2 vols. (Budapest: Akadémiai kiadó, 1989), 507–627, 931–84, with immensely copious bibliographies 1371–400, 1430–61; see also the useful survey by Wellmann, "Kontinuität und Zäsur in Ungarns Bauernleben zur Zeit Maria Theresias und Josephs II," in *Österreich im Europa der Aufklärung,* 1:87–120.

21. Komlos's view is developed at length in his controversial study, *Nutrition and Economic Development in the Eighteenth-Century Habsburg Monarchy* (Princeton, N.J.: Princeton University Press, 1989). Freudenberger's claims, as can be seen in this volume, are more modest, but his *Industrialization of a Central European City: Brno and the Fine Woollen Industry in the Eighteenth Century* (Edington, Wilts.: Pasold, 1977) represented the first thorough analysis of the achievements of the textile industry in the Habsburg lands during a period exactly corresponding to that of the early Industrial Revolution in Great Britain. Unfortunately, the important work by Walter Endrei, *Magyarországi textilmanufaktúrák a XVIII században* (Budapest: Akadémiai kiadó, 1969)—remarkably informative on the technical side, too—remains unknown outside Hungary.

22. See, in general, Stuart Woolf, *The Poor in Western Europe in the Eighteenth and Nineteenth Centuries* (London: Methuen, 1986); and Olwen Hufton, *The Poor of Eighteenth-Century France* (Oxford: Oxford University Press, 1974). The mechanics of the English poor law are examined by Paul A. Slack, *Poverty and Policy in Tudor and Stuart England* (London: Longman, 1988).

23. This aspect of Habsburg policy is the one least explored in the present context. Johann C. Allmayer-Beck and Erich Lessing, *Das Heer unter dem Doppeladler* (Munich: Oldenbourg, 1981); and Christopher Duffy, *The Army of Maria Theresa* (London: Routledge, 1977), yield little on the army as an institution of state. In a valuable recent contribution to the debate about *Polizei*, Roland Axtmann, "'Police' and the Formation of the Modern State," *German History* 10 (1992): 39–61, shows how welfare aspects of the regulation of the civilian population in Austria came to the fore by the mid-eighteenth century but were then displaced by new repressive instruments of official surveillance.

24. Komlos, *Nutrition and Economic Development;* Melton, *Origins of Compulsory Schooling.*

25. These issues are discussed at length by Franz Szabo in the first volume of his biography of Kaunitz, which is forthcoming from the Cambridge University Press.

26. Jiří Kroupa, *Alchymie štěstí: Pozdní osvícenství a moravská společnost* (Kroměříž/Brno: Muzeum/Muzejní a Vlastivědná Společnost, 1986). Important work on Hungarian Masonry by Éva H. Balázs is summarized in *Magyarország története*, 4:831–926, 1023–1123, also published separately as *Bécs és Pest-Buda a régi századvégen, 1765–1800* (Budapest: Magvető, 1987). Studies of the subject in Austria proper have begun to yield diminishing returns: see, for example, *Aufklärung und Geheimgesellschaften: Zur politischen Funktion und Sozialstruktur der Freimaurerlogen im 18. Jahrhundert,* ed. Helmut Reinalter (Munich: Oldenbourg, 1989), with useful bibliography.

27. The limited notion of "Josephinism" espoused by Eduard Winter, *Der Josephinismus und seine Geschichte* (Brünn: Rohrer, 1943), has stood the test of time better than the broader definition proposed by Fritz Valjavec, *Der Josephinismus* (Vienna: Verlag für Geschichte, 1945). There is helpful discussion by Elisabeth Kovács, "Was ist Josephinismus?" in *Österreich zur Zeit Kaiser*

Josephs II (Vienna: Niederösterreichische Landesregierung, 1980), 24–30; Karl Otmar von Aretin, "Der Josephinismus und das Problem des katholischen aufgeklärten Absolutismus," in *Österreich im Europa der Aufklärung,* 1:509–24; and Derek Beales, *Joseph II* (Cambridge: Cambridge University Press, 1987), 1:439–41 and passim. Important recent contributions to the overall issue have been Peter Hersche, *Der Spätjansenismus in Österreich* (Vienna: Österreichische Akademie der Wissenschaften, 1977); and *Katholische Aufklärung und Josephinismus,* ed. Elisabeth Kovács (Munich: Oldenbourg, 1979), which consider the nature of the religious ideas of the Josephinists; and Josef Karniel, *Die Toleranzpolitik Kaiser Josephs II.* (Tel Aviv: Institut für deutsche Geschichte der Universität, 1985), which examines the motives of Joseph's policy of confessional tolerance.

28. This subject still stands in need of detailed investigation. P. G. M. Dickson, "Joseph II's Reshaping of the Austrian Church," *Historical Journal* 36 (1993): 89–114, reaches important conclusions about the (inadequate) funds available for such reform.

29. The classic Hungarian case receives fresh and incisive investigation by E. H. Balázs in *Magyarország története,* 4. Reappraisal of the Bohemian nobility's response to Josephinism is a major desideratum.

30. See the important discussions in Jonathan I. Israel, *European Jewry in the Age of Mercantilism, 1550–1750* (Oxford: Oxford University Press, 1985), 15–16, 38–44, 64–69, 87–105, 124–59 passim, 192–95.

31. Valuable recent work includes William O. McCagg, *A History of Habsburg Jews, 1670–1918* (Bloomington: Indiana University Press, 1989), 11–43; László Gonda, *A zsidóság Magyarországon, 1526–1945* (Budapest: Századvég, 1992), 32–56, with excellent bibliography by Gyula Zeke, 330–89; and chapters by Benjamin Braude and Lois Dubin in *Il mondo ebraico: Gli ebrei tra Italia nord-orientale e Impero asburgico dal medioevo all'età contemporanea,* ed. Giacomo Todeschini and Pier Cesare Ioly Zorattini (Pordenone: Studio Tesi, 1991), 329–51, 289–310. Long neglect of the subject in Austria is now being remedied: see, e.g., Dorothea McEwan, "Jüdisches Leben im mährischen Ghetto: Eine Skizzierung der Stetl-Geschichte von Lomnitz bis 1848," *Mitteilungen des Instituts für Österreichische Geschichtsforschung* 99 (1991): 83–145.

32. Raffaella Gherardi, *Potere e costituzione a Vienna fra Sei e Settecento* (Bologna: Il Mulino, 1980), seems to believe these plans viable. John W. Stoye, in his biography of Count Marsigli, forthcoming with Yale University Press, is more balanced. An edition of the famous blueprint for Hungary, the *Einrichtungswerk,* is at last in prospect: see J. J. Varga, "Berendezési tervek a török kiűzésének az időszakában: az Einrichtungswerk," *Századok* 125 (1991): 449–86.

33. See, for example, Beales, *Joseph II,* 272–305, 386–438. See also idem, "Die auswärtige Politik der Monarchie vor und nach 1780"; and Robert A. Kann, "Ideengeschichtliche Bezugspunkte der Außenpolitik Maria Theresias und ihrer Söhne, 1740–92," *Österreich in Europe der Aufklärung,* 1:557–74.

34. There is particularly good evidence in James A. Vann, *The Swabian Kreis: Institutional Growth in the Holy Roman Empire, 1648–1715* (Brussels: International Commission for the History of Representative and Parliamentary Institutions, 1975); but contrast the conclusions, for a slightly later period, of Reinhard von Neipperg, *Kaiser und Schwäbischer Kreis, 1714–33* (Stuttgart: Kohlhammer, 1991).

35. There is no general treatment of these themes. One aspect is briefly surveyed by Roger V. Paxton, "Identity and Consciousness: Culture and Politics among the Habsburg Serbs in the Eighteenth Century," in *Nation and Ideology: Essays in Honor of Wayne S. Vucinich,* ed. Ivo Banac et al. (New York: East European Monographs, 1981), 101–19; and by Strahinya K. Kostič, "Kulturorientierung und Volksschule der Serben in der Donaumonarchie zur Zeit Maria Theresias," in *Österreich im Europa der Aufklärung,* 2:847–66. Roider's own article, ibid., 87–100, takes up some matters related to the subject of his paper here. For Austrian diplomatic perceptions, see his *Austria's Eastern Question, 1700–90* (Princeton, N.J.: Princeton University Press, 1982).

36. I have presented some evidence of this in my *Habsburg Monarchy,* chap. 8. The subject has been illuminated in a series of magisterial articles by Volker Press, e.g., in *Klientelsysteme,* 19–46.

37. See, from Joseph's perspective, Beales, 1:110–33; from the perspective of the *Reich,* Karl Otmar von Aretin, *Heiliges Römisches Reich, 1776–1806: Reichsverfassung und Staatssouveranität,* 2 vols. (Wiesbaden: Harrassowitz, 1967), 1:13–27 and passim.

Part 1

**Religion in
the Counter-Reformation**

Introduction

Paula Sutter Fichtner

The house of Austria became a major player in European affairs at a time when religious concerns preoccupied the entire continent. Confessional upheavals during the sixteenth and seventeenth centuries spawned social, political, and economic issues that perplexed all Christian rulers. The Ottoman conquest of the Danube valley threatened to Islamicize Europe from the east, even as the remnants of an earlier Muslim presence left the Iberian peninsula for good. Both geographically and institutionally, the Habsburgs were on the frontlines of these developments. As Holy Roman emperors from 1440 on, Frederick III and his descendants served, at least in theory, as the worldly guardians of all Christendom. If anything, they gave the role renewed credibility upon becoming kings of Bohemia and Hungary in 1526, for the latter realm had long been a bulwark against the Turks. Most members of the dynasty fulfilled that duty seriously, if, from several viewpoints, idiosyncratically, since by the sixteenth century, Protestantism had given rise to multiple understandings of the term "Christian." Charles V was the last emperor to be crowned by a pope—in this case Clement VII—and that in Bologna, not Rome itself.

Christianity and Christian institutions received wide support from those who ruled Europe throughout the Middle Ages, the Habsburgs and earlier Austrian dynasties among them. On the personal level, the Austrian houses, as well as the medieval kings of

Hungary and Bohemia, actively advanced the causes of the church of Rome in the belief that their faith required it. Habsburgs and Babenbergs, Árpáds and Přemyslides, Luxemburgs and Angevins—all counted among them those who soldiered through crusades, endowed religious orders and bishoprics liberally, and used their authority to enforce Christian doctrines. Their subjects who neglected such teachings or defied them altogether risked stern punishment at the hand of local government.

But these rulers were secular officials as well, driven by the concerns normal to the breed. Long and often painful experience had shown that their claims to dominion in their lands were often hard to reconcile with the legal and financial immunities of the church. Medieval Austrian history is, among other things, a chronicle of tension between territorial princes and the great sees of Central Europe—Passau, Salzburg, Brixen, Trent—whose holdings stretched deeply and broadly into Austria above and below the Enns, the Tyrol, Styria, and Carinthia. As late as 1549, Ferdinand I declared to a provincial council in Salzburg that he would tolerate no interference from bishops in his Austrian governments.[1] The Habsburg relationship with the papacy itself in such matters was equally troubled. Ferdinand's great-grandfather Frederick III regularized at least one aspect of this to dynastic advantage when, in 1446, Pope Eugene IV allowed him to nominate suitable candidates for bishoprics that lay within Habsburg Austrian holdings, namely, Brixen, Trent, Chur, Gurk, Trieste, Laibach, Vienna, and Wiener Neustadt. Frederick's heirs, both the pious and the less observant, continued this policy. Rudolph II, Ferdinand III, and Leopold I firmly upheld the *placetum regium,* their right to allow the promulgation of papal decrees in their lands. On the other hand, tempting as it was to commandeer local ecclesiastical revenues for military and other fiscal emergencies, the Habsburgs carefully respected the general principle of an independent and universal church. When, in 1534, Ferdinand I forbade the religious foundations of his Austrian lands to sell their property unless he permitted it, the financial well-being of religious institutions was not foremost in his mind. Yet, while he and his successors frequently drew upon these resources to meet the Ottoman challenge, they usually did so only after Rome had given its consent.[2]

Hungarian and Bohemian kings had been equally aggressive when dealing with these issues. The Árpáds early established their right to found bishoprics and cloisters. By the thirteenth century, no episcopal election was valid unless the king had assented to a chapter's choice. Toward the end of the Middle Ages, expanded papal authority and fiscal privileges granted to the Hungarian clergy weakened the royal position, but monarchs recovered much lost ground during the fifteenth and early sixteenth centuries. Sigismund of Luxemburg, in 1404, and later Matthias Corvinus once again proclaimed the royal right to appoint bishops. In both instances, the Hungarian diet supported their sovereign.

Similar conditions prevailed, at least generally speaking, in Bohemia. After 1198, when the bishops of the realm were no longer regarded as German territorial princes, they received their investiture from their king directly. The end of the Hussite wars brought the dissolution of the bishopric of Prague in 1431, so that from then on Bohemian rulers worked in a somewhat different institutional context than did their Austrian or Hungarian counterparts. Nevertheless, the kings continued to bend religious establishments to their will in significant ways. Even before the Hussite conflict, the Bohemian estates had allowed the king to tax church lands as he wished, the privileges of the clergy to the contrary notwithstanding. In 1500, the otherwise ineffectual Vladislav II forbade clerical establishments to pawn or exchange their holdings without royal consent. Such measures often reflected fiscal weakness as much as they did strength. Nevertheless, they clearly bespoke the principle that an effective prince was one who could assert significant control over the territorial, judicial, and fiscal independence of the church.

Until the Protestant Reformation, however, the disputes that complicated the relationship of religious and political establishments in the Habsburg lands were largely institutional. While these were sometimes heated and spewed forth large cohorts of partisans on all sides, they did not end, Bohemia excepted, in systemic confessional innovation. From a contemporary standpoint, one should not even dwell overly long on Rome's failure to reincorporate the Utraquists into the body of the traditional faith. In the face of widespread spiritual restlessness, the Council of Constance upheld church unity and condemned Jan Hus in 1415, not the other way around.[3] Indeed, many participants in the deliberations had made up their minds on that score long before they met the Czech reformer face-to-face.[4]

The Reformation added a distinctively new dimension to these issues. Luther, Calvin, and religious radicals of all kinds wholly disavowed the sacramental core of the orthodox church. Worse yet, in calling upon Christians to validate their teachings through an examination of individual consciences, they opened the arena of religious controversy to broad masses of people. In so doing, the Protestant reformers created the problem of not only how one ruled a confessionally divided people but whether it could be done at all. Earlier princes and clerical officials had argued over their respective spheres of influence; these controversies did not vanish. But now territorial rulers were called upon to make decisions on the role of confession in their lands, a process that could alienate some, if not all, of those whom they governed.

That the Habsburgs themselves, with the possible exception of Maximilian II, kept true to the faith of Rome did not immunize their peoples to the appeals of the new sects, most notably Lutheranism in its various forms. By 1600, Bohemia, with wealth that rulers beginning with Ferdinand I had hoped to exploit, was overwhelmingly Protestant. Figures differ on just how many of their number were in the Habsburg Austrian holdings as the sixteenth century drew to a close. However, it seems safe to say that at least in Austria above and below the Enns—today's Upper and Lower Austria—they came close to, or actually constituted, the majority. Carinthia and Styria, or Inner Austria, as it was called, had large groups of converts as well. The Tyrol was perhaps the most important exception. Hungary, where Calvinism made significant inroads, would prove to be a problem in the seventeenth century, even though, as Robert Bireley points out in this volume, the Habsburgs controlled so little of its territory until after 1683.

Indeed, the Austrian Habsburgs were among those rulers most afflicted by the religious controversies of the Reformation. They governed subjects often angrily divided in faith among themselves and, in massive numbers, from their rulers as well. As emperors, they faced the same dilemma in Germany. Politically speaking, the situation had proven earlier to be advantageous only in very exceptional cases. Both Babenbergs and Habsburgs in the Middle Ages had used their claims to protect a true religious minority, for example the Jews, as part of an overall effort to limit the legal competence of the nobility, towns, and even ecclesiastical institutions in their territories.[5] As R. Po-chia Hsia shows, this strategy lived on in Habsburg dealings with the principalities of the empire. But Jews were only a small part of the population and spoke for no one other than themselves. Protestants voiced the concerns of all Christendom as they defined it, and the Habsburgs had to take account of them in all their political calculations.

The sixteenth-century Habsburgs of Central Europe therefore had little choice but to seek religious compromise and Catholic renewal at the same time. Beginning with Ferdinand I, they showed that they could trim doctrinal niceties to fit the circumstances, especially when military and political survival were at stake. Purely instrumental though it ordinarily was, such flexibility both distinguished and divided them from their Spanish cousins and in-laws. It was the impeccably Catholic Ferdinand I who, desperate for aid in the face of Ottoman attack, accepted the temporary *cuius regio, eius religio* formula at the diet of Speyer in 1526. Under similar pressure, he endorsed the arrangement again in the Peace of Augsburg of 1555. At the same time, he pushed through the so-called Ecclesiastical Reservation, which called for church property in ecclesiastical principalities to remain under Rome's control should the territory otherwise opt to become Lutheran. The arrangement provoked Charles V's vehement opposition and finally moved him to step down as emperor a year later. Shortly after, Philip II went to war with his rebellious subjects in the Netherlands against the persistent counsel of his cousin and brother-in-law, Maximilian II. This was not because the latter was a principled pacifist—they were few and far between in the sixteenth and seventeenth centuries—but because he feared that the conflict would set off a wider war in Germany itself. His sons, emperors Rudolph II and Matthias, both agreed to protect Protestantism in 1609 when their political positions were at stake. Rudolph issued the Bohemian Letter of Majesty to win the support of the Bohemian estates in his struggle to retain the crown in that kingdom; his younger brother did much the same thing with the estates in Austria above the Enns in order to remain territorial ruler there.

Ferdinand I may or may not have seen the Augsburg agreement as an immediate instrument of re-Catholicizing his Austrian lands. His energies in the last few active years of his reign were taken up with bringing the Council of Trent to a successful conclusion. Only if the church cleansed itself spiritually and morally and raised the general level of its intellectual life did he think that it could regain lost ground in Central and Eastern Europe. Maximilian II, though he was sincerely concerned for the moral condition of the traditional faith in his domains, came to regard the Augsburg settlement as something more durable, an attitudinal, if not structural, model for any realm forced to live with confessional pluralism within its borders. But this arrangement and the smaller compromises that the Habsburgs accepted did much to compound their troubles. Ferdinand and Maximilian discovered that they had only fostered expectations of greater religious freedom among Protestants within their lands. The estates of Lower Austria quickly and persistently asked for more public liberty in the exercise of their faith, however clear it was that if the *regio* belonged to the Catholic Habsburgs, their *religio* would be privileged in those lands as well. Maximilian II confronted the issue in 1568 and again in 1571. Burdened with a crushing load of debt and the ever-present Turkish menace, he yielded to the confessional demands of those who spoke for Lower Austria in return for financial support, though he managed to restrict his concessions to the nobility and their vassals, thus excluding the towns. His brother, Archduke Charles, who had inherited Inner Austria from his father, faced the same constellation of circumstances that led to the Pacification of Bruck in 1578.

Nevertheless, as Geoffrey Parker reminds us,[6] the Habsburgs were Catholic princes, not Protestant, the hopes of some among their subjects to the contrary notwithstanding. The Augsburg Peace supported those interests as well, though it was not immediately obvious. If the religious revolution of the early modern era initially made governing and defending the Habsburg lands much harder, it eventually gave these tasks an overarching purpose. By the late sixteenth century, signs began to mount that the Habsburgs were preparing to defend their ancestral faith more confidently. Ferdinand of the Tyrol and Charles of Inner Austria met with the duke of Bavaria in 1579 and resolved to stop compromising with rival confessions. This determination temporarily slackened during the reign of Rudolph II, whose neurotic withdrawal from affairs of state led his brother, Archduke Matthias, to surrender time and again to Protestant wishes in order to win their support for his own bid to rule both the Habsburg territories and the empire. But, as Bireley points out, Ferdinand II was of sterner stuff, willing to enforce confessional conformity throughout Inner Austria, and when the opportunity finally came, in the rest of the Habsburg holdings and the empire as well. He was not altogether without the appreciation for political reality found in his immediate predecessors. Bireley reminds us that it was the secular rather than religious challenge to the Habsburg role in the empire, where they were electors of Bohemia, and in that kingdom itself, that moved him to armed action. He continued, at least for a short time, to allow some confessional freedom in Lower Austria, where a sizeable number among the Protestant estates were willing to render fealty to him. Once strategically situated to clear the way for Catholic uniformity, however, he moved decisively, making it amply clear that political and religious hegemony did indeed, as almost all early modern rulers believed, go hand in hand.

Save for the Turkish preoccupation with internal troubles during the first half of the seventeenth century, the Habsburgs were not ideally positioned in 1618 for military action of any kind, much less long-term conflict. Their greatest success was the short, punitive campaign in Bohemia at the outset of the Thirty Years' War. In hoping to roll back Protestantism in the empire, Ferdinand II overreached his moral appeal and material resources. Yet, even in partial defeat, the Habsburg response to confessional issues was of singular importance. Out of it came a comprehensive Catholicism—theological, sociopolitical, and aesthetic all at once—which brought real cultural coherence to their otherwise fragmented polity by the beginning of the eighteenth century.[7] Past historians have stressed the special nature of this development and the equally special sense of identity this gave to the dynasty's peoples.[8] Along with

many recent scholars, however, Anton Schindling points out that
the Habsburgs behaved much as did other German princes, Protestants included, in shielding and advancing their faith before the
twin demons of heresy and the infidel and using it to more mun-
dane ends as well. The entrenchment of the various confessions in
all the German states went hand in hand with political centralization, the fostering of princely absolutism, and the encouragement of
supportive social arrangements as well.[9] There were, as Schindling
reminds us, countless obstacles to this process in the Habsburg
lands and elsewhere. Institutional peculiarities, such as the overly
large parish structure of the Austrian lands, or popular opposition
were only two. Bireley's picture of the complex and stubborn negotiations between the future Emperor Ferdinand II and the estates of
Inner Austria over the matter of Protestant privilege is but one example of the formidable defense that Protestants were prepared to
mount for the new faith in the Habsburg patrimony itself. The dual
goals of confessional uniformity and more effective administrative
and political control of their lands did not come easily to either Protestant or Catholic princes, including the Austrian Habsburgs, even
though the latter were backed occasionally by their far wealthier
Spanish cousins or Rome itself.

But Schindling also notes that the Habsburgs were alone
among German princes in using violence—specifically in Bohemia—
to realize their internal confessional goals. In itself this was a dramatic demonstration of their exceptional religious dedication. It also
turned out to be a successful policy at home and abroad. Even
where, in the short run, the Habsburg willingness to wage war for
the sake of Catholicism backfired, defeat turned into long-term advantage. Ferdinand II's 1629 Edict of Restitution may have failed,
as Schindling observes, to restore Catholic hegemony, and through it
Habsburg dominance, in Germany. Curbing Habsburg influence in
the empire nevertheless smoothed the way for Christians of all per-
suasions near the end of the century to turn Leopold I into a local
and universal hero of another kind—the deliverer of Europe from
the Turk.

More important, force was but one part of a larger Habsburg
religious offensive. From participation in public ritual—the Feast of

the Eucharist being perhaps the most notable example—to the vivid triumphalism of baroque ecclesiastical architecture and ornamentation, the dynasty proclaimed its faith to its peoples, wherever the latter were. A traveler in East-Central Europe even today would have to be blind to miss the impact that the Habsburg baroque in all its manifestations has made on that part of the world. Local languages may not have changed with the advent of Habsburg rule, nor very often did local social and political practices. What was clear both then and now was that it was Catholicism which made ruler and subject one. While this message did not insure complete loyalty to the dynasty, as noble uprisings in Hungary during the seventeenth century proved, it turned the confessional orientation of the Habsburg lands into positive dynastic capital for the first time since the Reformation. The issue of religious pluralism would reopen during the Enlightenment, but in a far different context. In the meantime, the Habsburgs, for better or for worse, had begun to define the nature of their polity.

Notes

1. Ernst Hellbling, *Österreichische Verfassungs- und Verwaltungsgeschichte* (Vienna: Springer, 1956), 258.

2. Ibid., 257–58.

3. Gordon Leff, *The Dissolution of the Medieval World Outlook* (New York: Harper Torchbooks, 1976), 118–47.

4. Matthew Spinka, *John Hus at the Council of Constance* (New York: Columbia University Press, 1965), 67.

5. In general, see Klaus Lohrmann, *Judenrecht und Judenpolitik im mittelalterlichen Österreich,* vol. 1 of *Handbuch zur Geschichte der Juden in Österreich* (Vienna/Cologne: Böhlaus, 1990).

6. Geoffrey Parker, *The Thirty Years' War* (London: Routledge and Kegan Paul, 1984), 6.

7. This is the thesis of R. J. W. Evans, *The Making of the Habsburg Monarchy 1550–1700: An Interpretation* (Oxford: Clarendon Press, 1979).

8. E. g., Victor-L. Tapié, *The Rise and Fall of the Habsburg Monarchy,* trans. Stephen Hardman (New York: Praeger, 1971), 84–114; Anna Coreth, *Pietas Austriaca: Ursprung und Entwicklung barocker Frömmigkeit in Österreich* (Vienna: Verlag für Geschichte und Politik, 1959), 5.

9. R. Po-Chia Hsia, *Social Discipline in the Reformation: Central Europe 1550–1750* (London/New York: Routledge, 1989), 3.

Confessional Absolutism in
the Habsburg Lands in the Seventeenth Century

Robert Bireley, S.J.

Absolutism is a relative term, both in theory and in practice.[1] A minimalist definition assigns it two features: a degree of centralization of government and the establishment of the ruler's clear predominance over the estates or representative body. The ruler may well recognize traditional rights of the estates, but at the very least, when conflict emerges over their extent or interpretation, his is the final and effective word. Given this understanding of absolutism, Ferdinand II, emperor from 1619 to 1637, first established it in the Habsburg Monarchy.[2]

Yet his was also a "confessional absolutism," a term that emphasizes the role of religion in early-modern state-building.[3] My purpose here is to discuss the nature of Habsburg absolutism under Ferdinand II and Ferdinand III, characterized as it was by these three features: an element of centralization, princely predominance over the estates, and the advancement of Catholicism. Despite setbacks during the Thirty Years' War, the monarchy emerged from the conflict as a European power. This was no mean achievement, especially when we recall the difficulties encountered by Philip IV and the Count Duke of Olivares in holding together the not altogether dissimilar Spanish Monarchy at approximately the same time.

Yet Jean Berenger in a fine study rejects the term "absolutism" even in an attenuated sense for the monarchy under Leopold I (1658–1705), arguing convincingly that an oligarchy of aristocratic families effectively controlled the formation of policy even in foreign affairs. "Ainsi l'absolutisme autrichien était un vain mot" by the end of the century.[4] The powerful families of the *Herrenstand* were able to reassert their power, perhaps as a result of Ferdinand II's policies themselves. So we have to raise the question whether there was a regression in the Habsburg rulers' power in the course of the century. My treatment does not include Hungary, or the sliver thereof under Habsburg control. There neither Ferdinand II nor Ferdinand III ever held the clear upper hand over the estates that they possessed in the Austrian and Bohemian lands, nor were they able to mount the systematic Counter-Reformation efforts in Hungary that they did elsewhere in the monarchy.

Paula Sutter Fichtner has pointed out the importance of primogeniture for the growth of a more centralized state in Germany.[5] Ferdinand II introduced it into the Habsburg lands. On 10 May 1621, shortly after the defeat of the Bohemian rebellion, he signed his last will and testament. He realized that if he was not to fall victim to disruptive confessional forces and if he was to hold the line against the Turks, the threat of whom had long occupied him as archduke in Inner Austria, he would have to create a greater unity among his lands.[6] His testament prescribed that "all our hereditary kingdoms, archduchies, principalities, lands and peoples, with all that is incorporated or belongs with them," be passed on by strict primogeniture "forever together," never to be divided. Indeed, in 1623 Ferdinand seems even to have envisioned the creation of a kingdom out of his Austrian lands. Later he solemnly confirmed his testament on 8 August 1635, about eighteen months before he died and after he had been compelled by the Peace of Prague to call off his Counter-Reformation program in the empire.[7] His efforts to maintain his inheritance as a single entity did not meet with complete success. For family reasons, he was compelled to make concessions to his brothers, Archduke Charles, then bishop of Breslau, who died in 1624, and Archduke Leopold, who was eventually made head of a collateral line that governed the Tyrol and Further Austria until 1665.[8] Yet his action was a decisive step in consolidating the monarchy.

Ferdinand took measures leading to greater concentration in Vienna of administrative and judicial authority for the Austrian lands and Bohemia. Most important was the creation in 1620 of an Austrian chancery distinct from the imperial chancery. Four years later, the chancery for Bohemia was moved from Prague to Vienna, and henceforth communication with Moravia and Silesia was directly from Vienna rather than through Prague. Ferdinand took steps to make Vienna a genuine capital city, one of which was to establish his own permanent residence there. He effected the elevation of the bishopric of Vienna to the level of an imperial principality in 1631, thus raising the status of the city.[9] He put in place governors (*Statthalter*) for different territories, such as Hans Ulrich von Eggenberg in Inner Austria and Cardinal Franz von Dietrichstein in Moravia, the nature and exercise of whose offices need further investigation.[10] Yet he never attempted to develop a system of judicial or financial officials reaching down to the local level, either for the monarchy as a whole or for individual territories, even though Maximilian of Bavaria had advised him to take this course in Bohemia with the help of confiscated lands.[11] A feature of the Habsburg Monarchy until the reforms of Maria Theresa was the lack of a graded bureaucracy and a class of government officials.

Under Ferdinand II, progress was made toward the development of a standing army under Vienna's control and the restriction of the power of the estates and of recruiters in military affairs. Following the Thirty Years' War, Ferdinand III decreed the maintenance under arms of nine infantry and ten cavalry regiments, and consequently 1649 has come to be recognized as "the birth date of a standing army in Austria." The following year, the *Hofkriegsrat* underwent reorganization. It was during the long war that the need for such a force became evident; in the midst of such a conflict, one could not dismiss the troops in the winter to enroll them again the next spring. Wallenstein, the ultimate *condottiere* who raised a huge permanent force, greatly reduced the power of regimental colonels and recruiters in his army, and these changes remained in the imperial army after his death. Ferdinand II also took steps to prohibit the estates from keeping under arms troops who were able to undertake offensive action. In a decree of 1635, he claimed that the "jus belli ac armorum" was his alone, thus asserting a monopoly of military force and foreign policy for himself as territorial ruler.[12]

Most importantly, Ferdinand established clearly that he, the prince, held the upper hand in his territories, and thus he broke the power of the estates and ended the *Ständestaat*. His discouragement of a common meeting of the estates of all his territories was undoubtedly dictated by the frequent anti-Habsburg turn such meetings had taken earlier in the century. At the same time, the mild nature of his absolutism and his successful effort to obtain the cooperation of the estates and their leading group, the lords, or *Herren*, set the direction for future Habsburg rule. Ferdinand's respect for the estates of the different territories encouraged a sense of regional identity that characterized the monarchy and still does the Republic of Austria today.[13] The Peace of Augsburg granted him, as it did all princes of the empire, the right to determine the religion of his territories, thus greatly extending princely claims to control and regulate the church. Otherwise his constitutional position varied in the different territories.

In Inner Austria, where the seventeen-year-old Ferdinand assumed power in late 1596 and early 1597, two intertwined issues immediately confronted him: the Turkish threat—the perennial conflict with the Turks had escalated into war by 1593—and the growth of Protestantism, which had made substantial inroads among the Inner Austrian nobility. Ferdinand immediately clashed with the estates over the religious issue.[14]

Much to his own consternation, Archduke Charles, Ferdinand's father, had been compelled to make religious concessions to the estates of Inner Austria culminating in the Pacification of Bruck in 1578.[15] Encouraged by his father's testament, which imposed upon him the task of leading Inner Austria back to Catholicism; the urging of his Bavarian mother, Archduchess Maria; and the Jesuits, Ferdinand was determined to re-Catholicize the territory, and this resolve to restore Catholicism was the driving force toward absolutism throughout his lands.[16] Protestant nobles, for their part, hoped to secure his written agreement to the concessions made at Bruck before the estates formally recognized him as ruler.

Ferdinand refused to make any such commitment, and the three estates still accepted his rule with a readiness that surprised the Catholic party.[17]

His first major move came on 13 September 1598, when he decreed the expulsion of all Protestant preachers from the cities and domain lands of Styria. Despite warnings from some councillors that his measure might well provoke rebellion, Ferdinand acted, and the resultant ease with which the decree was implemented first in Graz itself confirmed him in the belief that God was on his side. Indeed, he subsequently told a delegation from the estates that his actions were based on an "inspiration of God the Holy Spirit."[18] Increasingly, measures were taken to implement the Counter-Reformation in Inner Austria, measures which also effectively asserted Ferdinand's authority over the estates. Ferdinand believed that he acted legally throughout this whole process, and his most recent biographer seems to agree.[19]

Ferdinand issued a long, forceful response, dated 30 April 1599, to the Protestant members of the Inner Austrian estates that Hans Sturmberger has called the "magna carta" of the Counter-Reformation in Inner Austria.[20] His father had not bound his successors, he argued, a point some adversaries had earlier conceded.[21] Moreover, the preachers had violated conditions of the Pacification in many ways, for example, by pressuring peasants to abandon Catholic practices and by attacking him and Catholic prelates in their sermons. Ferdinand had to protect the rights of the church, he contended. As to his authority, the estates had no right to appeal over his head to emperor or empire. In fact, they had sought the intervention of Emperor Rudolph II without success.[22] Ferdinand's contention that he was a "princeps absolutus," not a "princeps modificatus," as he alleged the estates to have implied, must be seen in the context of his denial of the estates' right to take their case to the emperor. The term did not exclude respect for the legitimate privileges and liberties of the estates. Later, in his testament of 1621, Ferdinand instructed his son to honor these.[23] But here he argued that the religious privileges they claimed had no basis either in the "consent of all the people" ("consensus totius populi") or in the "assent of the spiritual or temporal prince, to whom it belongs to es-

tablish laws and approve customs" ("principis vel spiritualis vel
temporalis assensu, cuius est condere leges et Consuetudines appro-
bare").[24] The estates then acknowledged him as their "rechten
natürlichen erbherrn" and, thus, their "principem absolutum." But
they implied that this did not give him the right to govern their consciences.[25] The issue was essentially religious, and both sides appealed to conscience. With the Peace of Augsburg on his side,
Ferdinand won out.

Another factor in Ferdinand's negotiations with the Inner Austrian estates was the Turkish danger, which generally functioned as
a stimulus to greater unity within the monarchy. Since the Pacification of Bruck, the government in Inner Austria and the estates together had assumed nearly full responsibility from the emperor for
defense of the borders. This made it extremely difficult for the estates to withhold funds for defense, and it also compelled cooperation between government and estates in maintaining an adequate
military, which in turn played a major role in the development of an
Inner Austrian state.[26]

More than twenty years later, the decisive Battle of the White
Mountain in early November 1620 established Habsburg political
and military predominance in the Bohemian lands and in Upper
and Lower Austria. Yet before the battle, on 13 July 1620, Ferdinand
had come to a settlement with the estates of Lower Austria. After he
confirmed the nobility's free exercise of religion, the Catholic and
many of the Protestant members of the estates recognized him as
their ruler. Later there would be disagreements over the interpretation of this concession, but throughout the war the estates convened
annually—sometimes more frequently—and voted taxes regularly.[27]
The emperor retained their support.

Bohemia and Upper Austria, Ferdinand claimed, were in a different constitutional situation. By their rebellion the estates had
forfeited their rights, and Ferdinand felt free to impose his settlement on them. But here too, despite the well-known public hanging
of twenty-four rebels in Prague in June 1621, he eventually took a
relatively soft line. To be sure, he secured clearly the Habsburgs'
hereditary right in Bohemia and the establishment of Catholicism, a move that would later be followed up with vigorous

Counter-Reformation measures. But in the *Verneuerte Landes-ordnung* imposed upon Bohemia in 1627, he did not seek to set aside the estates and their functions. The new constitution, which would remain in force until 1741, was "not an instrument of absolutism in the French style." The estates kept nearly the whole administration of the kingdom in their hands, and they retained the right to approve taxes. The old Bohemian nobility generally remained in control of the major offices at court, and the *Herren* continued to exercise direct *Herrschaft* over most inhabitants. The principle of the *Ständestaat* and the estates themselves were so built into the structure of the kingdom that the political role of the estates could not be radically reduced. Even the foreign nobility introduced into the kingdom tended in the long run to identify with Bohemian interests.[28] Upper Austria received analogous treatment: strictness on the religious issue, otherwise incorporation of the estates into the government.

Why did Ferdinand not proceed more aggressively against the estates? This is a crucial question. Certainly, one reason applicable in the territories that had not rebelled was his sense for law. This was the case even in matters of religion, where he always claimed to have acted legally. In 1620 he wrote to the elector of Cologne regarding Lower Austria "that he had acted and would act only within the traditional limits 'as this land's indisputable hereditary Lord and Prince.'"[29] He remained within the bounds of the territorial constitutions, as he understood them, just as he believed, according to his Jesuit confessor, William Lamormaini, that as emperor he always acted within the constraints of the imperial constitution.[30]

In Bohemia and Upper Austria, Ferdinand did not attempt to reduce the power of the estates more than he did because he did not consider this necessary. His sovereignty was in place, and this was enough to carry out the religious changes he envisioned. He recognized that the estates had long played an important role in the administration of the Austrian lands and Bohemia, and he was not about to upset this tradition of the *Ständestaat*.[31] Moreover, he was wise enough to recognize that he needed the estates.[32] He had taken to heart what was taught as an axiom of government by both Machiavelli and anti-Machiavellian writers, such as Giovanni Botero and

Justus Lipsius, whose *Ragion di stato* and *Politicorum sive civilis doctrinae libri sex,* respectively, both published in 1589, were at hand in his library:[33] a prince could not rule effectively in the long run without the support of the governed and especially the dominant group, in this case the *Herren,* or aristocracy.[34]

To win their political, financial, and administrative support, Ferdinand conceded to the magnates a large measure of control over the peasants. First, he made no attempt to develop a class of civil servants or judicial or financial officers who would threaten to usurp the magnates' position, as had the rulers of Bavaria or France.[35] Perhaps there was no real alternative, in that there did not exist in the Habsburg lands a sufficient urban population from which to draw bureaucrats.[36] Second, magnates' demands upon the peasants were allowed to increase. In the sixteenth century in Lower Austria, twelve days of required work (*Robot*) by the peasant for the lord was the normal load. By the eighteenth century, this sometimes amounted to as many as 153 days.[37] Ferdinand followed this policy because he needed the estates not only for the payment but also the collection of taxes, a function they had traditionally performed, as the war devoured more and more money. Both he and his son successfully raised the funds they needed throughout a war that was often fought close to home. Ferdinand's consent to the magnates' control of the peasants also grew out of the desire to make use of an effective instrument to maintain order among a peasantry perceived to be increasingly unruly. It was part of the pursuit of order so characteristic of the early seventeenth century.[38]

Ferdinand pursued a further policy of creating a "Habsburg nobility" whose lands would be distributed over the territories of the monarchy and whose loyalty would be to the dynasty rather than to a region. Imperial favor and the bestowal of offices and lands would be a useful tool in securing the nobility's loyalty.[39] Prince Eggenberg, Ferdinand's chief minister and close friend, a convert who accompanied him from Graz to Vienna, acquired enormous lands spread over the monarchy in this way.[40]

A third element in Habsburg absolutism was governmental advancement and growing control of the church, a feature of the emerging state that has gained increasing recognition in recent years. Heinz Schilling has argued that it was a "motor" for the state's development equal in importance to a financial bureaucracy or a standing army.[41] By their championship of Catholicism, Ferdinand II and Ferdinand III set in place a foundation stone of the monarchy and enhanced their own position. One can rightly see in Ferdinand II the beginnings of the policy that will later be called Josephinism.[42]

That both rulers took seriously the obligation of a Christian prince to defend the church and to foster the religious development of his subjects is beyond doubt. Yet they were well aware of the temporal advantages to be gained through the "reformation of religion" in their lands. I can only mention two here. The first was the creation of a bond to hold the various territories together. As R. J. W. Evans puts it, "For all the diversity of its territories and institutions the Habsburg Monarchy, by the later seventeenth century, basically supported a single culture," at least at the top, and Habsburg Catholicism was a leading feature of this culture. "A revived cosmopolitan (Catholic) Church" helped the dynasty to triumph.[43]

The second political advantage of the reformation of religion was to bring the power of government to bear on subjects, nobility, burghers, and especially peasants in a new fashion. "In this way the individual felt for the first time the breath of the modern state."[44] Ferdinand II did not endeavor to extend the reach of government to the lower levels of society through financial or judicial officers; rather, it was through the church that he and his son sought to circumvent the magnates and influence the life of the peasants.[45] Already in Inner Austria under Archduke Ferdinand, the government took a much more direct role in Counter-Reformation measures than previously, when the bishops had usually been in charge and had been supported by the prince.[46] Later, in 1627, Ferdinand's confessor, Lamormaini, argued in a paper that was to serve as the basis for a Counter-Reformation program in Bohemia that both the ecclesiastical and secular officials of the Reformation Commission ought to appear in the king's name because the heretics would not recognize the authority of the ecclesiastical authority, and "piety can only be restored in Bohemia by a powerful authority."[47]

In a sweeping move, Ferdinand ordered the expulsion of all Protestant preachers and teachers from Lower Austria on 14 September 1627, a measure similar to the one taken in Graz in 1598.[48] In 1624 he had extended the jurisdiction of the secular courts over disputes regarding ecclesiastical property in his Austrian lands, in 1628 he reorganized tithe payments in Upper Austria, and in 1631 he decreed that non-Catholic wards were to have Catholic guardians and were not to be sent out of the country.[49] These are only a few examples of his legislation touching ecclesiastical affairs, the implementation of which was another matter. In 1633, at a low point in his fortunes during the Thirty Years' War and perhaps in an effort to win divine favor, Ferdinand issued for his Austrian subjects a lengthy mandate entitled *Tugendsame Lebensführung,* which was later reissued twice by Ferdinand III, in 1641 and again after the war in 1652 as part of a renewed program of reform. It called for the use of informers to check on Sunday observance and established measures to oversee and enforce the required Easter confession and communion.[50] Indeed, Ferdinand III continued very much in the tradition of his father, as he had been bidden to do, and he moved further in controlling ecclesiastical matters, introducing in 1641, for example, as a regular requirement the *Placet* before the promulgation of papal bulls in the Austrian lands.[51]

A principal instrument for the implementation of Counter-Reformation measures and the restoration of Catholicism in the Habsburg lands and elsewhere was the Reformation Commission, a variation on the age-old ecclesiastical visitation, in which government now played a heightened role. Ferdinand's first commission in Inner Austria, in 1599–1600, was led by Bishop Martin Brenner of Seckau, who was accompanied by a privy councillor, often a treasury councillor, a secretary, and a military captain with a band of two to three hundred soldiers for protection should this be necessary. Upon arriving in a town or village, the commission's first business was to expel the Protestant preacher if he still remained. Then the local community was called together, and the bishop began a series of instructions on the Catholic faith, the evils of Lutheranism, and the benefits of conversion, which was often presented as a form of obedience to the prince. Usually non-Catholics were then given a fixed period of time, often a month, to decide whether to convert, though in fact their Protestantism was often tolerated for years. If they did not convert, they could then be forced into exile, an option, however, not usually afforded peasants. The commission then generally installed a Catholic pastor and placed the village school under his charge. It looked into the state of the church building, inspected parish finances, and laid down regulations for services and for conduct, for example, the observance of Sundays and feast days.[52]

Ferdinand II and Ferdinand III later instituted Reformation commissions of this type in Upper and Lower Austria and in Bohemia. Except for Inner Austria, these commissions seem to have enjoyed only limited effectiveness in rural areas until after the Thirty Years' War. Between 1650 and 1652, Ferdinand III inaugurated a new *Generalreformation* in Bohemia, Moravia, Silesia, and Upper and Lower Austria, whose work continued into the reign of Leopold and brought the project to an end. We should note that for the most part the authorities realized that the work of such commissions was only the start of a long period of evangelization that, it was hoped, would eventually lead to genuine conversion.[53] Catholicism was thus eventually restored, despite the long perdurance of a crypto-Protestant remnant. In the process, many were forced into exile: from Inner Austria perhaps 11,000 townspeople between 1598 and 1605 and 1,000 nobles in 1628, from Upper and Lower Austria perhaps 50,000 people altogether between 1620 and about 1660, and from Bohemia as many as 200,000.[54] These figures indicate that the government was strong enough to implement its policy.

At this point, we can merely ask whether Ferdinand II and Ferdinand III intended to use the clergy, secular as well as regular, as a form of ersatz bureaucracy. The Habsburgs' generosity to the Jesuits and to other religious orders is well known, as is the orders' devotion to the dynasty, and their members served on Reformation commissions and, especially in the case of the Jesuits, founded and administered schools and universities. But in the long run, the restoration of parishes with effective parish priests was essential. Ferdinand II attempted to exploit his position as *Landesherr* in Lower Austria in order to secure a voice in the appointment to pastorates,[55] and with this came a role in the selection of schoolteachers, cantors, and sacristans. Ferdinand III required in 1652 that pastors in Lower Austria report each year after Easter directly to the government about the state of their parish and especially about those who failed to make the required Easter confession and communion. In 1659, as a result of church protests, an agreement was reached that these reports would first go to the diocesan officials in Passau and then be sent on to the government authorities.[56] Yet many obstacles stood in the way of the reestablishment of parishes, especially the lack of native parish priests and the retention of rights of patronage by nobles who were reluctant to appoint priests and assign them adequate income and so lose revenues themselves. Progress was slow.[57]

Confessional absolutism thus took shape in the Habsburg Monarchy with a degree of centralization, the subordination and cooperation of the estates, and extensive control of religion leading to an increasing *Staatskirchentum*. Robert Chesler concludes that "of the major powers only Austria avoided a crisis in the 1640s, and we find here the true measure of the success of Ferdinand II and Ferdinand III." Throughout the war they were able regularly to draw funds from the estates.[58] Yet, according to Berenger, as we have seen, by 1700 the *Herren* had reasserted their power to the point that by their control of government finances through the estates, they were able to dictate policy, even in foreign affairs. If this is the case, and the evidence suggests that it is, it represents a waning of the ruler's power in the second half of the century. So we have a problem that calls for an explanation and for further research.

Notes

1. See Werner Näf, *Die Epochen der neueren Geschichte: Staat und Staatengemeinschaft vom Ausgang des Mittelalters bis zur Gegenwart,* vol. 1 (Aarau: H. R. Sauerländer, 1945), 412ff., cited in Hans Sturmberger, *Kaiser Ferdinand II und das Problem des Absolutismus* (Munich: Oldenbourg, 1957), 7.

2. This is the position of Sturmberger, *Ferdinand II und das Problem des Absolutismus,* esp. 3–8, 45–46; see also Robert Bireley, "Ferdinand II, Founder of the Habsburg Monarchy," in *Crown, Church and Estates: Central European Politics in the Sixteenth and Seventeenth Centuries,* ed. R. J. W. Evans and Trevor Thomas (London: Macmillan, 1991), 226–44, which covers some of the same ground as this essay but from a different perspective. On absolutism, see Rudolf Vierhaus,

"Absolutismus," in *Absolutismus,* ed. Ernst Hinrichs (Frankfurt: Suhrkamp, 1986), 56–57; and Vierhaus, *Deutschland im Zeitalter des Absolutismus,* vol. 6 of *Deutsche Geschichte,* ed. Joachim Leuschner (Göttingen: Vandenhoeck und Ruprecht, 1978), 116–19, 141; and Otto Brunner, *Land und Herrschaft: Grundfragen der territorialen Verfassungsgeschichte Österreichs im Mittelalter,* 4th ed. (Vienna: R. M. Rohrer, 1959), 389–90, 438. For a discussion of recent trends in the study of absolutism, see Heinz Duchhardt, *Das Zeitalter des Absolutismus,* Oldenbourg Grundriss der Geschichte, vol. 11 (Munich: Oldenbourg, 1989), esp. 166–71; and Richard Bonney, "Absolutism: What's in a Name?" *French History* 1 (1987): 93–117.

3.   Karl Eder seems to have introduced this term; see his *Kirche im Zeitalter des konfessionellen Absolutismus (1555–1648),* vol. 3, part 2 of *Kirchengeschichte,* ed. Johann Peter Kirsch (Freiburg: Herder, 1949), 1–8.

4.   Jean Berenger, *Finances et absolutisme autrichien dans la seconde moitié du xviie siècle* (Paris: Imprimerie nationale, 1975), 484. See also 155, 234, 497–503. Disappointingly, Berenger does not really take up the issue in his *Histoire de l'Empire des Habsbourg, 1273–1918* (Paris: Fayard, 1990).

5.   Paula Sutter Fichtner, *Protestantism and Primogeniture in Early Modern Germany* (New Haven, Conn.: Yale University Press, 1989).

6.   Winfried Schulze, "Hausgesetzgebung und Verstaatlichung im Hause Österreich vom Tode Maximilians I. bis zur pragmatischen Sanktion," in *Der dynastische Fürstenstaat: Zur Bedeutung von Sukzessionsordnungen für die Entstehung des Frühmodernen Staates,* ed. Johannes Kunisch, Historische Forschungen, vol. 21 (Berlin: Duncker und Humblot, 1982), 264–66, 270–71.

7.   "Testament Kaiser Ferdinands II. Wien, 10. Mai 1621," and "Zweites Kodizill Kaiser Ferdinands II. Wien, 8 August 1635," in Gustav Turba, *Die Grundlagen der pragmatischen Sanktion,* vol. 2: *Die Hausgesetze,* Wiener Staatswissenschaftliche Studien, vol. 11, part 2 (Vienna/Leipzig: F. Deuticke, 1913), 335–51, 359–61. The quotation is on page 341. For the conflict in Vienna between those favoring a vigorous policy in the empire and those advocating a focus on the monarchy, see Bireley, "Ferdinand II, Founder of the Habsburg Monarchy," 228–30; and, much more extensively, idem, *Religion and Politics in the Age of the Counterreformation: Emperor Ferdinand II, William Lamormaini, S.J., and the Formation of Imperial Policy* (Chapel Hill: University of North Carolina Press, 1981). For Ferdinand's short-lived project of an Austrian kingdom, see Hermann Bidermann, *Geschichte der österreichischen Gesammt-Staats-Idee 1526–1804,* vol. 1: *1526–1705* (Innsbruck: Wagner, 1867), 27–28.

8.   Schulze, "Hausgesetzgebung und Verstaatlichung," 265–66. Even after 1665, these territories retained considerable autonomy; see Berenger, *Finances et absolutisme autrichien,* 5–6.

9.   Hugo Hantsch, *Die Geschichte Öcsterreichs,* 4th ed. (Graz: Styria Verlag, 1959), 1:343–44; Eila Hassenpflug-Elzholz, *Böhmen und die böhmischen Stände in der Zeit des beginnenden Zentralismus,* Veröffentlichungen des Collegium Carolinums, vol. 30 (Munich: Oldenbourg, 1982), 72, 75–77; Friedrich Walter,

Österreichische Verfassungs- und Verwaltungsgeschichte von 1500–1955, Veröffentlichungen der Kommission für neuere Geschichte Österreichs, vol. 59 (Vienna:
Böhlau, 1972), 70–74.

10. Albert Starzer, *Beiträge zur Geschichte der niederösterreichischen Staathalterei: Die Landeschefs und Räte dieser Behörde von 1501 bis 1896* (Vienna:
Selbstverlag der k.k. niederösterreichischen Staathalterei, 1897) has not been
available to me.

11. Hassenpflug-Elzholz, *Böhmen und die böhmischen Stände,* 21, 53.

12. John A. Mears, "The Thirty Years' War, the 'General Crisis,' and the Origins
of a Standing Army in the Habsburg Monarchy," *Central European History* 21
(1988): 125–39, quotations on pages 126, 132. See also Robert D. Chesler, "Crown,
Lords, and God: The Establishment of Secular Authority in the Pacification of
Lower Austria" (Ph.D. diss., Princeton University, 1979), 399.

13. Hans Sturmberger, "Der absolutistische Staat und die Länder in
Österreich," in *Der österreichische Föderalismus und seine historischen Grundlagen* (Vienna: Institut für Österreichkunde, 1968), 75–76.

14. By the estates of Inner Austria, I mean the estates of Styria, Carinthia, and
Carniola; they were separate institutions but usually worked closely together.

15. Sturmberger, *Ferdinand II und das Problem des Absolutismus,* 16–18;
Johannes Loserth, ed., *Akten und Korrespondenzen zur Geschichte der Gegen-
reformation in Innerösterreich unter Erzherzog Karl, 1578–1590,* Fontes Rerum
Austriacarum, section 2, vol. 50 (Vienna: Alfred Hölder, 1898), x–xxxiv.

16. Sturmberger, *Ferdinand II und das Problem des Absolutismus,* 16–17.

17. Loserth, ed., *Akten und Korrespondenzen zur Geschichte der Gegenreformation in Innerösterreich unter Ferdinand II,* vol. 1: *1590–1600,* Fontes Rerum
Austriacarum, section 2, vol. 58 (Vienna: Alfred Hölder, 1906), xxxiii–xliii, l–li.

18. Response of Ferdinand II to a protest of the Styrian estates, Graz, 25 July
1599, Loserth, *Akten und Korrespondenzen zur Geschichte der Gegenreformation in
Innerösterreich unter Ferdinand II,* vol. 1: *1590–1600,* #787 (593–94); Bireley, *Religion and Politics,* 14.

19. Johann Franzl, *Ferdinand II: Kaiser im Zwiespalt der Zeit* (Graz: Styria
Verlag, 1978), 71.

20. Sturmberger, *Ferdinand II und das Problem des Absolutismus,* 18.

21. Loserth, *Akten und Korrespondenzen zur Geschichte der Gegenreformation
in Innerösterreich unter Ferdinand II,* vol. 1: *1590–1600,* xxxvi.

22. Committee of the Styrian Estates (Verordneten) to Emperor Rudolph II,
Graz, 8 Nov. 1598, Loserth, *Akten und Korrespondenzen zur Geschichte der Gegen-
reformation in Innerösterreich unter Ferdinand II,* vol. 1: *1590–1600,* #542 (404–9).
The Committee of the Styrian Estates to Committees of the Carinthian and
Carniolan Estates, Graz, 9 April 1599, ibid., #710 (541–42), reports the emperor's
negative response.

23. "Testament Kaiser Ferdinands II. Wien. 10. Mai 1621," in Turba, *Grundlagen der pragmatischen Sanktion,* 2:349.

24. This document is published in Friedrich Hurter, *Geschichte Kaiser Ferdinands II und seiner Eltern* (Schaffhausen: Hurtersche Buchhandlung, 1851), 4:496–522, who calls it a "Meisterstück einer Staatsschrift" (203n.28). It is summarized in detail in Leopold Schuster, *Fürstbischof Martin Brenner: Ein Charakterbild aus der steirischen Reformations-Geschichte* (Graz/Leipzig: U. Moser, 1898), 399–409. Bishop Brenner may well have been the author.

Ferdinand's charge that the Protestant preachers operated even in the cities and domain lands, where his "absolutum et merum imperium" was uncontested, was intended in the first instance to emphasize their audacity, not to state a constitutional position. "Merum imperium" is a term from Roman law that designates legislative power as well as the right to impose capital and lesser punishments. This *Herrschaftsrecht* was the principal ingredient of the concept of "superioritas territorialis," which increasingly after 1600 was attributed to rulers of the German territorial states. In a sense, "merum imperium" is a forerunner of "superioritas territorialis." See Dietmar Willoweit, *Rechtsgrundlagen der Territorialgewalt: Landesobrigkeit, Herrschaftsrechte, und Territorium in der Rechtswissenschaft der Neuzeit,* Forschungen zur deutschen Rechtsgeschichte, 11 (Cologne/Vienna: Böhlau, 1975), 11, 18, 20–21, 46, 123–25, 187–88.

One of Ferdinand's principal arguments was that the Styrian estates had excluded the clergy and towns and even some Catholic nobles and then—without his permission, which was required—had summoned Protestant nobles from the estates of Carinthia and Carniola to join them. Thus the estates were not truly representative. Ferdinand did threaten the estates with unspecified dire consequences if unrest did break out as a result of his Counter-Reformation measures and they did not come to his aid as he expected. Earlier in the document, he warned that should they fail to make the necessary contributions to defense against the Turks, he would consider them enemies of the beloved fatherland.

25. Response of the Protestant Estates to Archduke Ferdinand, Graz, 24 Feb. 1600, Loserth, *Akten und Korrespondenzen zur Geschichte der Gegenreformation in Innerösterreich unter Ferdinand II,* vol. 1: *1590–1600,* #946 (esp. 727–28). See Sturmberger, *Ferdinand II und das Problem des Absolutismus,* 18–20, whom, apart from a few emphases, I follow in this matter.

26. Winfried Schulze, *Landesdefension und Staatsbildung: Studien zum Kriegswesen des innerösterreichischen Territorialstaates (1564–1619),* Veröffentlichungen der Kommission für neuere Geschichte Österreichs, vol. 60 (Vienna: Böhlau, 1973), esp. 18, 54–55, 71–73, 88, 95, 104, 135, 168–69, 214–15, 235–36.

27. Bireley, *Religion and Politics,* 9, 30; Grete Mecenseffy, *Geschichte des Protestantismus in Österreich* (Graz: Böhlau, 1956), 155–58; Chesler, "Crown, Lords, and God," 199–200, 218, 281–82, 291, 344, 370–74. For the Lower Austrian estates during the last period of the war, see Gunther Ortner, "Die niederösterreichischen Landtage von 1635–1648," (Ph.D. diss., University of Vienna, 1975).

28. Hassenpflug-Elzholz, *Böhmen und die böhmischen Stände,* 25–27, 61–64, 364, 435–43 (quotation on p. 25); and idem, "Die böhmische Adelsnation als

Representantin des Königreiches Böhmen von der Inkraftsetzung der Verneuerten Landesordnung bis zum Regierungsantritt Maria Theresias," *Bohemia Jahrbuch,* 15 (1974): 75–79. The Bohemian estates also lost the right to initiate legislation. Similar constitutions were issued shortly thereafter for Moravia and Silesia, which were no longer governed from Prague but from Vienna.

29. Chesler, "Crown, Lords, and God," 162, citing a letter of 24 March 1620.

30. *Ferdinandi II Romanorum Imperatoris Virtutes* (Vienna: Gelbhaar, 1638), author's copy, Vienna, Österreichische Nationalbibliothek, Handschriftensammlung, Codex 7378, 61.

31. For a general treatment of the role of the estates in the Austrian lands, see Herbert Hassinger, "Die Landstände der österreichischen Länder: Zusammensetzung, Organisation, und Leistung im 16–18 Jahrhundert," *Jahrbuch des Vereins für Landeskunde von Niederösterreich und Wien* 2 (1964): esp. 989, 994, 1015, 1020, 1022–24, 1033–35; for Bohemia, see Hassenpflug-Elzholz, *Böhmen und die böhmischen Stände.*

32. See, for example, Hassenpflug-Elzholz, *Böhmen und die böhmischen Stände,* 20, 79, for Bohemia. Sturmberger, *Ferdinand II und das Problem des Absolutismus,* 28–29, thinks Ferdinand's desire to retain the support of the Upper Austrian estates against the Bavarian occupation explains his conciliatory approach to them. But the reasons for his general policy, which applied to the estates of all his territories, must have been more fundamental.

33. "Cathologus Serenissimi Principis Ferdinandt Archiducis Austriae Librorum," Österreichische Nationalbibliothek, Handschriftensammlung, Codex 13,531. This seems to have been drawn up about 1615, perhaps with a view to the move from Graz to Vienna.

There are also resonances of Botero and Lipsius in the anonymous *Princeps in compendio,* which was initially published in Vienna in 1632 and often attributed to Ferdinand; see Heinz Dollinger, "Kurfürst Maximilian von Bayern und Justus Lipsius," *Archiv für Kulturgeschichte* 46 (1964): 259 and n.80. A new edition of the *Princeps in compendio,* edited by Franz Bosbach, has recently appeared in *Das Herrscherbild im 17 Jahrhundert,* ed. Konrad Repgen (Münster: Aschendorff, 1991), 79–114.

34. Botero, *Della ragion di stato,* ed. Luigi Firpo, Classici politici, vol. 2 (Turin: Unione Tipografico-Editrice Torinese, 1948), 1.8 (67–68); and Botero, *Aggiunte alla ragion di stato,* 1.2–4 (415–24) (*Aggiunte* appeared in 1598 and usually was published with the *Ragion di stato* thereafter); Lipsius, *Politicorum sive civilis doctrinae libri sex* (Frankfurt: Wechel, 1590), 4.8–12 (103–47). The prince's need for the support of the governed is a constant theme in Machiavelli's *Principe* and *Discorsi.*

35. For a comparison of French and Habsburg styles of absolutism, see Wolfgang Hans Stein, "Formen der österreichischen und französischen Herrschaftsbildung im Elsass in 16. und 17. Jahrhundert: Ein Vergleich," in *Vorderösterreich in der frühen Neuzeit,* ed. Hans Maier and Volker Press (Sigmaringen: Thorbecke, 1989), 285–314.

36. I should like to thank Volker Press for pointing this out to me.

37. Brunner, *Land und Herrschaft,* 299.

38. Chesler, "Crown, Lands, and God," 190–95, 199–200, 218, 363–66, 370.

39. See Josef V. Polisensky (with the collaboration of Frederick Snider), *War and Society in Europe, 1618–1648* (Cambridge: Cambridge University Press, 1978), 210–16, esp. 211.

40. R. J. W. Evans, *The Making of the Habsburg Monarchy, 1550–1700: An Interpretation* (Oxford: Clarendon Press, 1979), 172.

41. *Konfessionskonflikt und Staatsbildung: Eine Fallstudie über das Verhältnis von religiösem und sozialem Wandel in der Frühneuzeit am Beispiel der Grafschaft Lippe,* Quellen und Forschungen zur Reformationsgeschichte, vol. 48 (Gütersloh: Verlagshaus Mohn, 1981), 365–66; and idem, "The Reformation and the Rise of the Early Modern State," in *Luther and the Modern State in Germany,* ed. James D. Tracy, Sixteenth Century Essays and Studies, vol. 7 (Kirksville, Mo.: Sixteenth Century Journal Publishers, 1986), 21–30.

42. Theodor Wiedemann, *Geschichte der Reformation und Gegenreformation im Lande unter der Enns,* vol. 1 (Prague: F. Tempsky, 1879), 629.

43. See Evans, *The Making of the Habsburg Monarchy, 1500–1700;* the quotes are on pages xxiii, 311.

44. Inge Gampl, *Staat-Kirche-Individuum in der Rechtsgeschichte Österreichs zwischen Reformation und Revolution,* Wiener Rechtsgeschichtliche Arbeiten, vol. 15 (Vienna: H. Böhlaus Nachfolger, 1984), 6.

45. This is a main thesis of Chesler, "Crown, Lords, and God."

46. Schuster, *Fürstbischof Martin Brenner,* 198, 422–56.

47. Bireley, *Religion and Politics,* 36–37. A copy of this paper composed by Lamormaini along with another Jesuit, Heinrich Philippi, is found in the Archivum Romanum Societatis Jesu, Rome, Austria 23, fols. 1–21, and it is summarized in Alois Kroess, *Geschichte der böhmischen Provinz der Gesellschaft Jesu,* vol. 2, part 1: *Beginn der Provinz, des Universitätsstreites und der katholischen Generalreformation bis zum Frieden von Prag 1635,* Quellen und Forschungen zur Geschichte Österreichs, vol. 13 (Vienna: Verlag Mayer, 1927), 193–98.

48. Bireley, *Religion and Politics,* 45.

49. Gampl, *Staat-Kirche-Individuum,* 14, 22, 27.

50. Ibid., 4, 18, 29, 30.

51. Ibid., 13.

52. Schuster, *Fürstbischof Martin Brenner,* 198, 422–56.

53. On the Reformation commissions in Lower Austria under Ferdinand II as well as Ferdinand III see the fine dissertation by Kurt Piringer, "Ferdinands III. Katholische Restauration" (Ph.D. diss., University of Vienna, 1950); and for Upper Austria, Gunter Khinast, "Beiträge zu einer Geschichte des Landes ob der Enns unter dem Landeshauptmann Hans Ludwig von Kuefstein (1630–56)" (Ph.D. diss., University of Innsbruck, 1967). Kuefstein, who converted in 1627, served as the leading figure in a number of commissions during his years in office. For Bohemia,

see Kroess, *Geschichte der böhmischen Provinz der Gesellschaft Jesu,* vol. 2, part 2: *Die böhmische Provinz der Gesellschaft Jesu unter Ferdinand III. (1637–1657),* Quellen und Forschungen zur Geschichte Österreichs, vol. 14 (Vienna: Verlag Mayer, 1938), 556–82, who also indicates the opposition of some ecclesiastics to rigorous procedures. In Bohemia the great nobles also dispatched commissions on their own lands.

54. Berenger, *Histoire de l'Empire des Habsbourg,* 329; Othmar Pickl, "Glaubenskampf und Türkenkriege in ihren Auswirkungen auf das Siedlungswesen und die Bevölkerungsstruktur der österreichischen Länder," in *Siedlungs- und Bevölkerungsgeschichte Österreichs* (Vienna: Institut für Österreichkunde, 1974), 97–102. Pickl notes that much of this movement came only after 1650 and that it was prompted as much by new economic opportunities in Germany as by religious pressure.

55. Ludwig Wahrmund, *Das Kirchenpatronatsrecht und seine Entwicklung in Österreich* (Vienna: Alfred Hölder, 1896), 2:16–18.

56. Piringer, "Ferdinands III Katholische Restauration," 123–27, 208–9.

57. Berenger, *Finances et absolutisme autrichien,* 143–45.

58. Chesler, "Crown, Lords, and God," 363–64.

Delayed Confessionalization

Retarding Factors and Religious Minorities in the Territories of the Holy Roman Empire, 1555–1648

Anton Schindling

It was a consequence of the Reformation that, instead of the one Christian church of the Western world, there emerged several confessions, such as Catholicism, Lutheranism, Calvinism, and Anglicanism. German-speaking historians describe the process of church building with the terms *Konfessionsbildung* and *Konfessionalisierung*. The term *Konfessionsbildung* emphasizes the process of spiritual and theological discussion and definition within the church that resulted in the formulation of a binding confession (such as the Lutheran Augsburg Confession, Catholic Council of Trent, or Dutch Reformed Synod of Dordrecht). By contrast, the more comprehensive term *Konfessionalisierung* embraces the implications for state, politics, society, and culture that resulted from the definition of the confession. In fact, the different confessions not only had a formative influence on theology, liturgy, piety, and morals but also penetrated large parts of society with specific elements, so that the confessions became an essential factor of differentiation in political, social, and cultural life. Nowhere is this more evident than in the confessionally diverse German lands, as the important work of historians Ernst Walter Zeeden, Volker Press, Wolfgang Reinhard, Heinz Schilling, and Walter Ziegler attests.

Ever since the pioneering research by Ernst Walter Zeeden,[1] the comparative study of confessions has been one of the central developments in the scholarly treatment of early modern German history. First, the new approach had to win acceptance from an older, confessionally bound, both church and secular historiography. Similar work by French and English-language historians—for example, research on the history of religious mentality combined with social history—was helpful. A new picture of the Reformation unfolded that did not fit the classical division into the age of Reformation and Counter-Reformation that had existed ever since Leopold von Ranke and Moriz Ritter. Despite the fundamental significance of Martin Luther and his reformatory breakthrough, his renunciation of the Roman Church could no longer be seen as an eruptive and comprehensive new beginning. Older structures and mentalities limited the impact of Luther's innovations, and what changes took place became a topic of controversy for more than a century.

Luther's reformatory publications of 1520 (the famous "ABC-Schriften": "An den christlichen Adel deutscher Nation," "De captivitate babylonica ecclesiae," and "Von der Freiheit eines Christenmenschen") and the discussions about Holy Communion and the Augsburg Confession did bring about confessional separation from Rome and the creation of the Protestant churches.[2] At the same time, confessionalization began as a program for carrying out theological, organizational, and disciplinary norms of the developing confessional churches in the territories and cities. Not until the century following the Religious Peace of Augsburg did this process, with its all-encompassing social consequences, become a distinctive feature of the age, not only in the German Empire but in Europe as a whole.[3]

Catholicism, Lutheranism, and Calvinism achieved internal confessional maturity in the 1560s and 1570s with the conclusion of the Council of Trent, the Heidelberg Catechism, the Second Helvetic Confession, and the Formula of Concord. Yet decades passed before the theological and disciplinary norms associated with these beliefs were asserted in the territorial churches and imperial cities or achieved even marginal acceptance from parishioners. The formation of individual and group identities through the confessions, with their normative impact on society, was not completed until around 1700. Only then, after the main Christian confessions had ended their missionary efforts among the population, can one speak of an internally, coherently structured Christian Occident (except-ing Jews). This aspect is emphasized in modern French historiogra-phy, especially by Jean Delumeau and Louis Châtellier.[4]

Such methods have encouraged today's scholars to treat these issues in the German territories by closely connecting the history of the empire with the history of the territories or the history of the cit-ies, respectively. Above all, Volker Press has pursued Zeeden's ques-tions independently and most productively by correlating them with an analysis of the development of the territorial state based on a broad empirical synthesis of the history of the empire, its territories, and its cities.[5] His overall presentation of the seventeenth century is at present the best German-language study in this field.[6]

Using Calvinist examples from northwest Germany, Heinz Schilling has also looked at the process of confessionalization from a broadly comparative perspective and has emphasized the similari-ties and parallels.[7] Through his research on the papacy during the Counter-Reformation, Wolfgang Reinhard has analyzed the paral-lelism of "modernizing" elements in the confessionalization pro-cess.[8] Walter Ziegler has addressed the problem by studying territo-ries of the old church in the empire.[9] Such a comparative approach has aroused much controversy.[10] It has, however, proven to be very productive and has generally prevailed, especially in several impor-tant studies by pupils of the aforementioned historians, most nota-bly Paul Münch on Nassau, Georg Schmidt on the counts of the Wetterau, and Manfred Rudersdorf on Hesse-Marburg.[11]

Indeed, the success of the approach suggests that further in-vestigation of the problem of delayed confessionalization should also include a comparison of the Habsburgs' Austrian and Bohemian possessions with other imperial territories. The greater part of this essay will thus be devoted to such a comparison.

What exactly were the retarding factors that obstructed confes-sionalization and the development of a closed confessional state in many German territories? I would like to begin with the Catholic Reform and Counter-Reformation. As factors hindering Tridentine reform, one must mention first, besides the expansion of Protestant-ism, the traditional diocesan and parish structures of the old church as well as the mentality of the benefice-holding clergy, especially the aristocratic members of the cathedral chapters.[12] Even though pastoral activity suffered because dioceses and parishes were far too large, their borders were seldom changed as part of the Catholic reform. Not even the replacement of the archdeaconry by the more flexible constitution of the deanery was possible in all dioceses. The overly extended parishes in the Austrian lands and in the ecclesiastical territory of Salzburg were the main reason for the survival of rural *Geheimprotestantismus* in the mountainous regions. Only under Maria Theresa and Joseph II was the long-overdue reorganization of the parish districts in Austria undertaken. By this time, *Geheimprotestantismus* was already confessionally established, as was seen after Joseph II's *Toleranz-Patent* in 1781.[13]

The extraordinary missionary activity of the religious orders could not compensate for the weakness of the parish structures in those territories that remained Catholic. Nevertheless, with the help of additional orders brought in from France and Italy, the Catholic reform inspired by the Council of Trent did foster a wide variety of missionary activities, pastoral work, and spiritual and educational activity. The Jesuits and the Capuchins were especially active, but the Observant Franciscans, the Observant Carmelites, the Piarists, and the Ursulines also made important contributions. The Jesuits especially influenced the early and main phases of Catholic confessionalization, whereas in the last phase, after the Thirty Years' War, other religious orders became more dominant, apparently partly to counterbalance the influence of the Jesuits. Yet the delay of the Catholic reform in German territories, especially when compared to Italy and France, accounts for the far smaller number of initiatives for founding new religious orders in the empire.

The monasteries of the old orders, especially the Benedictines, first had to reform themselves before they could implement the Catholic reform through pastoral work and educational efforts. The foundation of the University of Salzburg by the Benedictines in 1622 should be seen in this context. This university is an example of delayed confessionalization, especially when measured against the Jesuit educational offensive, which had, by this time, already been underway for six decades. It was, in fact, only possible because of the intensive efforts of the Jesuits in reforming Benedictine monastic life in the south of the empire.[14]

The benefice-holding clergy were particularly opposed to the Jesuits as the leaders of Catholic confessionalization. Of the clergy adhering to the old church, only some were eager for reform; many cathedral chapters were unenthusiastic, as were Catholic university corporations, such as *Vorderösterreich*'s University of Freiburg im Breisgau. Here the reigning prince, Archduke Leopold of Tyrol, was able to introduce the Jesuits only in 1620 after battling long and tenacious opposition.[15]

As Hansgeorg Molitor has pointed out, the beginning of pre-Tridentine reform—a reform that partly had an inspiration different from that later on promulgated by the Council of Trent ("untridentinische Reform")—alongside old church traditionalism, was able to stem the advance of Protestantism in sixteenth-century Germany;[16] but it also delayed the further implementation of reforms inspired by the Council of Trent. Catholic confessionalization, coming from Trent and carried by the reformed papacy and its nuncios, the Jesuits, and other new orders, brought a superior conception of Catholic reform to Germany that was clearly more effective, since it had a European character and international support. Along with modernization, the Counter-Reformation from the south led to what Wolfgang Reinhard sees as a Europeanization of the lands of Catholic Germany.[17] One feature of this was the importation of the Roman baroque style into the empire; a very early example is the cathedral in Salzburg. The diocese of Strasbourg in Alsace took a different course; here the Catholic reform was not a complete success until after the Thirty Years' War and was linked to the Frenchification of Alsace, with the result that a significant link developed between French and Rhenish Catholicism.[18]

The cautious, traditionalist attitude of the cathedral chapters, which, for example, looked upon the Jesuits with great mistrust, was often responsible for hindering Catholic confessionalization in the ecclesiastical territories.[19] The Religious Peace of Augsburg, with its Ecclesiastical Reservation and Declaration of Ferdinand, reinforced opposition to reform. In many ecclesiastical territories, the prince-bishops, cathedral chapters, and increasingly Protestant nobility and cities found themselves stalemated. The religious question became mingled with conflicts between princes and estates, for example in Münster, Paderborn, Osnabrück, Hildesheim, and Fulda. Only in Münster and Paderborn did the prince-bishops bring about a complete re-Catholicization. This did not happen until the seventeenth century, which is late compared to southern and western Germany.[20] In the ecclesiastical territory of Münster, re-Catholicization came to a successful conclusion only after the Thirty Years' War.

The dynamic prosecution of a Counter-Reformation in the ecclesiastical territory of Osnabrück during the Thirty Years' War ended far short of its goal and resulted in the terms for parity for Osnabrück that were laid down by the Peace of Westphalia. Attempts at re-Catholicization following the Edict of Restitution in 1629—for example in Hildesheim, Minden, and Verden—were not successful. Late examples of Catholic confessionalization with varying success were found on the contested border of Catholicism in northwestern Germany. In the ecclesiastical territory of Osnabrück, the chance possession of parishes by one of the two confessions on 1 January 1624 was finally responsible for the definite assignment of those parishes to the Catholic or Protestant confessions by the Peace of Westphalia.[21]

In many territories, it was the estates that delayed or prevented the confessionalization desired by the princes. After the Peace of Westphalia, territorial rulers had to tolerate the legalized religious practice of local minorities that diverged from the territorial confession if their position had been established by the normative year of 1624. So the situation in a large number of territories was characterized by delayed confessionalization attempted by the sovereign, obstruction by the estates, and the continued presence of religious minorities. Most of these territories had not participated in the large wave of confessionalization at the end of the sixteenth century, and their confessionalization was caught up in the events of the Thirty Years' War.

Generally speaking, this finding holds for several ecclesiastical territories where confessionalization came late. It is also true, in a different way, for the territories of the so-called Second Reformation, to be discussed later, and the emperor's own Austrian and Bohemian crownlands. Here, however, the conflict with the Protestant estates was resolved violently, ending in the forced re-Catholicization of entire countries. In Austria and Bohemia, delayed Catholic confessionalization resulted in a military victory for the Counter-Reformation—though the triumph was incomplete, as is shown by the number of exiles and the continued existence of *Geheimprotestantismus*. In Bohemia, the Counter-Reformation Catholicism that emerged after the Battle of White Mountain was forced and artificial, as the subsequently lukewarm Bohemian Catholicism and Czech anti-Catholicism suggest.[22] In any case, it was an important factor for the history of Catholic confessionalization in the empire that the Counter-Reformation of the emperor was a late one, delayed but successful, violent but also accompanied by the splendid intensity of Habsburg Catholicism. Austria was now the most important example of a confessionally closed state in the empire, an example of confessional absolutism.

The history of Catholic confessionalization in Lower and Upper Austria after the unsuccessful revolt of the Bohemian estates provides another case in point.[23] There is no doubt that the radical policy of the Calvinist leaders of these bodies undermined the Protestant church. They succeeded in confederating the estates in Upper and Lower Austria with the Bohemian rebels and in refusing homage. In 1620, however, Ferdinand II persuaded a part of the Lower Austrian estates to pay homage, but in return he promised to allow them to continue practicing their religion in the same form they used during the reign of Emperor Matthias. Yet, after his Bohemian triumph, he submitted the remaining estates, including Upper Austria's, to proscription and confiscation. In 1627 even this promise to the Lower Austrian nobility was restricted to them personally; Protestant preachers and schoolmasters were removed from the courts with the explanation that they would profess Calvinism and blaspheme the Catholic religion, thereby encouraging rebellion among his subjects.

The punishment of the territorial sovereign hit Upper Austria with full force. Its estates in Linz were forced to pay homage to Ferdinand following its conquest by Elector Maximilian I of Ba-

varia, to whom it was temporarily pawned; they received no promises concerning religion, nor did a prior commitment exist, anyway.
Ferdinand II fully re-Catholicized Upper Austria while it was still
mortgaged to Maximilian, who was himself cautious with religious
edicts. Here the long-standing policy of moderation that had begun
under Ferdinand I was abandoned for the first time. The sharp divisions between the two sides were aggravated by the peasants' rising
in Upper Austria in 1626, which was defeated with military force by
the Bavarians. It was at this point that the Bavarian governor,
Count Herberstorff—himself a convert from Styria—executed
seventeen rebels in Zwiespalten and Frankenburg after forcing
them to follow the military custom of throwing dice to determine
whether they would live or die.[24] Distorted accounts of the "Frankenburg game of dice" ultimately became the subject of liberal and Protestant polemics in nineteenth-century Austria.

As a consequence, re-Catholicization, which at the beginning
was genuinely religious and was carried through by a traveling Reformation Commission, became more or less a regulation forced by
sovereignty. Once again, however, these conditions did not take hold
immediately. Inner re-Catholicization was clearly predominant in
Vienna and Lower Austria, as witnessed, for example, by the voca-
tion of Capuchins and other orders and their successful work, the
partial transfer of the University of Vienna to the Jesuits, persistent
attempts of conversion through sermons, and the leading role of the
court in religious practice. In Upper Austria, however, it spread
slowly and initially with less success.

Re-Catholicization also provoked a large wave of emigration
from Austria, especially from above the Enns, mostly into the empire via the imperial city of Regensburg. The exodus has been estimated at 100,000—a huge number of bitter exiles whose departure
seriously weakened those parts of the population which often were
intellectually and politically the most active. Of course, not all Protestants went into exile. Despite a high number of conversions, some
Protestant aristocrats and their subjects survived, particularly in
Lower Austria. Article V/13 of the Treaty of Osnabrück did reiterate
the emperor's promise of 1620 that the "Comites, Barones et
Nobiles" (though not their subjects) were not obliged to emigrate

because of their religion and were allowed to attend services in neighboring villages. In the future, this inspired close relations between these groups and the Protestant church in Hungary. Yet, in the closing stages of the Thirty Years' War, the Swedes were wholly unable to recruit supporters in Upper and Lower Austria during their occupation of the neighboring Bohemian lands. Even in Bohemia and Moravia, support was sporadic among a population that now viewed the Swedes as an enemy of the country.

To summarize, confessionalization started very late in Austria because the emperor's religious policy prevented a Protestant confessionalization but for a long time did not promote a Catholic one. When in 1620 this religious policy changed, the delay in confessionalization was made up for—though their ultimate success still depended on the outcome of the war.

It is a curious parallel that the *Territorialstaat* Brandenburg-Prussia, which a century later would be the major opponent of Austria in the empire, was also molded by a delayed confessionalization, but one that focused on Calvinism and the Second Reformation. When in 1613 Elector John Sigismund of Brandenburg converted to Calvinism, he could not force a change of confession in the Mark Brandenburg from Lutheranism to Calvinism.[25] Nor did he succeed in doing this in the other Hohenzollern lands.

In 1615, John Sigismund had to come to terms with the Lutheran estates of the Mark and guaranteed the Lutheran church. In Berlin Calvinism became the religion of an elite minority—the dynasty, the court, and the civil servants. The bourgeoisie in the capital and the surrounding country continued to adhere to a kind of Lutheranism that, even around 1600, was marked by many Catholic customs in liturgy and pastoral practice. These practices in the church of Brandenburg were compatible with the Lutheran Formula of Concord,[26] but strong resistance developed to a Calvinist confessionalization. On the other hand, remaining Catholic traditions aroused the opposition of determined Calvinists. This resulted in the spectacular iconoclastic outburst in the cathedral in Berlin in 1615.

In the German lands, Calvinism had to overcome the initial handicap of lack of imperial recognition. It also had to work against the opposition of the population, whose mentality did not readily accept the rationalist, Calvinist structure of the service and the strict morality. Calvinist confessionalization, compared to Lutheran or Catholic, appears to have been stifled by a lack of closeness between church and population and by the exclusion of popular religion. But more comparative research is necessary. Still, it is notable that territories that had come under Calvinist influence could be successfully re-Catholicized even at a late date, as witnessed by the Upper Palatinate,[27] the kurmainzische Bergstraße (a region between Darmstadt and Heidelberg), Nassau-Hadamar, and partly Nassau-Siegen. But the Calvinist movement retained an elitist, nonpopular character, and thus gained a special force, which was especially effective in the success of Brandenburg-Prussia.

The history of Brandenburg-Prussia leads to a final basic concept necessary for the comprehension of the age of confession—tolerance. In nearly all of the territories, the process of Lutheran, Catholic, or Calvinist confessionalization never fully eradicated religious minorities. In some Protestant territories, such as the former ecclesiastical principalities of Magdeburg, Halberstadt, and Minden, Catholic monasteries and cathedral chapters survived due to the imperial guarantee given by the so-called Contract of Passau, the Augsburg Religious Peace, and the Peace of Westphalia.[28]

The normative year 1624, determined by the Peace of Westphalia, stabilized the confessional possessions in the empire and secured the existence of minorities belonging to other confessions in the territories, as long as they could prove that they had held private or public services in 1624. This normative year therefore brought a legal solution to manifold problems that had been caused, since the beginning of the seventeenth century and during the Thirty Years' War, by the late and delayed confessionalizations with their successes, partial successes, and failures.

Pragmatic tolerance and legal parity between the two or three Christian confessions had become principles of the secular law of the empire through the Peace of Westphalia.[29] At first this affected and regulated confessional conflicts. Eventually a genuine tolerance emerged with the evolution of the Enlightenment concept of natural law. Thus an intellectual line leads from the Peace of Westphalia to the laws of tolerance of enlightened absolutism in Austria and Prussia.[30] The achievement of the Peace of Westphalia, in the history of the confessionalizations, is one of political and legal balancing, particularly of the delayed and the only partially successful confessionalizations. A rule of tolerance toward the other confessions and neighbors belonging to other confessions developed in the empire and its territorial structure, which now was understood in a secularized sense.[31]

The Holy Roman Empire in 1648 had changed from a Christian empire of the Middle Ages to a secular legal system guaranteeing confessional plurality, parity, and tolerance. None of the three competing confessions had succeeded in confessionalizing the empire quite to their satisfaction. Compared to the already strictly structured political and confessional powers, projects such as Emperor Ferdinand II's Catholic Edict of Restitution or Gustavus Adolphus's purported dreams of a Protestant emperorship were delayed efforts. These efforts had minimal chances of success and merely reinforced the movement toward a permanently deconfessionalized, secularized concept of policy. The delayed confessionalizations in their different variations led, after they had blockaded each other, to legal parity and a system of tolerance in the empire.

It was not the closed confessional state but rather the open, partly confessionalized state, continually moving toward a pragmatic policy of tolerance, that proved to be the superior model of the future. This was how Brandenburg-Prussia developed.[32] Yet one should not overemphasize the linear development from the still-Calvinist Great Elector to the agnostic policy of tolerance of Frederick the Great and to the *Allgemeines Landrecht*. In Austria the difficulties of the transition from a closed confessional state to the secular state of enlightened absolutism first became obvious in the debates on the necessity of a policy of tolerance during the reign of Maria Theresa and then in the resistance against the tolerance legislation of Joseph II.

The replacement of the confessional principle by the secular state was slow and often hard and painful. The historical result of the various confessionalizations, particularly of the delayed and unsuccessful ones, was religious freedom. Its implementation however, would still take a long time: 239 years of German history passed between the Religious Peace of Augsburg and the Prussian *Allgemeines Landrecht*.

This raises the final question: What did the confessionalizations lead to—and was it worth it? Obviously this question can only be answered subjectively, and the answers are open for discussion, but they can only be judgments from a historian's point of view.

I especially would like to point out that the age of confession does not constitute a lapse back to the Middle Ages, neither in theological aspects nor in social history. In their result, the confessionalizations were innovative: first of all, this is true for the history of early modern Christianity. All confessions were intensively committed to the religious education of laypeople: the lay Christian stands at the end of the long process of confessionalization in Europe and represents the new model, equally relevant for spiritual as well as social activity—whether as a member of a Marian congregation, as a Jansenist, a Pietist, or a Puritan.[33] Increased lay literacy was a by-product.[34] The success of the confessionalizations in Europe is spectacular, and I think that this must be seen as a fundamental factor in the development of the early modern era, even if this contradicts the theory of a religiously indifferent modernity. During the early modern period, confessionalization and Christianization on the one hand and secularization on the other one existed in a necessary, tense relationship, mutually dependent and making each other possible.[35]

Measured against the partially secularized ideas of Renaissance Humanism concerning the world and humanity, confessionalizations might appear as delayed efforts to reinstate a closed religious idea of state and society—delayed and condemned to fail. Still, all these attempts were not simply mechanical components of the modernization process. Each attempt was, in itself and in its relationship to its competitors, an important step away from the Middle Ages, away from medieval Christianity and its pre-Reformation ecclesiastical deficits. Seen in this way, the Catholic as well as Lutheran and Calvinist Reformations caused change and modernization—

modernizations in theology, devoutness, discipline, spirituality, and morality. Social discipline and the internalization of religious and moral ideals were central results of all three confessionalizations. They are also essential basic concepts of the modern world.

Notes

1. Ernst Walter Zeeden, *Die Entstehung der Konfessionen: Grundlagen und Formen der Konfessionsbildung im Zeitalter der Glaubenskämpfe* (Munich/Vienna: Oldenbourg, 1965); idem, *Konfessionsbildung: Studien zur Reformation, Gegenreformation und katholischen Reform* (Stuttgart: Klett-Cotta, 1985).

2. Erwin Iserloh, *Geschichte und Theologie der Reformation im Grundriß* (Paderborn: Schöningh, 1982); Bernd Moeller, *Deutschland im Zeitalter der Reformation,* 3d ed. (Göttingen: Vandenhoeck & Ruprecht, 1988); Horst Rabe, *Reich und Glaubensspaltung: Deutschland 1500–1600* (Munich: Beck, 1989).

3. Ernst Walter Zeeden, *Hegemonialkriege und Glaubenskämpfe 1556–1648* (Frankfurt: Propyläen, 1977); Heinrich Lutz, *Das Ringen um deutsche Einheit und kirchliche Erneuerung: Von Maximilian I. bis zum Westfälischen Frieden 1490–1648* (Frankfurt: Propyläen, 1983); Martin Heckel, *Deutschland im konfessionellen Zeitalter* (Göttingen: Vandenhoeck & Ruprecht, 1983); Marc Venard and Heribert Smolinsky, eds., *Die Geschichte des Christentums von den Anfängen bis zur Gegenwart,* vol. 3: *Das Zeitalter der Bekenntnisse (1530–1620/30)* (Freiburg im Breisgau: Herder, 1992).

4. Jean Delumeau, *Le catholicisme entre Luther et Voltaire,* 2d ed. (Paris: Presses Universitaires de France, 1979); idem, *Un chemin d'histoire: Chrétienté et christianisation* (Paris: Fayard, 1981); Louis Châtellier, *L'Europe des dévots* (Paris: Flammarion, 1987).

5. Volker Press, "Adel, Reich und Reformation," in *Stadtbürgertum und Adel in der Reformation,* ed. Wolfgang J. Mommsen (Stuttgart: Klett-Cotta, 1979), 330–83; Press, "Führungsgruppen in der deutschen Gesellschaft im Übergang zur Neuzeit um 1500," in *Deutsche Führungsschichten in der Neuzeit: Eine Zwischenbilanz,* ed. Hanns Hubert Hofmann and Günther Franz (Boppard: Boldt, 1980), 29–77; Press, "Stadt und territoriale Konfessionsbildung," in *Kirche und gesellschaftlicher Wandel in deutschen und niederländischen Städten der werdenden Neuzeit,* ed. Franz Petri (Cologne/Vienna: Böhlau, 1980), 251–96; Press, "Soziale Folgen der Reformation in Deutschland," in *Schichtung und Entwicklung der Gesellschaft in Polen und Deutschland im 16. und 17. Jahrhundert,* ed. Marian Biskup and Klaus Zernack (Wiesbaden: Steiner, 1983), 196–243.

6. Volker Press, *Kriege und Krisen: Deutschland 1600–1715* (Munich: Beck, 1991).

7. Heinz Schilling, *Konfessionskonflikt und Staatsbildung: Eine Fallstudie über das Verhältnis von religiösem und sozialem Wandel in der Frühneuzeit am Bei-*

spiel der Grafschaft Lippe (Gütersloh: Mohn, 1981); idem, "Die Konfessionalisierung im Reich: Religiöser und gesellschaftlicher Wandel in Deutschland zwischen 1555 und 1620," *Historische Zeitschrift* 246 (1988): 1–45; idem, *Aufbruch und Krise: Deutschland 1517–1648* (Berlin: Siedler, 1988); idem, "Nationale Identität und Konfession in der europäischen Neuzeit," in *Nationale und kulturelle Identität: Studien zur Entwicklung des kollektiven Bewußtseins in der Neuzeit,* ed. Bernhard Giesen (Frankfurt/Main: Suhrkamp, 1991), 192–252.

8. Wolfgang Reinhard, "Gegenreformation als Modernisierung? Prolegomena zu einer Theorie des konfessionellen Zeitalters," *Archiv für Reformationsgeschichte* 68 (1977): 226–52; idem, "Konfession und Konfessionalisierung in Europa," in *Bekenntnis und Geschichte: Die Confessio Augustana im historischen Zusammenhang,* ed. Wolfgang Reinhard (Munich: Vögel, 1981), 165–89; idem, "Zwang zur Konfessionalisierung?" *Zeitschrift für historische Forschung* 10 (1983): 257–77.

9. Walter Ziegler, "Reformation und Klosterauflösung: Ein ordensgeschichtlicher Vergleich", in *Reformbemühungen und Observanzbestrebungen im spätmittelalterlichen Ordenswesen,* ed. Kaspar Elm (Berlin: Duncker & Humblot, 1989), 585–614; Ziegler, "Territorium und Reformation: Überlegungen zur Entscheidung der deutschen Länder für oder gegen Luther," in *Ecclesia militans: Studien zur Konzilien- und Reformationsgeschichte. Remigius Bäumer zum 70. Geburtstag,* ed. Walter Brandmüller (Paderborn: Schöningh, 1988), 2:161–77; Ziegler, "Territorium und Reformation: Überlegungen und Fragen," *Historisches Jahrbuch* 110 (1990): 52–75.

10. Heinz Schilling, ed., *Die reformierte Konfessionalisierung in Deutschland: Das Problem der "Zweiten Reformation"* (Gütersloh: Mohn, 1986).

11. Paul Münch, *Zucht und Ordnung: Reformierte Kirchenverfassungen im 16. und 17. Jahrhundert (Nassau-Dillenburg, Kurpfalz, Hessen-Kassel)* (Stuttgart: Klett-Cotta, 1978); Georg Schmidt, *Der Wetterauer Grafenverein: Organisation und Politik einer Reichskorporation zwischen Reformation und Westfälischem Frieden* (Marburg: Elwert, 1989); Manfred Rudersdorf, *Ludwig IV. Landgraf von Hessen-Marburg 1537–1604: Landesteilung und Luthertum in Hessen* (Mainz: Zabern, 1991).

Through their study of the history of education, universities, and schools, Peter Baumgart, Notker Hammerstein, Anton Schindling, and others have found an independent approach to the problem of confessionalization. See Peter Baumgart and Notker Hammerstein, eds., *Beiträge zu Problemen deutscher Universitätsgründungen der frühen Neuzeit* (Nendeln/Liechtenstein: KTO Press, 1978); Peter Baumgart, "Humanistische Bildungsreform an deutschen Universitäten des 16. Jahrhunderts," in *Humanismus im Bildungswesen des 15. und 16. Jahrhunderts,* ed. Wolfgang Reinhard (Weinheim: VCH Acta humaniora, 1984), 171–97; Notker Hammerstein, "Humanismus und Universitäten," in *Die Rezeption der Antike: Zum Problem der Kontinuität zwischen Mittelalter und Renaissance,* ed. August Buck (Hamburg: Hauswedell, 1981), 23–39; Manfred Rudersdorf and Anton

Schindling, "Luthéranisme et université à l'époque confessionelle: Une comparaison entre Strasbourg, Tubingen et Marbourg," *Bulletin de la Société de l'histoire du protestantisme français* 135 (1989): 64–76; Manfred Rudersdorf, "Der Weg zur Universitätsgründung in Gießen: Das geistige und politische Erbe Landgraf Ludwigs IV. von Hessen-Marburg," in *Academia Gissensis: Beiträge zur älteren Gießener Universitätsgeschichte,* ed. Peter Moraw and Volker Press (Marburg: Elwert, 1982), 45–82.

Attempts toward a first assessment of the research results on the confessionalization processes have been made by the Verein für Reformationsgeschichte in symposia on the Calvinist and Lutheran churches and by the Gesellschaft zur Herausgabe des Corpus Catholicorum, with the volumes *Die Territorien des Reiches im Zeitalter der Reformation und Konfessionalisierung 1500–1650,* five of which have been published since 1989: Anton Schindling and Walter Ziegler, eds., *Die Territorien des Reichs im Zeitalter der Reformation und Konfessionalisierung: Land und Konfession 1500–1650,* vol. 1: *Der Südosten,* vol. 2: *Der Nordosten,* vol. 3: *Der Nordwesten,* vol. 4: *Mittleres Deutschland,* vol. 5: *Der Südwesten* (Münster: Aschendorff, 1989–93).

12.   Peter Moraw and Volker Press, "Geistliche Fürstentümer," in *Theologische Realenzyklopädie* (Berlin: de Gruyter, 1983) 11:711–19.

13.   Anton Schindling, "Theresianismus, Josephinismus, katholische Aufklärung: Zur Problematik und Begriffsgeschichte einer Reform," *Würzburger Diözesangeschichtsblätter* 50 (1988): 215–24.

14.   Rudolf Reinhardt, *Restauration, Visitation, Inspiration: Die Reformbestrebungen in der Benediktinerabtei Weingarten von 1567 bis 1627* (Stuttgart: Kohlhammer, 1960); Anton Schindling, "Die katholische Bildungsreform zwischen Humanismus und Barock: Dillingen, Dole, Freiburg, Molsheim und Salzburg. Die Vorlande und die benachbarten Universitäten," in *Vorderösterreich in der frühen Neuzeit,* ed. Hans Maier and Volker Press (Sigmaringen: Thorbecke, 1989), 137–76.

15.   Theodor Kurrus, *Die Jesuiten an der Universität Freiburg im Breisgau 1620–1773,* 2 vols. (Freiburg im Breisgau: Albert, 1963–77); Joachim Köhler, *Die Universität zwischen Landesherr und Bischof: Recht, Anspruch und Praxis an der vorderösterreichischen Landesuniversität Freiburg (1550–1752)* (Wiesbaden: Steiner, 1980).

16.   Hansgeorg Molitor, "Die untridentinische Reform: Anfänge katholischer Erneuerung in der Reichskirche," in *Ecclesia militans: Studien zur Konzilien- und Reformationsgeschichte,* 1:399–431.

17.   Reinhard, "Gegenreformation als Modernisierung?"

18.   Louis Châtellier, *Tradition chrétienne et renouveau catholique dans le cadre de l'ancien diocèse de Strasbourg (1650–1770)* (Paris: Ophrys, 1981); Francis Rapp, ed., *Le diocèse de Strasbourg* (Paris: Beauchesne, 1982).

19.   Anton Schindling, "Reichskirche und Reformation: Zu Glaubensspaltung und Konfessionalisierung in den geistlichen Fürstentümern des Reiches," *Zeitschrift für historische Forschung,* Beiheft 3: *Neue Studien zur frühneuzeitlichen Reichsgeschichte* (1987), 81–112.

20. Manfred Becker-Huberti, *Die tridentinische Reform im Bistum Münster unter Fürstbischof Christoph Bernhard von Galen 1650 bis 1678* (Münster: Aschendorff, 1978); Berthold Jäger, *Das geistliche Fürstentum Fulda in der frühen Neuzeit: Landesherrschaft, Landstände und fürstliche Verwaltung. Ein Beitrag zur Verfassungs- und Verwaltungsgeschichte kleiner Territorien des alten Reiches* (Marburg: Elwert, 1986).

21. Anton Schindling, "Westfälischer Frieden und altes Reich: Zur reichspolitischen Stellung Osnabrücks in der frühen Neuzeit," *Osnabrücker Mitteilungen* 90 (1985): 97–120; idem, "Reformation, Gegenreformation und Katholische Reform im Osnabrücker Land und im Emsland," *Osnabrücker Mitteilungen* 94 (1989): 35–60.

22. Franz Machilek, "Böhmen," in *Die Territorien des Reichs*, ed. Schindling and Ziegler, vol. 1: *Südosten*, 2d ed. (1992), 134–52.

23. Walter Ziegler, "Nieder- und Oberösterreich," in ibid., 118–33.

24. Hans Sturmberger, *Adam Graf Herberstorff: Herrschaft und Freiheit im konfessionellen Zeitalter* (Vienna: Verlag für Geschichte und Politik, 1976).

25. Peter Baumgart, "Zur Entstehung der Monarchie und des preußischen Staatsgedankens," in *Preußen-Ploetz: Eine historische Bilanz in Daten und Deutungen*, ed. Manfred Schlenke (Freiburg/Würzburg: Ploetz, 1983), 122–34; Manfred Rudersdorf and Anton Schindling, "Kurbrandenburg," in *Die Territorien des Reichs*, ed. Schindling and Ziegler, vol. 2: *Nordosten*, 3d ed. (1993), 34–66.

26. Ernst Walter Zeeden, "Katholische Überlieferungen in den lutherischen Kirchenordnungen des 16. Jahrhunderts," in *Konfessionsbildung*, ed. Zeeden, 113–91.

27. Walter Ziegler, "Die Rekatholisierung der Oberpfalz," in *Um Glauben und Reich: Kurfürst Maximilian I. Beiträge zur Bayerischen Geschichte und Kunst 1573–1657*, ed. Hubert Glaser (Munich: Hirmer, 1980), 2.1:436–47.

28. Wolfgang Neugebauer, "Die Stände in Magdeburg, Halberstadt und Minden im 17. und 18. Jahrhundert," in *Ständetum und Staatsbildung in Brandenburg-Preußen*, ed. Peter Baumgart (Berlin: de Gruyter, 1983), 170–207; Hans Nordsiek, "Zur Eingliederung des Fürstbistums Minden in den brandenburgisch-preußischen Staat," in *Expansion und Integration: Zur Eingliederung neugewonnener Gebiete in den preußischen Staat*, ed. Peter Baumgart (Cologne/Vienna: Böhlau, 1984), 45–79; Anton Schindling, "Kurbrandenburg im System des Reiches während der zweiten Hälfte des 17. Jahrhunderts: Eine Problemskizze," in *Preußen, Europa und das Reich*, ed. Oswald Hauser (Cologne/Vienna: Böhlau, 1987), 33–46; Schindling, "Der Große Kurfürst und das Reich," *Zeitschrift für historische Forschung*, Beiheft 8: *Beiträge zur Geschichte des Großen Kurfürsten von Brandenburg* (1990), 59–74.

29. Anton Schindling, *Die Anfänge des Immerwährenden Reichstags zu Regensburg: Ständevertretung und Staatskunst nach dem Westfälischen Frieden* (Mainz: Zabern, 1991).

30. Peter Baumgart, "Joseph II. und Maria Theresia 1765–1790," in *Die Kaiser der Neuzeit 1519–1918: Heiliges Römisches Reich, Österreich, Deutschland*, ed. Anton Schindling and Walter Ziegler (Munich: Beck, 1990), 249–76; Anton

Schindling, "Friedrichs des Großen Toleranz und seine katholischen Untertanen," in *Kontinuität und Wandel: Schlesien zwischen Österreich und Preußen,* ed. Peter Baumgart (Sigmaringen: Thorbecke, 1990), 257–72.

31. Dieter Stievermann, "Politik und Konfession im 18. Jahrhundert," *Zeitschrift für historische Forschung* 18 (1991): 177–99.

32. Peter Baumgart, "Grundzüge des preußischen Absolutismus", in *Preußen-Ploetz,* ed. Schlenke, 149–62.

33. Carl Hinrichs, *Preußentum und Pietismus* (Göttingen: Vandenhoeck & Ruprecht, 1971); Peter Hersche, *Der Spätjansenismus in Österreich* (Vienna: Verlag der österreichischen Akademie der Wissenschaften, 1977); Châtellier, *L'Europe des dévots.*

34. James Van Horn Melton, *Absolutism and the Eighteenth-Century Origins of Compulsory Schooling in Prussia and Austria* (Cambridge: Cambridge University Press, 1988).

35. Jean Delumeau, *Le christianisme va-t-il mourir?* (Paris: Hachette, 1977); idem, *Un chemin d'histoire.*

The Jews and the Emperors

R. Po-chia Hsia

On 17 April 1564, Sara, wife of Gumprecht of Schweigkhausen, wrote a petition to Emperor Maximilian II.[1] The innkeeper Gumprecht, Sara, and their children have been living in Schweigkhausen, in the vicinity of Memmingen, under the protection of the nobleman Sebastian Reichlin von Meldeck zu Sysenburg. Not long ago, when her husband was traveling on business, the nobleman came to their inn and inventoried and seized all their property, including her dowry, her husband's Hebrew books, her clothes, their bed sheets, their furniture—in short, "everything that is worth a penny." Although they owed their lord thirteen schillings in *Schutzgeld* and had some outstanding debts with other Jews, no one has come forward to sue them, declared Sara in her petition. And when she wrote to Sebastian, the nobleman answered that the confiscated goods would be sold to pay for their debts. Sara added that she had recently pleaded her case at the Imperial Diet that met in Augsburg. She is now asking the emperor for justice because he is the protector of all poor people.

Some time later, perhaps in 1565 or early 1566, in an undated letter, Sara addressed another petition to the emperor. She stated that although she had twice appealed to the emperor, the nobleman Sebastian had not restored their property. She and her children are in dire needs. She is now once again appealing to "His Majesty as the protector of all Jews" to order Sebastian to return the sixty marks and the properties taken away by force.

On 30 April 1566, Maximilian II wrote to Sebastian Reichlin and ordered him to return all possessions forcibly taken away from Sara. Another letter went out from Maximilian on 4 August 1566, ordering the nobleman to obey the previous imperial letter sent to him from Augsburg. In the meantime, Reichlin filed a countersuit at the Imperial Aulic Court.[2] In his statement of 22 May 1566, he asserted that Sara owed other Jews 150 reichstaler and that they had complained to him as their lord and protector. Moreover, Sara owed him *Schutzgeld,* which brought the total to 210 reichstaler. He only confiscated her property when she failed to pay up.

Apparently Sara did not give up. On 24 November 1566, Sebastian wrote to the emperor, asking that Sara be told to desist from pestering him. The dispute dragged on until 22 February 1571, when Maximilian appointed a commission to arbitrate. After further correspondence, on 11 August 1572 the commissioners, Karl Welsen, *Landvogt* of the margraviate of Burgau, and Isaac Hanen, *Rentmeister,* summoned the nobleman to appear in Günzburg on 17 August for a hearing, urging him to settle his differences with Sara.

Sara's case may be a dramatic one: a poor Jewish woman appealing to the emperor as the protector of all Jews against her lord. But it was by no means unique. Between the 1540s and the outbreak of the Thirty Years' War, there were dozens of cases that came before the Imperial Aulic Court in which Jews were one or both of the parties.[3] Appeals by Jewish parties continued throughout the seventeenth and eighteenth centuries, albeit at a lower volume compared to the period from the 1540s to 1618. The cases fall into two broad categories: lawsuits and appeals for repayment of debt, and appeals against infringement of Jewish privileges. The majority of the former cases were brought by Jewish creditors against debtors who were members of the imperial estates (*Reichsstände*), and sometimes against another Jewish party. Cases of infringement of justice, as in the example of Sara, were based on the *jus commune* of the empire and on the particular privileges and ordinances governing Jewish life in various localities of the empire.

In the remainder of this essay, I shall offer some preliminary observations based on a reading of several of these cases at the Imperial Aulic Court. I shall then suggest some significant themes in the relationship between the emperors and the Jews within the Holy Roman Empire of the sixteenth and seventeenth centuries, both in terms of the actual workings of Habsburg power and from the perspective of a religious and ethnic minority.

First of all, a distinction must be made between the person of the emperor and the institution of the emperorship. In regard to Jewish policies in the Holy Roman Empire, the personal disposition of individual emperors was secondary to the long-term objectives of imperial institutions, or to the articulation of the dynastic and imperial interests of the Habsburgs. Indeed, a policy of *Judenschutz* (protection of Jews) did not necessarily imply a favorable disposition. A brief comparison among the three emperors—Maximilian I, Maximilian II, and Rudolph II—may illustrate this point.

Maximilian I was a strong supporter of the cult of Simon of Trent, who was allegedly killed in 1475 in a ritual murder. His devotion went back as early as 1479; when he was archduke, he erected a monument of silver in Simon's honor; in 1495, he ordered Simon's coffin to be opened for pious viewing; and when he was proclaimed emperor in 1508, Simon's relics were displayed in a procession in his honor.[4] These feelings, it would seem, played a role in the Pfefferkorn Affair of 1508, when the emperor gave permission to the Jewish convert to confiscate and burn Talmudic books in the empire, contrary to the privileges he had earlier granted to the Frankfurt Jewish community. Similarly with Maximilian II, one can discern a personal dislike of Jews. In his diary entries, Maximilian II described Jews as a quarrelsome and deceitful people who denounced one another, gave usurious loans to miners and artisans, and traded in inferior metals.[5] Between 1567 and 1573, the emperor repeatedly issued mandates to expel Jews and prohibit usury in Lower Austria, orders whose executions apparently were less than complete.[6] The Habsburgs did not all dislike Jews. In the well-known case of Rudolph II, who was favorably disposed toward the Jews of Prague, his interest in the occult even led to an audience with the leading Jewish cabalists of Prague, an event that assumed legendary proportion in later Jewish folklore.[7]

These episodes aside, and in spite of the different personal reactions of the emperors, it was rather the routine workings of the imperial institutions, through the Imperial Aulic Court in Prague and later Vienna and through the government of Further Austria in Tyrol with the attendant local officials, that shaped the contours of Jewish policies. A sharp differentiation must be made, however, between Habsburg Jewish policy in the empire and in the *Erblande* (the hereditary lands). Within the empire, the Habsburg emperors acted as the guardians of peace, tradition, and privileges; the protection of Jews not only strengthened a traditional regalian right but also gave opportunities for imperial intervention in the affairs of the imperial estates. Within the hereditary lands, however, the ruling house was subjected to the direct pressure of the provincial estates, which included periodic expressions of anti-Jewish grievances and calls for expulsion.

Let us first examine Habsburg Jewish policy in the empire itself. The overall objective of the Habsburgs was already well established by Emperor Frederick III in the 1460s and 1470s: a vigorous policy to regain regalian rights over the Jews of the empire in order to strengthen the authority and the finances of the dynasty. The policy of *Judenschutz,* therefore, represented a consolidation of Habsburg rule and was continued, with occasional reversals under Maximilian I, by all the Habsburg emperors into the seventeenth century.

Under Maximilian I, chronic fiscal needs resulted in an inconsistent and ad hoc Jewish policy. Eager to raise funds from all possible sources, the emperor granted privileges of toleration to Jews while allowing imperial cities to invalidate those privileges in order to expel or exclude Jews. In spite of the general ineffectiveness of Maximilian's Jewish policy, the first steps were taken to regain the *Judenregalien* that had been lost to the various imperial estates during the previous two centuries.

During the reign of Charles V, the constitutional framework for toleration was laid in a series of Jewish privileges in return for Jewish financial contributions to the imperial war effort against the Protestants. The regulation of interests on loans, the prohibition of ritual murder trials, the protection of the person and property of the Jews, the allowance of free travel, and the stipulation of Jews as subjects of the emperor constituted the legal basis for a more secure presence of Jewish communities within the empire during a time of heightened religious tensions among Christians and renewed calls for expulsions of Jews.

During the next eighty years, between the 1540s and 1618, in spite of occasional contradictions and inconsistencies, this imperial policy of *Judenschutz* asserted itself against long-standing legal obstacles and prejudices against the Jews. I shall select two case studies to illustrate the workings of the Habsburg Jewish policy and its effectiveness and limitations. The first example is that of the bishopric of Würzburg; the second concerns the imperial city of Worms.

In 1543, several Jews of Würzburg were arrested on the charge of ritual murder. Acting on the appeal of Josel of Rosheim, the leader of the Jewish communities in the empire, Charles V wrote on 3 March 1544, asking the bishop to free the Jews, who included several women and one sixteen-year-old girl. They had been held for a long time and were denied the food and clothing brought to them by friends and relatives. Charles asked the bishop to be merciful in judgment, and in view of the fact that the Jews were being held against imperial law, he urged they be released.[8] Twenty-six years later, in 1570, another accusation of ritual murder arose in Würzburg: accused of murdering a boy, Moses and Gumpen of Dertzbach were imprisoned by Bishop Friedrich. Again, the emperor, this time Maximilian II, wrote to the bishop to intercede and free the Jews.[9]

These two accusations of ritual murder occurred in a period of anti-Jewish agitation in the territory of Würzburg. Responding to the numerous grievances against Jewish moneylending in the territory, Bishop Friedrich obtained a privilege from Emperor Ferdinand, dated 28 July 1559, that allowed him to expel all Jews from his territory.[10] Simply moving onto the neighboring estates of the Imperial Knights, the Jews carried on their business within the territory of Würzburg. The execution of this mandate was thus largely ineffective, and some Jewish families remained in the city of Würzburg.

A more vigorous policy of Jewish exclusion was carried out later by Bishop Friedrich and by his successor, Bishop Julius, between 1567 and 1575. On 9 February 1575, Bishop Julius publicized a mandate of expulsion forbidding his subjects to trade with the

Jews. In response to petitions from the Imperial Knights and the Jews in Franconia, Maximilian reversed the policy of his father and on 20 June 1575 wrote to Würzburg on behalf of the Jews.[11] In his reply, Bishop Julius cited the decree granted by Ferdinand to his predecessor that invalidated all the privileges of the Jews. In protecting his subjects against Jewish usury, Bishop Julius claimed that he was doing his duty as an imperial prince. Faced with new repressive measures, the Franconian Jews again appealed in 1576. On 18 October 1576, the new Emperor Rudolph II forwarded the petition of the Franconian Jews to Bishop Julius and asked the bishop to accede to his wishes in granting the Jews more liberties. Petitions and correspondence continued until 18 June 1578, when Bishop Julius agreed to the appointment of an imperial commission.

The second example of imperial Jewish policy concerns the imperial city of Worms. This conflict first came before the Imperial Aulic Court in 1558, when the "Gemainer Judischait in Teutscher Nation in Worms" appealed to Emperor Ferdinand, and was only resolved in 1616 with the forcible expulsion of Jews and their restitution by imperial forces. The details of the uprising between 1613 and 1617 have been recently reconstructed by Christopher Friedrichs, so I shall limit myself here to analyzing the expulsion conflict in the mid-sixteenth century.[12]

Although historians have generally considered Regensburg 1519 as the final act in a long series of expulsion of Jews from imperial cities, they have overlooked the strong undercurrent of anti-Jewish resentment in imperial cities throughout the sixteenth century, as represented by, for example, the expulsion of Jewish communities from Esslingen (1543) and Dortmund (1595).[13] The events in Worms were part of this larger pattern.

Under mounting pressure from burghers' complaints against Jewish moneylending, the magistrates of Worms sought permission in 1558 to terminate the *Geding* (residence contract) of the Jewish community. On 8 June 1559, the city received a privilege from Ferdinand I allowing Worms to rescind the residency of the Jews in two years. Immediately, the Jewish community appealed, citing this as an infringement of the privileges they had received from previous emperors. The bishop of Worms also interceded, claiming injury of his liberties in case of an expulsion. After charges and counter-charges, in 1561 Ferdinand appointed an imperial commission of seven to deliberate. The commission itself split on the question, with Archbishop Daniel of Mainz supporting the bishop of Worms and the Jews, and Frederick Count Palatine arguing for expulsion. Two new commissioners were added in 1563—Duke Christoff of Württemberg and Bishop Marquardt of Speyer. In August 1563, the commission reported to Ferdinand but did not come up with any recommendations because of the unwillingness of the bishop of Worms to cooperate.

In any case, the conflict died down after 1563, when an investigation of ritual murder by the city council in Worms backfired on the city. Relatives of the accused Jew, Abraham zum Bock, filed a lawsuit against the city at the Imperial Chamber Court; and the city was cited as a defendant for violation of the rights and privileges of the Jews and for conducting a ritual murder trial against imperial law. In 1564, Abraham was released from jail, and the calls for expulsion also died down.

Six years later, another attempt by the magistrates to expel the Jews met with similar protests from the bishop of Worms and the Jewish community. Thereafter, things got quieter, although anti-Jewish resentment never went away. By 1612, guild grievances came to the fore again, eventually leading to the expulsion of the Jewish community and to the turmoil associated with the uprising of Vincent Fettmilch in Frankfurt, the history of which is well known and does not need repeating.[14]

A short penultimate remark may be in order for the period after 1648, which this essay cannot discuss at length. As I suggested earlier, the Habsburg policy toward Jews in the empire and in the hereditary lands followed different imperatives and reacted to different political structures. In the empire, the emperors upheld the residence and religious rights of Jews, a policy that was most successfully carried out in the territorially and politically weaker areas under the imperial cities and the Imperial Knights. Volker Press has alluded to some of the salient characteristics of the seventeenth-century empire: the channeling of potentially violent conflicts into legal disputes, the primacy of reason of state over religious conformity, and the protection of privileges against aggression.[15] The Jewish policy of the emperors within the empire was very much a reflection of this general pattern, which also characterized the toleration of Jews by many territorial princes. Compared to the fifteenth and sixteenth centuries, the expulsion of Jews, a violation of imperial peace and privilege, was no longer tolerated, as the failure of the citizen uprisings in Frankfurt and Worms clearly demonstrate. The Jewish community in Frankfurt, the largest in the empire, continued to enjoy the protection of emperors Leopold I, Joseph I, and Charles VI, in spite of persistent anti-Jewish resentment among broad segments of the urban population.[16] The contrast between Frankfurt and Vienna after 1648 is therefore all the sharper when considered in light of the 1670 expulsion of Viennese Jews. The mandate of expulsion, which was not signed by Leopold I but issued in his name, resulted in part from the anti-Jewish violence in the capital that the urban magistrates did not and could not control.[17] Although the Jewish community was able to reestablish itself in the capital within three years, the episode exposed not only the persistent anti-Jewish resentment of the Lower Austrian estates but also the narrower confines of Jewish toleration within the dynastic lands.

While a definitive study of the Habsburgs and the Jews is still to be written, four concluding observations may be permitted as working hypotheses:

1.   The anti-Jewish agitation in the empire was embedded in a larger structure of constitutional and social conflict between imperial estates, between ruler and ruled, and between social groups. In Würzburg the Imperial Knights supported the Jews against the bishop; in Worms, the bishop played the role of protector against the city. This constitutional conflict was further complicated by confessional antagonism: although most Franconian Imperial Knights and the city of Worms professed Lutheranism, their opposition to the Catholic bishops took different forms on the Jewish issue. The effectiveness of imperial Jewish policy in the empire, and of Habsburg rule in general, depended on the skillful manipulation and balancing of these constitutional and confessional tensions.

2.   The general effect of imperial Jewish policy aimed to channel anti-Jewish conflicts into established legal and institutionalized forms of resolution. Through the use of the Imperial Aulic Court and the ap-

pointment of imperial commissions, common practices in the instrumentalization of Habsburg policy in the empire, the regulation of Jewish life became more exclusively matters of *Polizei* and constitutional rights, and not of religion and theology.

3.   In the long run, imperial policy integrated the Jews of the empire into the clientage system of the Habsburgs.[18] In addition to the obvious fiscal contributions of the Jews that prepared the way for the court factors of the seventeenth and eighteenth centuries, the protection of Jewish privileges gave the Habsburgs the opportunity to intervene in the affairs of the imperial estates, especially in the politically fragmented German southwest.[19]

4.   The effective protection of Jewish life and property helped to give German Jews a more effective organization and a sense of loyalty to both the emperor and the empire. In spite of the failure of the Jewish communities to develop an imperial rabbinate, the major Jewish communities in Frankfurt, Worms, and Prague helped to give Jewish life an imperial dimension and cohesion. Thus, the transformation of Jews into a quasi-*Reichsverband* acted as one of the countering forces to the territorialization of the early modern empire.

Notes

1.   The documents of Sara's case are deposited in Vienna, Haus- Hof- und Staatsarchiv (hereafter HHStA), Reichshofrat (RHR), Alte Prager Akten J1.

2.   The documents of Reichlin's countersuit are deposited in HHStA, RHR, Antiqua 665, no. 10.

3.   The files are found in two depositories of the HHStA, RHR: Alte Prager Akten and Antiqua.

4.   Archivio di Stato, Trent, Archivio Principesco-Vescovile, Sezione Latine, Capsa 69, no. 1e, no. 137; Hermann Wiesflecker, *Kaiser Maximilian I: Das Reich, Österreich und Europa an der Wende zur Neuzeit* (Munich: Oldenbourg, 1981), 4:9–10; Benedetto Bonelli, *Dissertazione apologetica sul martirio del Beato Simone da Trento nell'anno 1475 dagli ebrei ucciso* (Trent, 1747), 212a. On the cult of Simon, see R. Po-chia Hsia, *Trent 1475: Stories of a Ritual Murder Trial* (New Haven, Conn.: Yale University Press, 1992).

5.   Communication of Professor Paula Sutter Fichtner, Brooklyn College.

6.   See A. F. Pribram, ed., *Urkunden und Akten zur Geschichte der Juden in Wien,* part 1, *Allgemeiner Teil 1526–1847 (1849),* Quellen und Forschungen zur Geschichte der Juden in Deutsch-Österreich, vol. 8 (Vienna: Braumüller, 1918), 1:21–34.

7.   Cf. Bedrich Thieberger, *The Great Rabbi Loew of Prague: His Life and Work and the Legend of the Golem* (London: East & West Library, 1954); R. J. W. Evans, *Rudolf II and His World: A Study in Intellectual History 1576–1612* (Oxford: Clarendon, 1973).

8. HHStA, RHR Antiqua 1159, no. 6.

9. HHStA, RHR Antiqua 1157, no. 4.

10. Staatsarchiv Würzburg, Würzburger Urkunden 41/40.

11. Documents for Würzburg are found in HHStA, RHR Antiqua 1157, no. 4.

12. For documents of the Worms conflict, see HHStA, RHR Antiqua 1143; Baden-Württembergisches Hauptstaatsarchiv (HStA) Stuttgart, A125, Bü. 32; Stadtarchiv Worms, 2020/1–74. On the uprising, see Christopher R. Friedrichs, "Anti-Jewish Politics in Early Modern Germany: The Uprising in Worms, 1613–1617," *Central European History* 23 (1990): 91–152.

13. On Esslingen, see HStA Stuttgart A56 Bü 7; on Dortmund, see R. Po-chia Hsia, "Printing, Censorship and Antisemitism in Reformation Germany," in *The Process of Change in Early Modern Europe: Essays in Honor of Miriam Usher Chrisman,* ed. Sherrin Marshall and Philip N. Bebb (Athens: Ohio University Press, 1988), 135–48.

14. On the uprising in Worms, see Friedrichs, "Anti-Jewish Politics." On the Fettmilch Uprising, see Matthias Meyn, *Die Reichsstadt Frankfurt vor dem Bürgeraufstand von 1612–1614: Struktur und Krise* (Frankfurt: Kramer, 1980); Christopher R. Friedrichs, "Politics or Pogrom? The Fettmilch Uprising in German and Jewish History," *Central European History* 19 (1986): 186–228.

15. Volker Press, *Kriege und Krisen: Deutschland 1600–1715* (Munich: Beck, 1991).

16. See Gerald Soliday, *A Community in Conflict: Frankfurt Society in the Seventeenth and Early Eighteenth Centuries* (Hanover, N.H.: University Press of New England, 1974).

17. For documents related to the 1670 expulsion, see Pribram, *Urkunden und Akten,* 211–57. For a succinct narrative, see John P. Spielman, *The City and the Crown: Vienna and the Imperial Court 1600–1740* (West Lafayette, Ind.: Purdue University Press, 1993), 123–35.

18. On the Habsburg clientage system, see Volker Press, "The Habsburg Court as Center of the Imperial Government," in *Politics and Society in the Holy Roman Empire, 1500–1806, Journal of Modern History* (1986), Supplement, 23–45.

19. For the Habsburgs in the German southwest, see Volker Press, "Vorderösterreich in der habsburgischen Reichspolitik des späten Mittelalters und der frühen Neuzeit," in *Vorderösterreich in der frühen Neuzeit,* ed. Volker Press and Hans Maier (Sigmaringen: Thorbecke, 1989), 1–41. Although there is nothing in this volume on Jews and Habsburg Jewish policy, there is rich documentation in archives in Stuttgart, Ludwigsburg, Munich, Karlsruhe, and Tirol. For a description of sources related to Further Austria in Tirol, see Fridolin Dörrer, "Die für Vorderösterreich zuständigen Behörden in Innsbruck und die Quellen zur Geschichte Vorderösterreichs im Tiroler Landesarchiv," in *Vorderösterreich,* ed. Press and Maier, 367–93.

Part 2

Government and Culture
during the Baroque

Introduction

Nicolette Mout

Discussing the concept of "baroque" in Austrian intellectual history, Robert Kann somewhat dejectedly mentioned the "natural desire of the human mind to perceive the whole spirit of an era in one well-rounded concept" and proceeded to give a critical assessment of the shortcomings of the corresponding historiography.[1] An insouciant use of the terms "government" and "culture" during the baroque might easily incur similar censure, for it is impossible to provide a definition for either key concept in relation to the baroque that would have the clarity, brevity, and aptness sought after by most scholars. Government in the Habsburg Monarchy encompassed powers as diverse as the emperor himself and his court, the estates in the hereditary lands, Bohemia, and Hungary—all more or less curbed by princely absolutism—and the many highly differentiated administrative, judicial, and military institutions throughout the realm. These governmental bodies all functioned according to their own rules and competences and jealously guarded their privileges, even during the heyday of Habsburg absolutism. Culture in the Habsburg Monarchy can be interpreted as an immensely complex entity comprising the whole of sociocultural ideas and images with their manifestations, not only in the arts, the sciences, and education but also touching religious, political, and social life in general.

A combination of "government" and "culture" during the baroque points, on the one hand, toward the study of the culture of the elite, the dominant social stratum. The rulers, rather than the ruled, come most easily into focus and have consequently been the subject of many studies written on the basis of source material that is as abundant as it is attractive. It gave us, for example, splendid works on aspects of court culture and similar subjects.[2] On the other hand, the study of the links between government and culture can lead to the examination of the means the government had to influence and possibly even dominate the life of its subjects. Historians have long been aware of the importance of the impact of the various secular and ecclesiastical authorities on many aspects of religious, social, and cultural life and have written seminal works on this topic.[3]

Research carried out along both lines promises to extend our knowledge and deepen our understanding of an extremely complex society. It might possibly benefit, however, from a more profound contemplation of guiding concepts and key terms frequently used— but not always explained—by scholars, such as "representation," "propaganda," or even "social discipline," not to mention the difficult term *Polizei* for something like "civil order." *Begriffsgeschichte* is, also in this case, a useful addition to the historian's arsenal.[4]

Society in the Habsburg Monarchy during the early modern era was no different from the rest of Europe, in that it was strictly hierarchical and full of social antagonisms: magnates against lower nobles, nobles against townspeople, lords against peasants. This unsteady and yet fixed political, social, and cultural hierarchy was headed by the emperor. Since William Lamormaini, confessor to Ferdinand II, had painted the image of that pious emperor as the ideal Christian prince in his popular work *Ferdinandi II. virtutes* (1638), the special imperial position was preferably expressed in a religious context with political overtones. The members of the *Casa d'Austria* not only possessed the traditional thaumaturgic healing power for various afflictions, such as goiter, scabies, and stammer, but also were able to heal the state by stamping out religious and sociopolitical dissent. They were even depicted as sustaining the whole world by their extraordinary piety, like Christian Atlases.[5]

During the formative period of the Habsburg Counter-Reformation state—roughly the last decades of the sixteenth century and the first half of the seventeenth—a firm alliance was forged among the emperor and his government, a sizeable part of the aristocracy, and the Catholic church with the express intent to attack and subdue the forces of Protestantism and of social and political unrest. This alliance functioned most successfully in the fields of education, scholarship, and printing. Except in Hungary, Protestant institutions of higher education disappeared altogether and were replaced by the colleges and universities of the Jesuits and other religious orders. The press was not only censored but virtually monopolized by supporters of the government, among whom the Jesuits, again, played an important role. Gradually, a new Catholic intellectual establishment emerged under the aegis of the government and the church, upholding ideals not only of piety but also of social harmony and political unity. Soon this new intelligentsia was producing works of literature and scholarship that were in keeping with the precepts of the Counter-Reformation church and, at the same time, defending the sociopolitical order and hierarchy of the absolutist state.[6]

It has been argued that "for all the diversity of its territories and institutions the Habsburg Monarchy, by the later seventeenth century, basically supported a single culture."[7] The dominant feature of this elite culture was educated orthodox Catholicism of a special, Central-European brand. Patronage—by the church, the aristocracy, or the emperor himself—was essential to it, as was the use of Latin, although the vernacular had its own niche. Its blossoming was solidly founded upon humanist learning in all its different aspects. Its representatives were often, but by no means always, clerics, like the omniscient philosopher Athanasius Kircher. Good relations with the ecclesiastical authorities were, however, very important and often a sine qua non for the prospective author who wanted to see his works in print. Next to theology, philosophy—predominantly Aristotelian but with Platonist and Augustinian variations—and sciences such as astronomy, mathematics, and physics flourished. A certain amount of intellectual independence and nonconformism was allowed and was even accepted in this very "official" world of learning, which always needed the blessing of the authorities. The occult sciences, especially alchemy, remained popular in educated circles and were deemed to be completely compatible with Catholic orthodoxy. Emperors and magnates such as Leopold I and Karl Eusebius von Liechtenstein had a marked interest in the quest for the philosopher's stone and in transmutations. More important, however, was the fact that the church succeeded in encapsulating the occult sciences almost entirely, not so much in their experimental—transformatory—form, but as a spiritual power. The spiritual and intellectual quest for higher wisdom became permitted, even respectable in the eyes of the authorities. At the same time, popular magic, especially in the guises of divination, prophecy, and witchcraft, was vehemently attacked because it was considered to be incompatible with Counter-Reformation orthodoxy.[8]

It took a long time before the Counter-Reformation in all its aspects was brought to fruition in the Habsburg Monarchy as a whole. But in the end, the combined efforts of the ecclesiastical and secular authorities, the forced or voluntary conversions (or exile) of the Protestants, and the firm control to which the population was subjected proved to be successful. In the course of time, religious and political conformity also came to permeate the whole administrative system, as virtually no servants of the government were allowed to be outside the Catholic fold. Thus, true Christian morality in the style of the Counter-Reformation was finally introduced in almost all parts of the realm during the reign of Emperor Leopold I (1658–1705), taking the form of strict observance of the Catholic faith. Notable exceptions were Hungary and Silesia, where Protestantism remained relatively strong, and clandestine dissenting congregations were not unknown in Bohemia and even in the hereditary lands.

The *pietas austriaca,* that remarkable fruit of the Counter-Reformation, should certainly not be exclusively understood as an imposition on the population from above. Imperial piety was undoubtedly genuine—although it also satisfied some of the political, social, and cultural needs of the dynasty—as was the spirituality found in the ranks of the aristocracy and, naturally, in the church itself. It is not easy to understand how important and self-evident religious life in its new, disciplining garb was for the lower social strata. It is, however, a rewarding subject for further research, as especially the lower administrative and ecclesiastical powers kept many relevant records, such as the *Beichtzettel*—pieces of evidence that the holder had made his Easter confession—while other sources, including sermons, broadsheets, newsletters, and legal documents such as the numerous *Polizeiordnungen* can be, and have been, used to shed light on this problem. Famous preachers, such as Abraham à Sancta Clara, had much success with their homilies, which were full of social criticism and visionary piety. Members of the religious orders not only converted the Protestants and dispensed pastoral care but also exhorted the population to develop local religious customs, such as pilgrimages or the cult of a particular saint.[9]

Returning to the more specific subject of elite culture, attention must be drawn to the intertwinement of the absolutist government and the imperial court. It has been stated that "without the Habsburg court the Habsburg state would simply not have existed."[10] This development reached its peak in the long reign of Emperor Leopold I, the second half of the seventeenth century. Only then did Vienna become the permanent residence of the court and, consequently, the seat of the central government and the capital of the monarchy. In earlier times, emperors used to travel frequently, and Rudolph II had even preferred to reside in Prague rather than in Vienna.[11] Eventually, the central institutions of the monarchy were located there: the Privy Council and the imperial and Austrian chanceries; the *Hofkammer* (Court Chamber), a body responsible for government finances and taxation; the *Hofkriegsrat* (War Council); and the *Reichshofrat* (Imperial Aulic Court), which became de facto, if not de jure, the most important judicial body of the monarchy.[12]

Leopold's reign also brought the ascendancy of the Austrian branch of the house of Habsburg over the Spanish one, to which it was bound by a series of imperial marriages, and the beginning of the long-lasting rivalry between the two most important absolutist powers of the time, Austria and France. As the heir, albeit in a spiritual sense only, to the Spanish pretensions of world rule, the emperor put forward his claims to universality with some emphasis: the Austrian sun (*Sol Austriacus*) was pitted against the similar pretences of the "Roi Soleil," Louis XIV.[13]

In this image of the emperor as the universal und supremely Christian ruler par excellence lies a clue to a correct understanding of the role of the Habsburg court during the baroque. This court was not simply the central institution for an absolutist government—which was, incidentally, by far not as centralized as the Habsburgs would have wished it to be. It wanted to be considered the center of the world, a symbol of imperial sovereignty, the ultimate source of secular power, and, at the same time, a fountain of Christian virtues: in short, a cosmos in itself. On a more terrestrial level, it came to be seen as the highest possible form of high society, especially by the aulic entourage of the emperor. The very elaborate imperial court ceremonial was based on the example of the Spanish Habsburgs of the sixteenth century but became refined and developed even further over the course of time, reaching its height under Emperor Charles VI (1711–40). During the baroque, the aulic household grew in numbers, and court hierarchy and ceremony expanded with it. What remained unchanged was the prominent position of the most senior noble officers at the court, such as the *Obersthofmeister* (senior majordomo) and the *Obersthofmarschall* (senior court marshal). Court service could be very remunerative and yielded great prestige, with splendid titles into the bargain, like the one borne by the hereditary imperial postmasters, the Counts Paar, who were called *Reichs- Hof- und General-Erblandpostmeister.*[14]

The Habsburg court was as expensive as it was expansive. The reasons should be sought not only in the desire for prestige and display of power, qualities that beset any court, but also in the combination of political, social, and cultural operations peculiar to it. The ruling functions were subsumed, as it were, in a wide range of cultural events. Of these, court festivities were the most spectacular, celebrating major occasions in dynastic and political life. The traditional Habsburg patronage of the fine arts was combined with an increasing predilection for literature, music, and the theater. Since the accession of Emperor Leopold I to the throne, the court saw a number of amazingly lavish and artistically innovative opera productions, mainly the work of Italian composers and designers. These operas and other theatrical creations, such as equestrian ballets (*Rossballette*), were all designed to set off the august position of the emperor and his court and government. The importance of church music and the participation of the court in religious ceremonies underlined the close relations between the rulers and the Catholic faith. Court life became imbued with theatrical aspects, as every public function—from baptisms to coronations and from weddings to funerary ceremonies—was elaborated into pageantry of some kind. Imperial patronage was sometimes supplemented by imperial participation, as more than one member of the dynasty turned his hand to music making or even composing and versifying. Leopold I, for example, hunted Palestrina manuscripts and took a personal interest in the work of his court librarian, the renowned scholar Peter Lambeck. In this way, patronage and representation of the imperial idea went hand in hand. Representation was helped along, moreover, by a steady flow of printed propaganda, often in the form of historiography, eulogizing the dynasty and the institutions of the Habsburg Monarchy.[15]

It has often been remarked that the counterpart to the elaborate baroque court spectacle was the monumental representational architecture, which became especially prominent after the siege of Vienna (1683). These buildings, or at least their facades and their massiveness, were there for all to see, while court festivities were by no means always accessible to a wider public. The numerous religious orders built their houses, colleges, and churches. The Habsburg dynasty at first concentrated on the erection of ecclesiastical buildings and monuments, such as the plague columns in and outside Vienna. Only in the course of the eighteenth century was the imperial Hofburg expanded by building a chancery, a riding school, and a library. Around the turn of the century, a number of town palaces were built in the capital, and summer palaces appeared in the surroundings. The builders were magnates from all over the Habsburg Monarchy, all holders of grand names and high government offices: Auersperg, Trautson, Liechtenstein, Harrach, Esterházy, Schwarzenberg, Schönborn, Starhemberg-Schönburg, Eugene of Savoy, to name but a few. The palace has been an important political and social symbol throughout the ages, a manifestation of power, glory, and wealth. It has been called "a repository of the values of the ruling class," where "ideas were collected, ordered and expressed in visual form."[16] Not only in Vienna but everywhere in the Habsburg Monarchy, palaces sprang up in the main towns, while castles in the countryside were rebuilt in baroque style. Numerous ecclesiastical buildings and monuments were erected; some of them, such as Klosterneuburg or Melk, were very grand indeed. But the humble St. John of Nepomuk on almost every bridge or the valiant St. Florian or the Virgin herself at the street corner must not be overlooked, either. Together they came to dominate town- and landscape alike and reminded the population of the eminent presence and power of their secular rulers and of the church and of the ideals of secular and spiritual order, harmony, and unity.

Baroque art in a way mirrors and explains some aspects of the relation between government and culture in the Habsburg Monarchy. It expressed, no doubt, the intimate link between absolutist state and Counter-Reformation church to the contemporary beholder. It played a significant role in the representation of the imperial idea and stressed the power and prestige of the Habsburg dynasty and the noble families alike. Especially in architecture, but also in fresco painting and decorating, a style was created that left its mark even in the remotest corner of the realm. Learning during the baroque seemed to have possessed something of the same universal quality: the same or similar books are found in libraries all over the Habsburg Monarchy. The works of Justus Lipsius or Athanasius Kircher, for instance, were endlessly reprinted or re-edited.

There was a certain element of *folie de grandeur* in this: endearing in a way but also quite disturbing. Emperor Charles VI (1711–40) is known to have dried the ink of his letters with sand mixed with a liberal sprinkling of gold dust. The reader was confronted with greenish-golden scintillations emitted by the letters, representing the splendor of imperial majesty and thus reinforcing the authority of the contents of the *Handbillet* (autograph letter by the emperor). Nothing could symbolize the close association between government and culture in the Habsburg Monarchy during the baroque better than these sparkling pages, which are still the delight of the historian visiting the archives.[17]

Notes

1. Robert A. Kann, *A Study in Austrian Intellectual History: From Late Baroque to Romanticism* (London: Thames and Hudson, 1960), 2.

2. See, for example, Hubert Ch. Ehalt, *Ausdrucksformen absolutistischer Herrschaft: Der Wiener Hof im 17. und 18. Jahrhundert* (Vienna: Verlag für Geschichte und Politik, 1980).

3. See, for instance, R. Po-chia Hsia, *Social Discipline in the Reformation: Central Europe, 1550–1750* (London: Routledge, 1989).

4. Winfried Schulze explained, for instance, one useful concept of social discipline in his article "Gerhard Oestreichs Begriff 'Sozialdisziplinierung in der Frühen Neuzeit,'" *Zeitschrift für historische Forschung* 14 (1987): 265–302. For the concept *Polizei,* see Peter Nitschke, "Von der Politeia zur Polizei: Ein Beitrag zur Entwicklungsgeschichte des Polizei-Begriffs und seiner herrschaftspolitischen Dimensionen von der Antike bis ins 19. Jahrhundert," *Zeitschrift für historische Forschung* 19 (1992): 1–27.

5. *Ferdinandi II. Romanorum Imperatoris virtutes* (Vienna, 1638, and many other editions); cf. Robert Bireley, S.J., *Religion and Politics in the Age of the Counterreformation: Emperor Ferdinand II, William Lamormaini, S.J., and the Formation of Imperial Policy* (Chapel Hill: University of North Carolina Press, 1981); Anna Coreth, *Pietas Austriaca: Österreichische Frömmigkeit im Barock,* 2d ed. (Munich: R. Oldenbourg Verlag, 1982), 11, 17, and passim.

6. R. J. W. Evans, *The Making of the Habsburg Monarchy 1550–1700: An Interpretation* (Oxford: Clarendon Press, 1979), 100–116; Gernot Heiss, "Princes, Jesuits and the Origins of Counter-Reformation in the Habsburg Lands," in *Crown, Church and Estates: Central European Politics in the Sixteenth and Seventeenth Centuries,* ed. R. J. W. Evans and Trevor V. Thomas (London: Macmillan, 1991), 92–109; Helmut Engelbrecht, *Geschichte des österreichischen Bildungswesens,* vol. 2: *Das 16. und 17. Jahrhundert* (Vienna: Österreichischer Bundesverlag, 1983).

7. Evans, *The Making of the Habsburg Monarchy,* 311.

8. Ibid., 311–418 passim.

9. The older literature is still valuable, cf. Evans, *The Making of the Habsburg Monarchy,* 117–40 and passim.

10. R. J. W. Evans, "The Austrian Habsburgs: The Dynasty as a Political Institution," in *The Courts of Europe: Politics, Patronage and Royalty 1400–1800,* ed. A. G. Dickens (London: Thames and Hudson, 1977), 145.

11. Ibid., 121.

12. See Evans, *The Making of the Habsburg Monarchy,* 146–51, for a short description of the central institutions.

13. Anton Schindling, "Leopold I. (1658–1705)," in *Die Kaiser der Neuzeit 1519–1918. Heiliges Römisches Reich, Österreich, Deutschland,* ed. Anton Schindling and Walter Ziegler (Munich: Beck, 1990), 168–85; Friedrich Polleross, "'Sol Austriacus' und 'Roi Soleil': Amerika in den Auseinandersetzungen der europäischen Mächte," in *Federschmuck und Kaiserkrone: Das barocke Amerikabild in den habsburgischen Ländern* (Exhibition catalogue, Schlosshof, 1992), 54–84.

14. Ehalt, *Ausdrucksformen;* Evans, *The Making of the Habsburg Monarchy,* 177–78.

15.   Evans, "The Austrian Habsburgs," 139–43; idem, *The Making of the Habsburg Monarchy,* 152–53; Anna Coreth, *Österreichische Geschichtsschreibung in der Barockzeit,* Veröffentlichungen der Kommission für neuere Geschichte Österreichs, vol. 37 (Vienna: Böhlau, 1950).

16.   Jonathan Brown and John H. Elliott, *A Palace for a King: The Buen Retiro and the Court of Philip IV* (New Haven, Conn.: Yale University Press, 1980), vii.

17.   Hans Schmidt, "Karl VI. (1711–1740)," in *Die Kaiser der Neuzeit 1519–1918,* ed. Schindling and Ziegler, 200.

The Imperial Hofburg

The Theory and Practice of
Architectural Representation in Baroque Vienna

Hellmut Lorenz

Our general understanding of the representative role of art and architecture in a residence in the age of absolutism is normally taken from outstanding examples, such as the Louvre and Versailles of Louis XIV. Indeed, there can be no doubt that the king of France and his instrumentalization of the arts for making political power visible really did serve as model for several residences throughout all parts of Europe. Around 1700, we find nearly everywhere new and large palaces—suburban and city residences as well—whose main goal is to glorify the importance of the ruler and/or his dynasty with modern architecture and programmatic decoration.

Astonishingly enough, this seems not to have been the case in Vienna, the very center of political power in Central Europe. A comparison between two secondary residences in France and Austria offers an example of this phenomenon: Marly, built from 1679 on to be used while Versailles was under construction; and Laxenburg, where Leopold I also resided only temporarily during the spring, especially after 1683.

In both places, the ruler—king or emperor—was accompanied by the leading families at court. The position of the king of France and his relationship to the nobility is clearly expressed by architectural means in Marly (fig. 1): The King's Pavilion, placed in the very center of the site, dominates the entire composition and naturally (we would say) is bigger and more sumptuously decorated than the

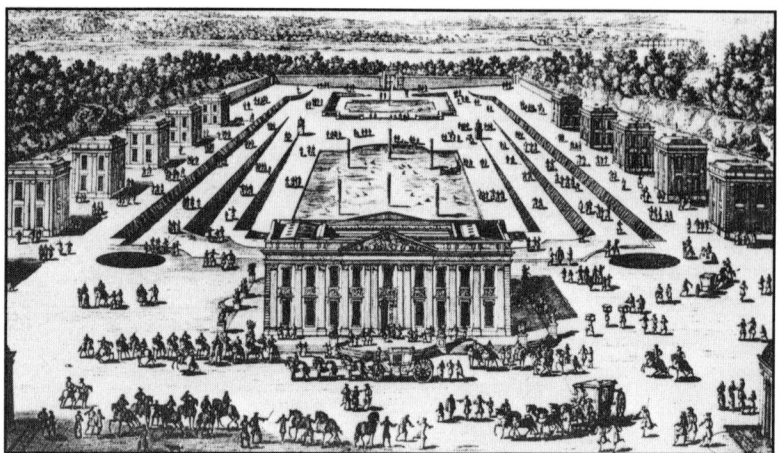

Fig. 1

small uniform pavilions for the noblemen allowed to join the king during his sojourn.

Just the contrary is true in Laxenburg (fig. 2), where it is the nobility that owns modern *maisons de plaisance*. They surround the residence of the emperor, which is a small castle still in medieval form, surrounded by an old-fashioned moat. There is no subordination of the nobility to the ruler as there is in France. And this constellation can also be taken as a paradigm of the promotion of the arts in the Habsburg monarchy in a more general respect: While noble families dominated the artistic scene of Vienna in these years, the emperor was still indebted to the value of tradition. The nobility— and not the monarch, as everywhere else—brought modern art and renowned artists to the capital and transformed the still-medieval town to a flourishing center of modern baroque art and architecture. No one ever described the famous "Vienna Gloriosa" as the "Vienna Gloriosa Habsburgica."[1]

In this essay, I would like to focus on the astonishing fact that the Habsburg rulers obviously did not rule the arts for a very long period during the epoch of baroque absolutism, when everywhere else in Europe sovereigns were following the example of Louis XIV. For the sake of brevity, I will concentrate on the center of Habsburg power, the imperial Hofburg in Vienna (fig. 3).[2]

The history of this site goes back to the second half of the thirteenth century, when a four-tower castle was erected near the city walls (no. 1 in fig. 3); this followed a very common custom in Central European residential palaces. Later additions were made in the sixteenth century, not by enlarging the medieval nucleus (which was only modernized superficially in 1550) but by raising new buildings of similar shape in the neighborhood: in 1556, the later Stallburg as a separate residence for Maximilian II (no. 3 in fig. 3), which was subsequently transformed into a museum and then to the stables for the "White [Lippizaner] Horses"); and after 1575, the Amalienburg for Rudolph II's brother, Archduke Ernest (no. 11 in fig. 3).

This somewhat accidental juxtaposition of different castles, interspersed with small houses for several offices and chanceries, was sufficient at this time; but problems arose when, after Rudolph II's temporary residence in Prague, the court moved back to Vienna in the early seventeenth century. The continuity of the site's use as a residence had been interrupted, and for several years the old buildings had to be used in a somewhat provisional way.

Only in 1660 did Leopold I made a decisive step toward architecturally unifying and modernizing this conglomerate. Obviously

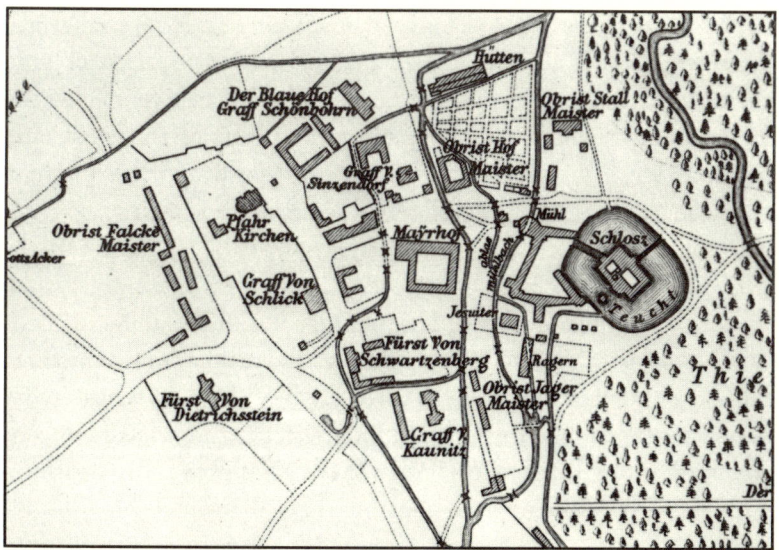

Fig. 2

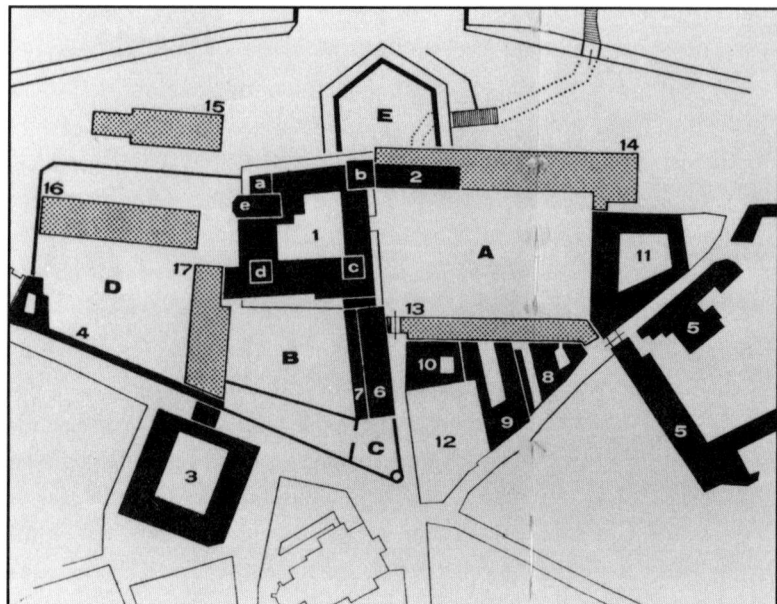

Fig. 3

impressed by the recently enlarged residence-castle at Munich,[3] he started with a long, new wing by the then-leading court architect Filiberto Lucchese (fig. 4). This new Leopoldine Tract served several purposes: First of all, it established a long-needed sequence of large rooms for living and ceremonial purposes, but it also connected the medieval castle with the Amalienburg, thus unifying the entire site; furthermore, it provided a large inner court for festivities; finally, it gave the entire residential area a large new facade facing the city's exterior.

Compared with the artistic standards of the time, this was a modern and typical solution. The addition of a large number of identical bays—which might look at first sight somewhat monotonous to us—responded to the architectural ideal of the age, whose most sumptuous example, the Czernin Palace in Prague, was under construction in the same years.[4] Soon there were projects to continue with this decoration of large pilaster strips all over the older buildings, in order to unify the appearance of the entire residential area.

Given the menacing danger of a siege or attack by the Turks, it is not surprising that no further construction was undertaken dur-

ing the following years. What is really astonishing is that the
residential area was not modernized during the period after the lib-
eration of Vienna in 1683 and remained as it was for nearly half a
century. After all, it was at the turn of the century that the climax of
modern baroque residential architecture flourished everywhere else
in Central Europe (e.g., in Berlin, Bonn, Dresden, Ludwigsburg, and
Rastatt).

For the last two generations, scholars have perceived Johann
Bernhard Fischer von Erlach's project for Schönbrunn, which was
conceived in 1688, as an attempt to represent architecturally the
increased power of the monarchy after 1683. This interpretation followed ideas put forward by Hans Sedlmayr in 1938.[5] But this so-
called *Reichsstil* is obviously more a castle in the air (by Fischer von
Erlach as well as Hans Sedlmayr) than a real, historical fact.[6] Looking at the evidence, we must assume that Leopold I and his artistic
advisers—for whatever reasons—refused to resort to architectural
splendor as an artistic device for official representation.

Leopold did, however, promote other artistic activities,[7] such
as opera, where the glory of the monarchy was celebrated in perfor-
mances such as the *Pomo d'oro,* or the highly interesting Plague
Column in Vienna, which was begun in 1687. A wonderful engraving

Fig. 4

of this column from 1696 (fig. 5) explains its meaning more clearly than the monument itself, showing the emperor in his function as mediator between earth and heaven, between humanity and the

Fig. 5

Holy Trinity—a position normally reserved for the Holy Virgin. This is a fine example of the meaning of illusion in baroque art, which can give interpretive keys for later generations. Coincidentally, it also provides eloquent testimony in support of Anna Coreth's assertions about the important confessional and political role that the *pietas austriaca* played in the visual arts.[8] Instead of architectural splendor to glorify the *Casa d'Austria,* we find devotion to the Catholic Church as the central feature of Leopold's patronage.

And when it came to an architectural representation of the house of Austria, it was rather traditional, as for instance in an engraving from 1705 (fig. 6),[9] which is taken from a printed *Castrum doloris* for Leopold I. Religious monuments such as the Plague Column or the column for the Virgin Mary support the *Domus Austriae*—but the architectural style of this *Casa d'Austria* is far from being up-to-date. Rather, it resembles the Spanish *Alcázar,* which had been in vogue in the early seventeenth century[10] but was rather out of fashion by the end of the century. Keep in mind that this was exactly the period when the leading patrons in Vienna, such as Prince Eugene of Savoy and Prince Johann Adam von Liechtenstein, built their splendid palaces and helped make Vienna one of the cultural centers of Europe. Both patrons employed

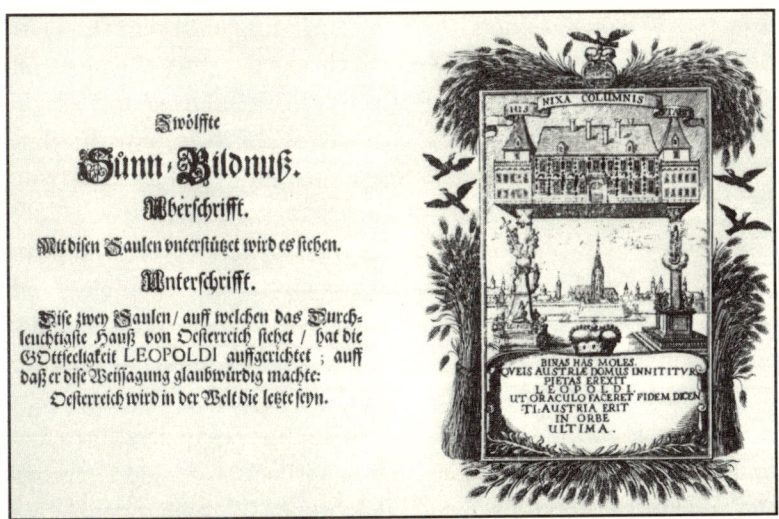

Fig. 6

Fischer von Erlach, who had scarcely anything to do in his official position as architect to the court.

The Habsburg monarchs' dismissal of modern architectural splendor continued during the reign of Joseph I (1705–11), even though he had been educated in architecture by Fischer von Erlach and might thus have been expected to evince a greater appreciation of his work. There is, however, only very vague evidence of any idea to build a new residence outside the fortifications. Otherwise, nothing really happened during his short reign. Nor did his younger brother and successor, Charles VI (1711–40), initially show much interest in building palaces. As late as 1715, the situation of the Hofburg was still the same as it had been more than half a century ago. Yet, after some delay, Charles VI did eventually begin to employ the monarchy's network of talented artists and architects in residential projects.[11] Fischer von Erlach finally got the chance to show his talents, as did another court architect, Johann Lucas von Hildebrandt, and a circle of learned men, such as Gottfried Wilhelm Leibniz, Carl Gustav Heraeus, and Konrad Adolph von Albrecht.

The construction of a new Austrian Court Chancery in 1717 began what could be termed a comprehensive building campaign. The very next year, construction began on the new imperial stables—a huge building with a facade more than 300 meters long. Although the stables were located outside the city's fortifications, they faced the palace and its Leopoldine wing and were thus put clearly in relation to the Hofburg. In the early 1720s, the imperial library was begun at the edge of the residential area as a single block without connection to the castle itself. In its interior, Fischer von Erlach and Daniel Gran created a magnificent hall glorifying Charles VI and his patronage of the arts and sciences. It was only after these buildings were well underway that Charles could start to renovate a part of the castle itself, since all the offices, stables, and collections had hitherto been housed there. Then in 1723, the new building of the Imperial Court Chancery (*Reichskanzlei*) was begun.

Measured by the standards of the decades before, this is an incomparable outburst of modern architecture, created within a few years by some of the leading architects of the time, including father and son Fischer von Erlach and Hildebrandt. Without a doubt this "imperial style" (or *Kaiserstil,* following Franz Matsche) of Charles VI deserves our attention as a climax of late baroque architecture in Central Europe. Finally, the Habsburg monarchy seems to have found its way to modern architecture. Two qualifying remarks are, however, necessary. First, this late imperial style is not an action but a reaction. After some delay, Charles VI decided that he had to compensate for the inactivity of his predecessors and catch up to the building campaigns in all other European residences—such as Dresden, where modern architecture had been utilized with the unconcealed intention of superseding the Imperial Court at Vienna.[12] Seen in context with the general situation of baroque architecture in Europe, the Caroline imperial style is a rather late flowering and did not establish new standards of residential architecture.

Second, Charles VI had now supplied new and quite representative houses for the members of his bureaucracy, for his books, and for his horses—but not for himself or the imperial family. His private and official rooms were still situated partly within the medieval nucleus of the castle (the Schweizerhof), and partly in the neighboring rooms of the Leopoldine Tract.[13] Moreover, the Hofburg was still the only residence in Europe without a great hall for festivities or a ceremonial staircase at a time when even a simple count or prince would have considered them a *conditio sine qua non* for his baroque palace. Even under Charles VI, the residence still had the general appearance of a *mixtum compositum* of old and new. The new buildings provided some highlights, but they did not transform the character of the residential area entirely, which still proudly presented its traditional features.

This is the other side of the coin of the imperial style: the enormous value that Habsburg rulers assigned to tradition within the residential area. Obviously, there never was a serious attempt to replace the entire area with modern buildings; instead, the embellishment was restricted to the addition of new parts to the already existing structure of different wings and courts. Most of the numerous visitors from abroad in the early eighteenth century expressed their surprise about the rather old-fashioned appearance of the emperor's seat; some of them did recognize, however, that this feature was maintained on purpose.[14]

It is for this reason that several of the leading architects of the age were unsuccessful in proposing the construction of an entirely new residence. Among them was Balthasar Neumann, who developed modern solutions, including large facades, symmetrical wings, and spacious courts (fig. 7).[15] But the process of modernizing the Hofburg according to the latest architectural trends would have forced the destruction of major parts of the old buildings, wiping out the site's historical legacy. Indeed, it was because all of the proposals would have eliminated the medieval castle that they were rejected, and that portion of the Hofburg has remained nearly unchanged until today.

Without question, this was due not only to the lack of money but also to the Habsburgs' conviction that the signs of history, the traces of tradition, should not be extinguished. Evidently, it was essential to the strategy of imperial building in Vienna—even at the climax of baroque architectural splendor under Charles VI—to keep visible the tradition of the residential building, thereby visually preserving the long history of the Habsburg dynasty all the way back to the Hofburg's late thirteenth-century origins.

This rejection of modern architecture led also to rather unusual situations that are hard to explain, even if we take into consid-

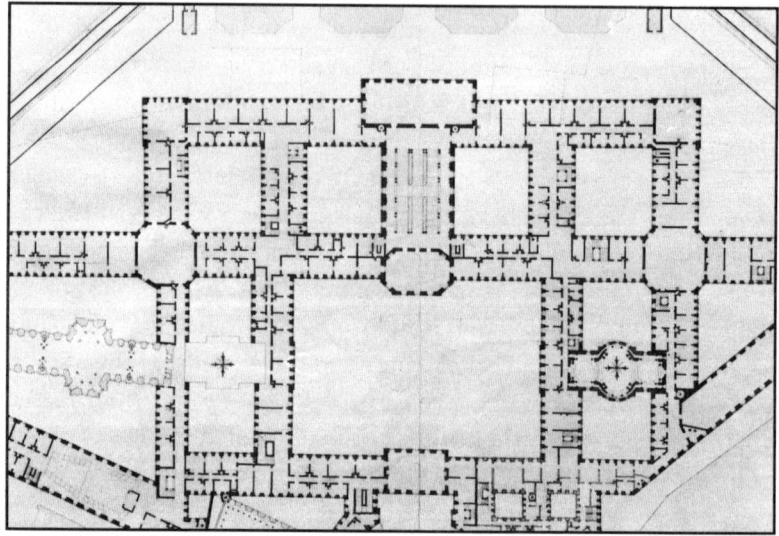

Fig. 7

Fig. 8

eration the importance of tradition. Thus, for instance, the story of Joseph Emanuel Fischer von Erlach's marvelous project for a new facade that would have faced the city (fig. 8). It was begun in the early 1730s but was then abandoned and left unfinished. With the decision in 1748 and again in 1756 to build the new Burgtheater at exactly the same spot, every attempt to unify the appearance and enhance the splendor of the Hofburg was condemned to total oblivion (figs. 9, 10).

There is a short epilogue to this project. King Frederick the Great of Prussia intentionally utilized Fischer's design for his new library in Berlin (built 1775–1780) at his Forum Friderizianum. His purpose was strictly political. The building should make clear that here, in the capital of Prussia, it was possible to build something like that within a few years, while in the capital of the recently defeated Habsburg Monarchy the state of this facade was still fragmentary. Indeed, it was only in the last years of the nineteenth century that the present facade of the Hofburg—the Michaelerfassade—could be completed, following the slightly modified plan of Fischer.

Thus we may conclude that the residential area of the Hofburg in Vienna, which had been the very center of imperial power in Central Europe, can hardly be called a center of the arts or architecture in baroque times. Even under Charles VI, the residence

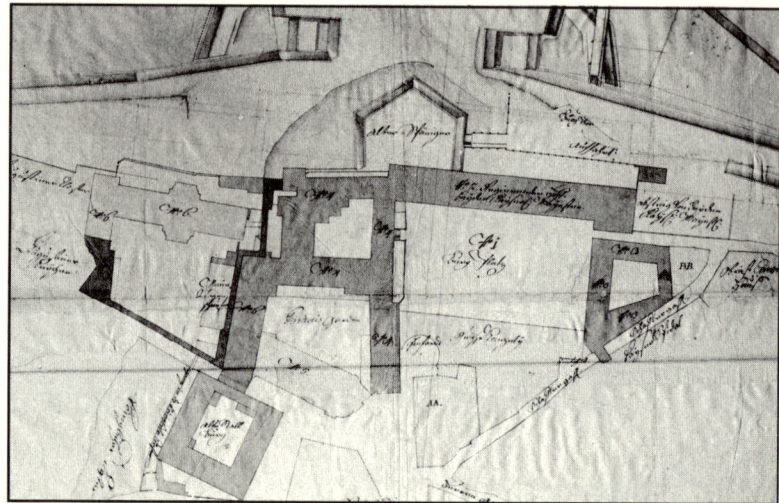

Fig. 9

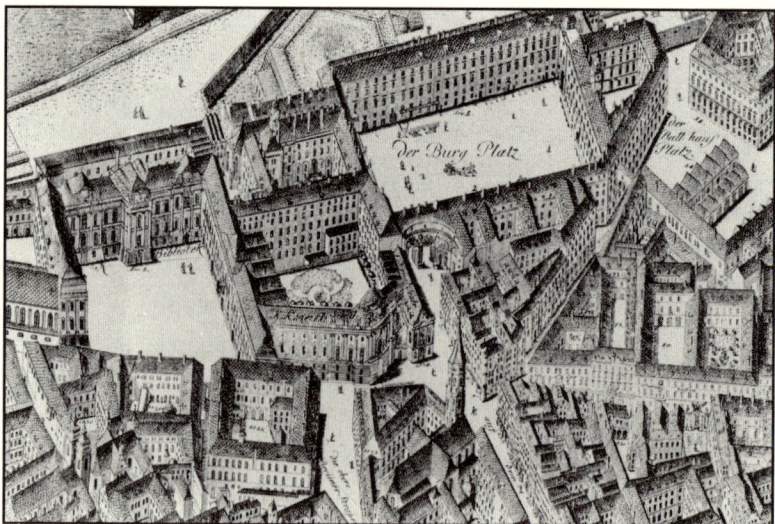

Fig. 10

remained a conglomerate of different buildings without any attempt to unify its structure by modern architectural means. It is
not by mere chance that this building has been always called the
Burg right up to the present rather than the more modern baroque terms *Schloß* or *Residenz*. As we have seen, the value of the

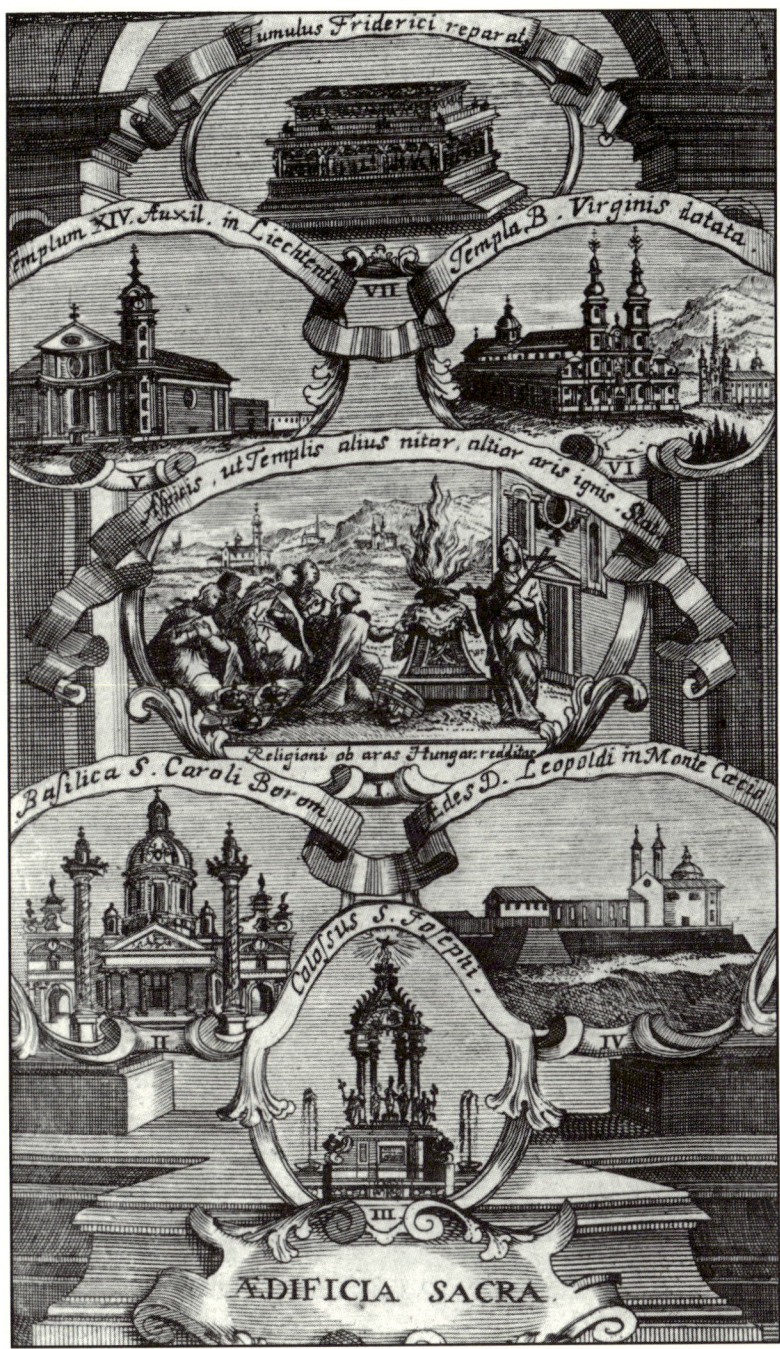

Fig. 11

historical tradition—dynastic as well as architectural—seems to be one reason for this phenomenon, while the glory of rigid modernization was left to "parvenus" such as Augustus the Strong or Frederick the Great.

Thus we are confronted with standards of value that differ somewhat from ours. An art historian of today (and probably a historian, too) would normally expect that the most distinguished solution would also be most modern, the most up-to-date, the most "baroque." A modern and prestigious building such as the Church of St. Charles (Karlskirche) strikes us as the climax of baroque architecture in Vienna. This was not the case for the contemporary Jesuit writer Anton Höller, who illustrated his treatise on the famous monuments erected during the reign of Charles VI with a copperplate (fig. 11) that essentially rates the *aedificia sacra* and grants the highest ranking to the reestablishment of Catholicism in the Hungarian countries.[16] Only after this do we see the Church of St. Charles amid an outlying subsidiary circle of buildings, few of which would be esteemed today as valuable contributions to the evolution of baroque architecture.

Building projects and architectural splendor did not rank very high with the Habsburgs. In this respect, even Charles VI—the only

Fig. 12

major patron of architects during the baroque—followed the path of his immediate predecessors, Joseph and Leopold. The models for residential buildings that had been established by contemporary architectural theory (for example, that of Paul Decker, fig. 12)[17] and executed at other courts were not valid in Vienna. Whereas other courts eagerly imitated Louis XIV and Versailles, the emperors did not find an adequate modern representation of their resurgent political power by means of architecture. Nor did they try especially hard to do so.

As an art historian, I can only call attention to this phenomenon. I can also provide possible explanations for this Habsburg timidity toward modern architectural splendor, such as the value of tradition, which also dominates baroque Habsburg historiography;[18] the already well-documented modesty of Leopold I and other Habsburg rulers;[19] and their greater devotion to religious rather than to secular art. A definitive answer to these questions raised by art history will, however, have to await the judgment of historians.

Notes

1. "Zum ersten Mal in der jüngeren deutschen Geschichte übernimmt der Adel . . . die Führung. Es ist ein einzigartiges Geschehen, das in anderen Residenz-städten des Reiches ohne Nachfolge blieb" (Wolfgang Braunfels, *Die Kunst im Heiligen Römischen Reich Deutscher Nation* [Munich: C. H. Beck, 1979], 1:49). See also Hellmut Lorenz, "Vienna Gloriosa Habsburgica?" *Kunsthistoriker: Mitteilungen des österreichischen Kunsthistorikerverbandes* 2 (1985): 84–89.

2. On this topic, Moriz Dreger, *Baugeschichte der k.k. Hofburg in Wien,* Österreichische Kunsttopographie, vol. 14 (Vienna: A. Schroll, 1914) is still indispensable. See also Harry Kühnel, *Die Hofburg,* Wiener Geschichtsbücher, vol. 5 (Vienna: P. Zsolnay, 1971); Christian Benedik, "Die Wiener Hofburg unter Kaiser Karl VI: Probleme herrschaftlichen Bauens im Barock" (Ph.D. diss., University of Vienna, 1989).

3. "Ihre Kayserliche Majestät sollen sich bey Ihrer jüngsten Anwesenheit zu München an dem Schloß daselbst verliebet haben" (quoted in Kühnel, *Die Hofburg,* 58).

4. The close connection between the Czernin Palace in Prague and the architecture in Vienna becomes even more evident in W. W. Praemer's project for the Hofburg, designed by around 1670; see Hellmut Lorenz, "Wolfgang Wilhelm Praemers 'Palaz zur accomodirung eines Landts-Fürsten,'" *Wiener Jahrbuch für Kunstgeschichte* 34 (1981): 115–30; 36 (1983): 191–202.

5. Hans Sedlmayr, "Die politische Bedeutung des deutschen Barock," in *Gesamtdeutsche Vergangenheit: Festgabe für Heinrich Ritter von Srbik zum 60. Geburtstag* (Munich: F. Bruckmann, 1938), 126–40.

6. Hellmut Lorenz, "Der habsburgische 'Reichsstil'—Mythos und Realität," in *"Künstlerischer Austausch—Artistic Exchange": Akten des XXVIII. Internationalen Kongresses für Kunstgeschichte Berlin 1992* (Berlin: Akademie-Verlag, 1993), 2: 163–76.

7. Friedrich B. Polleross, "Sonnenkönig und österreichische Sonne," *Wiener Jahrbuch für Kunstgeschichte* 40 (1987): 239–56.

8. Anna Coreth, *Pietas Austriaca: Ursprung und Entwicklung barocker Frömmigkeit in Österreich* (Munich: R. Oldenbourg, 1959).

9. Grete Lesky, "Das Leben des Heiligen Leopold in einem Emblembuch," *Jahrbuch des Stiftes Klosterneuburg,* n.s. 10 (1976), fig. 11.

10. See, for instance, Eggenberg castle near Graz, begun 1623.

11. Franz Matsche, *Die Kunst im Dienst der Staatsidee Kaiser Karls VI* (Berlin/ New York: W. de Gruyter, 1981); see also Benedik, "Die Wiener Hofburg unter Kaiser Karl VI."

12. The central pavilion of Pöppelmanns Zwinger in Dresden and its iconographic program clearly reflect the ambitions of August the Strong to become emperor himself; see Monika Schlechte, "HERCULES SAXONICUS—Versuch einer ikonographischen Deutung," in *Sachsen und die Wettiner: Chancen und Realitäten.* Papers of the international conference at Dresden, 1989 (Dresden: Kulturakademie des Bezirkes Dresden, 1990), 298–306.

13. Christian Benedik, "Die Repräsentationsräume der Wiener Hofburg in der ersten Hälfte des 18. Jahrhunderts," *Das achtzehnte Jahrhundert und Österreich, Jahrbuch der Österreichischen Gesellschaft zur Erforschung des achtzehnten Jahrhunderts* 6 (1990/91): 7–21.

14. For example, Montesquieu during his sojourn of 1728; see Grete Klingenstein, "Jede Macht ist relativ: Montesquieu und die Habsburger Monarchie," in *Festschrift Othmar Pickl zum 60. Geburtstag,* ed. Herwig Ebner et al. (Graz: Verlag Leykam, 1987), 307–23.

15. Hellmut Lorenz, "Balthasar Neumanns Pläne für die Wiener Hofburg," in *Balthasar Neumann: Kunstgeschichtliche Beiträge zum Jubiläumsjahr 1987,* ed. Thomas Korth and Joachim Poeschke (Munich: Hirmer, 1987), 131–42.

16. Anton Höller, *Augusta Carolinae Virtutis Monumenta* (Vienna: J. P. van Ghelen, 1733); see also Matsche, *Die Kunst im Dienst der Staatsidee Kaiser Karls VI,* 386–427.

17. Paul Decker, *Fürstlicher Baumeister oder: Architectura Civilis . . .* (Augsburg, 1711–16).

18. This is especially the case with the monumental volumes by Marquard Herrgott, *Monumenta Augustissimae Domus Austriae* (Vienna, 1750–72).

19. See, for instance, J. C. Lünig, *Theatrum ceremoniale historico-publicum . . .* (Leipzig, 1719–20), 2:670 (on the occasion of Leopold I's funeral): "Wie er in seinem

gantzen Leben mehr Majestät und Weißheit in seiner Regierung, als Pracht in seiner äußerlichen Aufführung gezeiget, so ist auch seine Beerdigung selbst nach dieser österreichischen Modestie eingericht gewest" (I am grateful to Anton Schindling for this reference).

List of Illustrations

1. Marly, summer residence of Louis XIV (engraving by Perelle; author archive).

2. Laxenburg, spring residence of Leopold I (engraving by Marinoni; author archive).

3. Vienna, Hofburg, schematic ground plan (reproduction from Kühnel, *Die Hofburg*): no. 1: medieval nucleus (Schweizerhof); no. 3 : Stallburg (residence for Maximilian II, begun 1556); no. 11: Amalienburg (residence for Archduke Ernst, after 1575); no. 14: Leopoldine Tract (begun 1660); no. 16: site of the imperial library (begun 1722).

4. Vienna, Hofburg, Leopoldine Tract (engraving by Kleiner; author archive).

5. Vienna, Plague Column (engraving by Nessenthaler; Vienna, Bundesdenkmalamt).

6. Allegorical representation of the "Casa d'Austria" (engraving from a "castrum doloris" for Leopold I, printed 1705 in Graz; reproduction from Lesky, "Das Leben des Heiligen Leopold").

7. Balthasar Neumann, project for an enlargement of the Hofburg in Vienna, 1746 (drawing; Berlin, Kunstbibliothek SMPK).

8. Joseph Emanuel Fischer von Erlach, project for the facade facing the Michaelerplatz of the Hofburg in Vienna (engraving by Kleiner; author archive).

9. Vienna, Hofburg, situation in 1745 (anonymous drawing; Berlin, Kunstbibliothek SMPK).

10. Vienna, Hofburg, situation in 1770 (engraving by Huber; author archive).

11. "Aedificia sacra" of Charles VI (engraving in A. Höller: *Augusta Carolinae Virtutis Monumenta* [Vienna 1733]; author archive).

12. Paul Decker, Ideal prospect of a Royal Palace (engraving in: *Fürstlicher Baumeister*, 1711–16; author archive).

Status as Commodity

The Habsburg Economy of Privilege

John P. Spielman

From the late seventeenth century down to our own day, one of the central problems addressed by those exploring the rise of the Habsburg Monarchy has been the obvious disjuncture between its achievements in its heroic age and the equally obvious paucity of its monetary resources to accomplish what it did. There have been many different answers to that question since Gottlieb Rinck attributed it to the justice of the Habsburg cause.[1] One suggestion holds that the monarchy assured the loyalty of its servants in large measure by delegating to them the right to collect honoraria or user fees from those needing government services from the crown.[2]

The more one examines the day-to-day functioning of the court of Leopold I, however, the more it appears that most of its activities were taking place in some realm beyond the cash nexus. Unlike his French cousin Louis XIV, Leopold I rarely had the cash on hand to reward his servants for their service and never enough to provide them with pensions, which were one of the Sun King's characteristic ways of showing favor.

Not that the monarch did not want to help his loyal servants when they were in financial trouble. In 1700 a countess Starhemberg was widowed with overwhelming debts to discharge. Leopold sent her a personally written letter (needless to say, with a secretary's transcription attached) granting her 20,000 gulden, and her children 30,000. But he had to add: "In deme aber der Zeith mit paaren mitteln aufzukhomen, schwär fallen wurde, als sollet Ihr dise summa, also in die Ämpter austheillen, des in einem oder lengstens zweÿ Jahren dieselbe bezahlt oder auf solche von Ihnen anticipirt werden khöne."[3] One other example from 1681, another of the few peaceful years during Leopold's reign, may stand symbolically for a host of such comments. This from a report by an agent at the court of Vienna to the Hoch- und Teutschmeister Johann Caspar von Ampringen: "Von gelt oder güthern is beÿ iezigen des Hoffs zustandt, wans auch schon versprochen würdt, kein sichere oder doch schlechte hoffnung zu machen . . ."[4]

Many of the Austrian crown's normal sources of revenue were anticipated beyond any reasonable expectation of redemption, its diets' contributions as well as its extraordinary taxes pledged against further loans. Salaries owed to functionaries were often three or more years in arrears. If any one of the many offices charged with collecting money due the crown actually received cash, it would be instantly besieged by an importunate throng of petitioners, all with valid claims on the crown. Doorkeepers would grow rich from gratuities, and the money would disappear, absorbed as if by capillary action.

Yet in spite of all this, the monarchy did function in its own way, and unusually successfully against tremendous odds in the late seventeenth and early eighteenth centuries. The answer is in part to be found in foreign subsidies for its wars; but it is also to be found in the fact that for much of its normal business it did not function in the cash economy at all, but in what may well be called an economy of privilege. It was an "economy" because this particular matrix of relationships was subject to what we think of as economic laws, involving such things as supply and demand, marginal utility, market pressures, and the like; and an economy of *privilege* because the exchanges in this matrix involved social status, private rights, or exemptions from normal legal procedure, rather than—or more precisely, as well as and beyond—hard cash. While at the beginning it must be made clear that money was usually involved in most of these exchanges, it was neither the primary reason for them nor the publicly visible symbol for the exchanges taking place. This matrix of relationships was also subject to all the contradictions, irrationality, and potential for abuse that one associates with a primitive command economy or an advanced capitalist economy.

In the Habsburg Monarchy of the seventeenth century, the only unlimited resource available to the crown was privilege. As *Landesfürst* in the hereditary lands and king in Bohemia and Hungary, the monarch was recognized as the primary creator of social status through his power to ennoble commoners or to confer higher estate upon those who were born to the aristocracy. As elected Roman Emperor, he had similar powers to reward all German princes, who were in theory at least his direct vassals. The power to confer status within the recognized social hierarchy made up a large part of the crown's political and potential financial capital. Creating a ninth electorate for Hanover or recognizing the Hohenzollerns as kings in Prussia were powerful acts of sovereign grace, made for what were presumed to be urgent political considerations. Granting Victor Amadeus II of Savoy the privilege of styling himself a "*Serene* Highness" was also political in the sense that it rewarded an unreliable prince for allying briefly with the Habsburgs. The 750,000 gulden he paid for this honor was doubtless more important. Victor Amadeus might turn his coat many times (and he did), but the cash once delivered produced one more "Miracle of the House of Austria."

In the world of honor and privilege, money mattered, but symbols of status and words also served as the coin of the realm. Like virtually every coinage in history, this one also experienced a progressive inflation over time as the monarchy exercised its sovereign power to create ever newer and finer distinctions within the social hierarchy over which it presided. The fate, for example, of the once meaningful title *Hofrat* is familiar to all, as is the distinction between real and titular *Kammerherrn*. Honors that once had graced a handful of advisers or attendants on the monarch's person had become by the second half of the seventeenth century little more than parking stickers allowing the bearer a place amidst the crowds in Hofburg antechambers.

Simply keeping track of the titles and proper forms of address became a profession in itself. In 1487 Max Ayrer published in Nuremberg a *Büechlein der Titel aller Staende*. It had twelve pages.[5] By the early seventeenth century, it had become a hefty handbook, now called the *Cantzleÿbüechlein,* an indispensable reference book for every private secretary and public office in the empire.

The general tendency toward inflation of symbols is nowhere more obvious than in the language used by members of the political elite. This was common throughout Europe but achieved a peculiarly grotesque efflorescence in court German, possibly because the structure of the empire itself produced so many different kinds of status within its noble ranks. One of the characteristic linguistic developments in seventeenth-century German was the rapid change that took place in forms of direct address, characterized by a proliferation of third-person abstractions and the shift to the plural verb in addressing persons of rank.[6]

Linguistic forms reinforced the external symbols of order and rank, turning all communication into an exercise in deference or condescension. Petitioners would flatter those above them from whom they hoped for favor by subtly (or not so subtly) increasing the angle of declination between their own status and that of the one addressed. Those above could encourage or discipline those below by carefully graded units of condescension expressed or withheld.

As court German became ever more rigidly structured in the seventeenth century, it served to limit the spontaneity of social intercourse in ways that have ever since been the subject of satire and ridicule. On closer examination, however, we can see this language of deference as one of the most basic elements of political culture. Clearly, one of its primary functions was exclusionary. It took a good education and a lot of practice to master the intricacies of it. Mistakes could be costly.[7] As Hubert Ehalt and others have pointed out, verbal expression of differences in rank was what gave them reality. A slip of the tongue in addressing a person of high station was more than a mistake; it was a threat, however small, to the social order itself.

The evidence for this use of new forms of address is massive, and mostly overlooked. The most common unit of exchange in this economy of privilege was the verbal or written compliment, the *Kompliment* uttered at the appropriate moment, or the epistolary *Gratulationsschreiben.* Most scholars working in this period have seen more than enough of the latter to be grateful that technology did not permit the preservation of the former. However much we may cavil at the dense archival underbrush of congratulatory epistles, these documents represent much more than empty ritual or formality. Clearly, the society that produced them took them seriously, thus it is useful to us to do so as well.[8] An interesting example of just how seriously these could be taken can be found in the correspondence of Johann Caspar von Ampringen, *Hoch- und Teutschmeister*, 1664–84, and Leopold's governor of Royal Hungary, 1673–79. Not only did Ampringen save every flattering scrap that came to him at New Years, he carefully underlined in pencil phrases he found worth noting and indicated in the margins any doubts he had about the sincerity of what he read. Perusing this correspondence is rather like watching a modern financier pour over his portfolio.[9]

If these formalities were received with considerable attention, what concentration must have gone into their composition! In Ampringen's case, at least, there is more than ample evidence that this was a matter too serious to be left to a secretary. He not only dictated his own drafts but carefully corrected them in his own hand, adding new turns of phrase, even holding back a clear copy when he found a more suitable formula.[10] Originality within the stilted form was desirable but not absolutely essential. On at least one occasion in 1681, Ampringen recycled a ten-year-old New Year's greeting to Leopold I.[11]

These incessant compliments were in one sense the small change in the economy of privilege. They were the means by which court society practiced its exclusive language and kept track of the changing relationships among themselves as some rose in rank while others stagnated. When Ampringen was elected *Hoch- und Teutschmeister* after Archduke Charles Joseph's death in 1664, he, who had been a mere administrator of the order for its Habsburg grand masters, suddenly became a *Hochfürstliche Gnaden*. In the following year, Leopold I elevated Dr. Johann Paul Hocher, a commoner, to the office of court chancellor and made him a baron. Both acts produced minor eruptions in the hierarchy, both called forth a flood of *Gratulationsschreiben*. These letters exalted the newly powerful, placed the recipients under some small obligation for the courtesy, and defended linguistically whatever might remain of the writer's own status. Both the obligation to common courtesy and the assertion of status at the proper angle of declination were universally understood exchanges within the social hierarchy.

The value of status could be exactly calculated; indeed, by the end of the seventeenth century, a certain amount of system had been introduced into social elevation, with tables specifying the sums payable for documents recognizing certain grants of status. The crown's need to use this source of income conflicted with the resistance of existing groups within the elite structure. Generally the noble houses of the various estates of the realm could be relied upon to add to their periodic grievances a challenge to the monarch's excessive generosity in granting titles and new status to people who neither inherited nor merited either.

For those who already had almost everything, there were other symbols of distinction available. One of the Habsburgs' most treasured awards was the coveted Golden Fleece, the *toison d'or*, inherited with the duchy of Burgundy. This knightly order had come to be valued by the European nobility above all other honors because its ranks were kept small and socially exclusive. Once granted, the Golden Fleece took precedence over all other decorations, as contemporary portraits reveal. The members of this order formed the *corps d'elite* of European nobility, with reigning princes and monarchs making up a substantial part of its cadre and the other high nobles admitted to the company only for very large gifts to the crown or as a reward for outstanding service, usually military.

In 1721 there was a convocation to honor twenty-four newly created knights of the Golden Fleece.[12] Their number included the electoral prince of Poland-Saxony, princes of Portugal, Hanover, Lorraine, Bavaria, Württemberg, Schleswig-Holstein, and Liechtenstein. Accompanying them were lesser nobles with names familiar to all observers of the monarchy—Fürstenberg, Herberstein, Martinitz, Schlick, Khevenhüller—alongside less well-known but, one assumes, equally well-heeled foreigners.

Status moved in one direction only: from above downward, a product of the sovereign's grace. Once granted, it could be recalled, but only under extraordinary circumstances, for status that could be recalled at the ruler's whim had little value to those seeking it. The first condition, therefore, for the operation of this system had to be the monarch's acceptance of the principle that once he used his power to grant status, he had to acknowledge that grant as permanent and hereditary. There was in seventeenth-century Austria nothing akin to the English bill of attainder, which extended criminal judgment to a whole family. Ferdinand II had Wallenstein put out of the world, but his family continued to serve the monarchy capably and honorably for generations.

Rank and title were the most obvious signs of status. There were other, less obvious but, from the crown's viewpoint, equally profitable forms of status production. Sumptuary laws dictating who could wear what sort of clothing attempted to regulate the fashion statements men and women could make. Leopold's *Policeÿ Ordnung* concerning court dress, which banned the wearing of some popular costumes by any but those who were explicitly privileged to wear them, was justified on moral and economic grounds: "dardurch er eine löbliche Ehrbarkeit/ sowohl in Klaidungen/ als anderm Politischen wande/ eingeführt/ und dargegen aller unnothwendiger überfluess abgestellt werde . . ."[13] Violations invited a fine and confiscation of unauthorized finery and encouraged accusations by offering a reward of one third of the fine to an accuser.

The list of outward symbols that could be permitted or forbidden could be extended: the number of horses permitted on a carriage (only the pope and the emperor could have six), the right to sit in another's presence, ceremonial keys worn by real *Kammerherren*, specific places in religious or secular ceremonies, exemption from a generally binding regulation (such as the sumptuary laws); all could be used as rewards for loyalty or special contributions. And it was the monarch, usually acting through his *Obristhofmeister*, who alone had the power to manipulate the system.

The temptation to extend the system of privilege even beyond the point of diminishing returns was almost irresistible. The case of gambling is instructive. This was a golden age for games of fortune: gaming became part of the aristocratic ethic, in many instances a social disease of major proportions. Condemned by every moralist of the age, it was easy for the Austrian crown to condemn it in the most vigorous terms, prohibiting every sort of gambling throughout the realm under threat of severe punishment and fines. Since such a blanket condemnation of a universal human propensity was clearly unenforceable, the only way to have some control of behavior was to privilege it. Thus the court provost, Martin Güttinger, was granted the privilege of licensing gambling establishments and charged with the task of shutting down all those he did not authorize. The provost made a fortune on selective enforcement, which he shared as a matter of course with his superior, the *Obristhofmarschall,* and with the crown itself. The crown then made further profit when it granted Güttinger's sons an *Expectanz,* or anticipated succession, to the provost's office and the gambling monopoly.

Like moonlighting palace guards who augmented their inadequate pay by selling wine and beer brought into the city without paying taxes, the monarchy itself used acts of sovereign grace and selective enforcement of its prohibitions to supplement its income. The power to confer special privileges could be *"versilbert"* in the same way as tax-exempt liquor.

The beginning of a new reign provided many opportunities for the new monarch. While all grants of privilege were presumed to endure, it became customary to seek reconfirmation of them to make sure that the authorities in the new regime would take cognizance of and actively enforce the privileges involved. Thus, at the beginning of Leopold's reign, we find new grants of privilege to all the chartered guilds of Vienna and the reconfirmation of Jewish privileges. The crown also confirmed private monopolies, exemptions, and the right to purvey certain products to the court.

All these grants had their price. They also had value to the groups and individuals who received them. The mutual interdependence of the crown and its subjects upon the flow of privilege from above downward in return for loyalty and money flowing upward created increasing cohesion in a very loosely structured empire. While it could not provide the fuel to sustain the Habsburg Monarchy, this current of status and privilege pouring out from the monarch's sovereign grace did serve as an economic lubricant that kept the system functioning.

Notes

1. Gottlieb Eucharius Rinck, *Leopolds des Grossen wunderwürdiges Leben und Thaten* . . . (Cologne, 12°, 1713).

2. John Spielman, "Austrian Political Culture, the Seventeenth Century" (Paper delivered at the meeting of the German Studies Association, St. Louis, 1986).

3. Haus- Hof- und Staatsarchiv, Vienna (HHStA), Familien Korrespondenz A-15. Leopold I to Graf von Starhemberg, 27 January 1700. "But since at this time it would be hard to come up with hard cash, she should parcel out these sums to various offices so that in one or at most two years they can either be paid or she can use as security for a loan (or an advance)."

4. Deutsches Ordens Zentralarchiv, Vienna (DOZA), Hoch- und Teutschmeister (HM) 496 III, Mairhofer to Ampringen, Vienna, 15 March 1681. "In the current situation at court there is no secure, or even bad, expectation for either money or estates, even when they have been promised."

5. Max Ayrer, *Büechlein der Titel aller Staende* (Nuremberg, 1487; facsimile edition, Weimar, 1921).

6. George G. Metcalf, *Forms of Address in German (1500–1800)* (St. Louis: Washington University Press, 1938), chap. 2, "The Seventeenth Century."

7. Hubert Ch. Ehalt, *Ausdrucksformen absolutistischer Herrschaft: Der Wiener Hof im 17. und 18. Jahrhundert* (Vienna: Verlag für Geschichte und Politik, 1980), 118.

8. HHStA, Grosse Correspondenz 30a and 30b, etc.; and DOZA, Varia 560, and HM 493–96 passim.

9. Ampringen's correspondence is preserved in two large batches in Vienna, with doubtless more in the order's archives at Ludwigshaven. DOZA, HM 493–96; and HHStA, Grosse Correspondenz.

10. DOZA, Varia 560.

11. Ibid. Draft of 1671 letter with Ampringen's note in pencil: "Ist mir '81 wieder gebraucht worden."

12. HHStA, Ältere Zeremonielakten (ÄZA) 30, 23 November 1721.

13. HHStA, Obristhofmarschallamt (OMaA) 519 IV, Leopold I to *Obristhofmarschall* von Starhemberg, 22 March 1659, transmitting official copy of the decree for enforcement by the *Hofgericht*. "So that he may thereby introduce a praiseworthy uprightness in dress as well as in other public circumstances, and eliminate thereby all unnecessary excess."

Public Opinion and the Phenomenon of *Sozialdisziplinierung* in the Habsburg Monarchy

Karl Vocelka

Problems of Definition

Sozialdisziplinierung is one of the most frequently used but least examined terms in the early modern European lexicon.[1] Based on a theory of civilization developed by Norbert Elias, a number of historians have observed that in the course of the sixteenth and seventeenth centuries, both the state and church initiated various disciplinary practices with the intention of creating obedient and faithful subjects. But the term *Sozialdisziplinierung* actually refers to a wider range of phenomena.

The founding father of German sociology, Max Weber, already stressed the importance of the term "discipline" in his theory on processes of rationalization. In his view, discipline constituted a fundamental category in the development of modern society.[2] Norbert Elias more specifically defined the phenomenon within the context of the monopolization of power. He traced disciplinary mechanisms of control back to medieval courtly society, in which the aristocratic community of courtiers developed regimes of self-control necessitated by a great number of people living together. According to Elias, these disciplinary regimes developed at the top of society (aristocrats, army, bureaucracy, clergymen) and were then adopted by, or forced on, the lower strata of society. Moreover, *Sozialdisziplinierung* as conceived by Elias also entailed the transfer of external mechanisms of control into the psyche of individuals.[3] This framework is a compelling explanation. What Elias describes so clearly—increasingly refined manners developed by the nobility in courtly society, including crucial attitudinal changes toward sexuality—seems obvious in the early modern period (though doubted by some scholars, such as Hans Peter Duerr).

Michel Foucault suggests a somewhat different but basically related idea. He analyzes the development of a network of control and the mechanisms of internalization in a new social formation based on discipline that replaced the traditional society of estates in the course of the seventeenth and eighteenth centuries.[4] Like Elias, Foucault stresses that the state establishes "mastery of the body" by controlling sexuality and by instrumentalizing the body through practices such as torture.[5] Robert Muchembled also emphasizes the "repression of sexuality."[6] Foucault's theory cannot, however, easily explain *Sozialdisziplinierung* in early modern Europe. Advocating an ahistorical—in his words, genealogical—approach, he challenges process-oriented models such as Elias's by postulating social formations or patterns without being in the least interested in processes of transition. Thus, where Elias explains history with an all-encompassing concept of development, Foucault establishes heuristic models of social formations. His model of social control exercised through, and internalized in, the control of the body is always connected with industrial production and an instrumentalized rationality. Although Elias might well be describing the first stages of Foucault's process of *Sozialdisziplinierung,* Foucault's model is not related to the sovereign power of the absolute state but rather to the anonymous power structures that are at the core of a modern, industrialized social formation. I hope, however, to demonstrate that Foucault's notions can and should be applied to early modern Europe in order to understand fundamental processes of social change in this period.

The theoretical frameworks discussed so far conceive of the term *Sozialdisziplinierung* as an abstract notion traced in long-term developments or social structures. The constitutional historian Gerhard Oestreich, on the other hand, uses the term to characterize a very specific development in the process of establishing the modern state.[7] He sees the eighteenth century as a period of programmatic *Fundamentaldisziplinierung* that climaxes in the age of enlightened absolutism—the "Sattelzeit der Sozialdisziplinierung"—after the social regulations of towns in the late Middle Ages and the *Stabsdisziplinierung* influenced by neo-Stoicism.

Thus *Sozialdisziplinierung* emerges as a fundamental concept for studying social structures and changes in the early modern period. Yet no comprehensive study for the Habsburg Monarchy has been published so far. One of the most important contributions is the unpublished doctoral thesis of Maximilian Grothaus,[8] who discusses the hostile image of the Ottoman Empire and the Turks and analyzes some of the mechanisms of *Sozialdisziplinierung* in the limited context of a case study. Gisela Felhofer also deals with this problem in her doctoral thesis, although she is less specific and does not focus on the early modern period.[9]

It is neither my intention to argue for or against one of the definitions outlined above nor to consider *Sozialdisziplinierung* in the Habsburg Monarchy from all possible angles. For our present purposes, I have chosen three aspects of this phenomenon that seem to illustrate the mechanisms at work in this period: the normative aspect, the educational aspect, and the propagandistic aspect. I will briefly relate each of these aspects to source material, then demonstrate which instruments serve as vehicles for *Sozialdisziplinierung* and how this issue permeates the media meant to influence public opinion.

The Normative Aspect

The normative aspect can best be observed in the so-called *Polizeiordnungen*[10] and, for the rural part of the country, in an analysis of the *Weistümer*. The fundamental changes taking place between the sixteenth and seventeenth centuries can best be observed through an interpretation of the *Polizeiordnungen*. In the *Polizeiordnung* published in 1542 for Lower Austria, the main prohibitions concern:

1. blasphemy and cursing
2. fortune-telling and sorcery
3. gluttony and drinking, especially toasting
4. gambling
5. adultery and fornication

6. luxurious clothes
7. wedding and baptizing banquets
8. the annual fixation of prices for inns
9. buying on credit
10. measures and weights
11. loans on future harvests
12. vagabonds
13. itinerant traders, "Scots" and "Saffoyer"
14. imported golden and silk textiles
15. servants and workers of vineyards—their laziness, disobedience, unjustified demand for higher wages, and frequent changes of jobs.[11]

This list—repeated in several new editions of the *Polizei-ordnung* and in other patents—gives an exhaustive program of social control. Apart from the economic measures concerning prices, weights, etc., the *Polizeiordnungen* attack immorality and luxury. Although some items also deal with fringe groups of society, neither Gypsies nor Jews are mentioned. Concerns with sexual morality can mainly be observed in the so-called *Weistümer* and also in legal protocols, but unfortunately few studies based on these serial sources exist for Austria.

By contrast, the seventeenth-century *Polizeiordnungen* mainly stress the prohibition of luxury, also a main topic of patents and manifestos. May one conclude that this narrowing of concerns reflects the success of *Sozialdisziplinierung* in the sixteenth century, that in the course of the seventeenth century a repetition of certain regulations was no longer necessary because they were being observed anyway? And does this then mean that the process of internalizing disciplinary regimes had already had some effect?

The *Polizeiordnung* for Carinthia of 1577 assumes an intermediary position between the regulations quoted above and the crafts and police laws of the seventeenth century. In this document, some disciplinary measures—differentiated according to various social groups—are still mentioned, including:

blasphemy and swearing;
soothsayers/magicians and like persons;
social drinking and gluttony;
playing games;

adultery and frivolous (thoughtless) extramarital intercourse; extraordinary expense for clothing.

Nevertheless, regulations for servants and craftsmen constitute the main bulk of this law.

The religious element, which forms the background to all these measures, is most overt in the norms concerning sexuality. For example, "Even if many irresponsible persons sleep with each other outside a marriage set up by God, or cultivate other dishonesties, and even adultery is permitted openly without being punished, the Almighty is extremely offended by it, as this is against his divine commandment and causes too much annoyance." "So we demand," the law states, "that our authorities not tolerate this."[12]

In contrast to the *Polizeiordnung* of 1542, in the seventeenth-century work it is possible to discern a distinct concern with social groups at the fringes of society. Not only are foreign workers and traders—Scots and Savoyards, Italian masons and chimney sweepers—mentioned, even beggars, Jews, and Gypsies are included in these regulations, which required that nobody beg, that beggars be removed to another town or to a hospital, and that Jews display their specific sign, *Judenzeichen,* permanently. In these anti-Jewish polemics, religious elements—Jews as non-Christians and murderers of Jesus Christ—blend with old accusations of ritual murder, well poisoning, blaspheming holy wafers, usury, theft, counterfeiting, and cavorting with the Turks, thus formulating an endlessly repeated stereotype, which also found its expression in various pamphlets of the period. RudolphII's *Polizeiordnung* for Bohemia (1605) also deviates from the sixteenth-century pattern of disciplinary measures by passing over general or moral issues in favor of regulations for different crafts.[13]

Another group of edicts that figures prominently in the *Polizeiordnungen* and other patents of the seventeenth century concerns sumptuary regulations governing clothing and various luxury products.[14] Their emergence stems from the evolution of early mercantile ideas and from the ruling elite's desire to maintain existing differences between the social classes. Sometimes moral reasons are also given for economic measures, such as one 1686 ordinance that appealed, "in these as such difficult times of scarce money and of sorrows, one should rather think of frugality, as well as good and irreproachable manners and behavior, than wastefulness."[15]

The Educational Aspect

Both the Protestants and Catholics gave a high priority to educational issues during the age of the Reformation and Counter-Reformation. Luther called for public schools and wanted to grant more influence to state authorities. He also called upon secular authorities to force parents to send their children to school by threatening various forms of punishment.[16]

With the victory of the Counter-Reformation, schools and the school system changed. Together the Jesuits and Piarists controlled most institutions of higher education, a dominance that they perpetuated by training future generations of teachers. Max Weber located the roots of social control in European society in the disciplinary regimes of monasteries; one can easily imagine how much influence a highly disciplined order such as the Jesuits must have exerted on people in the early modern period, especially on social elites, to which monastic discipline was taught via the educational system.

Although schools were not originally in the vanguard of Jesuit activities, education soon became a central issue for them. In contrast to the Protestants, the Jesuits did not allow any state influence in their schools. But this hardly mattered during the Counter-Reformation, when the goals of the Church and the state were mostly identical in the Habsburg Monarchy. In summarizing the Austrian educational system, Helmut Engelbrecht concludes that the "school as an institution thus moves from the periphery of general attention and public necessity to a position that attracted the attention of the relevant authorities. In the school system, they saw an instrument which allowed leveling the subjects [Untertanen] by controlling their religion."[17]

The Propaganda Aspect

Muchembled poses a very important question by asking exactly how the establishment of control works, how a consensus is established, and how submission is achieved.[18] Newsletters, chapbooks, and other forms of popular media prompted the authorities' increasing concern with "public opinion." Certainly the measures they took to influence public opinion must also be regarded as vehicles of *Sozialdisziplinierung*. Sermons were definitely the most important medium that the ruling elite could employ to reach and influence the masses. They facilitated the triumph of confessional absolutism—that characteristic blend of religious-counterreformational and secular-absolutistic ideas that is so typical for the Habsburg Monarchy. These sermons could induce fear of God's punishment and demand measures of social control that were conveniently supported by directives of the state.

A good illustration of this collaboration of state patents and church sermons is documents dealing with natural catastrophes. Catastrophes such as earthquakes or epidemics were presented as God's punishment against those who failed to curb their sexual and other material pleasures. By stirring up such irrational fears, the governmental and clerical elites rendered the masses more receptive by establishing power over their emotions and desires. Muchembled demonstrates how this new mechanism of domination suppressed popular culture, and Elias would probably stress the fact that these sermons and patents regarding vice and immorality are parts of the process of civilization and changes of micronorms, general phenomena indicative of social change in early modern Europe. Both authors concentrate on France, but the specific development of baroque piety, which was characteristic for the Habsburg Monarchy until Joseph II, shows the same dialectic at work between elite and popular culture, with propaganda serving as a mediator between them.

Atonement [Penitence] and
Amendment (*Busse und Besserung*)

As pointed out above, sermons were an important means for spreading the mores of *Sozialdisziplinierung* and its theological background. A theologian of the period realized very clearly that people could be addressed directly in schools and from the pulpit.[19] Sermons dealt with all the scourges of God, such as locusts, epidemics, inflation, malnutrition, and war, the last being especially effective in the Habsburg Monarchy, which was constantly threatened by the Turkish menace. All these were interpreted as God's punishment for sin, against which similar measures are always suggested, as we can see from this *Infections-Ordnung:* "That each head of a household should see to it that his subordinates refrain from any blasphemy, whoredom, excessive eating and drinking and other similar vices and bad habits."[20] In order to encourage atonement and amendment, propaganda had to reinforce fear. In the remainder of this section, I will examine three of the main sources of fear emphasized by the instruments of public opinion.

Earthquakes

In their sermons about earthquakes—which are already mentioned as God's punishment in the Old Testament—preachers often relate earthquakes to other punishments. We can find various passages linking earthquakes to the Ottoman danger, which was often connected with epidemics as well. Take the example of a sermon on the occasion of the conquest of Ofen/Pest by imperial troops in 1686: "Therefore, just as in times of an earthquake, salvation must only come from God; in times of war and accidents God alone must be implored for consolation, salvation and help."[21]

Printed sermons (undoubtedly the majority were never fixed in writing) were definitely not intended to provide eyewitness reports; rather, preachers dealt with this phenomenon from their very specific point of view. Indeed, Protestant as well as Catholic sermons proceeded from a religious interpretation of earthquakes. One did not regard earthquakes as natural events but rather as expressions of God's wrath in punishment for the sins of Christianity. The earthquake itself was considered a sermon, more powerful than the words of the preachers. Take, for example, the sermons of the twenty-three-year-old Protestant preacher David Schweitzer from Tübingen, who had worked on the estate of the Protestant aristocrat Andreas Teufel Baron zu Guntersdorf in Schöngrabern in Lower Austria since 1587. Schweitzer expresses this attitude very distinctly on the occasion of the earthquake of 15 September 1590 (one of the strongest earthquakes Austria ever had), saying:

> So that, in these days of the cruel, terrible and unprecedented
> earthquake, we shall not be in want of preachers, God has placed
> preachers for us not only into one pulpit, but in all churches, even
> every house and town all over the country. . . . Are those mighty
> and powerful preachers of repentance not sent by God?

The earthquake is, according to Schweitzer's interpretation, a "be-
sonderes Wunderzeichen und Straffruten Gottes." Only people who
do not believe in God, states Schweitzer, believe in natural reasons
for earthquakes.

We can find similar interpretations in Catholic sermons up to
the seventeenth century, and even later.[22] For example, the Viennese bishop Caspar Neubeck in Vienna delivered two sermons, also
on the 1590 earthquake. In his first sermon, he rhetorically asks
how God is praised by earthquakes and finds the answers to his
question in very learned quotations, all of them concluding that, in
this way, God demonstrates his power and strength to his subjects.[23]

This is a notable reversion from classical and Renaissance
modes of interpretation and distinguishes Austrian polemics from
those of more secular Italian scholars. This can easily be demonstrated by looking at the *tractatus* of Augustinus Galesius, published in Bologna in 1571, which gives a survey and critical analysis
of all classical theories of earthquakes.

Schweitzer's sermon shows also the interconnection between
state and church propaganda. Schweitzer takes the example of a
medieval earthquake and tells his audience that in 1226 the
Lombards plotted a mutiny against Emperor Frederick to prevent
him from going on a crusade to the Holy Land. So God sent an earthquake to Lombardy and proved in this way that "Erdbeben auch
umb der Auffruhren und Ungehorsams willen geschehen, damit
böse ungehorsame Unterthanen gestillt und die Obrigkeit geehrt
würde." This sermon clearly demonstrates how corrective mechanisms of the church—be it Catholic or Protestant—and the establishment of obedience by the state through regulatory practices
dovetail with each other. However, taking into consideration
Luther's reaction to the Peasants' War and Protestant attitudes
toward rulers, it is perhaps not a complete coincidence that this

outspoken example of political and moral control originated from a Protestant rather than a Catholic source.

It is the definite goal of the sermons about earthquakes and other catastrophes, whether natural or not, to bring the population to atonement and amendment and to make them faithful, obedient subjects of the state. To this end, God is presented as the God of the Old Testament, an avenging, wrathful deity who makes the earth tremble in order to punish the sins of humanity, but Caspar Neubeck also believes in God's Grace: "Die Güte und Barmhertzigkeiten deß Herrn erschienen daran, daß wir nit allesamt umbkommen und verzehrt sein."[24]

The sins of the world are the real reason for earthquakes, and these sins are minutely listed by preachers. In this list, the secular and the spiritual points of view are again interconnected and—surprisingly—there is also room for critical remarks on society: "of excessive eating, drinking, usury, miserliness, fraud and finance, of envy, rage, hatred and animosity, of adultery, fornication and whoredom, of disobedience toward the authorities, of swearing, scolding, and profanities, of stealing, robbery, and shedding blood, of injustice and bleeding the poor (miserable) subjects, etc." The attributes of earthquakes are sometimes connected to particular sins. Thus Neubeck interprets Plinius's observation that earthquakes are more frequent during the night by explaining that this is because the night is also the time of unchastity and alcoholic excesses.[25]

The apocalyptic conception of earthquakes as God's warning can also be found in pamphlets of the period. A good example is an obviously Protestant pamphlet, dealing again with the event of 1590. This pamphlet claims with the title *Newe Zeitung* to be an objective report of the event. The author, Markus Volmarius, informs his readers: "If you sum it all up, such mighty earthquakes—besides famine, pestilence, bloodshed, terrible chasimatis and signs in the skies—are certain forebodings and preparations for the Day of Judgment: that we shall be prepared and approach our dear bridegroom Jesus Christ in happy spirits and with joy."[26]

This pamphlet, which is rather a theological tract than an informative report, uses the opportunity to polemicize against everything—the pope, the Turks, the new calendar, and so on—but in other cases, the theological influence is more pronounced. A peculiar example with a strong connection to anti-Ottoman propaganda is a pamphlet about an earthquake in Amasia, Turkey, in 1598, in which the theological interpretation of earthquakes is applied to the Ottomans, who are considered subject to the same divine retribution as Christian society:

> Because there is no good administration of justice, and also no proper penitence, but they severely anger God and his prophet Mohammed with constant and grave sins and misdeeds, and also do not show the Turkish emperor the proper and due honor and obedience, such scourges and more punishments are sent, and more will follow, mark my words, which warn the people to examine themselves and to appease God's rage with prayers.[27]

The Turks

The almost interminable conflict with the Ottoman empire dominated Habsburg politics in the early modern period, thereby providing yet another justification for influencing public opinion within the monarchy. It was not long before Habsburg propaganda had ideologized the struggle for Hungary and against Ottoman expansion in the Balkans. Indeed, not only Catholic polemicists but also Protestants, such as Luther, portrayed the Turks as "the scourge of God" who were there to punish the sins of Christians. The Habsburg authorities readily accepted and reinforced this interpretation, which helped determine the collective mentality in the monarchy for a long time to come.

Stereotypes about the cruelty of the "archfoe of Christendom" stress the Turks' gruesome acts, while conveniently omitting any mention of similar atrocities by Christian forces.[28] Only a few pamphlets contain hints of the atrocities committed by imperial mercenaries.[29] Not only the conflict against the Ottoman Empire but also war in general was particularly—as Grothaus shows so well—conceived of as God's punishment of sin. Abraham à Sancta Clara sums it up impressively: "Die Sünd ist der Magnet, welcher das scharpffe Eysen und Kriegs-Schwerd in unsere Länder zieht."[30]

According to this interpretation, the real reason for the Turkish invasion of the Habsburg dominions was the widespread presence there of "idols, superstition, unbelief, weariness of, and contempt for, God's truth; sanctimoniousness and hypocrisy, gross ingratitude for God's charity; blasphemy and using God's holy name in vain, as well as the holy sacraments; excessive swearing, perjury; all kinds of magic."[31] This call for a moral armament of the people is again interspersed with the typical demands for social control that we have already encountered above.

A patent dating from November 1683 clearly shows the immediate connection that was made between the actual Turkish menace and people's refusal to obey state authorities. The patent criticizes that "some of the subjects there behave very objectionably toward the authorities and likewise fancy they need not show the obedience, nor the work or respect due to them."[32]

What concrete measures did the government propose in such a situation? Needless to say, it repeated the already familiar moral demands. In addition, it demanded that people pray intensively, as in 1598, when Rudolph II introduced a forty-hour prayer during the long Turkish war—a directive that was repeated in Vienna in 1663 and again in 1683. The observation of these demands, which were issued by the church, was controlled by the state. By threatening punishment, the Counter-Reformation church and the absolutist state cooperated in completely suppressing and disciplining their subjects.

The intention of the ruling class to guarantee law and order, obedience, and security was ideologically supported by the theological framework. The permeation of secular rule by Catholicism clearly contributes deeply to *Sozialdisziplinierung* by justifying domination and suppression of individuals under the ideological pretext of justly ruling by God's grace. In no other context are these ideas so frequently expressed as when conjuring up fears of the demonized Ottoman enemy, the *Erbfeind der Christenheit*.[33]

The Plague

Alongside earthquakes and the Turks, the plague intensified fear of God's punishments. "The visitation of pestilence, as the Holy Scriptures teach us, is the hand of God, God's rod, a sword of His fury, a divine revenge, an arrow sent by a furious god, thunder and lightening of God's rage; and finally it is unjustly called a War-God."[34] The combat against this disease was, like the one against the Turks, a religious task and therefore used religious means, described as "Geistliche Mittel zur Zeit der Pestilentz nutzlich zugebrauchen. Das erste Mittel. Die Bueßwerck"[35] in a sermon by Ferdinand Anton Hauck. Once again, penitence is most important, closely followed by other religious exercises, among them worshipping the Holy Sacrament or the Holy Virgin and all the saints; only then are natural means mentioned, such as flight, cleaning the air, sweating, temperance, a happy mood, and various (frequently very obscure) medication, including "Der Trunck deß Menschen-Harm vnnd was von der schwartzen Hennen distilirten Koth zu halten."[36]

The topos of the plague as God's punishment disappears from the *Infections-Ordnungen* by the mid-seventeenth century. This is rather surprising, especially when contrasted to the host of printed material on the Turks, which, as Grothaus shows, remained as evident as it had been in the sixteenth century. In the *Infections-Ordnung* of 1562, we can still read "that the almighty God let fall on us the torment of war, hunger, and mainly pestilence as just and well deserved reward for our incessant sinning,"[37] followed by admonitions to the clergy to preach against vices (followed by the usual list). Furthermore, the *Infections-Ordnung* of 1630 still threatens the justified wrath of God,[38] whereas the relevant texts of the late seventeenth and early eighteenth centuries are written without any ideological or religious arguments.[39]

Conclusion

As we have seen, the central aspect of *Sozialdisziplinierung* was religion. Regardless of whether they were of ecclesiastical or secular origin, official media were based on a religious interpretation of various events that helped to arouse fear of God's retribution for sins, a punishment that could be avoided only through atonement and amendment. Baroque Catholicism internalized these fears by producing a guilty conscience in its followers. Moreover, it promoted typical forms of piety in the service of authority, which were presented as the only possible remedy against sin. Through the media of propaganda, people gradually became convinced of their own responsibility for catastrophes—which were hardly rare in those days—and were thus brought to remodel their behavioral patterns along the lines suggested by official propaganda. Punishment of sins, long prayers, fasting, worshipping saints, pilgrimages, castigation, and whipping all develop in the sixteenth and seventeenth centuries with the Counter-Reformation, which sought and found support from an equally solicitous absolutist state. The church's call for moral behavior could only be successful with the help of state authorities. This characterization of confessional absolutism must be seen as the background to all individual measures.

The fact that this normalization of behavior was better developed—or at least better observed—in towns than on the estates of the aristocracy can possibly be explained by the specific circumstances of the Counter-Reformation in the Habsburg countries. The special and comparatively strong position of the Austrian nobility gave this social group more free play for a longer period, whereas the Counter-Reformation began earlier and with more force in the towns. Jean Delumeau perhaps overemphasizes the fact that the roots of *Sozialdisziplinierung* lie in urbanization and the centralization of power—a nevertheless important observation in this context. He is, however, undoubtedly correct in suggesting that absolutism and Catholicism contributed to the spread of this phenomenon.

Having developed later than in the towns, social control in the countryside flowed essentially from the top to the bottom of society. This is evident in various sources, such as sermons and patents, that constantly emphasize the responsibility of the ruling class, "der Obrigkeit, bzw. des Hausvaters"—a central term in Otto Brunner's "Herrschaft des ganzen Hauses" and the "Hausväterliteratur." Florentinus Schillig devotes a whole sermon to the motto "Es kann nicht wol zuegehen wo die Obrigkeit nichts nutz ist." Another sermon from the same series under the topic "Der redlich Haußvatter. Müssiggang ist aller Laster Anfang" describes exactly what tasks a *Hausvater* has to perform: He has to be careful and busy and just; he has to get up early and work hard; last, but certainly not least, he has to control the workers in his house to prevent idleness and disobedience.

The persecution of outsiders becomes increasingly common in the late seventeenth century.[40] In the last few years, many historical books and articles have reflected Foucault's influence by dealing with this fashionable topic, especially with the institutionalization of prisons (*Zucht- und Arbeitshäuser*).[41] The propagandistic aspect of this phenomenon has attracted less attention. It is, however, conspicuous in the *Polizei- und Infektionsordnungen* and patents of the sixteenth century that were directed at those people who lived at the fringes of society. Thus the *Infections-Ordnung* of 1562 makes dispositions "die Petler auß der Stat zu schaffen deßgleichen das müessig geendt gesindt" or "die offnen Spillen Fechtschuellen vnd Spilleut nit zuhalten."[42] This trend is even more clear in the documents of the seventeenth century, the best-known example definitely being the catalogue of measures against Jews issued by Leopold I, who had them deported from the hereditary lands.[43]

Another group that was severely persecuted is the Roma und Sinthi Gypsies. In Carinthia the *Polizeiordnung* of 1577 had already explicitly accused them of collaborating with, and spying for, the Ottoman empire, and had decreed that they no longer be tolerated in the province.[44] A century later, a patent of 22 November 1689 forbade them from entering any of the Austrian hereditary lands. If caught, they could be imprisoned and forced to work, "auff ihr Leben lang in Band vnd Eisen zur Arbeit condemniert."[45]

In the towns, the attempt to establish and guarantee law and order is especially evident in patents and various practical innovations. In 1687 the governor of Lower Austria, Johann Quintin Count Jörger, attempted to combat incidences of murder, fighting, and other criminal activities by installing Vienna's first streetlights with seventeen lanterns in the Dorotheergasse. One year later, the whole town was illuminated every night. In addition to such practical measures, various forms of propaganda contributed to the fight against crime, such as patents issued against "höchstschädliche Rauffhändel, Balgereyen, Außforderungen und Duellen."[46]

The foundation of workhouses and orphanages (*Arbeits- and Waisenhäuser*) fits well within the context of regulatory mechanisms especially directed against marginal social groups. The baroque era may have been an age of prodigal splendor, with aristocratic palaces, flamboyant churches, and an abundance of court festivities. Yet it was also a period of bitter poverty and strong social discrimination that witnessed a rise in the number of poor people, beggars, and criminals. The attempt to use the poor as a cheap work force and the idea to render criminals "useful" in penitentiaries instead of executing them derive from the same ideological background. For example, in Vienna the first orphanage for boys was founded in 1663, largely on the initiative of Johann Konrad von Richthausen Baron von Chaos. Eight years later, Emperor Leopold I ordered the construction of a penitentiary on the location of three houses of Jews who had been driven out of Vienna. This institution was meant not only for real criminals but also for healthy beggars, disobedient servants, people who did not want to work, prostitutes, and children of migrant families. Inmates were to be disciplined mainly by beating and by being made pious through religious instruction.

Both phenomena are to be viewed together: the propagandistic nature of discipline, which showed results at the end of the seventeenth century; and practical measures against the vestiges of indiscipline, especially healthy individuals who tried to escape the control of state authorities. At the end of the early modern period, this process of *Sozialdisziplinierung* was by no means finished, and total social control had not been achieved. Thus, many of the trends we have observed continued into more recent times, while others were abandoned altogether.

Notes

1. See R. Po-chia Hsia, *Social Discipline in the Reformation: Central Europe 1550–1750* (London: Routledge, 1989).

2. Max Weber, *Wirtschaft und Gesellschaft: Grundriß einer verstehenden Soziologie* (Tübingen: Mohr, 1956).

3. Norbert Elias, *Die höfische Gesellschaft: Untersuchungen zur Soziologie des Königtums und der höfischen Aristokratie,* Suhrkamp Taschenbuch Wissenschaft, vol. 423 (Frankfurt/Main: Suhrkamp, 1983); and *Über den Prozeß der Zivilisation: Soziogenetische und psychogenetische Untersuchungen,* 2 vols., Suhrkamp Taschenbuch Wissenschaft, vols. 158/159 (Frankfurt/Main: Suhrkamp, 1976). See also Markus Reisenleitner, "Die Bedeutung der Werke und Theorien Norbert Elias' für die Erforschung der Frühen Neuzeit," *Frühneuzeit-Info* 1 (1990): 47–57.

4. Michel Foucault, *Überwachen und Strafen: Die Geburt des Gefängnisses* (Frankfurt/Main: Suhrkamp, 1977), Suhrkamp Taschenbuch Wissenschaft, 184; there is a critical discussion of these theories in Hubert Treiber and Heinz Steinert, *Die Fabrikation des zuverlässigen Menschen: Über die "Wahlverwandtschaft" von Kloster- und Fabriksdisziplin* (Munich: Moos, 1980).

5. Richard van Dülmen, *Theater des Schreckens: Gerichtspraxis und Strafrituale in der frühen Neuzeit,* Beck'sche Reihe, vol. 349 (Munich: Beck, 1985).

6. Robert Muchembled, *Kultur des Volkes—Kultur der Eliten: Zur Geschichte einer erfolgreichen Verdrängung,* 2d ed. (Stuttgart: Klett-Cotta, 1984), 188.

7. Gerhard Oestreich, *Geist und Gestalt des frühmodernen Staates* (Berlin: Duncker & Humblot, 1960). For a thorough explanation of this theory, see Winfried Schulze, "Gerhard Oestreichs Begriff *Sozialdisziplinierung* in der frühen Neuzeit," *Zeitschrift für historische Forschung* 14 (1987): 265–302.

8. Maximilian Grothaus, "Der 'Erbfeindt christlichen Nahmens': Studien zum Türken-Feindbild in der Kultur der Habsburgermonarchie zwischen 16. und 18. Jahrhundert" (Ph.D. diss., University of Graz, 1986).

9. Gisela Felhofer, *Die Produktion des disziplinierten Menschen,* Dissertationen der Johannes-Kepler-Universität Linz, vol. 70 (Vienna: VWG, 1987).

10. Wilhelm Brauneder and Irmgard Helperstorfer: *Die österreichischen Polizeiordnungen des 16. Jahrhunderts,* Fontes rerum Austriacarum, third series: Fontes iuris, vol. 12 (Vienna-Cologne-Weimar, 1991).

11. Kristl Tönz-Leitich, "Laster- und Unsittenverbote der Frühneuzeit," *Österreich in Geschichte und Literatur* 14 (1970): 175; Thomas Winkelbauer, "Sozialdisziplinierung und Konfessionalisierung durch Grundherren in den österreichischen und böhmischen Ländern im 16. und 17. Jahrhundert," *Zeitschrift für historische Forschung* 19 (1992): 317–39.

12. *Des Ertzhertzogthumbs Khärndten verbesserte vnd New aufgerichte Policey ordnung/ Im ain tausend fünffhundert vnd Sibenvndsibtzigisten Jar* (Grätz: Zacharias Bartsch, 1578).

13. *K. Rudolphs II. Polizeyordnung für Böhmen, 1605* (Dresden: Walther, 1792).

14. For example, Patente Leopolds I. Wien 23. September 1682 (Vienna: Haus-Hof- und Staatsarchiv [HHStA]), Archivdepot Grafenegg Fasc. 200), and Laxenburg 5. Mai 1697 (HHStA, Archivdepot Grafenegg Fasc. 201).

15. *Der Röm. Kayserl. auch zu Hungarn vnd Böhaimb etc. Königl. Mayestät Herrn Herrn Leopoldi, Erthertzogen zu Oesterreich/ Vnsers Allergnädigsten Herrn vnd Landts-Fürstens/ etc. Policey-Ordnung/ in Oesterreich Vnter- vnd Ob der Ennß* (Vienna: Christina Losmerovin, 1686); similar in *Der Röm. Kayserl. auch zu Hungarn vnd Böhaimb etc. Königl.Mayest. Herrn/ Herrn Leopoldi Ertzhertzogens zu Oesterreich/ Vnsers Allergnädigsten Herrn vnd Landsfürstens/ etc. Policey-Ordnung/ In Oesterreich Vnter- vns Ob der Ennß* (Vienna: Matthäus Cosmerovius, 1671); or *Der Röm. Kayserl. auch zu Hungarn vnd Böhaimb etc. Königl. Mayest. Herrn/ Herrn Leopoldi, Erthertzogen zu Oesterreich/ Vnsers Allergnädigsten Herrn vnd Landts-Fürstens/ etc. Erneutes Policey-Patent/in Oesterreich Vnter- vnd Ob der Ennß* (Vienna: Christina Losmerovin, 1688).

16. Helmut Engelbrecht, *Geschichte des österreichischen Bildungswesens: Erziehung und Unterricht auf dem Boden Österreichs,* 2: *Das 16. und 17. Jahrhundert* (Vienna: Österreichischer Bundesverlag, 1983), 12.

17. Ibid., 13.

18. Muchembled, *Kultur des Volkes—Kultur der Eliten,* 185.

19. Christian August Pfalz, *Abominatio desolationis Turcicae, der Türckischen Verwüstungs-Grewel Durch Unsern Herrn und Heyland Jesum Christum Vorgesagt: Wann ihr sehen werdet den Grewel der Verwüstung/ daß er stehet an dam heiligen Orth* (Prague: Wilhelm Knauff, 1672), 405

20. *Der Röm. Kay. auch zu Hungarn vnnd Behaim etc. K. May. Erthertzogens zu Osterreich vnsers Allergnedigsten Herrn/ New verbesserte Infectionsordnung* (Vienna: Matthias Formica, 1630).

21. Elias Veieln, *Die prophetische Bitte und Dancksagung Deß hocherleuchteten und glückseligen Königs David In einer Sieges- und Dancks-Predigt . . . Wegen Eroberung der königl. Haubt-Statt Ofen/ Angestellten Freuden-Fest/ Der christlichen Gemeinde in Ulm* (Ulm: Matteus Schultes, 1686).

22. Caspar Neubeck, *Zwo Catholische Predigten. Gehalten zu Wienn in Österreich/ in offentlicher Versammlung zum gemeinen Gebett/ wider die Schröckliche Erdtbidem/ so sich Anno 1590 den 15. September/ vnd nachmals vilfeltig erzeigt haben* (Vienna: Nassinger, 1591), 10; and David Schweitzer, *Ein Christliche Bußpredigt/ Auch Gründtliche vnnd außführliche Erklärung/ der erschröcklichen/ grausamen vnd schälichen Erdbeben, so sich im verlauffenen 90. Jahr den 15. Septemb. vnd nachmals vielfältig in Oesterreich/ vnd andern vmbligenden gräntzenden Ländern vnd Königreich/ erzeigt haben: Gehalten Zu Schöngrabern in Nider Oesterreich/ Anno 1590. den 14. Sontag nach Trinit* (Frankfurt/Main: Johann Spieß, n.d.), 35.

23. Ibid., 6.

24. Ibid., 2.

25. Ibid., 52–53; see Plinius, lib. 2.nat. hist, cap. 30.

26. Marcus Volmarius, *Newe Zeittung vom schröcklichen Erdbidm/ den 15. nach dem Newen/ aber den 5. tag Septembris/ nach dem alten Calender/ deß 1590. Jars/ zu Wien in Oesterreich geschehen* (No place/publisher, 1591).

27. *Zwo newe Zeitung/ Die erst/ Wie der Allmächtige Gott, in der Türckey/ gegen der Landschafft Amasia/ zwo Türckische Städt/ der eine schwartz Tauris/ die ander Castille genandt/ sampt 6.Dörffern/ vnd sechtzig tausent Personen/ in disem 1598.Jar zu ende deß Mertzens/ durch einen Erdbidem jämmerlich versenckt hat. Die ander . . .* (Augsburg, n.d.).

28. See Helmut Lamparter, "Luthers Stellung zum Türkenkrieg" (Ph. D. diss., University of Fürstenfeldbruck, 1940); Richard Lind, "Luthers Stellung zum Kreuz- und Türkenkrieg" (Ph.D. diss., University of Giessen, 1940); Johan W. Bohnstedt, *The Infidel Scourge of God: The Turkish Menace as Seen by German Pamphleters of the Reformation Era,* Transactions of the American Philosophical Society, n.s., vols. 58–59 (Philadelphia: The American Philosophical Society, 1968); Richard Ebermann, "Die Türkenfurcht: Ein Beitrag zur Geschichte der öffentlichen Meinung in Deutschland während der Reformationszeit" (Ph.D. diss., University of Halle, 1904).

29. Martin C. Mandlmayr and Karl G. Vocelka: " 'Christliche Triumphfreude über herrliche Victorien und stattliche Kriegsprogressen:' Die Eroberung Ofens

1686: Fallstudie über Zahl, Verbreitung und Inhalt propagandistischer Medien in der Frühen Neuzeit" *Südost-Forschungen* 44 (1985): 99–138.

30.   Abraham à Sancta Clara, *Auf, auf ihr Christen! Das ist/ Eine bewegliche Auffrischung der christlichen Waffen wider den Türckischen Blut-Egel etc.* (Vienna: Johann van Ghelen, 1683), 30.

31.   *Klagendes Teutschland forschet Wehemütig nach den Ursachen deß Türckischen Kriegsüberzugs. Darauf werden dieselben umbständig erzehlet von denen Astrologis, Theologis, Politicis, Oeconomicis, Militaris Rei Pewriti & Justitiaris: Das hierüber betrübtre Teutschland wird treulich verwarnet/ wahre Buß zu tun* (No place/publisher, 1664) fols. 9v–10r.

32.   Vienna, 27 November 1683 patent (HHStA, Archivdepot Grafenegg Fasc. 200).

33.   See Grothaus, "Der 'Erbfeindt christlichen Nahmens,'" especially 584.

34.   Ferdinand Anton Hauck, *Schuß-Frey In dem Krieg Gottes. Das ist: Geistlich- vnd Natürliche Mittel wider die Pestilentz nutzlich zu gebrauchen sambt etlichen schönen Fragstucken/ vnd der Infections-Ordnung so zu Palermo und Florentz gehalten* (Vienna: Peter Paul Vivian, 1679).

35.   Ibid.

36.   Ibid.

37.   *Der Röm. Kay. auch zu Hungarn vnnd Behaim etc. Kü. May. Erthertzogens zu Osterreich vnsers Allergnedigsten Herrn etc. Verwalter Statthalter Ambts/ Cantzler/ Regenten vnnd Camer Räthe der Niderösterreichischen Lande/ New fürgenomene Infections Ordnung* (Vienna: Michael Zimmermann, 1562).

38.   *Der Röm. Kay. auch zu Hungarn vnnd Behaim etc. Kü. May. Erthertzogens zu Osterreich vnsers Allergnedigsten Herrn/ New verbesserte Infectionsordnung* (Vienna: Matthias Formica, 1630).

39.   *Der Hoch- vnd Löblichen Herren Fürsten/ vnd Stände im Hertzogthum Ober- vnd Nieder-Schlesien Neue Infections-Ordnung de dato Breslau den 14. Februarii 1680* (Breslau: Baumannische Erben/ durch Gottfried Gründern, 1680); *Neue Infections-Ordnung im Marggrafenthumb Mähren de dato Brünn den 6. Februarij Anno 1705* (Brünn: Maria Elisabetha Sinapin Wittib/ durch Georg Strnadt, 1705).

40.   See, among many others, Norbert Schindler, "Die Entstehung der Unbarmherzigkeit: Zur Kultur und Lebensweise der Salzburger Bettler am Ende des 17. Jahrhunderts," *Bayerisches Jahrbuch für Volkskunde* (1988): 61–130.

41.   See, for example, Hannes Stekl, *Österreichs Zucht- und Arbeitshäuser 1671–1929: Institutionen zwischen Fürsorge und Strafvollzug* (Vienna: Verlag für Geschichte und Politik, 1978).

42.   *Infectionsordnung* 1562.

43.   Vienna, 6 August 1669 patent (HHStA, Archivdepot Grafenegg, Fasc. 200).

44.   *Des Ertzhertzogthumbs Khärndten verbesserte vnd New aufgerichte Policey ordnung/ Im ain tausend fünffhundert vnd Sibenvndsibtzigisten Jar* (Grätz: Zacharias Bartsch, 1578).

45. Vienna, 24 October 1701 patent (HHStA, Archivdepot Grafenegg, Fasc. 201).

46. Vienna, 23 September 1682 patent (HHStA, Archivdepot Grafenegg Fasc. 200), repeated in Vienna 26 January 1712 patent (HHStA, Archivdepot Grafenegg, Fasc. 201).

Part 3

Government and Economy

Introduction

Herman Freudenberger

In 1666, not long after Jean-Baptiste Colbert began his career as reformer of the French economy, the Habsburg Monarchy—like France and other countries, an overwhelmingly agrarian country—took its own first halting steps in the same direction. It was in that year that J. J. Becher, an alchemist and political economist, came to Vienna from Munich at the request of Emperor Leopold I and one of his chief ministers, Count Georg Ludwig Sinzendorf.[1] He was a "projector" and founded a silk-manufacturing company on an estate of Count Sinzendorf's. Beside Sinzendorf, a number of wholesalers were the investors. At the same time, Becher saw to it that a government agency for the promotion of commerce and industry (*Kommerzienrat*) was formed. Becher also was responsible for the establishment of an Oriental-trade company, owned for the most part by a number of so-called warehousers (*Niederlagsverwandten*) in Vienna, a group of foreign merchants with special privileges who were engaged in the export and import business.[2] In this way, Becher initiated a tradition for effecting economic development that was adhered to for at least the following 130 years, namely, a combination of government leadership and private ownership. In his writings, Becher shows himself to be a foe of monopolies but nevertheless a great admirer of the British and Dutch large-scale companies, such as the British East India Company, indicating that he did not realize that it was indeed a monopoly. While emphasizing the basic position of the peasantry in the economy and the parasitic nature of nobility, he had few proposals for the improvement of agriculture. He did not remain very long in the Habsburg Monarchy, and his projects did not enjoy much success. Nevertheless, he was a pioneer for the so-called cameralists.

One of these was Philipp Wilhelm von Hörnigk, Becher's brother-in-law, like him an immigrant from Germany proper, who nevertheless wrote a flaming patriotic tract in 1683 entitled *Österreich über alles, wann es nur will*. This small book envisioned the entire Habsburg Monarchy as a small, self-sufficient world that no longer needed to purchase so many goods from France. It went through at least sixteen editions, the latest coming out in the 1780s. It was obviously influential, so that a leading member of the council of state (*Staatsrat*), Egid Valentin Baron Borié, could proudly proclaim that Austria was indeed over all in the world.[3]

A third member of this group was Wilhelm von Schröder, who also came from Germany proper and arrived in Vienna in 1673.[4] He, more than the other two, emphasized the importance of a strong economy for the income of the royal exchequer. He was strongly influenced by the British mercantilists Sir Thomas Mun and Sir Josiah Child and himself resided in England for three years, apparently to observe the working of its economy. In his writings, he proposed, among other things, the formation of a central bank guaranteed by the state but operated for the benefit of the private economy. Accordingly, a large bank was founded in Vienna in 1703, which eventually was called the Municipal Bank of Vienna.[5] It did not function well because it was unable to resist the crown's demands for credit. Nevertheless, the idea was still influential later in the eighteenth century, especially in the founding of an economic development bank in Brno in 1751 and a similar but much larger bank in Vienna in 1787, the latter owned by some of the greatest aristocrats in the Habsburg Monarchy, including Prince Schwarzenberg.[6]

One of the central facts of life with which the officials and the emperor of the Habsburg Monarchy were faced was the chronic shortage of revenues in the exchequer, especially in view of the numerous wars that were being fought at that time. It comes consequently as no surprise that Prince Eugene of Savoy at one point expressed his frustration when he said that if it were to take only a few thousand gulden to save the monarchy, it would be impossible to do so. Similarly, when Maria Theresa acceded to the throne in 1740, she found the treasury empty. This lack of resources was a catalyst for the government to act in the economic sphere. But it was frustrated by the vested interests within the monarchy and its own lack of will. While it had great opportunities to centralize its administration and reduce the power of the estates and other vested interests after defeating the aristocrats and the burghers in Bohemia in the Thirty Years' War and the reconquest of Hungary from the Turks in the 1680s, the state was hamstrung until the time of Maria Theresa. Hörnigk had written his book while the war with Turkey was at its height, and he hoped that the war emergency would shake up society enough so that some basic economic changes could be made.

It was after another great war, one that threatened to tear the monarchy completely apart, that a further series of publications engages our attention. In this case, too, it was a man from Germany proper whose works proved to be very influential. Published in 1758, the first work of Johann Heinrich Gottlob Justi was based on the new supreme authority in the Habsburg Monarchy, the *Directorium in publicis et cameralibus,* and supposedly read by its officials prior to publication. According to Justi, the basic goal of government was to provide for the welfare and happiness (*Glückseligkeit*) of its people. The role of government was thus to eliminate the obstacles that impeded free commerce. Both the state and the individual citizens wanted to acquire wealth and to use it for the common welfare. Justi, a rationalist, dealt to a large extent in abstractions. He did not remain long in the Habsburg Monarchy and left Vienna for Prussia. He can be considered a late cameralist.

The same was true of Joseph von Sonnenfels, a professor at the University of Vienna and a member of some government agencies from time to time. Like Justi, he believed in the complete rationalization of society. The highest ethical purpose of the state, he thought, was to aid the common welfare and to protect its citizens. One of his basic principles was that the state should provide the maximum population that a country could employ. Consequently, he favored the elimination of labor dues by peasants to their lords and the division of large estates into small peasant holdings. He also believed in free market competition. This enlightened cameralism was a valuable predecessor of economic liberalism, of which the brothers Ludwig and Karl Zinzendorf were the best practitioners. Sonnenfels's major work, first published in the 1760s, was used as a textbook until 1848.

I pointed out above that the efforts at economic development from time to time enjoyed the support of the government and of private persons within the monarchy. Until the reign of Maria Theresa, this happened, however, in a fairly haphazard way. Becher's commercial council did not last long and was at any rate ineffective during its existence. The government in Vienna made an attempt in 1698 to analyze the condition of the economy by requesting the chanceries for Bohemia, Lower Austria, and Hungary to submit descriptions of the economies of the area under their jurisdiction to evaluate the citizens' ability to pay taxes. Out of this request came an edict in 1710 by which the Bohemian Commercial College (*Commerzcollegium*) was formed to propose measures for the improvement of the Bohemian economy. Not much happened in its deliberations. Similar agencies were established for several other crown lands with equally dismal results. By 1740, when Maria Theresa came to power, the entire organization had been destroyed through the shortsightedness of the highest authorities in the government and the narrow egotism of the vested interests. Finally in 1746, a new agency was formed with competence for all the lands of the monarchy. This was part of the movement toward greater centralization in the monarchy, led by the Silesian nobleman Friedrich Wilhelm Count Haugwitz. In 1749 subordinate agencies for the various lands were established. Under this system, Austrian mercantilism reached its apogee in the 1760s, with the prohibition of the import of various goods from abroad and the import of foreign craftsmen to introduce the manufacture of commodities that had previously been made abroad. One might even say that a certain amount of primitive economic planning was developed through the so-called operational plans (*Operationspläne*) of the 1760s. This government intervention was modified in the 1770s as a result of the actions of two key officials, Count Karl Zinzendorf, who, according to his diary entry, was nevertheless very upset when the agency was abolished;[7] and Franz Anton von Raab, whose greatest claim to fame was that he was in charge of a central-government move to break up latifundia and settle them with small peasants. In 1818 a leading government official, Anton von Krauss-Elislago, said that these agencies could have functioned effectively if competent officials, merchants, and industrialists had been its members. Instead, they became a foul bureaucratic mess.[8] This may be an overly harsh evaluation, as they did serve as catalysts for industrial development.

To be sure, it was not the government agencies alone that were responsible for a push in the direction of more industrial production. Private investors did exist in the monarchy, though not in great numbers. There were manufacturing units on many noble estates, such as distilleries, breweries, and iron foundries. Many, while not insignificant producers of income for the manor, were small and sold their products mostly to the local peasants. The first large industrial undertaking was established in Linz when a local merchant, Christian Sind, built a wool-textile factory[9] in 1672, which at one point in the eighteenth century had more than 30,000 employees, both within and outside the factory. Founded by a private capitalist investing his money, it passed into state ownership in the middle of the eighteenth century and finally went out of business in 1851. As was the case with many other new industrial undertakings, the Linz factory had many problems with sales, partly without doubt because of poor quality but also because of the disinclination of Habsburg merchants to break their relations with foreign suppliers.

Early in the eighteenth century, the Linz firm became the property of the Vienna Poor House and not long thereafter that of the Oriental Company, a new firm which began operations as a shareholding corporation (*Aktiengesellschaft*) in 1719. It was closely connected with the government, and Emperor Charles VI was one of the investors. It had been founded to take advantage of the Treaty of Passarowitz (1718) and open Turkey and the Near East to Habsburg products. Charles VI ordered the Vienna Municipal Bank, a supposedly private bank, to invest 100,000 gulden in the company. The Oriental Company also established a large cotton factory with several thousand employees in Schwechat, outside of Vienna.

These enterprises were without doubt significant in the first half of the eighteenth century. There were also several factories on the manors of noblemen. The government seems to have been involved in these cases on a very peripheral basis. One of these was a wool stocking factory erected on Slavkov (Austerlitz), the Moravian estate of Count Kaunitz, the grandfather of the famous statesman of the reigns of Maria Theresa, Joseph II, and Leopold II.[10] Kaunitz brought in foreign specialists to instruct the peasants on his estate. The other noteworthy enterprise belonged to Count Waldstein, who built a fine woolen cloth factory on his estate in Horní Litvínov (Oberleutensdorf). Proud of his accomplishment, he had a group of artists make copper engravings of the factory in the 1720s, affording us an excellent view of the textile technology of the time. This same area in northwestern Bohemia already enjoyed some industrial employment with a woolen stocking factory on a monastic estate in nearby Osek (Ossegg). Like Kaunitz, Waldstein brought in foreign experts, in his case from England and Holland, to teach his peasants the art of making fine cloth. This firm enjoyed indifferent success while under direct control of the Waldstein family. For some twenty years in the nineteenth century it was operated by Ferdinand Römheld, a bourgeois industrialist, with substantial success.

Probably the greatest industrialist of this time in the Habsburg Monarchy was Maria Theresa's consort, and from 1745 to his death in 1765, emperor of the Holy Roman Empire, Francis Stephen, formerly the duke of Lorraine. The Prussian representative in Vienna estimated his wealth at 20 million gulden in 1755. In 1736, shortly after his marriage, he established a large cotton mill at Šaštin (Sassin) and an earthenware factory in Holič (Hollitsch) in today's Slovakia. The cotton factory later went into private hands, with a substantial profit for Francis Stephen. He also was responsible for the recruitment of a number of Belgian craftsmen, who were brought in during the 1740s to teach the guildsmen of the Moravian cloth center Jihlava (Iglau) the art of making fine woolen cloth. Unappreciative of this favor from Vienna, the cloth masters pushed the Belgians out of Jihlava, whereupon the emperor settled them on the manor Pardubice (Pardubitz), a large estate belonging to the central government but operated by Francis Stephen as his own after he paid off its debts. This endeavor proved to be unsuccessful, and after more than ten years on the rural estate, the workers were brought to Brno, where after years of difficulties, a solid industrial base was established. With this factory, the government in Vienna invested a considerable amount of money without ever gaining a direct benefit. But by that time, it was under bourgeois control.

In the second half of the eighteenth century, a considerable number of new factories were established on the estates of aristocrats. All this, including what happened in the late eighteenth century, might be considered the era of protoindustrialization, a learning period for full industrialization and market orientation. In this period, peasants were often employed part-time for money wages. The nobility of Bohemia and Moravia was probably more engaged in industry than were their counterparts in other countries. Such names as Kinsky, Blümegen, Haugwitz, Schwarzenberg, and others come to mind.

Merchants also began to participate more actively in the formation and support of industrial undertakings. Prominent among them were Viennese warehousers, many of them merchant bankers from Switzerland. The most prominent of these was Johann Fries, who rose to the rank of count before he died in 1785. Serving as the Austrian intermediary, he collected the English subsidy after the Treaty of Aix-la-Chapelle. Involved in various financial operations, he also participated in a large wool-textile factory in Bohemia with Baron Neffzer, cotton factories in Kettenhof and in Fridau (Lower Austria), and a brass factory and was in charge of silk manufacturing in Vienna. His heir could report to the new emperor Leopold II in 1790 that the cotton factories at Fridau and Kettenhof alone had an investment of more than one million gulden and employed 20,000 persons.[11] Moreover, Fries and Company ran a silk factory of 120 looms in Wiener Neustadt, employed a number of ribbon producers in Mödling, founded a factory city (*Fabriks-Stadt*) in Werow (Galicia), and was engaged in various other commercial activities. Fries without question benefited from his connections with the government and may have been encouraged by high officials of the government to go into industry. The firms, however, took the risks and, according to the evidence, received no direct aid from the state.

Although Fries was the most outstanding Austrian entrepreneur of his time, there were other warehousers in Vienna who were involved in industry. One of these was Bernhard von Tschoffen, also from Switzerland.[12] We first meet him in the 1760s, when he headed a consortium of Viennese merchants brought together by the government commercial college to purchase all goods produced by a brass-buckles manufacturer by the name of Matthew Rosthorn, who had recently been recruited in England. Incidentally, Rosthorn's firm existed well into the nineteenth century and was one of the first to use the British method of producing iron with the puddling method. Tschoffen was responsible for bringing other British specialists to Austria. He quite nearly also became the first one in the Habsburg Monarchy to install a Boulton and Watt steam engine. He already had a tentative agreement with the British firm in the 1790s.[13] He also was a partner in a wool-textile factory located in Naměšt (Namiest), Moravia, an estate belonging to Count Haugwitz.

It was thus through government initiative and encouragement as well as private investment that there was some progress in industry during the second half of the eighteenth century. Moreover, following the cameralists' suggestion, the government was active in removing some of the obstacles to industrial development. One step in that direction was the creation of decrees of protection (*Schutzdekrete*) in the early eighteenth century for especially skilled, non-Catholic, foreign artisans. Also, the government of Maria Theresa in the 1750s created a distinction between what were called policed and commercial crafts in order to extend industrial production. The policed crafts, such as bakers, were restricted by guild rules and produced only for a local market. On the other hand, the commercial crafts, such as cloth makers, produced for a distant market and were completely free of guild limitations.

It would be going too far to suggest that the Habsburg economy was free by 1790, when Joseph II died. A forward momentum had, however, been created that even the more reactionary rule of his nephew Francis I of Austria could not completely disrupt. Significant enterprises were created under the latter's reign, such as the large cotton spinning factory at Pottendorf, not far from Vienna, which used mechanical spinning machines. Other firms, such as the textile mills of Leitenberger in Bohemia, the brass and iron works of Rosthorn in Lower Austria and Carinthia, and the wool manufacturer Offermann in Brno, to mention only a few, greatly expanded their operation during this time. As Jerome Blum wrote many years ago, this period laid the basis for Austria's further development in the late nineteenth century.[14]

While it is fair to say that the state in the first half of the nineteenth century did not greatly inhibit the progress of industry, this cannot be said for agriculture. For example, repeated petitions from noble landowners to be permitted to eliminate serfdom on their estates were turned down by the central government. During this time, landlords were becoming profit maximizers. Writers on agricultural history often insist that, as Otto Brunner wrote, the old science of economy (*Ökonomik*) did not teach about the market. *Oikonomia* in the seventeenth century meant the ordering of the house. This may be true, but, it seems clear, the landowners also wanted to enrich themselves. They may not have conducted their operations in a fully "rational" way before the nineteenth century, but they were interested in the power that wealth brought with it. As William Wright states, they became more profit oriented in the fifteenth and sixteenth centuries and certainly did so again from roughly 1750 on.[15]

To be sure, Roman Sandgruber comes to a more pessimistic conclusion.[16] He sees very little improvement in agriculture in the first half of the nineteenth century when compared with state-of-the-art techniques in Germany and Western Europe. Even though Bohemia, Moravia, Silesia, and Lower Austria were the most advanced areas in the Habsburg Monarchy, he sees even here progress only from 1850 on. There were, however, efforts made in the direction of agricultural progress going back at least to the 1760s, when a number of agricultural societies were established. One fairly successful endeavor of that time was the importation of merino sheep and other fine breeds to provide better wool for the growing wool-textile industry. That it did not completely succeed at first is suggested by a new effort in 1803 to bring merino sheep secretly out of Spain. Bernhard Petri, a high official of the estates of Prince Liechtenstein, reported on this adventure in the *Öckonomische Neuigkeiten und Verhandlungen* (1812), a journal published in Brno under the editorship of Christian Carl André, who was very active in the promotion of agriculture and industry, to which end he published another journal, *Hesperus*. It might be said here in passing that

André; his aristocratic landowner patron, Hugo Altgraf zu Salm-Reifferscheidt; and Abbot Franz Cyrill Napp of the local Augustinian monastery were responsible for the founding of a number of other specialized agricultural associations in Brno. It was Napp who accepted the great geneticist Gregor Mendel in his monastery and encouraged him in his experimentation, after having promoted improving the breeds of sheep and refining several types of plants.[17] We find here an excellent example of the cooperation of agriculture, industry, and science.

Another example of the collaboration between industry and agriculture, on a somewhat less exalted level, was the founding of the Carinthian Agricultural Society in 1765, which owed its origin to Jean Thys, a Belgian native who had only recently started a wool-textile factory in Klagenfurt. Out of this association came Johann Burger, called by some the founder of practical agricultural science in Europe, at the beginning of the nineteenth century.

Above, I mentioned the interest of the landed aristocrat Salm-Reifferscheidt in agricultural progress. He, too, was engaged in industry, having iron works in operation on his estate at Rájec (Raiz) and being personally involved in scientific and technological research. There were a number of other aristocratic landowners who were pursuing similar goals. One of these was Prince Joseph II Schwarzenberg, who deserves to be better known in the economic history of the Habsburg Monarchy.[18] The head of the senior branch of the family, he was certainly one of the richest landowners of the Habsburg Monarchy, his house having under its control prior to 1848, and certainly not much different at the beginning of the century, 640,000 hectares of land, or roughly 10 percent of Bohemia alone. Schwarzenberg believed in using the latest methods on his estates, and to educate his officials in this respect, he established a school of agriculture on his estate at Český Krumlov (Krumau). Besides being interested in agriculture, he participated in commerce and industry. He was the leading investor in the Wiener *Kommerzial- Leih- und Wechselbank,* which existed from about 1787 to 1811, making numerous loans to agriculturalists and financing a number of manufacturing establishments. One of the most prominent of these firms was the Pottendorf Yarn Manufacturing Company, which was managed by the Englishman John Thornton. By

1811, it worked 38,880 mechanical spindles and employed 1,800 persons, making it one of the largest factories in Europe. For the rest of the nineteenth century, members of the Schwarzenberg family were engaged in the promotion of the Habsburg economy, most prominently in the founding of the *Creditanstalt* in Vienna and the construction of the *Franz-Josefs-Bahn.*

Prince Josef II Schwarzenberg also was among the early landowners who wanted to solve what was unquestionably the biggest social problem facing the monarchy, the elimination of the peasants' servile dependency on their landlords. He negotiated with his peasants for a mutually agreeable solution to their obligation to provide free labor on the lords' fields. There is at present no analysis of this process in the case of Schwarzenberg, but the suspicion exists that the peasants found the terms not very advantageous.

All in all, Habsburg agriculture was still in the thrall of a fairly rigid peasant-lord relationship. There is a consensus that most of the peasants were abysmally poor and therefore could not function as demanders of goods. Maybe their condition was better than that of the Polish peasants, as Lord Stormont, the British ambassador in Vienna, asserted in the 1760s. Owing often at least three days a week of free labor, *Robot,* on the lord's fields, they had little time to take care of their own needs and to produce some marketable surplus to pay taxes and fees. Even worse off were the landless rural workers, many of whom rented living quarters in the huts of the peasants. Michael Mitterauer estimates that in the 1760s a third or more of the population in several Austrian provinces was "unhoused."[19] Cotters and others with little or no land were in the majority in a number of provinces, as James Van Horn Melton has recently discovered.[20] While living in a near-subsistence condition, they were apparently not anxious to take on industrial work that paid higher wages than agricultural labor. This at least was the complaint of publicists and government officials. There is, however, some contrary evidence. According to official statistics, the number of spinners in Bohemia increased sharply between 1768 and 1787. One should, of course, be cautious in the use of such figures.

Deeply concerned about the income of the royal exchequer, the government began in the seventeenth century to intervene in the lord-peasant relationship. It was also impelled by the rebellions that occurred from time to time on the various estates. Thus a number of *Robotpatente* were issued, starting in 1680. Until the peasant emancipation decrees of 1781 and 1783, most of these were poorly enforced, if at all. Joseph II, like some of the cameralist writers, believed in principle in the virtue of small holdings. This was above all tried out on estates under the direct control of the government and was introduced and managed by Hofrat Raab in the 1770s.[21] The labor obligation of the peasants was commuted to money payment. Even though this system proved quite profitable, it was not widely emulated by other landowners. And, although the lot of the peasants was somewhat improved as a result of the decrees of Maria Theresa and Joseph II, the *Robot* obligation was not eliminated until 1848. By that time, the Habsburg Monarchy was fairly well along the way to a modest industrial evolution.

Notes

1. Herbert Hassinger, *Johann Joachim Becher 1635–1682* (Vienna: A. Holzhausens Nachfolger, 1951).

2. Herbert Hassinger, "Die erste Wiener orientalische Handelskompanie 1667–1683," *Vierteljahrschrift für Sozial- und Wirtschaftsgeschichte* 35 (1942): 1–53.

3. Henryk Grossmann, "Die Anfänge und geschichtliche Entwicklung der amtlichen Statistik in Österreich," *Statistische Monatschrift*, n.s., 21 (1916): 425.

4. Wilhelm von Schröder, *Fürstliche Schatz- und Rentkammer* (Leipzig, 1686); Louise Sommer, *Die österreichischen Kameralisten* (Vienna: Verlagsbuchhandlung Carl Konegen, 1925), 2:85.

5. Hermann Ignaz Bidermann, "Die Wiener Stadtbank," *Archiv für österreichische Geschichte* 20 (1859): 343–455.

6. Herman Freudenberger, *The Industrialization of a Central European City: Brno and the Fine Woollen Industry in the Eighteenth Century* (Edington, Wilts.: Pasold, 1977), 58–63; Fritz Rager, *Die Wiener Commerzial- Leih- und Wechselbank (1787–1830)* (Vienna: Alfred Hölder, 1918).

7. Hans Wagner, ed. *Wien von Maria Theresia bis zur Franzosenzeit* (Vienna: Wiener Bibliophilen Gesellschaft, 1972), 8.

8. Karl Pribram, *Geschichte der österreichischen Gewerbepolitik von 1740 bis 1860* (Leipzig, 1907), 116–18.

9. Viktor Hofmann, "Beiträge zur neueren Wirtschaftsgeschichte," part 1: "Die Wollenzeugfabrik zu Linz an der Donau," *Archiv für österreichische Geschichte* 108 (1920): 345–778.

10. Jindřich Šebánek, "Textilní podniky moravských Kounicù," *Časopis Matice Moravské* 60 (1931): 95–168, 418–68; 56 (1932): 101–80.

11. Hofkammerarchiv (Vienna), Red. No. 147, fols. 805–10; Herbert Matis, "Die Grafen von Fries," *Tradition* 5 (1967): 484–96.

12. Herman Freudenberger, "Technologie-Transfers von England nach Deutschland und insbes. Österreich im 18. Jahrhundert," in *Technologischer Wandel im 18. Jahrhundert,* ed. Ulrich Troitsch (Wolfenbüttel: Herzog August Bibliothek, 1981), 105–24.

13. Jennifer Tann and Michael Brecking, "The International Diffusion of the Watt Engine 1775–1825," *Economic History Review,* n.s., 31 (1978): 541–64.

14. Jerome Blum, "Transportation and Industry in Austria, 1815–1848," *Journal of Modern History* 15 (1943): 24–38.

15. Otto Brunner, *Neue Wege der Sozialgeschichte* (Göttingen: Vandenhoek & Ruprecht, 1956), 33–61; William E. Wright, *Serf, Seigneur and Sovereign* (Minneapolis: University of Minnesota Press, 1966), 8.

16. Roman Sandgruber, *Österreichische Agrarstatistik 1750–1918* (Munich: Verlag für Geschichte und Politik, 1978).

17. Rudolf Hurt, "Die Funktion des Augustinerklosters unter den Abten Napp und Mendel," *Folia Mendeliana* 6 (1971): 227–30.

18. Franz Blaschko, "Die Ahnenreihe," *Schwarzenbergisches Jahrbuch* 29 (1950): 36–39. See also Herman Freudenberger, "Die proto-industrielle Entwicklungsphase in Österreich," in *Von der Glückseligkeit des Staates,* ed. Herbert Matis (Berlin: Duncker und Humblot, 1981), 376–78.

19. Michael Mitterauer, "Lebensformen und Lebensverhältnisse ländlicher Unterschichten," in *Von der Glückseligkeit des Staates,* ed. Matis, 321.

20. James Van Horn Melton, *Absolutism and the Eighteenth-Century Origin of Compulsory Schooling in Prussia and Austria* (Cambridge: Cambridge University Press, 1988), 124.

21. Anon., *Nachricht über die Einführung des neuen Robot-Abolitions-Systems im Markgraftum Mähren* (Brno, 1778).

Between East and West

Lower Austria's Noble *Grundherrschaft,* 1550–1750

Herbert Knittler

Historians have long recognized that the sixteenth century was a period of remarkable agrarian expansion throughout Europe. There is also general agreement that it was then that differences in agrarian circumstances and production first arose between Western Europe on the one hand and Eastern and East Central Europe on the other. In its most extreme form, this separate development in land ownership, legal rights, and entrepreneurship can be seen in the progress of agrarian commercialization in England and refeudalization in Eastern Europe. In Central Europe, there was an effort to clarify the distinction between the terms *Grundherrschaft* and *Gutsherrschaft.* In the case of *Grundherrschaft,* the peasant proprietor was free to work the land for his own benefit in exchange for the payment of fees in cash or in kind; by contrast, *Gutsherrschaft* generally existed on great feudal estates that were worked by serfs who were simultaneously tied to the land and obliged to work for the owner. Nevertheless, the absence of clearly identifiable geographical or structural divisions between the two systems—especially in East Central Europe—raises questions about the validity of regional differentiation as well as about the existence of hybrid models of manorial enterprise. These questions are the focus of this essay.

A definitive agrarian profile of the Habsburgs' Danubian lands necessitates a quantitative analysis of manorial dues and services rather than an examination of the circumstances of enserfed producers themselves. A comparison of the two archduchies of Austria below and above the Enns (*Nieder-* and *Oberösterreich*) during the mid-eighteenth century indicates that compulsory labor service (*Frondienst*) was very significant in only some parts of eastern Lower Austria and did not approach the dimensions that obtained east of the Elbe or in the Bohemian lands. At the same time, the picture of agrarian and commercial entrepreneurship, monopolies, dues, and labor services deviates so greatly from our preconceived model of manorial overlordship that it appears to justify the formulation of a transitional category of manorial enterprise akin to that proposed by Alfred Hoffmann. In reality a single, uniform model was neither envisioned nor applied in the Austrian lands.

During 1774 the Lower Austrian Estates remonstrated against the restrictions on labor services instituted in the *Robotpatenten* of 1772–73, arguing that landlords "who have treated their subjects leniently would be punished, while those who have exercised their power most rigorously would essentially be rewarded."[1] They pointed out that whereas the *Patent* reaffirmed the customary maximum service of 104 days, it also compensated for the elimination of unlimited *Zugrobot* (labor service with a team of horses or oxen) for full tenants and *Halblehner* (half tenants) by allowing landlords to increase labor services up to a maximum of 208 days.[2] The Estates therefore asked the prince to amend the *Patent* by reinstating unlimited labor services as provided in the *Tractatus de iuribus incorporalibus* of 1679. They argued that the peasantry had not been adversely affected by the present system. The existence of unlimited labor service had not prevented their subjects from extending their holdings by purchasing additional land (*Überländgründe*).[3] Nor would landlords be likely to extract four or more days of labor service, because it was in their interest to keep their subjects in an "upright position" and because the Lower Austrian regime would investigate reported excesses.

The question of labor service is crucial to understanding the development and structural conditions of *Grundherrschaft* in early modern Lower Austria and to comparing them with neighboring regions and countries.[4] Today there is no longer any question that labor service is the central criterion for distinguishing among *Grund-herrschaft*, *Gutsherrschaft*, and their regional variations. It is also important that we take into account the two other forms of feudal rent, money rent and rent in kind, since an increase in labor service might result in a reduction of the previously demanded tribute in money and kind.

Hartmut Harnisch has devised an especially sophisticated model for analyzing labor services in Central European *Gutsherr-schaft*. Although one must take into account that increased rent in kind might compensate for lower labor services, Harnisch's data suggests that labor services of more than two to three days per week constitute a "threshold value" for determining whether regions were characterized by either *Grundherrschaft* or *Gutsherrschaft*.[5] His conclusions demonstrate that the same regional differentiation be-tween the central and eastern German regions also applies to the Austrian lands. Once again, it is necessary to take extraeconomic criteria into account, such as the legal status of the direct producer or his title to the land he cultivated. This yields a classification scheme for special developmental patterns that is superior to sim-pler classification models, such as those based on the Elbe, Saale, Enns, and Leitha river valleys.[6]

In early modern times, the grain-producing zones of the east-ern German *Gutsherrschaft* as well as of the adjoining areas in Po-land and the Baltic countries comprised a region that fits Engel's description of the so-called second serfdom; to the south and west were regions that retained various elements of a rent economy (*Rentenwirtschaft*), such as rent in money and kind, despite the clear dominance of labor service. In addition, export-oriented grain cultivation was beginning to be overshadowed by livestock, fish, wine, timber, industrial products, and especially beer. This is par-ticularly true in Bohemia, Moravia, Hungary, Slovakia, and Croatia, which were categorized either as a transitional zone of Eu-ropean agricultural dualism or even as one where *Gutsherrschaft* predominated.[7] For example, Władyslaw Rusiński emphasizes the existence of a bridging region that includes Lower Austria.[8] Leonid Żytkowicz's model for regionalization also lumps parts of Austria to-gether with Hungary-Slovakia-Croatia but compares them structurally with those parts of western Elbia where labor service was of importance.[9] None of these statements have, however, been tested against quantitative material.

In 1952 Hoffmann was the first to introduce an economic model that was based not on labor service but on a form of *Herrschaft* (domain) and was designed to identify the transition from *Rentenherrschaft* to *Gutsherrschaft* that emerged in the sixteenth and seventeenth centuries.[10] Based on the circumstances prevailing in Upper Austria, this so-called *Wirtschaftsherrschaft* describes a type of *Herrschaft* in which arable land was mostly owned by independent peasants. By centralizing the dues and increasing the services to be paid to the lord, these holdings were more closely bound together in an economic union than before. Important characteristics of this capitalized *Grundherrschaft* were the promotion of demesne lands, peasant trades,[11] and monopolized domestic markets.[12] An indispensable precondition for *Wirtschaftsherrschaft* was the use of manorial prerogatives and monopoly rights (*Bann- and Zwangsrechte*), which the noble Estates had wrung from the prince in the sixteenth century. Friedrich Lütge, Thomas M. Barker, and Immanuel Wallerstein have categorized *Wirtschaftsherrschaft* as the transitional stage between *Grundherrschaft* and *Gutsherrschaft,* with Wallerstein assigning it to the "more semi-peripheral zones of central Europe."[13] Others, however, have continued to stress labor service as a distinctive feature, including László Makkai, who places the Austrian lands under the sway of *Grundherrschaft* while characterizing Bohemia and Hungary as mostly a "region of *robot* economy."[14]

An unfortunate limitation in assessing the importance of labor service for the development of different manorial systems in Austria is the very uneven state of research. Although Georg Grüll's studies on Upper Austria have laid a solid foundation for a quantitative approach to the problem,[15] there is very little published on Lower Austria.[16] Obtaining useful data is further hindered by the fact that source material has been only partially studied, with the result that scholars have often arrived at opposite conclusions. In addition, before the eighteenth century it was rare to describe the extent of labor services in terms of days per year or days per week, thereby making it difficult to draw comparisons between regions. More typically, officials only identified the peasants who had to work certain units of demesne and the villages from which they came.[17]

If we start with the upper limits of labor service stipulated by the *Robotpatenten* of the 1770s[18] and assume that these new limits eased the burden for at least some of the peasants, we arrive at relative values that are largely confirmed by additional criteria. Thus the reduction of unlimited labor service to 156 days in Bohemia, Moravia, and Styria and to 104 days in Lower Austria indicates that previously existing labor service was now regulated, whereas in Upper Austria, with an average of fourteen days per year,[19] no need for regulation on a broader basis seemed necessary. This structure of labor service roughly corresponds to the division between the landlord's own "dominical" land and peasant-run ("rustical") holdings that is reflected in the Josephine tax assessment rolls.[20] It is impossible to arrive at exact figures because of differences in the time span and the hypothetical cultivation of the demesne by wage laborers.[21]

	arable land		pastures		vineyards		wood	
	d	r	d	r	d	r	d	r
Lower Austria*	9.3	90.7	20.3	79.7	4.3	95.7	61.6	38.4
VUWW	10.0	90.0	31.8	68.2	3.9	96.1	59.1	40.9
VOWW	5.4	94.6	10.6	89.4	5.1	94.9	64.2	35.8
VUMB	9.3	90.7	20.3	79.7	4.3	95.7	61.6	38.4
VOMB	8.0	92.0	14.1	85.9	9.6	90.4	56.1	43.9
Upper Austria	1.9	98.1	4.6	95.4	11.5	88.5	59.9	40.1
Styria	11.7	88.3	22.3	77.7	79.6	20.4	46.3	53.7
Bohemia	23.7	76.3	33.4	65.6	50.4	49.6	76.7	23.3
Moravia	11.8	88.2	21.7	78.3	2.9	97.1	86.3	13.7

TABLE 1. Percentage share of demesne and peasant holdings in agricultural land in Austria, Styria, Bohemia, and Moravia in 1788: (d = dominical, r = rustical)
*Lower Austria is divided into four parts, or *Viertel*: VUWW: Viertel unter dem Wienerwald; VOWW: Viertel ober dem Wienerwald; VUMB: Viertel unter dem Manhartsberg; VOMB: Viertel ober dem Manhartsberg

A comparative view of the relationship between demesne and peasant land in the second half of the eighteenth century clearly shows that, even within neighboring regions, marked differences existed that cannot be attributed only to the prevailing natural preconditions. Taking arable land as the most important production area and the area with highest labor services, this results in a division into three parts, with Bohemia (23.7 percent) and Upper Austria (1.9 percent) representing the two extremes and an extensive middle group including Moravia, Styria, and Lower Austria (11.8–9.3 percent). Within Lower Austria, there is a clear distinction between the Viertel ober dem Wienerwald and the other three parts of the province; by contrast, Styria has an even gradation of index numbers, with the extremes between 13.8 percent in the Marburg (Maribor) area and 5.1 percent around Bruck. The figure for Bohemia, which was slightly higher in the late seventeenth century than after the regulation of labor service, is comparable to Hungary, where demesne holdings amounted to about 15 to 30 percent of the peasant-owned land.[22] In Poland and eastern Germany, where *Gutsherrschaft* dominated, the *Vorwerksareal* increased from more than 30 percent to as much as 50 percent of the total land.[23] The ratio of 1:1 or 2:3 (in favor of peasant land) seems to have presented the economically viable limit for the expansion of *Vorwerkswirtschaft* (manorial economy).[24]

As has been suggested above, the sequence in proportion roughly corresponds with the information relating to the extent of labor service of peasant holdings in each country. In Bohemia labor service was limited to three days a week by the *Robotpatent* of 1680 but could be raised by the landlords in times of increased workload (grain or hay harvest, clearing of fishponds).[25] Yet there were also cases of daily labor service, with the landlord "graciously" giving peasants Saturday off (1674).[26] The reconstruction of daily labor service in western and eastern Styria given in the Theresian cadaster records of 1752[27] does not seem very realistic; the limited farmland available to demesnes clearly decreased the need for labor. Moreover, the tax amendments after 1750 often used random rateable values,[28] as demonstrated by the dominical tax declaration of the Lower Austrian estates, which, in contrast to those in Upper Austria, listed labor service performed *in natura* separately, as part of the estate's income.

It was obviously the variety in both the quality and quantity of labor services and the gap between the total labor service to which a landlord was entitled and that which was actually extracted that led to all those liable to labor service in Lower Austria being classified into two distinct categories: *Zugroboter* or *Handroboter,* who performed manual labor service; and an exempted class of cottars (*Kleinhäusler*) and landless peasants (*Inleute*). Assessments were to be made "equally but moderately" and seem to have been based on formal claims to "unlimited" (daily?) labor service dating back to 1563.[29] Thus we can only calculate the number of those liable for labor service but not the actual labor service rendered. In some cases, estates handed down differentiated information that indicates a distribution of twelve days per year or two days per week.[30] As we shall see, the two- or three-day level of labor service that Harnisch defines as the "threshold value" for *Gutsherrschaft* prevailed on the majority of estates in the Viertel unter dem Manhartsberg and the Viertel unter dem Wienerwald.[31] Since sources from 1667 and 1732[32] indicate that the large Liechtenstein estates in the northeastern Weinviertel, Rabensburg, and Wilfersdorf also did not exceed this level of labor service, Martin N. Baumann's generalization that labor service "from the beginning of spring to late fall was required almost twice to thrice weekly in the form of carrying or manual service"[33] seems exaggerated. Only during harvest time did labor service reach the upper limit of three to four days per week stipulated in 1772–73.[34] The government seems to have been referring to this increase on 20 November 1738 when it directed Count Koháry, lord of the Ebenthal estate, to "mitigate" the burden on "his subjects with a labor service of four, five, and even more days per week."[35]

Although the data on labor service from the late seventeenth and the eighteenth centuries cannot present a uniform picture, it indicates that some *Grundherrschaften* in Lower Austria faced the same transition to *Gutsherrschaft* experienced in Bohemia and Moravia, at least as far as labor service is concerned. This raises questions concerning the conditions and phases of a development that Zsigmond Pál Pach, writing from a Hungarian point of view, characterized as "branching off from the western European development."[36]

Despite the number of divergent and contradictory arguments, today's vast literature on the development of Eastern European *Gutsherrschaft* largely agrees on two things: the increase in *Eigenwirtschaft* (demesnes farmed directly by landlords) and the development of manorial commodity production.[37] We can only conclude that this situation was brought about by the pressure to counteract the devaluation of manorial rents, to prevent loss of status, and to keep one's social position in a competition that was often conducted through conspicuous consumption.[38]

In assessing the quantity of land available for cultivation and the income structure of the estates, it is worth repeating that at the end of the Middle Ages Austrian *Grundherrschaft* on both sides of the Enns primarily involved traditional feudal rents in money and kind from its subjects. There were, however, two exceptions: income from the landlord's own fisheries in the northern part of Lower Austria; and a number of indirect taxes (*regalia*), such as tolls, *Ungelder* (tax on alcoholic beverages), and market fees, which were especially the prerogative of estates owned by higher nobility or princes.[39] It is impossible to ignore the advantageous starting position of such well-equipped demesnes when comparing their income structure with that of medium-sized and small knightly demesnes during the inevitable sixteenth-century transformation. In 1510–11 regalian revenue on the estates of Count Hardegg amounted to 44.2 percent of the overall income in cash, as opposed to a mere 25.7 percent from money dues; and the sales of grain, flour, beer, etc. only accounted for 9.3 percent. On the other hand, the Veste Schmida estate, also owned by the same family, drew 68.2 percent of its income from money rents and 31.8 percent from rents in kind.[40] In 1529–30 the Upper Austrian estate of Wartenburg derived 67.5 percent of its cash income from money dues and 32.5 percent from sales of grain originating from rents in kind.[41] As a rule, dominical arable land was attached to a *Meierhof* (manorial farm) near the actual manor house and usually did not exceed the dimension of a large peasant holding.

A comparison of the above-mentioned data with the results of an inquiry into the structure of income and expenditure of the estates of the princely *Kammergut* in 1569–70 shows that at least the *Pfandherrschaften* (estates leased to noblemen) were characterized by *Rentenherrschaft* in the first two thirds of the sixteenth century. On the whole, income from sovereign rights (especially indirect taxes) dominated with a 35.9-percent share of overall revenue, followed by proceeds from services and dues (20.4 percent), tithes (15.2 percent), the landlord's own production and monopolies (14.9 percent), as well as commutation fees for labor services (10.4 percent). In the aggregate, the different kinds of money rents amounted to 60.3 percent of the total income, whereas rent in kind only took 24.8 percent and the landlord's own production and monopolies a mere 14.9 percent. This means that about 85 percent of the income stemmed from the noble's own manorial rights.[42] Receipts from limited farming usually corresponded with expenditures for labor services and the demesne's own laborers, which might mean that labor service was complemented by wage labor. As landlords often entered revenues from leased properties as income, we can assume that rents from leased properties must generally have been higher than the gains expected from farming the land wholly or partly by themselves.

In spite of the seemingly unchanged situation around 1570, we should not underestimate the first signs of a feudal reaction to the sixteenth-century price revolution and the enhanced market opportunities. These were twofold, combining initiatives for the expansion and restructuring of the landlord's own production with an intensification of extraeconomic pressure. Since the 1550s, wool-trade oriented sheep farming was on the increase; fisheries were improved and extended. In the following decade, more efforts were made to foster the trades within the framework of the feudal economy and especially to establish breweries, taverns, mills, fulleries, and brickyards, for which market monopolies were sought.

Comparing the development of feudal income in Upper and Lower Austria shows the different approaches that landlords chose to increase revenue. The above-mentioned characteristics are predominantly found in the Viertel ober dem Manhartsberg, unter dem Manhartsberg, and unter dem Wienerwald, whereas the Viertel ober dem Wienerwald and Upper Austria were not so much marked by an expansion of the landlord's own production as by a massive increase and diversification of feudal rent, especially in money.[43] The generalization of *Freigeld* (a commutation fee based on the value of the peasant holding and introduced in connection with *Freistifte* being made inheritable) and the increase of extraseigneurial fees and rates led to the development of a system that not only allowed for a rapid adaptation to price development but also recaptured the increased value of the peasant holdings that had been caused by the the sixteenth-century agricultural boom. The preference for cash led to the conversion of labor services into money rent as well as a reduction in *Robot* to an annual standard of fourteen days (1597), albeit with some exceptions.[44] *Robotgeld* (income converted from labor service) became a very important source of income for Upper Austrian *Grundherrschaften*. On the one hand, it led to the registration of all subjects liable to service; and on the other hand, it enabled the demesnes to make calculated use of the labor market, hiring wage laborers for work that was actually required and raising the number of servants.[45] Thanks in part to the incentive provided by the peasant rising of 1595–97, the structure established at the end of the sixteenth century is clearly reflected in the demesnial tax declaration of 1752, as shown in table 2.[46]

	Hausruckv.	Traunv.	Machlandv.	Mühlv.
Meierschaften	3.1	2.1	1.9	2.7
woods, fisheries	2.9	3.7	2.8	7.6
trades, monopolies, tolls	13.2	7.7	11.7	13.7
money dues	66.1	62.9	67.0	62.9
dues in kind	14.7	23.6	16.6	13.0
total	100.0	100.0	100.0	100.0

TABLE 2. Distribution of income of Upper Austrian *Grundherrschaften* according to Landesviertel in 1752 (in percentages).

It would not be at all sufficient to attribute the differentiation of Austrian *Grundherrschaft* at the end of the sixteenth century solely to the fact that the region of *Rentenherrschaft* coincided with the zone mainly occupied by hamlets and single peasant holdings and that the region of the transformed *Rentenherrschaft* overlapped with the zone dominated by villages; this differentiation based on types of settlement also corresponds with differing economic and constitutional characteristics. The east, dominated by villages based primarily on farming, was far more strongly affected by the agricultural depression of the late Middle Ages than areas in the west, which specialized in cattle breeding. This difference can also be seen in the uneven distribution of wasteland as reserves that could be absorbed by the demesnes.[47] During the late Middle Ages, deserted villages were found primarily in the Lower Austrian Viertel ober dem Manhartsberg, unter dem Manhartsberg, and unter dem Wienerwald, whereas in Upper Austria the crisis left hardly any trace.[48] On the other hand, this uneven distribution prevented the development of strong peasant communities and favored the grip on single holdings. Improved conditions for the absorption of surplus value in the west are clear in the far more detailed records on dues in land registers and estimates. Lastly, it would be a mistake to view the peasant holdings' rents and dues from the perspective of the eighteenth or nineteenth centuries.[49] Especially the peasant surveys at the end of the sixteenth century, which concentrated on the west, support the thesis that feudal pressure reached its height earlier in Upper Austria than in most of Lower Austria, where the increase in labor services was only speeded up by the extension of the landlord's own production.[50]

While the 1597 *Robotpatent* for Upper Austria stipulated a labor service of 14 days (down from between 15 and 40 days, with peaks of up to 100)[51] or an equivalent in money, developments in Lower Austria had taken a different course. The following examination is based on the Privilege of 1563, by which Ferdinand I granted the clerical and noble estates the right to unlimited labor service.[52] For the preceding thirteen years, the right to forced servant labor (*Gesindezwangsdienst*) had allowed them to draw upon the labor force of their subjects' children[53] and, in combination with their legal sovereignty, had enabled them to use extraeconomic means of coercion, which are usually regarded as the precondition for the development of the so-called second serfdom.[54] This poses the question why Lower Austria did not move toward the more prevalent type of *Gutsherrschaft*.

Already in 1895, Joseph Redlich compared the agrarian constitutions in the lands of the Bohemian crown with those of Upper and Lower Austria and pointed out the importance of constitutional law. He also linked peasant enserfment and the enormous increase in labor service in Bohemia with the strong position of the noble estates.[55] It is no coincidence that the same privileges emerged with the weakening of princely power in the Austrian archduchies; admittedly, they were only granted at a time when they appeared to make economic sense if they resulted in an increase in money rent. When, a few decades later, the expansion of demesnial land demanded the increase of a low-cost work force, the central power had regained its strength and could check the expansion of the estates.[56]

A further factor is the reduced market, especially for grain, on the macro- as well as the microeconomic level. The Western European markets could not be reached due to inadequate roads and transport facilities. Except for iron and salt mining, neighboring regions and countries also faced a surplus in production. On the whole, the modest demand of the home market could be met by peasant production. Only Vienna and the army figured as major consumers. Hence incentives to increase the market quota beyond the yield provided by rents in kind were restricted to certain periods and to certain areas.[57]

Unfortunately, our information on the extent of labor services in Lower Austria in the late sixteenth century comes primarily from the crown's estates (*Kammergut*), which is a special case, since it hardly needed labor service.[58] Some crown domains did not demand any labor service at all, others levied less than stipulated in the regulation, and still others varied the amount within a single demesne. In some cases, increases had already amounted to 60 days per year before 1570 (Weitra), and the peasants especially opposed the accumulation of labor obligations in times of increased work or special exactions, such as building service (*Burgwerk*) or chores that demanded "long carriages" drawn by several horses. The attempt to reduce competition between crown and noble-owned estates to include the latter in a standardized regulation of labor services had never gotten beyond the planning stage. This suggests unequal developments in the expansion of the landlords' own production.[59]

If we assume that during the transition from the sixteenth to the seventeenth century, feudal *Grundherrschaft* in Lower Austria gave priority to reducing costs and not to increasing productivity, then the increase in land under cultivation necessitates new conclusions concerning the development of labor services. Comparing the quantity of land available for farming on estates in the Viertel ober dem Manhartsberg, the Viertel unter dem Manhartsberg, and the Viertel unter dem Wienerwald between 1570 and 1620 suggests a twofold increase.[60] A qualitative analysis, however, shows that the increase in area per holding is only partly attributable to the inclusion of wasteland or reverted peasant holdings. Very often it is due to a process of consolidation whereby smaller knightly demesnes or manors were incorporated into bigger *Grundherrschaften*. Therefore the demand for more unpaid or cheap labor remained limited. If labor services expanded slowly before 1620, it was because some demesne lands had been leased or left uncultivated. The great importance of wage labor during these prewar years can be seen in the enormous number of 252 wage laborers employed by the Har-

degg estates on the Danube, 44 of whom were farm laborers at
Meierhöfen.[61]

Since the Thirty Years' War not only destabilized the economy
as a whole but also adversely affected the quantity and quality of our
data, we can only make generalizations about structural changes in
Lower Austrian *Grundherrschaft* and the changing importance of
labor service for the second half of the century. Again, we must start
with developments in arable land[62] and an analysis of demesnial
income.

According to tax assessments, 28 percent of all houses in
Lower Austria were depopulated or "despoiled" in 1656; by 1684 this
figure had risen to 60 percent.[63] Although we should weigh these
figures with a certain amount of caution, there was a decrease in
population perhaps from 600,000 to 560,000 during the Thirty
Years' War and—after a momentary increase—a further drop in
1683 to the original starting point. During the first half of the century, it was primarily the northern part of Lower Austria that was
most affected, while the Viertel unter dem Wienerwald suffered
most in the 1680s. Only later is there a continuous population increase—to about 922,000 in 1750.[64]

This demographic crisis not only prolonged the decline in grain
prices that had begun in 1620 but also added to the reserves of uncultivated land, especially in those areas most affected by the war.
As a result, many estates increased greatly in size while labor was in
very short supply. Thus, in 1671 the Heidenreichstein estate in the
Viertel ober dem Manhartsberg cultivated not only its original area
but also twelve deserted peasant holdings; an additional fifty-four (!)
deserted holdings were leased to subjects for a cash rent.[65] In other
cases, peasant holdings without an heir were incorporated into
Meierhöfe that could not be sold for decades, thanks to a dearth of
buyers.[66]

Thus, the mid-seventeenth-century increase in demesnial
land within the Waldviertel resulted from extraeconomic factors
rather than from market conditions. By way of contrast, those areas
which had shown favorable conditions for production and had generated demand experienced a short-term decline. Arable land was
turned into pastures and meadows, and numerous sheep farms
were established. This is especially true for the Viertel unter dem

Manhartsberg and, to a lesser extent, for the Viertel unter dem Wienerwald, which was oriented toward the Viennese market and military supply depots.

The renewed increase in grain price during the last third of the seventeenth century can be associated with the rise in the landlords' own production and the increasing labor service. This in turn led to the separate development of those regions especially favored by natural advantages and proximity to markets. Whereas toward 1700 in the Viertel ober dem Manhartsberg big demesne farms were partly dissolved or *Meierhöfe* were rusticated and labor service was turned into money rent,[67] demesnial land in the black-soil zones of the Viertel unter dem Manhartsberg and the Viertel unter dem Wienerwald actually increased. In 1750 these areas included about three quarters of all demesnes, with more than 300 *Joch* (about 427 acres) of arable land. As compared with labor service between twelve and forty days in the west and south, the Viertel unter dem Manhartsberg witnessed a relative increase in the number of demesnes extracting two or three days' labor service.

It is safe to assume that the overall amount of labor service at the disposal of the lord often included a larger reserve, analogous to the well-known conditions on the Bohemian demesnes.[68] Thus, the Neulengbach estate's 371 *Joch* of arable demesnial land (Viertel ober dem Wienerwald) provided 3,848 days of *Zugrobot* and 6,512 days of *Handrobot* (i.e., 14,208 days) (1750),[69] and the Weitra estate's 500.5 *Tagwerk* disposed of 7,738 days (2 days of manual labor = 1 day of labor with draught animals) (1704),[70] whereas the Wilfersdorf estate in the northeast of the Viertel unter dem Manhartsberg, which consisted of 1,146 ⅜ *Quanten* of arable land and 158 *Viertel* of vineyards (1732), had 9,568 days of *Zugrobot* and 50,908 days of *Handrobot* (i.e., 70,044 days).[71] Assuming that an average of 30 days were spent per *Joch*,[72] Weitra fell 7,277 days short, which had to be covered by wage labor, while Wilfersdorf (excluding the vineyards) had a surplus of 26,000 days. If applied to the problem of the development of different types, this means that also in areas with high labor service the "threshold value" for the transition from *Grundherrschaft* to *Gutsherrschaft* was not actually reached.[73]

The thesis that Lower Austrian demesnes "got stuck" on their way to *Gutsherrschaft* is further supported by an analysis of the income and rent structures around the mid-eighteenth century. Basically it has to be emphasized once more that an increase in labor services over a certain period had to result in a decrease in rent in money or kind if subjects were pushed below the limit of their reproductive capacity. A comparison of the figures for 1750 shows that, in addition to the aforementioned special situation in the Viertel ober dem Wienerwald, even in the Weinviertel the 35.6-percent share of *Gutswirtschaft* (including income from monopolies and trades and excluding labor service, which does not have an actual income character) lags well behind the 47.8-percent share of *Rentenwirtschaft*.[74] A more detailed analysis demonstrates the great importance of the grain and wine tithes, especially for the big estates of the region, which resulted in the demesnes' being able to trade considerable amounts of grain.[75] If we take into account that, since the sixteenth century, an increasing share of the estates' surplus was skimmed off by public taxes, which required more participation of the peasants in the local market, then we can conclude that a development toward *Gutsherrschaft* never took place. Neither can we perceive either a reduction of the peasants' usufruct or a lessening of their personal legal status, both of which are characteristics of *Gutsherrschaft*.[76]

	VOMB	VUMB	VOWW	VUWW
arable land, meadows, gardens, vineyards	7.86	10.43	8.04	9.78
woods, scrub, ponds, fishing waters	14.56	16.14	7.74	7.78
trades, monopolies, tolls	6.63	9.05	3.45	15.63
cash holdings	2.57	1.14	3.77	5.15
rent in money	30.65	22.42	41.80	28.28
rent in kind	15.00	25.42	15.60	17.11
labor service	21.20	14.02	16.84	14.61
other income	1.63	1.39	2.76	1.67
total	100.00	100.00	100.00	100.00

TABLE 3. Distribution of income of Lower Austrian noble estates (over an estimated 10,000 florins), according to Landesviertel, around 1750 (in percentages).

As mentioned at the beginning of this essay, research into feudalism in the East Central and East European regions has regarded labor service and its extent as the main criterion for distinguishing between different types of productive structures in agriculture. Figures concerning the structure and development of Austrian noble demesnes confirm that the Austrian lands did not form part of the zone of *Gutsherrschaft*.[77] Yet we would be stretching the term *Grundherrschaft* too far if we included the whole range of estates receiving a mixed income from the landlord's own production and from feudal rent. This is illustrated by the comparison of two examples dating back to the seventeenth century that show two widely differing budgets in size and composition.[78]

income	in florin	in %	expenditure	in florin	in %
regular cash income	1073	31.4	ecclesiastical donations	100	20.8
special cash income	300	8.8			
income from leased properties	84	2.4	building costs & special services	235	49.0
monopolies	130	3.8	board and clothing	130	27.1
income in kind	1114	32.6	servants	15	3.1
own production	719	21.0			
total	3420	100.0		480	100.0

TABLE 4. Average income and expenditure of the Hainstetten estate in 1677 (taxes excluded).

income	in florin	in %	expenditure	in florin	in %
regular cash income	524	3.8	wages	1466	19.9
special cash income	3280	23.9	building costs	329	4.5
income from leased properties	163	1.2	craftsmen and living expenses	864	11.7
regalia	1464	10.6			
forest	842	6.1	forest	275	3.7
own production	3858	28.1	own production	1924	26.1
trades	3242	23.6	trades	2014	27.4
other	372	2.7	other	489	6.7
total	13745	100.0		7361	100.0

TABLE 5. Income and expenditure of the Weitra estate (average 1689–92) (taxes excluded).

Apart from the absolute figures, the above examples differ especially regarding the net product arising from the landlord's agrarian production and trade, as well as from monopolies, which were primarily rendered in the form of indirect taxes. Admittedly, necessary expenditures sharply reduced the returns, cutting income from agricultural production by half and from trade to about 38 percent of the gross amount. The peasants' labor service, which had been substantially reduced within *Rentenwirtschaft,* could be used within all mentioned sections, with the retention of rent in money and in kind. These developments, which to the west of the Elbe were called *Gutswirtschaften* outside the region of *Gutsherrschaft,*[79] were widely spread within a zone reaching from the Baltic Sea and the provinces of the Bohemian crown to Styria, Hungary, and Croatia.

In substance, this clearly approaches the concept of *Wirtschaftsherrschaft* mentioned at the outset of this essay; yet this term bears the disadvantage of having been developed to identify a special regional development[80] that does not apply in this case. Neither can we assume that examples of this type were found in large adjoining areas of Lower Austria, where the share of the net income from the landlords' own production amounted to more than 40 percent.

Notes

1. Niederösterreichisches Landesarchiv, Ständisches Archiv (NÖLA, SA), HS 1013/I: Kurz gefasste Nachricht Über die beschafenheit des alten und des neuen Steuer Fusses in dem Land Oesterreich unter der Ennß, fol. 124v, dated 22 January 1774.

2. Robotpatent 6 June 1772, Nachtrag 12 June 1773, Erläuterung 24 October 1773. Cf. Kurz gefasste Nachricht, fols. 119–29; Ferdinand Edler v. Hauer, *Praktische Darstellung der in Oesterreich unter der Enns für das Unterthansfach bestehenden Gesetze,* 3d ed. (Vienna: J. G. R. v. Mösle sel. Witwe, 1824),1:78–147.

3. NÖLA, SA, HS 1013/I, fol. 125r.

4. Selected literature on the topic includes: Hartmut Harnisch, "Die Gutsherrschaft: Forschungsgeschichte, Entwicklungszusammenhänge und Strukturelemente," *Jahrbuch für Geschichte des Feudalismus* 9 (1985): 189–240; idem, "Probleme einer Periodisierung und regionalen Typisierung der Gutsherrschaft im mitteleuropäischen Raum," *Jahrbuch für Geschichte des Feudalismus* 10 (1986): 251–74; Witold Kula, *An Economic Theory of the Feudal System: Towards a Model of the Polish Economy 1500–1800* (London: N. L. B., 1976); Jerzy Topolski, "Continuity and Discontinuity in the Development of the Feudal System in Eastern Europe (Xth to XVIIth centuries)," *Journal of European Economic History* 10 (1981):

373–400; idem, "Autour des modèles de l'explication du passage au système de la corvée en Europe centrale et orientale (XVI⁰–XVII⁰ siècles)," *Studia historiae oeconomicae* 19 (1988): 1–15; Władyslaw Rusiński, "Über die Entwicklungsetappen der Fronwirtschaft in Mittel- und Osteuropa," *Studia historiae oeconomicae* 9 (1974): 27–45; idem, "Some Remarks on the Differentiation of Agrarian Structure in East Central Europe from the 16th to 18th Century," *Studia historiae oeconomicae* 13 (1978): 83–95; idem, "Die Agrarkrise des 17. Jahrhunderts in Ostmitteleuropa," in *Schichtung und Entwicklung der Gesellschaft in Polen und Deutschland im 16. und 17. Jahrhundert,* ed. Marian Biskup and Klaus Zernack (Wiesbaden: Franz Steiner, 1983), 258–72; Alois Míka, "Problém počátku nevolnictví v Čechách" (The problem of the origins of serfdom in Bohemia), *Československý časopis historický* 5 (1957): 226–48; Josef Válka, "Le grand domaine féodal en Bohême et en Moravie du 16ᵉ au 18ᵉ siècle: Un type d'économie parasitaire," in *Grand domaine et petites exploitations en Europe au moyen âge et dans les temps modernes,* ed. Péter Gunst and Tamás Hoffmann (Budapest: Akad. Kiadó, 1982), 289–315; Eduard Maur, "Geneze a specifické rysy českého pozdněfeudálního velkostatku" (The origins and principal characteristics of Czech demesnes in the late feudal period), *Acta Universitatis Carolinae: Philosophica et Historica* 1 (1976): 229–58; Arnošt Klíma, "Agrarian Class Structure and Economic Development in Pre-industrial Bohemia," in *The Brenner Debate: Agrarian Class Structure and Economic Development in Pre-industrial Europe,* ed. T. H. Aston and C. H. E. Philpin (Cambridge: Cambridge University Press, 1985), 192–212; Zsigmond Pál Pach, *Die ungarische Agrarentwicklung im 16.–17. Jahrhundert: Abbiegung vom westeuropäischen Entwicklungsgang,* Studia Historica Academiae Scientiarum Hungaricae, vol. 54 (Budapest: Akad. Kiadó, 1964); idem, "Labour Control on the Hungarian Landlords' Demesnes in the 16th and 17th Centuries," in *Grand domaine,* ed. Gunst and Hoffmann, 157–73; idem, "Fronarbeit und Lohnarbeit auf den ungarischen Herrengütern im 16.–17. Jahrhundert," in *Studien zur deutschen und ungarischen Wirtschaftsentwicklung (16.–20. Jahrhundert),* ed. Vera Zimányi (Budapest: Akad. Kiadó, 1985), 31–41.

5. Harnisch, "Probleme einer Periodisierung," 252.

6. Rusiński, "Some Remarks on the Differentiation," 83; Sándor Gyimesi, "Frühkapitalistische Entwicklung und Spätfeudalismus im 16. und 17. Jahrhundert in Ungarn," *Jahrbuch für Wirtschaftsgeschichte,* 1987, no. 2:51; Jenő Szücs, *Die drei historischen Regionen Europas* (Frankfurt: Neue Kritik, 1990), 13.

7. See the survey in Rusiński, "Some Remarks on the Differentiation," 92–95; also Roman Rosdolsky, "On the Nature of Peasant Serfdom in Central and Eastern Europe," *Journal of Central European Affairs* 12 (1952–53): 128–39; Jerome Blum, "The Rise of Serfdom in Eastern Europe," *American Historical Review* 62 (1957): 807–36; László Makkai, "Neo-Serfdom: Its Origin and Nature in East Central Europe," *Slavic Review* 34 (1975): 225–52 and other contributions in the same issue; Anton Špiesz, "Die neuzeitliche Agrarentwicklung in der Tschechoslowakei: Gutsherrschaft oder Wirtschaftsherrschaft?" *Zeitschrift für bayerische Landesgeschichte* 32 (1969): 222–37; Arnošt Klíma, "Probleme der Leibeigenschaft in

Böhmen," *Vierteljahrschrift für Sozial- und Wirtschaftsgeschichte* 62 (1975): 214–28; Josef Macek, "The Emergence of Serfdom in the Czech Lands," *East-Central Europe / L'Europe du Centre-Est* 9 (1982): 7–23; Josef Kočí, "Die Reformen der Untertänigkeitsverhältnisse in den böhmischen Ländern unter Maria Theresia und Joseph II.," in *Österreich im Europa der Aufklärung,* ed. Richard G. Plaschka et al. (Vienna: Österreichische Akademie der Wissenschaften, 1985), 1:121–37; Gerhard Heitz, "Wirtschafts- und sozialgeschichtliche Aspekte der 'Zweiten Leibeigenschaft,'" in *Studien zur deutschen und ungarischen Wirtschaftsentwicklung,* ed. Zimányi, 43–51; Holm Sundhaussen, "Der Wandel in der osteuropäischen Agrarverfassung während der frühen Neuzeit," *Südost-Forschungen* 49 (1990): 15–56.

8. Rusiński, "Some Remarks on the Differentiation," 93n.18; idem, "Agrarkrise," 260.

9. Leonid Żytkowicz, "W sprawie badań prónawczych nad genezą i rozwojem folwarku pańszczyźnianego" (On the comparative research on the origin and development of the domain based on servile labor), in *Społeczeństwo, gospodarka, kultura: Studia ofiarowane Marianowi Małowistowi w 4o-lecie pracy naukowej* (Warsaw, 1974), 438; see also Miroslav Hroch and Josef Petráň, *Das 17. Jahrhundert: Krise der Feudalgesellschaft?* Historische Perspektiven, vol. 17 (Hamburg: Hoffmann und Campe, 1981), 138–41.

10. Alfred Hoffmann, *Wirtschaftsgeschichte des Landes Oberösterreich,* vol. 1, *Werden, Wachsen, Reifen* (Salzburg: O. Müller, 1952), 98; idem, "Die Grundherrschaft als Unternehmen," *Zeitschrift für Agrargeschichte und Agrarsoziologie* 6 (1958): 123–31 (reprinted in Hoffmann, *Staat und Wirtschaft im Wandel der Zeit: Studien und Essays* [Vienna: Verlag für Geschichte und Politik, 1979], 1:294–306); cf. Werner Berthold, "Die Einkommensstruktur der adeligen Herrschaften um die Mitte des 18. Jahrhunderts," in *Nutzen, Renten, Erträge: Struktur und Entwicklung frühneuzeitlicher Feudaleinkommen in Niederösterreich,* ed. Herbert Knittler (Vienna/Munich: R. Oldenbourg, 1989), 204–5.

11. This aspect is emphasized in Eckart Schremmer, "Agrarverfassung und Wirtschaftsstruktur: Die südostdeutsche Hofmark—eine Wirtschaftsherrschaft?" *Vierteljahrschrift für Sozial- und Wirtschaftsgeschichte* 20 (1972): 42–65.

12. See also Georg Grüll, "Weinberg: Die Entstehung einer Mühlviertler Wirtschaftsherrschaft," *Mitteilungen des oberösterreichischen Landesarchivs* 4 (1955): 7–203; and Peter Stenitzer, "Der Adelige als Unternehmer? Das Wirtschaften der gräflichen Familie Harrach in Oberösterreich im 16. und 17. Jahrhundert," *Frühneuzeit-Info* 2, no. 1 (1991): 41–60.

13. Friedrich Lütge, *Die mitteldeutsche Grundherrschaft und ihre Auflösung,* 2d ed., Quellen und Forschungen zur Agrargeschichte, vol. 4 (Stuttgart: G. Fischer, 1957), 296–97; Thomas M. Barker, "Military Entrepreneurship and Absolutism: Habsburg Models," *Journal of European Studies* 4 (1974): 27; Immanuel Wallerstein, *The Modern World-System II: Mercantilism and the Consolidation of the European World-Economy, 1600–1750* (New York: Academic Press, 1980), 201.

14. Makkai, "Neo-Serfdom," 230–31.

15. Georg Grüll, *Die Robot in Oberösterreich*, Forschungen zur Geschichte Oberösterreichs, vol. 1 (Linz: Oberösterreichisches Landesarchiv, 1952); idem, *Der Bauer im Lande ob der Enns am Ausgang des 16. Jahrhunderts,* Forschungen zur Geschichte Oberösterreichs, vol. 11 (Linz: H. Böhlaus Nachf., 1969); idem, *Bauern-haus und Meierhof: Zur Geschichte der Landwirtschaft in Oberösterreich,* Forschungen zur Geschichte Oberösterreichs, vol. 13 (Linz: Oberösterreichisches Landesarchiv, 1975).

16. See Knittler, *Nutzen, Renten, Erträge,* 16; Johann Wöhrer, "Robot-Verhält-nisse im Viertel unter dem Wienerwald: Ein Beitrag zur Geschichte des Untertan-wesens in Niederösterreich" (Ph.D. diss., University of Vienna, 1930).

17. E. g., Archive of the Weitra Estate, Nr. 143a, Partikularbeschreibung der Meier- und Schäfereihöfe der Herrschaft Weitra samt den dazugehörigen Haus-und Überländgründen; NÖLA, Archive of the Stetteldorf Estate, HS 3/25, Hausbuch und Nachrichtsbeschreibung über die hochgräflich Hardeggischen "negst der Thonau" gelegenen Herrschaften . . . 1696; NÖLA, SA, Archive of the Retz-Gatterburg Estate, HS 109, Handbuch über die gräflich Hoyosische Herr-schaft Retz . . . 1664.

18. Lower Austria (1772–73), Bohemia, Moravia (1775), Styria (1778). Karl Grünberg, *Die Bauernbefreiung und die Auflösung des gutsherrlich-bäuerlichen Verhältnisses in Böhmen, Mähren und Schlesien* (Leipzig: Duncker & Humblot, 1893–94), 2:237–70; Friedrich Lütge, "Die Grundentlastung (Bauernbefreiung) in der Steiermark," *Zeitschrift für Agrargeschichte und Agrarsoziologie* 16 (1968): 190–209.

19. Grüll, *Robot in Oberösterreich,* 174–85.

20. Hofkammerarchiv (HKA) Vienna, Steuerregulierung, Summarien, 5–8, 9–12, 30–34, 58, 69–75; a slightly deviating *Summarium* for Austria below the Enns also in NÖLA, SA, Normalien- und Informations-Buch für das Catastral-Departement, I, fols. 54–60; rough totals of the Maria-Theresian *Kataster* records ibid., HS 1013/I, fols. 34–35; see also Knittler, *Nutzen, Renten, Erträge,* 118.

21. According to the source material, the following were classed as arable land: ponds comparable to arable land and *Drieschfelder;* and the following were classed as meadows: ponds comparable to meadows and gardens as well as *Hutweiden,* scrub, etc. Slightly deviating figures for Bohemia in Leonid Żytkowicz, "Trends of Agrarian Economy in Poland, Bohemia and Hungary from the Middle of the Fif-teenth to the Middle of the Seventeenth Century," in *East-Central Europe in Tran-sition,* ed. Antoni Mączak et al. (Cambridge: Cambridge University Press, 1985), 72. According to the 1750–51 Theresian *Fassion* for Lower Austria, the ratio be-tween rustical and demesnial land was 89.9:10.1 for arable land and 81.3:18.7 for meadows.

22. Pach, *Ungarische Agrarentwicklung,* 47; Pach mentions in "Über einige Probleme der Gutswirtschaft in Ungarn in der ersten Hälfte des 17. Jahrhunderts," in *Deuxième conférence internationale d'histoire économique* (Paris/The Hague: Mouton, 1965), 2:225, 25–30 percent; László Mákkai, "Die Hauptzüge der wirtschaftlich-sozialen Entwicklung Ungarns im 15.–17. Jahrhundert," *Studia*

Historica Academiae Scientiarum Hungariae 53 (1963): 41, mentions 25–33 percent for grain and 12–14 percent for wine; about 10 percent of the total agrarian area is indicated by Zs. Kirilly and István N. Kiss, "Production des céréales et exploitations paysannes en Hongrie," *Annales: Économies, sociétés, civilisations* 23 (1968): 1212–31. See also Żytkowicz, "Trends of Agrarian Economy," 79.

23. There is a good survey in Władysław Rusiński, "Das Bauernlegen in Mitteleuropa im 16.–18. Jahrhundert," *Studia historiae oeconomicae* 11 (1976): 21–56, especially 48–49; see also Harnisch, "Probleme einer Periodisierung," 272; idem, "Gutsherrschaft," 230; Leonid Żytkowicz, "Production et productivité de l'économie agricole en Pologne aux XVIe–XVIIIe siècles," in *Troisième conférence internationale d'histoire économique* (Paris/The Hague: Mouton, l968), 2:155; with regard to the sixteenth century, see Andrzej Wyczański, "L'exploitation seigneuriale (folwark) et l'exploitation paysanne: Subordination ou rivalité?" *Studia historiae oeconomicae* 17 (1983): 5–14.

24. Rusiński, "Über die Entwicklungsetappen der Fronwirtschaft," 43.

25. Klíma, "Agrarian Class Structure," 196.

26. Alés Chalupa, "Venkovské obyvatelstvo v Čechách v tereziánských katastrech, 1700–1750" (The rural population of Bohemia in the Teresian cadastres, 1700–1750), *Sborník Národního Muzea* 23 (1969): 320–21; Peter Kriedte, *Spätfeudalismus und Handelskapital* (Göttingen: Vandenhoeck & Ruprecht, 1980), 89.

27. Gerhard Pferschy and Heinrich Purkarthofer, "Die Robotbelastung der steirischen Bauern um 1750," in *Atlas zur Geschichte des steirischen Bauerntums,* ed. Fritz Posch (Graz: Akademische Druck- u. Verlagsanstalt, 1976), map 21; there is a critical assessment in Othmar Pickl, "Herren und Bauern in den Ostalpenländern Kärnten und Steiermark vom Mittelalter bis zur Neuzeit," in *Grand domaine,* ed. Gunst and Hoffmann, 93.

28. Berthold, "Einkommensstruktur der adeligen Herrschaften," 218–19. This is also true for the rent commutation statistics after 1848: the number of one-horse labor days to be commuted in Lower Austria was as high as the number of two-horse labor days, one-ox *Zugrobot* amounted to exactly one fifth, etc.; see Ernst Mischler and Josef Ulbrich, eds., *Österreichisches Staatswörterbuch* (Vienna: A. Hölder, 1895), 1:958–59. Cf. also Lütge, "Grundentlastung," 192–93.

29. NÖLA, SA, Normalien- und Informations-Buch, I.

30. NÖLA, SA, Theresianische Fassion, Dominikalfassion.

31. Three days on Marchegg, Propstei of Gloggnitz and two days on Prinzendorf (?), Hauskirchen, Erdberg, Steinebrunn (?), Zistersdorf, and Achau, among others. Marchegg (VUMB) Nr. 651, Propstei Gloggnitz (VUWW) Nr. 1237, Prinzendorf (VUMB) Nr. 1051, Hauskirchen (VUMB) Nr. 114, Erdberg (VUMB) Nr. 390, Steinebrunn (VUMB) 1094, Zistersdorf (VUMB) Nr. 1311, Achau (VUWW) Nr. 1262. Fifty-four houses had to pay "unlimited labor rent in kind," which the state "graciously" waived against payment of rent in money.

32. Hausarchiv der Regierenden Fürsten von Liechtenstein Wien (HALW), H 1344 (15 March 1667, confirming the two-day *Zug-* and *Handrobot* of the subjects of

the *Markt* Mistelbach); H 1257 ("Extract" on the overall land, arable land, vineyards, and subjects liable to labor service of the Wilfersdorf estate of 8 June 1752). See also Thomas Winkelbauer, "Haklich und der Korruption unterworfen: Die Verwaltung der liechtensteinischen Herrschaften und Güter im 17. und 18. Jahrhundert," in *Der ganzen Welt ein Lob und Spiegel: Das Fürstenhaus Liechtenstein in der frühen Neuzeit,* ed. Evelin Oberhammer (Vienna/Munich: R. Oldenbourg, 1990), 107–8.

33. Martin N. Baumann, *Abhandlung von Verbesserung der Niederösterreichischen Landwirthschaft* (Vienna: Joh. Thomas Edler v. Trattner, 1767), 49.

34. In the case of unlimited labor service (upper limit of 104 days per year), a maximum of three days per week could be demanded; for a limit between 104 and 156 days per year, also three days; and for a limit between 156 and 208 days, a maximum of four days per week. On the concentration of labor service during the seasons, the example being a demesne with agriculture, woods, ponds, and glass production, see Thomas Winkelbauer, *Robot und Steuer: Die Untertanen der Waldviertler Grundherrschaften Gföhl und Altpölla zwischen feudaler Herrschaft und absolutistischem Staat* (Vienna: Verein für Landeskunde von Niederösterreich, 1986), 99–101.

35. Codex Austriacus IV, 1045; Grüll, *Robot in Oberösterreich,* 239.

36. Pach, *Ungarische Agrarentwicklung.*

37. Rusiński, "Über die Entwicklungsetappen der Fronwirtschaft," 29; Harnisch, "Probleme einer Periodisierung," 268.

38. Werner Stark, *Ursprung und Aufstieg des landwirtschaftlichen Großbetriebs in den böhmischen Ländern* (Brno: Rohrer, 1934).

39. Knittler, *Nutzen, Renten, Erträge,* 20–85, 146–81.

40. NÖLA, Archive of the Stetteldorf Estate, Alte Herrschaften Nr. 46; more examples in Herbert Knittler, "Zur Einkommensstruktur niederösterreichischer Adelsherrschaften 1550–1750," in *Adel in der Frühneuzeit: Ein regionaler Vergleich,* ed. Rudolf Endres (Cologne/Vienna: Böhlau, 1991), 99–118.

41. OÖLA, Archive of the Wartenburg Estate, Sch. 73 (values without share of *Landsteuer*).

42. Knittler, *Nutzen, Renten, Erträge,* 57.

43. Grüll, *Bauer im Lande ob der Enns,* 102–203; Ernst Bruckmüller, "Die Grundherrschaft," in *Bauernland Oberösterreich: Entwicklung seiner Land- und Forstwirtschaft,* ed. Alfred Hoffmann (Linz: R. Trauner, 1974), 40; Hermann Rebel, *Peasant Classes: The Bureaucratization of Property and Family Relations under Early Habsburg Absolutism 1511–1636* (Princeton, N.J.: Princeton University Press, 1983), 120–37.

44. Such an exception is the Schwertberg estate, which extracted 71.5 days in addition to the tobacco rent. Grüll, *Robot in Oberösterreich,* 136.

45. Rebel, *Peasant Classes,* 135.

46. Oberösterreichisches Landesarchiv, Neuerwerbungen HS Nr. 76 (175), which is not statistically analyzed in Georg Grüll, "Die Herrschaftsschichtung in

Österreich ob der Enns 1750," *Mitteilungen des oberösterreichischen Landesarchivs* 5 (1957): 311–39.

47. See Kurt Klein, "Quantitative Informationen zu den Veränderungserscheinungen des 14.–16. Jahrhunderts in Niederösterreich," in *Mittelalterliche Wüstungen in Niederösterreich,* ed. Helmuth Feigl and Andreas Kusternig (Vienna: Niederösterreichisches Institut für Landeskunde, 1983), 55–74; Alfred Grund, *Die Veränderungen der Topographie im Wiener Walde und Wiener Becken* Geographische Abhandlungen, vol. 8/1 (Leipzig: B. G. Teubner, 1901).

48. Othmar Hageneder, "Die spätmittelalterlichen Wüstungen in der Grafschaft Schaunberg," *Jahrbuch für Landeskunde von Niederösterreich,* n.s., 33 (1957): 65–81.

49. In comparing the causes of the backwardness of Lower Austrian agriculture to other provinces, such as Upper Austria, Baumann, *Abhandlung,* 49, refers to the advantage of labor rent in money instead of labor services.

50. On the peasant rising of 1596–97, see Gottfried E. Friess, *Der Aufstand der Bauern in Niederösterreich am Schlusse des XVI. Jahrhunderts* (Vienna: Verein für Landeskunde von Niederösterreich, 1897); Grüll, *Bauer im Lande ob der Enns;* Helmuth Feigl, *Der niederösterreichische Bauernaufstand 1596/97,* 2d ed., Militärhistorische Schriftenreihe, vol. 22 (Vienna: Österreichischer Bundesverlag für Unterricht, Wissenschaft und Kunst, 1978); idem, "Die Ursachen der niederösterreichischen Bauernkriege des 16. Jahrhunderts und die Ziele der Aufständischen," in *Die Bauernkriege und Michael Gaismair,* ed. Fridolin Dörrer (Innsbruck: Tiroler Landesarchiv, 1982), 197–209; Jean Bérenger, "La révolte paysanne de Basse-Autriche de 1597," *Revue d'histoire économique et sociale* 53 (1975): 465–92; Alfred Hoffmann, "Zur Typologie der Bauernaufstände in Oberösterreich," in *Der oberösterreichische Bauernkrieg 1626,* ed. Dietmar Straub (Linz: Amt der oö. Landesregierung, 1976), 15–22 (reprinted in *Europäische Bauernrevolten der frühen Neuzeit,* ed. Winfried Schulze (Frankfurt/Main: Suhrkamp, 1982), 309–22.

51. Grüll, *Robot in Oberösterreich*, 109, 118.

52. This basically unlimited labor service was confirmed in the *Tractatus de iuribus incorporalibus* of 13 March 1679, although it was also stipulated that subjects were not to be burdened beyond their means or against old conventions. Hauer, *Praktische Darstellung,* 1:79; Friess, *Aufstand der Bauern,* 64–65; Erna Patzelt, "Bauernschutz in Österreich vor 1848," *Mitteilungen des Instituts für österreichische Geschichtsforschung* 58 (1950): 646–47, 650–51; Fritz Wisnicki, "Die Geschichte der Abfassung des Tractatus de iuribus incorporalibus," *Jahrbuch für Landeskunde von Niederösterreich,* n.s., 20, no. 2 (1926–27): 69–92.

53. Helmuth Feigl, *Die niederösterreichische Grundherrschaft vom ausgehenden Mittelalter bis zu den theresianisch-josephinischen Reformen* (Vienna: Verein für Landeskunde von Niederösterreich und Wien, 1964), 103–4.

54. Harnisch, "Probleme einer Periodisierung," 255, 257; Rusiński, "Some Remarks on the Differentiation," 93; Blum, "Rise of Serfdom," 830–31.

55. Joseph Redlich, "Leibeigenschaft und Bauernbefreiung in Österreich," *Zeitschrift für Social- und Wirtschaftsgeschichte* 3 (1895): 273–75; see also Eduard Maur, "Vrchnosti a poddaní za třicetileté války" (Authorities and subjects in the Thirty Years' War), *Folia Historica Bohemica* 8 (1985): 241–64.

56. Volker Press, "Adel in den österreichisch-böhmischen Erblanden und im Reich zwischen dem 15. und dem 17. Jahrhundert," in *Adel im Wandel: Politik—Kultur—Konfession 1500–1700,* ed. Herbert Knittler et al. (Vienna: Amt der NÖ Landesregierung, 1990), 26–27.

57. Knittler, *Nutzen, Renten, Erträge,* 60.

58. This can be seen from surveys aiming to limit labor service to twelve days on all *Kammerherrschaften.* Ibid., 42–43n.56, 65–66; see also the data in Wöhrer, *Robot-Verhältnisse,* 45–46.

59. For Upper Austria, see Grüll, *Robot in Oberösterreich,* 74–75.

60. Knittler, *Nutzen, Renten, Erträge,* 123.

61. NÖLA, Archive of the Stetteldorf Estate, Angestellte Nr. 35/1, Vertzaichnus aller officierer, diener unndt dienstbotten besoldung und underhalttung, beschriben 24ten Xbris 1616.

62. Knittler, *Nutzen, Renten, Erträge,* 124.

63. Karl Lechner, "Türkenschäden in Niederösterreich: Ein Beitrag zum Türkeneinfall 1683," *Unsere Heimat* 6 (1933): 272.

64. Kurt Klein, "Die Bevölkerung Österreichs vom Beginn des 16. bis zur Mitte des 18. Jahrhunderts," in *Beiträge zur Bevölkerungs- und Sozialgeschichte Österreichs,* ed. Heimold Helczmanovszki (Vienna: Verlag für Geschichte und Politik, 1973), 47–112.

65. Herbert Knittler, "Die Grundherrschaft: Organisationsprinzip und wirtschaftliche Unternehmung," in *Prinz Eugen und das barocke Österreich,* ed. Karl Gutkas (Vienna/Salzburg: Residenz, 1985), 197.

66. Knittler, *Nutzen, Renten, Erträge,* 128.

67. Ibid., 131. A similar development took place in Slovakia; see Špiesz, "Die neuzeitliche Agrarentwicklung," 229.

68. Emanuel Janoušek, *Historický vývoj produktivity práce v zemědělství v období pobělohorském* (The historical development of labor productivity in agriculture in the period after the Battle of the White Mountain) (Prague: Československé zemědělské muzeum, 1967), 188–89; Klíma, "Agrarian Class Structure," 206–7.

69. Knittler, *Nutzen, Renten, Erträge,* 145n.66.

70. Archive of the Weitra Estate, Nr. 140, Ausführlicher Anschlag über die Grafschaft Weitra . . . de Anno 1704.

71. See note 32 above.

72. Janoušek, *Historický vývoj,* 190–91; Franz X. Bohdanowicz, *Die Linzer Vorstädte und Vororte, dargestellt nach dem "Josephinischen Lagebuch" und "Franciceischen Kataster,"* Linzer Regesten, appendix (Linz, 1953–).

73. That in addition to labor service ploughing and carrying could be offered against wages to other villagers who did not have horses or oxen proves that labor service must have been low. See Herbert Knittler, "Zum Viehbesatz Weinviertler

Bauernwirtschaften um die Mitte des 16. Jahrhunderts," *Unsere Heimat* 62 (1991): 28–29.

74. Calculations based on Berthold, "Einkommensstruktur der adeligen Herrschaften," 204–35.

75. Knittler, *Nutzen, Renten, Erträge,* 134; concerning a large ecclesiastical estate, see Knittler, "Zwischen Stabilität und Veränderung: Ein Beitrag zur Melker Wirtschaftsgeschichte der frühen Neuzeit," in *900 Jahre Benediktiner in Melk* (Stift Melk, 1989), tables 3, 4.

76. The latter question could not be dealt with in detail in this essay. Basically, a contradiction seems to exist between the concentration of feudal rights concerning the subject (such as marriage consent, *Gesindezwangsdienst* and *Waisendienst,* and various legal rights) on the one hand and far-reaching personal freedom of movement on the other, which could only be checked by a fee (*Abfahrtsgeld*), which was not customary in all places.

77. Considerable deviations can occur concerning the income structure as presented in table 4 above if the estimates (*Anschläge*) of the estates are made the basis of the calculation, especially as they tend to record gross revenues, and forest is usually estimated according to the area covered and not according to the actual revenue. This can be shown by the average values for the four *Viertel* of Lower Austria based on data of twenty-four estates between 1650 und 1680:

	Own production and monopolies	Dues in money and kind
VOMB	70.2 (66.9)	29.8 (33.1)
VUMB	59.5 (49.1)	40.5 (50.9)
VOWW	35.4 (26.3)	64.6 (73.7)
VUWW	44.9 (40.5)	55.1 (59.5)
total	52.1 (45.1)	47.9 (54.9)

TABLE 6. Income of Lower Austrian noble estates 1650–1680 (in percentages; figure in parentheses excluding income from forest). Sources: Arbesbach: OÖLA, Schlüsselberger Archiv (SchA), HS 16/1, 3–10; Horn: Archive of Rosenburg Castle, Horn, Fasz. I/II, Nr. 8; Primersdorf: OÖLA, SchA, HS 16/5, 613–18; Schrems: OÖLA, Archive of the Weinberg Estate (AW), Akten 1301; Schwarzenau: OÖLA, SchA, HS 16/1, 296–302; Waidhofen/Thaya: OÖLA, SchA, HS 16/5, 393–99; Gobelsburg: OÖLA, SchA, HS 16/1, 85–89; Jedenspeigen: HALW, H 101; Niederkreuzstetten: OÖLA, SchA, HS 16/1, 434–48; Sierndorf: OÖLA, AW, Akten 1303; Sonnberg-Raschala-Oberhollabrunn: OÖLA, SchA, HS 16/1, 459–68; Weierburg: OÖLA, AW, Akten 1302; Freidegg-Schönegg: OÖLA, SchA, HS 16/2, 103–6; Grünbichl-Kilb: OÖLA, SchA, HS 16/1, 90–96; Karlstetten-Doppel: OÖLA, AW, Akten 1300; Plankenstein: OÖLA, SchA, HS 16/5, 577–97; Schallaburg-Sichtenberg: OÖLA, SchA, HS 16/1, 283–95; Wieselburg: OÖLA, SchA, HS 16/1, 480–84; Rauhenstein: OÖLA, AW, Akten 1301; Seibersdorf: OÖLA, SchA, HS 16/5, 37–42; Stixenstein: OÖLA, SchA, HS 16/1, 412–34; Trautmannsdorf: OÖLA, AW, Akten 1301; Vösendorf: AW, Akten 1302; Wartenstein: OÖLA, SchA, HS 16/5, 28–36.

78. Hainstetten: OÖLA, SchA, HS 16/1, 98–100; Weitra: HALW, H 104. Data for estates in Upper Austria, Ort 1723–78 and Windhaag 1734–39 cf. Bruckmüller, "Grundherrschaft," 48; for Aschach 1640–80 cf. Stenitzer, "Adelige als Unternehmer," 60.

79. Harnisch, "Gutsherrschaft," 210, 219; Harnisch, *Bauern—Feudaladel—Städtebürgertum: Untersuchungen über die Zusammenhänge zwischen Feudalrente, bäuerlicher und gutsherrlicher Warenproduktion und den Ware-Geld-Beziehungen in der Magdeburger Börde und dem nordöstlichen Harzvorland von der frühbürgerlichen Revolution bis zum Dreißigjährigen Krieg* (Weimar: H. Böhlaus Nachf., 1980).

80. Hoffmann, Wirtschaftsgeschichte, 98.

Translated by Désireé Verdonk, Vienna

Between Mercantilism and Physiocracy

Stages, Modes, and Functions of Economic Theory in the Habsburg Monarchy, 1748–63

Grete Klingenstein

The Platonic notion that rulers should follow the concepts of philosophers became a standard ingredient of public opinion in the second half of the eighteenth century. Or rather, it then emerged as the secularized version of the traditional expectation that religion be the foremost guide of politics. The ideological programs that political parties chiseled out during the nineteenth and twentieth centuries in order to attract and hold a mass following have colored this vision of eighteenth-century rulers, particularly those of Central European enlightened absolutism. As a result, the actions of Maria Theresa, Joseph II, Leopold II, and Frederick II have often been measured against the precepts and critiques of the eighteenth-century *philosophes,* and the relations between the theory and practice of enlightened rule have become a major subject of historical scholarship.[1]

In the case of the Habsburg Monarchy, Joseph von Sonnenfels (1733–1817) figures as the most prominent enlightenment thinker who reputedly influenced the reforms of Maria Theresa and Joseph II.[2] Indeed, Sonnenfels was not only the monarchy's leading *philosophe* of economy, society, and culture but also the first and most eminent representative of the new profession of journalism. As professor of *Polizey- und Kameralwissenschaften* in Vienna since 1763, he was the first academic teacher who, by using German instead of Latin, introduced the widening reading public to the discourse of the *philosophes.* But did Sonnenfels really influence the policy making of Maria Theresa and Joseph II? More specifically, did his ideas help determine Habsburg political economy? Such questions may seem banal, but they beg an inquiry into the origins, orientations, intent, standards, and dissemination of economic theory, as well as into the administrative levels of economic planning and decision making.

In assessing the extent of Sonnenfels's impact, it is important to analyze oral and written discourse of as wide a circle of private and public figures as possible.[3] Hence, rather than limiting ourselves to a relatively narrow examination of personal correspondence among a few key individuals, we should study a much wider group of economic administrators and other experts who worked alongside the monarch and *philosophes*. An analysis of their discourse might also help to determine the validity of the assertion—which first arose in the nineteenth century—that Enlightenment ideas flowed in a linear, almost mechanistic fashion from their cradle in France to the "less developed" states and nations of Southern, Central, and Eastern Europe.[4]

However, such an analysis suggests a more variegated pattern to the European Enlightenment. What emerges is a multiplicity of national centers where ideas with a general European appeal were not only discussed and adopted but also transformed, or even rejected, and transplanted to other regions further east, depending on each society's individual circumstances and needs.[5] Indeed, this multipolar intercourse of Enlightenment ideas involved a variety of national cultures and languages. Therefore, translations into a country's native language or into a third, intermediary tongue played an important role in the process of disseminating and transforming ideas throughout Europe.[6]

This new concept of multipolar Enlightenment intercourse invites a reappraisal of Sonnenfels's person in particular and economic theory and practice in the Habsburg Monarchy in general. What emerges is not so much a picture of the transition from cameralism to physiocracy and protoliberalism as one of the perseverance of cameralistic doctrines and practices in the face of budding liberalization. This essay is, however, of a more limited scope and covers only the fifties and early sixties. New source material indicates that this was the initial phase, when the international discourse on economic matters was firmly implanted in the Habsburg Monarchy by a group of economic administrators under the protection of State Chancellor Wenzel Anton Prince Kaunitz (1711–94).[7]

At the top levels of administration, the group included men such as Johann Karl Philipp Count Cobenzl (1712–70), Kaunitz's man in the Austrian Netherlands. This reform-minded minister promoted the publication in Brussels of the first economic journal in the Habsburg Monarchy, the *Journal de commerce* (1759–62).[8] Another key member was Ludwig Count Zinzendorf (1720–80), who was promoted in 1762 to the presidency of the newly instituted *Hofrechenkammer.* He was the group's outstanding theoretical mind. In 1761 he called his half brother, Karl (1739–1813), from Saxony to Vienna, where he gave him a thorough theoretical and practical training for later governmental services. Also worth mentioning are Philipp Joseph Count Sinzendorf (1726–88), the president of the Lower Austrian *Kommerzienrat;* and Egid Valentin Baron Borié (1719–93), a member of the recently established *Staatsrat.* None was, however, more important than the brothers Zinzendorf. What kept the group together was apparently Kaunitz's protection and a firm determination to learn from Western European economic patterns. Yet none of them publicly participated in the international discourse. This role was played by Sonnenfels alone, who, as if by coincidence, began teaching at the University of Vienna in 1763. By his numerous publications, he established his reputation as Austria's foremost theorist and authority on economic matters.

Furthermore, it is important to note that it was during this time that both Joseph II and Leopold II received their education. The two rulers will be mentioned only briefly, for my main concern is the juxtaposition of the Zinzendorf brothers as economic administrators on the one side and Sonnenfels as academic teacher on the other. In this context, the Viennese interlude of the cameralist Johann Heinrich Gottlob Justi (1717–71) is important largely because it elucidates the limited function that was granted by economic administrators and policy makers to academic economists.

In addition, it witnessed the first, but unsuccessful, attempt to establish Vienna as Central Europe's foremost interlocutor and intermediary of international economic discourse under the direction of Friedrich Wilhelm Count Haugwitz (1700–1765), Maria Theresa's most eminent minister during the first reform phase (1746–1759/ 61). By 1761, Haugwitz's system was replaced by new policies and institutions, designed by State Chancellor Kaunitz.

As the Seven Years' War (1756–63) drew to a close, Maria Theresa's advisors shifted their primary attention to economic problems, especially the enormous state debt.[9] As de facto prime minister, Kaunitz argued that improving the economic, social, and cultural conditions of the empress's subjects was the main prerequisite for raising overall economic productivity, which he considered indispensable for making Austria more competitive in European power politics. Kaunitz's orientation meant a radical shift in all internal politics from merely quantitative considerations of state revenue to quality consciousness. Henceforth, the government would have to focus upon the living conditions, social attitudes, and mentalities of the population—explicitly including religion and education—since each was a factor in determining economic productivity and, consequently, the state's wealth and power. This ideological shift was strongly prompted by Montesquieu's De l'esprit des lois (1748).[10]

The principal venue for discussing Kaunitz's program was his newly created Staatsrat (1760/61), which included all of the empress's key ministers and, occasionally, Crown Prince Joseph.[11] A memorandum written by Joseph in 1765 still echoes the vivacity of the discussions. Although very critical, he mentions "the modern French," and ironically he presents himself as "almost as wise as Colbert."[12] He clearly alludes to the neo-Colbertist and physiocratic schools, which had arisen in France in the fifties. Furthermore, Joseph hints at a general control of state revenues and expenditure. Such an institution, patterned after the French model, was designed by Kaunitz's protégé Ludwig Count Zinzendorf and introduced as the Hofrechenkammer in 1762, with Ludwig acting as first controller general.[13]

Kaunitz emerges as the main pivot for the transfer of the new currents of economic thought that swayed Western Europe after the Peace of Aix-la-Chapelle (1748). While preoccupied with securing support from Austria's allies during his diplomatic missions in Turin (1742–44), Brussels (1744–46), and Aix-la-Chapelle (1748),[14] he had become acquainted with the great Western European financial revolution that had established land, trade, and credit as the main sources of public wealth, state stability, and national power.[15] Following his return to Vienna in 1749, he hired Ludwig Zinzendorf as his collaborator to copy memoranda and to translate foreign writings.[16] Ludwig's linguistic abilities were truly exceptional. He mastered Italian and French, the latter surpassing the former as the most favored language at the court of Vienna. He had also become one of the first in multilingual Vienna to acquire a sound knowledge of English.[17]

Although the Zinzendorfs were of Lower Austrian origin, Ludwig, ten years younger than Kaunitz, had taken a circuitous route to the center of Habsburg power. Since his branch of the family was Protestant, it had emigrated to Saxony in the second half of the seventeenth century. Yet he converted to Catholicism in Dresden in 1739 and soon came to Vienna to inherit the family estates. At the age of twenty-six, he returned to the University of Leipzig, where Kaunitz himself had studied fifteen years earlier. The university was held in high esteem at the court of Vienna as the very center of modern law studies and as the seat of language reform.[18] Ludwig's Lower Austrian inheritance afforded him a seat in Vienna on the Lower Austrian court of nobility (*Landrecht*), where he developed an expertise in the financial affairs of the estates at the very time of Haugwitz's reforms. By September 1750, he had produced his *Essai sur l'etablissement d'une banque générale des états.*[19] Since Kaunitz was already keenly interested in the credit of crown and estates, he decided to take Zinzendorf to Paris as his *elève* (i.e., trainee) (October 1750–January 1753).

As in his earlier missions, Kaunitz's diplomatic responsibilities in Paris also involved economic and financial issues. Indeed, his embassy acted as the fulcrum for the monarchy's diplomatic and economic activities in Western Europe.[20] Kaunitz probably had the Adriatic port of Trieste and current commercial negotiations with Spain in mind when, in October 1752, he sent Ludwig to the French ports of Lorient and Brest to observe and learn the sale of overseas commodities.[21] Four months earlier, he apparently instructed Ludwig to compose an essay on the economic resources of France, entitled *Mémoire sur les richesses, le commerce et les finances de la France.*[22]

Further research is needed to determine which *salons* he preferred, whether he frequented the circles of the Pâris-Marmontel family, other financiers, or the aristocratic Stainville of Lorraine, who helped to forge and sustain the Austrian alliance under the auspices of Madame de Pompadour.[23] Although Ludwig was well versed in the books, prints, and manuscripts that were then circulating in Paris, it is impossible to trace all the books and pamphlets that he read during his stay in Paris or on his short trip to London. For sure we only know that, while still abroad, he conceived of a plan to have the most important economic tracts translated into German, and that the enterprise was to be located in Leipzig.[24]

Ludwig's obsession with translations is a clear indication that he was familiar with the seminal group of economists who were close to the intendant of commerce, Jean Claude Marie Vincent de Gournay (1715–59), to whom we attribute the phrase *"laissez faire et laissez passer."*[25] In Paris, economics was already considered a proper science, encompassing population, agriculture, manufactures, the trades and crafts, traffic and commerce, shipping and the colonies, taxation, and currencies and banking. Most of the group were either entrepreneurs themselves—manufacturers, merchants and ship owners, tax farmers, bankers, landholders, physicians—or were employed by the government. Indeed, the basic ingredients to their systematic inquiries into economy as a proper field of study stemmed from a combination of the maxims of natural law, the principles of the natural sciences, and a wide range of indigenous economic experiences.

Among these economists were François Louis Véron de Forbonnais (1722–1800) and his cousin Louis Joseph Plumard de Dangeul (1722–77), who both translated from English and Spanish.

They were joined by Anne Robert Jacques Turgot (1727–81), who translated from English; Claude Jacques Herbert, who wrote on the trade of grain; and Henri Louis Duhamel de Monceau, who, following the lead of Englishman Jethro Tull, specialized in agriculture, later also in trade. Notable is the group's preoccupation with Spanish and, above all, British authors, past and contemporary. Britain was France's partner and rival in commerce and politics, and at the same time the object of general admiration and emulation. In comparison to Central European cameralism, conspicuous features of the Western European economic discourse of the fifties are the absence of codification by means of university teaching, and proper economic experiences of the participants. In addition to the *salons,* the wider public was already fully involved in these discussions, and French authors, as in Britain, appealed to public opinion. Economic topics had established themselves as proper themes of political writing and journalism.

In the absence of more direct evidence, a provisional reconstruction of Ludwig's intellectual orientation must rely heavily on the contents of the library that he offered to his twenty-two-year-old brother Karl upon his arrival in Vienna in February 1761.[26] Karl had studied law and related subjects at the University of Jena, including courses on cameralist economy and on "statistics" (i.e., the demographic and political conditions of the European states). For the following three years, Karl underwent a systematic training in the theory and practice of "governing economy," as it was conceived by Ludwig and like-minded friends, above all Philipp Joseph Count Sinzendorf, the president of the Lower Austrian council of commerce.[27] All were opposed to protective tariffs and other prohibitive measures. The Lower Austrian council of commerce was Karl's first training ground. It was not long, however, before Sinzendorf, and then Kaunitz, sent him to explore the economic policies of the major European states (1763–69) and to analyze the economic situation of all the Habsburg lands (1771–76). During these journeys, he compiled an enormous trove of analytical works, none of which has ever been published.[28]

The details of Karl's economic education are too extensive to recount here. I should, however, like to review those elements which are also relevant to a reappraisal of Sonnenfels's position in the governing economy of eighteenth-century Austria. Of major influence was the policy- and action-oriented, yet intimate social climate of the economic discourse that surrounded Karl at his brother's home and in the *salons* of Vienna's international court society. Then there are the texts that Ludwig himself wrote or translated, both in print and in manuscript form. Again and again, Karl took to the voluminous manuscript that Ludwig had composed in 1758 on the history of European banking under the title *Beschreibung der vornehmsten europäischen Banken.*[29] Furthermore, Ludwig had translated John Locke's treatise on money and interest rates, which also remained in manuscript form, under the title *Übersetzung aus dem Englischen des Locke Geld und dessen Ausmünzung und Erhöhung der Münzen, auch die diesfällige Meinung des Herren Lowndes [sic] betr.*[30] In 1758 Vienna's most enterprising publisher, Johann Thomas Trattner, printed Ludwig's copiously annotated German translation of John Law's famous tract *Money and Trade Considered* (1720) under the title *Gedanken vom Gelde und von der Handlung nebst einem Vorschlage dem Geldmangel in Schottland abzuhelfen. Aus dem Englischen übersetzt.* It made no mention of either the author or translator.[31]

Karl also learned the bookkeeping and accounting method that Ludwig had imported from France and that was the mainstay of the *Hofrechenkammer*'s business of control. The bookkeeper Matthieu de la Porte's *Le Guide (La Science) des négocians et teneurs des livres* (Paris, 1685) had long been the standard handbook of this métier. It had been edited several times, most recently in 1748. Finally, in 1762, Trattner published the first German-language edition, together with a series of model instructions. It presented the double-entry bookkeeping used by merchants as a rational tool in civil-law inheritance cases, in the management of a landed property, as well as in the estates' credit operation of 1761 that Kaunitz and Ludwig had instigated and managed. There is enough evidence in the book to ascertain Ludwig's responsibility and the hand of the *Hofrechenkammer*'s chief accountant, Johann Matthias Puchberg.[32]

The readings cited above were directly connected to Ludwig's special fields of banking, accounting, and controlling. Since commercial experts were in great demand,[33] Kaunitz suggested that Ludwig secure a position for Karl in the Lower Austrian council of commerce, which was then being reorganized. Karl's was among several nominations that were made on 15 March 1762. Between April 26 and July 20, the council's president, Sinzendorf, assembled three of the nominees and his secretary to discuss the most controversial questions of the monarchy's industrial and commercial politics, such as the continued reliance on monopolies and privileges, the permanence of governmental intervention, and the principles of free competition.[34] In fact, although the council's activity was technically restricted to Lower Austria, these meetings, so-called academies, were committed to training their members to view every province as part of the monarchy as a single economic entity.

Karl's orientation now took a definite turn toward commerce. Previously, Sinzendorf had already advised him to read Forbonnais's *Elemens du commerce* (1754).[35] Indeed, Forbonnais emerges from Zinzendorf's diary as the most important author of Vienna's governing economy.[36] Kaunitz himself had a copy of the *Elemens* in his library,[37] and Sonnenfels labeled it "the commercial bible."[38] To all those who were intent on transforming the still-separate economies of the provinces into a unified national economy, or *Universalkommerz*,[39] Forbonnais supplied such important concepts as interior market and competition and gave technical advice on the business of currency and foreign exchange.[40]

Karl also studied those Spanish mercantilists who had tried to revive Spain's economy during the opening decades of Bourbon rule. In his *Théorie et pratique du commerce* (Spanish 1724/1742) Gerónimo de Uztáriz (1670–1732) had opposed monopolies and internal tariffs and had decried the impediments that the Catholic church had imposed on economic activities through holidays, fasting, the distribution of alms, and celibacy. It was in much the same vein that Bernardo de Ulloa (1690–1750) had composed his *Retablissement du commerce et de manufactures d'Espagne* (Spanish 1740). Indeed, Forbonnais himself had introduced Uztáriz to the French-speaking public of Europe in 1753, the same year that his cousin, Plumard de Dangeul, translated Ulloa's tract.[41] The Spanish authors were very popular among the economists of Catholic Europe in general, and among reform Catholics in particular.[42] It was the Jansenist abbot Ignaz Müller of the Viennese monastery of St. Dorothea who had first advised Karl to read Uztáriz when he steered the lad through a long-drawn-out conversion process.[43] Karl himself noted that Uztáriz's book was very pleasant to read. Karl thus directly encountered the Spanish sources of Catholic reform economics, as did probably most of Vienna's leading administrators, while clerics and other laymen were acquainted with the economic critique of religious traditions by the intermediation of Lodovico Antonio Muratori (1672–1750). Although Muratori was very popular in Austria, his writings were absent from Karl's reading list.[44]

But religion, particularly dissent and toleration, as topics of the economic discourse, were not confined to Catholic countries. By 1750, the question of the naturalization of foreign Protestants and of Jews had become a major political issue in Britain and caused the Anglican clergyman Joshua Tucker to expand on his economic analyses.[45] Today, Dean Tucker is considered an immediate precursor of Adam Smith. Then, he was one of the favorites of the Parisian group, and Turgot, who was fascinated by the economic implications of religion, in 1755 translated Tucker's *Reflections on the Expediency of a Law for the Naturalisation of Foreign Protestants* (1751–52).[46] It took Karl three months—from 20 October 1762 to 15 January 1763—to translate Turgot's anonymous *Questions importantes sur le commerce* into German as *Einige wichtige Fragen den Handel betreffende bey Gelegenheit der Wiedersprüche, die die letzte Bill zu Naturalisation der Ausländer in Großbritannien erlitten, aufgeworfen durch Josiah Tucker, Rectoren des S.Steffens Collegii zu Bristol und Caplan des dasigen Bischoffs, London 1755. Aus dem Französischen ins Teutsche übersetzt durch Carl Christian Heinrich Grafen und Herren von Zinzendorff und Pottendorff, Wien 1763.*[47] A conspicuous example of the international network of communication, copies of the German translation were bound and handed over to Sinzendorf and Ferdinand Count Harrach (1708–78), the president of the *Reichshofrat*, another great friend of the Zinzendorf brothers.[48] Just as Paris had served as a conduit for Tucker's ideas, it also helped to introduce David Hume with the publication of his *Discours politiques* (1752).[49] His reflections disbanded the deeply rooted doubts about the compatibility of commerce and luxury with virtue, happiness, and freedom and spread confidence in the beneficence of economic progress.

It was during these formative years in the early sixties—much earlier than historians have assumed[50]—that Karl was first exposed to the emerging physiocracy of the coterie of Madame de Pompadour's personal physician, François Quesnay (1694–1774), which now superseded the earlier ideas of Gournay. Due to his later positions in the eighties as president of the *Hofrechenkammer* and of the tax reform commission, Karl is generally considered the herald of physiocracy in the Habsburg Monarchy. But as his education and later readings and writings show, the encounter in no way conflicted with his mercantile interests in manufacture and commerce.[51] Or rather, one might define his attitude as protoliberalism. By 1761, he was captivated by Victor Riqueti Marquis Mirabeau's *L'ami des hommes* (1758). He later studied the economist Charles-Etienne Pesselier's refutation of Mirabeau's *Théorie de l'impôt* and reveled in the humanitarianism that emanated from Mirabeau's *Mémoire*, which was published in 1759 in the *Mémoires et observations recueillies par la société oeconomique de Berne*.[52] And then there were the *Journal économique* (1751–72) and the *Gazette de commerce* (1763–1783), both prominent examples of the rising trade of economic journalism, which reproduced the disputes between the proponents of physiocracy and their adversaries.[53]

Among all these publications, the proportion of Central European ones is small. Given the exceptional weight that is generally attributed to German and Austrian cameralism, this fact deserves closer attention. The most eminent representatives on the Austrian side were Johann Joachim Becher (1635–82), Wilhelm Schröder (1640–88), and Philipp Wilhelm Hörnigk (1640–1714).[54] They had established their science as special advisors to Leopold I and his ministers, who were still intent on accumulating a large state treasury. With their knowledge of *Polizei* (i.e., the good order, security, welfare, and peace of the commonwealth), the *Kameralisten* were expected to produce guiding principles of *Staatsklugheit* that were to serve as the exclusive catechism of the ruling elite. The rise of bureaucratic government, however, necessitated the transfer of these *Hof- und Kanzleiwissenschaften* to the universities. This first occurred in Prussia in 1727, and other, smaller territories of the *Reich* followed. These sciences were added to the other courses that liberally surrounded the core of law studies.[55] It is significant that economic theory remained geared to the needs and possibilities of the medium-sized and small states of the empire. As Justi's case will demonstrate, there was little interest in teaching the central-state-oriented cameralist doctrine within the Habsburg Monarchy until midcentury because there was such a great variety of regional and local economies that were largely run by the provincial estates. Moreover, as Sonnenfels's experiences show, the traditional Jesuit framework of Austrian universities also militated against such an innovation until 1762–63.[56]

However, Karl had become acquainted with Central European cameralism at the University of Jena in 1759. His teacher was Johann Joachim Darjes (1714–91), a councillor to the duke of Weimar, who taught him the branches of natural, international, and public law from 1757 to 1760. Darjes was an innovative thinker who criticized coercion and constraint in economic affairs and established the idea that circulating money was preferable to hoarding.[57] But, like other contemporary cameralists, Darjes did not transgress the boundaries of his small principality. Thus, none of the cameralists, neither traditional nor innovatory, appear in Zinzendorf's reading list.

The only exception is Justi. He had risen to prominence with his *Staatswirthschaft oder Systematische Abhandlung aller Oekonomischen und Cameral-Wissenschaften, die zur Regierung eines Landes erforderlich werden* (1755). As a former protégé of Haugwitz, he had based this book on his Austrian experience from 1750 to 1754.[58] But this treatise does not appear to have been held in high esteem by the men around Kaunitz, especially the economic administrators of Ludwig's intellectual standing and international horizon. Instead, Ludwig recommended only Justi's latest treatise on manufacturing, *Vollständige Abhandlung von denen Manufacturen und Fabriken* (1758–61). It served as a preparation for Karl's visits to the workshops of Vienna.[59] But Justi's prolific pen had more to offer. His *Vergleichungen der europäischen mit den asiatischen und andern vermeintlich barbarischen Regierungen* (1762) effected a comparison between Asiatic and European governments.[60] This political typology was fascinating since Montesquieu had introduced it to the reading public. Karl also read Justi's tract on the usefulness of the German language, which the Zinzendorfs, as translators, and like-minded men in Vienna considered most appropriate. Justi was the first to introduce this subject in Vienna when he delivered his inaugural lecture as professor of rhetorics at the *Theresianum* in 1750.[61]

Much more to the liking of Vienna's governing economists was the two-volume treatise *Institutions politiques* by Jakob Friedrich Bielfeld (1717–70). Of commercial origins, Bielfeld combined diplomatic experience in Hanover and London with a scholarly bent when he became tutor to Frederick II's brother Ferdinand.[62] Written in French and untinged by German academic pedantry, the *Institutions* gave a sensible survey of the latest Western European discussions not only on economy but also on politics, society, and religion, including Montesquieu, Melon, and Forbonnais. The proposals therein were supported by broad evidence taken from history and contemporary affairs. Suffice it to say that Ludwig advised his brother to read Bielfeld the very day after his arrival in Vienna on 8 February 1761; two years later, Bielfeld was also recommended to Archduke Leopold, who assiduously made long extracts from the French original.[63]

For members of the ruling elite, such as Zinzendorf, manuscripts were of equal importance for the shaping of a theoretical mind. Karl read most of the state papers that Ludwig composed, and he had easy access to other key economic texts that emerged from governmental activities, past and present. Karl's diary gives ample evidence that a host of manuscripts circulated among the ruling elite of Vienna.[64]

In this context, it is of far-reaching importance that Karl studied the detailed descriptions of all the Habsburg provinces that had been originally composed in 1759–60 for the express purpose of Joseph's education.[65] Such a work had never been compiled before, whether for governmental or academic purposes, because such knowledge had been considered the reserve of the provinces' estates and of the respective court ministers. Hardly an administrator—or even the emperor himself—possessed an overview.[66] Things changed with Haugwitz's administrative unification of the Bohemian and Austrian lands. The crown prince was the first to profit from such an endeavor. This is not the place to correct the wrong impression that has been given of Joseph's education.[67] But one must stress the fact that these so-called *Verfassungen* had been compiled under the supervision of Johann Christoph Bartenstein (1689–1767), who was state secretary until 1753 and afterwards vice president of Haugwitz's *Directorium*. Maria Theresa often requested his advice on economic, particularly commercial questions. It is also important to note that the *Constitutions,* as they were termed in Karl's diary, were patterned after the intendants' reports on the French provinces. Originally collected for the education of the duke of Burgundy in 1697, the reports had been published in 1727 and 1728 in Henry de Boulainvilliers's (1658–1722) version under the title *État de la France.* Since 1758 Karl had been familiar with a similar approach, called *Statistik.* Combining geographic, demographic, economic, political, and social perspectives, it had been developed at the University of Göttingen. At Jena, Gottfried Achenwall's (1718–72) *Staatsverfassungen der heutigen vornehmsten Europäischen Reiche,* first published in 1749, was Karl's textbook.[68] It is also important to note that the *Verfassungen* contain full assessments of the economic situation of each province. As translating was considered an excellent mental training, Karl had rendered the Latin text on Transylvania into German in his *Kurzgefaßte Nachricht von dem Fürstenthum Siebenbürgen und denen demselben einverleibten Stücken des Königreichs Ungarn, 1760, aus dem Lateinischen ins Deutsche übersetzt 1763 durch C.G.U.H.V.Z.V.P.*[69]

Karl thus shared with Joseph II, who was two years younger, a compact, empirical view of the provinces. It was a highly innovative *Herrschaftswissen* that was to be restricted to the top levels of decision making and administration, never to be divulged in print to commoners and foreigners. The veil of secrecy continued to surround this empirical description, especially if the Prussian enemy was to be prevented from taking advantage of it. As we shall see, the research endeavors of both Justi and Sonnenfels were crippled by this grave restriction. Of more immediate concern to Zinzendorf, and equally indicative of the government's precaution, is the case of the *Anmerkungen über die natürliche Beschaffenheit deren k.k. Erbländer und derselben bequeme Lage nicht allein zu ihrem eigenen inländischen Commercio, sondern auch den Kaufhandel in andere Reiche und Länder zu treiben* (Augsburg, 1763).[70] The book was banned in 1763, when peace already had been concluded at Hubertusburg. The *Hofkommerzienrat,* the board above the Lower Austrian council, did not consider it appropriate to reveal to the public either the economic resources and future economic opportunities or the deficiencies of the Habsburg Monarchy.[71] Zinzendorf regretted the ban. If also Sonnenfels judged the *Anmerkungen* to be "inapplicable, dreamlike designs," it was probably because he had just submitted his own *Probeschrift* to the economic authorities for approbation.[72]

In light of Zinzendorf's training and background, Justi's brief stay in Vienna (1750–54) and Sonnenfels's hasty training as an economist (1762–63) deserve a reappraisal. It was Haugwitz who summoned Justi in 1750, first to teach a reformed German language as an efficient instrument of administrative communication, then to hold private and public courses in *Kameral- und Polizeywissenschaften* at the *Theresianum.* Founded in 1746 for the training of administrators and run by a group of reform-minded Jesuits, this academy was open for such an innovation, while the university, entangled in conventional Jesuit and corporate structures, was not yet ready. As was customary, the cameralist was also employed by Haugwitz in the mining department of the *Directorium.* Justi also experimented, albeit unsuccessfully, in a silver mine of the Lower Austrian Alps.[73] In the absence of a competent academic body, the plan of the public course was approved by the councillors of Haugwitz's *Directorium.* Because Justi soon left Vienna, the plan was published in Leipzig in 1754 under the title *Auf höchsten Befehl an Seiner Römischen Kayserlichen und zu Ungarn und Böhmen Königlichen Mayestät erstattetes allerunterthänigstes Gutachten von dem vernünftigen Zusammenhange und practischen Vortrage aller oeconomischen und Cameralwissenschaften, wobey zugleich zur Probe die Grundsätze*

*der Polizeywissenschaft mit denen darzu gehörigen practischen
Arbeiten vorgetragen werden, benebst einer Antrittsrede von dem
Zusammenhange eines blühenden Zustandes der Wissenschaften mit
denjenigen Mitteln, welche einen Staat mächtig und glücklich
machen.* Rumor has it that Justi declined to convert to Catholicism.[74] It seems more likely that a combination of several circumstances induced Haugwitz, himself a convert, to withdraw his
protection, and therefore caused Justi to leave.

A major reason for Justi's departure was the inhibitions imposed upon his teaching, which had hardly begun. Justi intended to
extend it from theoretical to practical courses—as was customary at
the law faculties of Protestant universities—thus combining theory
and practice, teaching and research.[75] For this purpose, Justi requested access to registrars' offices and archives and proposed to
interview ministers and councillors. The *Directorium* and the *Hofkommerzienrat* reacted negatively.[76] They considered the available
economic data and the whole process of policy and decision making,
particularly in regard to taxation, a matter too important to be com-
municated to an outsider or to be divulged to students and to the
public. One must take into consideration that Justi was still a foreigner and a Protestant, not yet subject to the empress, and had
even served in the Prussian army (1742–44).

From abroad, Justi carried his case to the public and in 1754
published the request for access to registrars' offices and archives
that he had submitted to the Austrian authorities in 1752. When
Sonnenfels in 1765 sent a petition to Maria Theresa for the same
purpose, he cited Justi's earlier plea.[77] With no prospect of gaining
insight into the government's everyday practices, Justi left Vienna.
Thus failed Haugwitz's attempt to institutionalize the teaching of
Kameral- und Polizeywissenschaften in Vienna. The *Staatswirthschaft,* Justi's first great work of 1755, was based on his Austrian
experience. He dedicated it to Maria Theresa.

In turning to Sonnenfels, we bridge a gap of eight years, from 1754
to 1762. It was most likely in the newly founded *Staatsrat* that the
general lack of education and public communication in economic
affairs caused alarm. Borié, one of its members, approached Son-

nenfels in 1762 to publish an economic journal in German. It was to be patterned after the *Journal de commerce,* which, as we have already seen, had been published in Austrian-ruled Brussels since 1759. It was Borié who, at the same time, proposed the teaching of *Polizey- and Kameralwissenschaften* at the university.[78] Having undergone far-reaching changes in the fifties, the University of Vienna could now serve as an efficient instrument for reform.[79] The shift from the noble-dominated *Theresianum* to the more broadly based university was to meet the dire need for a distribution of such knowledge to a wider and socially lower segment of the bureaucracy, especially the new generation of provincial *Kreishauptleute.*

Again, as with the Zinzendorfs and Justi, language played an important role. Having worked at his father's side in translating Hebrew into German, Sonnenfels was enthusiastic about the German language. This enthusiasm was shared by many a secretary, civil servant, military officer, and minister, including Kaunitz and Karl Zinzendorf,[80] as well as by ordinary citizens. When Borié sought Sonnenfels out, he was the most active member of the *Deutsche Gesellschaft,* which had just been founded in Vienna for promoting German as a literary language. In addition to his language skills, Sonnenfels had acquired some aptitude in economics when briefly working as an accountant to the imperial horse guard.

Three aspects of Sonnenfels's preparation as an economist deserve our attention. First is the importance of German in teaching the new sciences dealing with economy, politics, and society. Although Latin remained the language of instruction at the university until 1782, the new sciences were propagated all over Europe in the national languages, be it in the original or in translation.[81] Therefore, foreign terms had to be translated and by explanation and adaptation made intelligible to the German public.[82] In Vienna, even the contemporary German cameralist literature and German translations from foreign languages had to be adapted, since the vocabulary did not quite fit the situations existing in the various provinces of the monarchy. Fortunately, Justi's *Staatswirthschaft* was an exception, since it had been based on his Austrian experiences. Sonnenfels was, therefore, able to adopt it as his model. On the whole, however, the teaching of *Polizey- und Kameralwissenschaften* in

German must have seemed a great challenge to a man who had originally aspired to obtain the new chair in German rhetorics at the university. Moreover, the prospect of starting an economic journal held forth the promise of yet another career, in the budding business of publishing.

In November 1762, Sonnenfels submitted a detailed financial plan for his economic journal. There are several likely explanations why the project was stillborn. Teaching and handbook writing probably consumed too much of his time and energy. He was also handicapped by a dearth of empirical contributions. Indeed, there were as yet only a few economic societies to promote such publications, and those that did exist were still in their infancy. Most of these had been established by members of various provincial diets, which still wielded enormous influence in economic matters. In 1764, the first economic society was founded by the estates of Carinthia.[83] In March 1765, Maria Theresa ordered the estates of the other provinces to follow its example. Her directive was apparently inspired by the recommendation of the council of commerce, following its commentary on the report that Karl Zinzendorf had brought back from his journey through Saxony.[84] For Sonnenfels's plans, however, there was a considerable drawback, as the estates stressed agriculture over commerce. In Vienna the preconditions for commercial societies were palpably less favorable. There was no attempt made among Vienna's merchants to found a commercial society.

Lack of information was, therefore, a severe obstacle to Sonnenfels's journalistic enterprise. His 1765 *Versuche in politischen und ökonomischen Ausarbeitungen zum Nutzen und Vergnügen* was short-lived. It consisted of only one volume, which contained three articles.[85] But Sonnenfels did, by his own efforts, considerably widen the circle of economic communication. Besides writing textbooks, he had his students defend and publish theses in German, many of them translations of foreign tracts or extracts.[86] In addition, he held an annual lecture to open his course at the university. Though this was an academic tradition, it was a novelty insofar as it was given in German and was open to the general public. Justi already had made use of this institution to introduce himself and the new sciences. Like Justi, Sonnenfels published these lectures.[87]

Besides using his linguistic skills and journalistic talents, Sonnenfels had to acquaint himself with a complicated network of theories. Keith Tribe has raised "doubts as to the solidity of Sonnenfels' [course] proposal . . . and of his grasp of the material."[88] Indeed, the span of time was very short from the day that Sonnenfels was recruited to his petition to the empress (November 1762), to his submission of a model chapter of his future course to the *Studienhofkommission,* the *Hofkammer,* and the *Hofkommerzienrat* (June 1763), to his first university lecture (November 1763), and, finally, to the publication of the first volume of his trilogy under the title *Sätze aus der Polizey, Handlungs- und Finanzwissenschaft* (1765). It contained only *Polizei.*

Under these circumstances, it is highly probable that it was not Sonnenfels himself who selected the sources but rather Borié and other men whom he consulted. From Zinzendorf's diary, we know that Sonnenfels paid a visit to Philipp Sinzendorf on 17 November 1762. We also know that his model chapter was patterned after Justi and that, when the experienced *Hofkanzlei* and *Hofkommerzienrat* councillor Karl Holler von Doblhof reviewed it, he praised the stylistic qualities and the purity of the sources—and commented that it contained nothing new.[89] This was the opinion among Vienna's governing economists. It is indicative that Zinzendorf's entry of 17 November 1762 is the only one concerning Sonnenfels among years of meticulous notes and other writings.[90] In his June 1763 petition to the empress, Sonnenfels confessed that his knowledge would become more perfect in the future as he applied his zeal to the preparation of his lectures. Indeed, his plan for the economic journal included the exorbitant annual sum of fl. 2,000–3,500 for purchasing books. In 1766, in his fourth year of teaching, he received fl. 800 for that express purpose from the empress, together with an extra fl. 800 from the *Staatsrat.*[91]

It is, therefore, evident that Sonnenfels's theoretical framework was grounded in the same discursive structures that had already been articulated by Kaunitz and the *Staatsrat,* the Zinzendorfs, Sinzendorf, and other architects of Vienna's governing economy. It is striking that most of the authors whom Karl Zinzendorf studied during his formative years in Vienna reappear in

Sonnenfels's commentaries, in his book list, and in the theses of his students. The list includes Locke, Law, Melon, Montesquieu, Uztáriz, Ulloa, Forbonnais, Dangeul, and Hume.[92] Sonnenfels's task as a teacher, therefore, was to retrieve the economic discourse on commerce, national credit, population, society, and culture that had germinated in Western Europe's nation-states and to adapt it to the conditions in the Habsburg Monarchy.

In this respect, France occupied a prominent place in this transfer, for contemporaries perceived a striking resemblance between the two states, at least as far as sheer size of territory and population and form of government were concerned.[93] By contrast, Sonnenfels dismissed the contemporary German cameralists Simon Peter Gasser, Julius Christoph von Dithmar, Johann Jakob Moser, Johann Joachim Georg Darjes, and Georg Heinrich Zincke as "superficial," at least in matters of *Polizei*.[94] Indeed, their principles were geared to the small- and medium-sized territories of the *Reich* and, as such, were not adequate to cope with the acute problems arising in Central Europe's largest town, Vienna, or in the monarchy's vast and highly diverse rural areas. Furthermore, the German cameralists operated within the cultural matrix of the Protestant churches and were not familiar with Catholicism, the predominant denomination in the Habsburg Monarchy. This is probably the reason why Sonnenfels would have preferred the *Institutions politiques* as a textbook model, for Bielfeld's horizon was not parochial but rather oriented toward France and England. In addition, as Sonnenfels stated, the German cameralists only briefly dealt with commerce, and then solely in the traditional context of foreign trade. They did not discuss how to establish an interior market, whereas Forbonnais and the Western European authors visualized economies that were geared to large territories and the colonial expanses of the Western European nation-states.[95] Therefore, with the single exception of Justi, the contemporary German cameralists are absent from Zinzendorf's training as an economist.

Thus, the Zinzendorfs and Sonnenfels built upon the same theoretical grounds. Their paths diverged, however, as soon as practical training, actual experience, journeying, and personal contacts with merchants, manufacturers, and bankers at home and abroad were concerned.[96] Sonnenfels was aware of the problem. In the plan for his economic journal of 1762, he stipulated that he required insight into the "inner manipulation" of the *Kommerzienrat* and the personal assistance of a copyist. In 1765, after two years as a university professor and the completion of his volume on *Polizei,* he submitted a request for access to the registrar's office and to the archives for the unrestricted use of official papers. He cited Justi's plea of 1752.[97] Again, Karl Holler von Doblhof formulated the negative vote, which contained practically the same arguments raised against Justi.[98] Doblhof agreed to grant Sonnenfels access, but he would not allow him to take the papers out of the office. Since Sonnenfels had no assistants, he was apparently too overloaded with work to profit immediately from the *Kommerzienrat's* offer. In 1767, however, he repeated his request before issuing the volume on commerce.[99] This time the secretaries and registrars were ordered to cooperate with him. They were directed to mark all theoretical sentences that were in accordance with already existing practices and institutions. Sonnenfels finally had the explicit consent to lay open deficiencies and to propose reforms that had originally been intended by all those in the *Staatsrat* who supported him.[100] For this purpose, Sonnenfels formulated a questionnaire to be answered by the staff of the *Kommerzienrat.* It was previously approved by the councillors in their session of 26 November 1767.[101] But on 23 July 1768, the main registrar, speaking for his colleagues, who were bogged down in routine work, declined to approve the professor's demands.[102] Indeed, the extensive subjects in Sonnenfels's questionnaire would have mustered the experience, diligence, and entire work force of a dozen secretaries and registrars for several years.

What in Vienna was conceived of as a one-man enterprise was in Western Europe the object of a broad discourse that was oral and written, private and public. In Paris and in London, the economic discourse was backed up by proper experience and practice in government and in enterprise and sustained by national languages that already had mastered all the technical vocabulary and necessary stylistic means. Considering Sonnenfels's starting position in Vienna, his achievements in economic theory and communication were respectable.

Similarly, Sonnenfels's endeavors to travel to Interior Austria and to the shore of the Adriatic came to naught already in 1765.[103] He himself had no private means to finance such an undertaking of six months' duration. Since he wanted to travel in his capacity as public professor, he needed a travel permit and the official recommendation for visits of all sorts. The *Staatsrat's* support did not overrule the negative vote of the *Hofkommerzienrat,* which was the decisive body.[104] Again it was Doblhof who expressed the profound distrust that economic administrators harbored against Sonnenfels, the academic and writer. First, he contended, there was Sonnenfels's zeal for publishing, and then the low standing of his economic experience and knowledge: "The applicant still has little comprehension of the nature and wide scope of the practical cameral and commercial sciences." How could he ever in such a short time acquaint himself with the provinces and learn about the great differences that existed among them?

Sonnenfels was never given an opportunity for practical work or investigative travel. In economic matters, he had few connections and no correspondence at home or abroad. By contrast, Zinzendorf met in Paris and in London with the prominent authors whose books he had read previously, including Forbonnais, Mirabeau, Turgot, Plumard de Dangeul, Hume, Galiani, and Helvétius. He collected information from merchants, financiers, and other economic experts all over Europe and visited the great ports and commercial centers where goods were produced and sold.[105] It has escaped historians, except Karl-Heinz Osterloh,[106] that Sonnenfels never occupied a seat on an economic board. Therefore, he could hardly ever have exerted direct influence on the shaping of economic policies in the Habsburg Monarchy.

From this investigation thus emerge two distinct stages and different modes and functions of economic theory in the Habsburg Monarchy during the decisive phase of modernization between the War of the Austrian Succession and the Seven Years' War. The subject matter was closely interrelated, if not identical. Yet the political and cultural institutions in which they operated were distinct, and their social milieus and appearance in the emerging public sphere differed significantly.

The first stage opened with Austria's survival as a European power in 1748 and the general intensification of international competition in the brief span of peace until 1756. As ambassador to France in the early fifties, Kaunitz was most zealous to receive firsthand information on the latest economic discourse that had been generated about the state debt, national credit, strength, and wealth of the rivals France and Great Britain. Insight into economic developments in Europe and overseas had long become prerequisites of foreign-policy decision making. In his Parisian retinue, we therefore find the multilingual Ludwig Count Zinzendorf, already an expert on financial and commercial matters at home and abroad. Upon his return to Vienna, Zinzendorf was to become the leading financial mind of Vienna's bureaucracy. He was active in translating and publishing the most important tracts in the German language. Together with Kaunitz, he therefore must have harbored the notion of economy as a proper field of study and subject of discourse not only in the councils of state and in the estates' assemblies but also in the wider public, as it existed in Western Europe. Ludwig Zinzendorf, a nobleman and member of the high bureaucracy, did not, however, unveil his identity as author or translator. Nor did his brother Karl, an equally hardworking man and prolific writer, leave his elevated station. A public economic discourse did not ensue; the main notions of modern economy remained restricted to Vienna's governing elite.

At the same time, in the early fifties, Haugwitz, as head of the *Directorium in publicis et cameralibus* (i.e., internal administration and taxation, public safety, social welfare, education, church matters, mining, and commerce), also attempted to promote the study of economy. He chose to implant modern economic thought at the *Theresianum,* a recently founded school for training civil servants of noble descent. For this purpose, he recruited a Protestant foreigner, Johann Heinrich Gottlob Justi, and, as was customary, Haugwitz also used his practical skills in one of the offices that dealt with primary resources. Justi's first commission, however, was to contribute actively to the reform and teaching of the German language in Vienna. This is a clear indication that it was also Haugwitz's intention to establish a forum for public economic discourse. Yet the scope was limited, and the experiment failed. The science that Justi conceived was grounded in large-scale empirical investigation and local case studies. But this kind of information was considered top secret in view of the international competition and therefore was not made available to him. As a foreign Protestant and former Prussian soldier, he did not carry the necessary badge of loyalty.

The second stage opened during the closing phase of the Seven Years' War in an atmosphere of high economic tension and exertion. The dissemination of economic knowledge to a wider public by way of German-language journals and other publications had become as imperative as the teaching of economics to the broad mass of law students who were to serve in the local and provincial administrations after the war. Joseph von Sonnenfels, who had already established a reputation as a writer and, in addition, possessed some accounting experience, was chosen for this new task. He was a beginner in the field. Notions of the latest economic discourse were transmitted to him by the high financial and commercial bureaucracy. His main task was to adapt and codify the international economic knowledge for teaching purposes, not to investigate and research. Though Catholic and an Austrian subject, Sonnenfels's enterprise experienced the same limits as Justi's experiment.

Economic thought in this decisive phase of the Habsburg Monarchy's modernization thus was channeled into two distinct institutions and milieus. One was the high aristocratic bureaucracy, Vienna's governing economy properly speaking. Keen on foreign publications, its members could investigate freely and thus possessed a vast treasure of firsthand information. They wrote prolifically, yet it was for official or personal use only and not destined for the public. The other institution was the university, which later, and on a lower level of discourse, entered the scene to educate regional and local administrators. Slowly, through Sonnenfels's efforts as author and teacher, the techniques of economic analysis and argumentation were imparted to the growing public.

It will be a fascinating task to examine how the numbers of economic publications steadily rose in the seventies and what their subject matter was, until the eighties witnessed a veritable outburst of economic tracts with the lifting of censorship.

Notes

For stylistic improvements, I am greatly indebted to Prof. Charles W. Ingrao.

1. See my "Revisions of Enlightened Absolutism: 'The Austrian Monarchy Is like No Other,'" *Historical Journal* 33 (1990): 161–62; Günter Birtsch, "Der Idealtyp des aufgeklärten Herrschers: Friedrich der Große, Karl Friedrich von Baden und Joseph II. im Vergleich," *Aufklärung* 2 (1987): 9–47; Leonard Krieger, *An Essay on the Theory of Enlightened Despotism* (Chicago, Ill.: University of Chicago Press, 1975).

2. Robert A. Kann, *Kanzel und Katheder: Studien zur österreichischen Geistesgeschichte vom Spätbarock zur Frühromantik* (Vienna: Herder, 1962), 156; Helen Liebel-Weckowicz, "Physiocrat Economics and the Economic Reforms of Maria Theresa and Joseph II" (revised typescript), n. 15; Terence Hutchison, *Before Adam Smith: The Emergence of Political Economy 1662–1776* (Oxford: Basil Blackwell, 1988), 252.

3. See Keith Tribe, *Governing Economy: The Reformation of German Economic Discourse 1750–1840* (Cambridge: Cambridge University Press, 1988), 90.

4. Louis Réau, *L'Europe française au siècle des Lumières* (1938; reprint, Paris: Edition Albin Michel, 1971); Hans Wagner, "Der Höhepunkt des französischen Kultureinflusses in Österreich in der zweiten Hälfte des 18. Jahrhunderts," *Österreich in Geschichte und Literatur* 5 (1961): 507–16.

5. Siegfried Jüttner and Jochen Schlobach, eds., *Europäische Aufklärungen-Einheit und nationale Vielfalt* (Hamburg: Felix Meiner Verlag, 1992).

6. See Kenneth E. Carpenter, *Dialogue in Political Economy: Translations from and into German in the 18th Century* (Boston: Baker Library, Graduate School of Business Administration, Harvard University, 1977); John Reeder, "Economía e illustración en España: Traducciones y traductores 1717–1800," *Moneda y crédito* 147 (1978): 47–70; Wilhelm Graeber and Geneviève Roche, *Englische Literatur des 17. und 18. Jahrhunderts in französischer Übersetzung und deutscher Weiterübersetzung: Eine kommentierte Bibliographie* (Tübingen: Max Niemeyer Verlag, 1988) concentrates on *belles lettres*.

7. Haus- Hof- und Staatsarchiv (HHStA), Vienna, Nachlaß Karl Graf Zinzendorf. Zinzendorf's diary has been used extensively for this essay. Christine Lebeau's important dissertation, submitted to the Sorbonne, Paris, in November 1991, "Ludwig et Karl von Zinzendorf, administrateurs des finances: Aristocratie et pouvoir dans la Monarchie des Habsbourg, 1748–1791," has been available to me only since June 1992. While I am in general accordance with Lebeau's findings, I do underscore subjects and themes that Lebeau overlooked or neglected. The first to

discover the diary's politicoeconomic value were Elisabeth Rainer, "Karl von Zinzendorf und das Eisenwesen in Innerösterreich," *Mitteilungen des österreichischen Staatsarchivs* 13 (1960): 258–330; and Helen Liebel-Weckowicz, "Count Karl Zinzendorf and the Liberal Revolt against Joseph II's Economic Reforms 1783–1790," in *Sozialgeschichte Heute: Festschrift für Hans Rosenberg zum 70. Geburtstag,* ed. Hans-Ulrich Wehler (Göttingen: Vandenhoeck und Ruprecht, 1974), 69–85; idem, "Physiocrat Economics and the Economic Reforms of Maria Theresa and Joseph II"; and idem, "Modernisierungsmotive in der Freihandelspolitik Maria Theresias," in *Maria Theresia und ihre Zeit,* ed. Walter Koschatzky (Salzburg: Residenz Verlag, 1980), 153–58.

8. Jeroom Vercruysse, "Journal de commerce," *Dictionnaire des journeaux, 1600–1789,* ed. Jean Sgard (Paris: Universitas, 1991), 2, no. 643.

9. P. G. M. Dickson, *Finance and Government under Maria Theresa 1740–1780* (Oxford: Clarendon Press, 1987), 2:36–79, 114–56.

10. On Montesquieu's theory of the relationship between a state's internal and external forces, see my article "Jede Macht ist relativ: Montesquieu und die Habsburger Monarchie," *Festschrift Othmar Pickl,* ed. Herwig Ebner et al. (Graz: Verlag Leykam, 1987), 307–24. On Kaunitz, see Franz A. Szabó, "Haugwitz, Kaunitz and the Problem of Absolutism" (typescript), 19 (we are looking forward to the publication of his Ph.D. thesis on Kaunitz [University of Alberta, 1976]); Harm Klueting, *Die Lehre von der Macht der Staaten: Das außenpolitische Machtproblem in der "politischen Wissenschaft" und in der praktischen Politik im 18. Jahrhundert* (Berlin: Duncker und Humblot, 1986), 167–235. For the influence of Montesquieu on Kaunitz, which Klueting ignores, see my review in *English Historical Review* 20 (1988): 134–38.

11. Carl Hock and Hermann Ignaz Bidermann, *Der österreichische Staatsrat 1760–1848* (Vienna: Wilhelm Braumüller, 1879).

12. Cited by Derek Beales, *Joseph II in the Shadow of Maria Theresa, 1741–1780* (Cambridge: Cambridge University Press, 1987), 106–9.

13. Dickson, *Finance and Government,* 2:82; Gaston von Pettenegg, ed., *Ludwig und Karl Grafen und Herren von Zinzendorf, Minister unter Maria Theresia, Josef II., Leopold II. und Franz I: Ihre Selbstbiographien* (hereafter cited as *Zinzendorf*) (Vienna: Wilhelm Braumüller, 1879), 83–89.

14. Kaunitz's early career needs a reassessment; William J. McGill, "The Political Education of Wenzel Anton von Kaunitz-Rittberg" (Ph.D. diss., Harvard University, 1961) is disappointing in this respect.

15. Georges Weulersse, *Le mouvement physiocratique en France de 1756 à 1770* (Paris: Felix Alcan, 1910), 23–42; Hutchison, *Before Adam Smith,* part 4; Antoine Murphy, "Le développement des idées économiques en France, 1750–1756," *Revue d'histoire moderne et contemporaine* 33 (1986): 521–41; Thomas E. Kaiser, "Money, Despotism, and Public Opinion in Early Eighteenth Century France: John Law and the Debate of Royal Credit," *Journal of Modern History* 63 (1991): 1–28. Christine Lebeau has drawn my attention to Simone Meysonnier, *La balance et l'horloge: La genèse de la pensée liberale en France au XVIII siècle* (Montreuil: Les Editions de la

Passion, 1989), but it was not available to me in time, as well as Jean-Claude Perrot, *Une histoire intellectuelle de l'économie politique, XVIIe–XVIIIe siècle* (Paris: Ecoles des Hautes Etudes en Sciences Sociales, 1992).

16. Pettenegg, *Zinzendorf,* 58–59. In this context, the French translations of English political tracts in the HHStA, Staatskanzlei, England Varia, Karton 11, deserve further attention.

17. As the example of the Milanese chief minister, Karl Count Firmian (1756–82) demonstrates, the imperial envoy to London, Ignaz von Wasener, was an influential source of such early Anglophilia. See Elisabeth Garms-Cornides, "Überlegungen zu einer Karriere im Dienst Maria Theresias: Karl Graf Firmian, 1716–1782," in *Österreich im Europa der Aufklärung,* ed. Richard Plaschka et al. (Vienna: Verlag der Österreichischen Akademie der Wissenschaften, 1985), 2:547–56.

18. Hilde Haider-Pregler, *Des sittlichen Bürgers Abendschule: Bildungsanspruch und Bildungsauftrag des Berufstheaters im 18. Jahrhundert* (Vienna: Jugend und Volk, 1980), 269–350. See Kaunitz's study program at Leipzig in my *Der Aufstieg des Hauses Kaunitz: Studien zur Herkunft und Bildung des Staatskanzlers Wenzel Anton Kaunitz* (Göttingen: Vandenhoeck und Ruprecht, 1975); and Lebeau, "Ludwig et Karl von Zinzendorf," 178–80.

19. Pettenegg, *Zinzendorf,* 59; HHStA, Nachlaß Zinzendorf, vol. 105, 26 September 1750. See Lebeau, "Ludwig et Karl von Zinzendorf," 308–19, and the reprint of *Essai sur l'etablissement* in appendix 8, 534–40.

20. See my article "Kommerz und Außenpolitik: Habsburgische Kommerzialreisen im Vorfeld der Diplomatischen Revolution, 1756," in *Wirtschaftsbeziehungen zwischen den Österreichischen Niederlanden und den Österreichischen Erblanden im 18. Jahrhundert,* ed. Othmar Pickl (Graz: Selbstverlag der Abteilung für Wirtschafts- und Sozialgeschichte des Instituts für Geschichte, 1991), 55–71.

21. HHStA, Staatskanzlei, Spanien Varia, Karton 55; Frankreich Varia, Karton 22, Kaunitz to Koch, Paris, 10 October 1752.

22. Österreichische Nationalbibliothek, Ms. 14.302, anonymous, carries the *ex libris* of Karl Zinzendorf.

23. Dickson, *Finance and Government,* 2:156–84; Guy Chaussinand-Nogaret, *Gens de finance au XVIIIe siècle* (Paris: Bordas, 1972), 57–66; Rohan Butler, *Choiseul: Father and Son 1719–1754* (Oxford: Clarendon Press, 1980). Lebeau, "Ludwig et Karl von Zinzendorf," 320, relies mainly on the brief remarks by Marmontel and the marquis d'Argenson.

24. Pettenegg, *Zinzendorf,* 62.

25. Cf. note 15 above for the following.

26. See Lebeau's chapter on Karl's education. A selection of Karl's diary, 1747–62, is being prepared for publication by Maria Breunlich and Marie-Louise Mader under the auspices of the *Kommission für Neuere Geschichte Österreichs,* Vienna.

27. Little is known about Sinzendorf. Cf. Constant von Wurzbach, *Biographisches Lexikon des Kaiserthums Österreich* (Vienna: Hof- und Staatsdruckerei, 1877), 35:20; Karl Pribram, *Geschichte der österreichischen Gewerbepolitik von 1740 bis 1860* (Leipzig: Duncker und Humblot, 1907), 1:32, 34, 101. In

1754 Sinzendorf served as a councillor to the *Intendenza* in Trieste and in 1760 as councillor to the Lower Austrian council of commerce, cf. *Kaiserlich und Königlicher, wie auch Erz-Herzoglicher, dero Haupt- und Residenz-Stadt Wien Staats- und Standes-Calender, auf das Gnaden-reiche Jahr Jesu Christi 1754. Mit einem Schematismo gezieret* (Wien: Leopold Johann Kaliwoda, 1754 and 1760).

28. The *Kommission für Neuere Geschichte Österreichs*, Vienna, has commissioned an international group, including myself, Christine Lebeau (Paris), Antonio Trampus (Trieste), Helmut Waclawik (Geneva), Eva Faber, Elisabeth Fattinger, and Erwin Reisinger (all Graz), with the edition of the most important journeys, and of Karl von Zinzendorf's activity as governor of Trieste, 1776 to 1782. The reports were first requested by Sinzendorf, and then by Kaunitz, and submitted to Maria Theresa and Joseph II. The diaries, the memoranda, and the documentary material are in HHStA, Nachlaß Zinzendorf. His vast correspondence and further biographical material are in the Deutschordenszentralarchiv, Vienna.

29. Diary, 9 September 1761 and 21, 22 November 1761; Nachlaß Zinzendorf, vol. 103 (vol. 104 is identical). See Pettenegg, *Zinzendorf,* 72; and Lebeau, "Ludwig et Karl von Zinzendorf," 324–29.

30. Diary, 6 November 1762; Nachlaß Zinzendorf, vol. 93, which is currently missing. See Lebeau, "Ludwig et Karl von Zinzendorf," 309.

31. Diary, 8 February 1761. This translation is listed in Carpenter, *Dialogue in Political Economy,* 29, but the translator is not identified. Nor could Lebeau, "Ludwig et Karl von Zinzendorf," 305, trace the printed version, as the manuscript in Nachlaß Zinzendorf, vol. 106, is missing.

32. Diary, 16, 20, 26, 27, 29, 30 January and 4–6, 11 February 1762; Pettenegg, *Zinzendorf,* 59; Österreichische Nationalbibliothek 48.E.13, *Einleitung zur doppelten Buchhaltung. Erster Teil. Wissenschaft der Kaufleute und Buchhalter. Aus dem Französischen des Herrn de la Porte übersetzt* (Vienna: Johann Thomas Trattner, 1762); 48.E.13, *Einleitung zur doppelten Buchhaltung. Zweyter Teil. Enthaltend eine Erbschaftsabtheilung, eine Wirtschaftsrechnung und eine Finanzoperation* (Vienna: Trattner, 1762). The *Erbschaftsabtheilung* was a German translation from the Genevan tract by Pierre Girandeau, with examples drawn from the year 1745. The *Finanzoperation der Stände,* 43, gives the amount that Ludwig Zinzendorf himself received for his translation of relevant legal texts into French, Italian, and Latin; 48.G.42, *Einleitung zu einem verbesserten Cameral-Rechnungs-Fuße auf die Verwaltung einer Herrschaft angewandt* (Vienna: Trattner, 1762). Ludwig himself had first applied the new method to the administration of his own estates; see Dickson, *Finance and Government,* 2:82–83. The *Einleitung zur doppelten Buchhaltung* was also in Kaunitz's library, Slavkov (Austerlitz), catalog no. 667.

33. Christian d'Elvert, *Zur österreichischen Verwaltungs-Geschichte unter besonderer Rücksicht auf die böhmischen Länder* (1880; reprint, Vienna: Geyer, 1970), 419. Pribram, *Gewerbepolitik,* 15; Lebeau, "Ludwig et Karl von Zinzendorf," 197.

34. Diary, 15 March 1762. Hofkammerarchiv, Niederösterreich Kommerz, rote Nummer 50. Lebeau, "Ludwig et Karl von Zinzendorf," chap. 6.

35. Diary, 21 November 1761.

36. Forbonnais has a remarkable lead in Lebeau's statistics of Karl's economic reading; see "Ludwig et Karl von Zinzendorf," appendix 11.

37. Slavkov (Austerlitz), catalog no. 629; Leyden, 1776.

38. Hofkammerarchiv, Niederösterreich Kommerz, rote Nummer 117, Sonnenfels to Studienhofkommission, n.d., probably August 1762.

39. The term, already used before 1750, was apparently derived from France; see my article "Kommerz und Außenpolitik."

40. See Louise Sommer, *Die österreichischen Kameralisten in dogmengeschichtlicher Darstellung* (1920–25; reprint, Aalen: Scientia Verlag, 1967), 354–69; Joseph J. Spengler, *Economie et population: Les doctrines françaises avant 1800: De Budé à Condorcet* (Paris: Presses Universitaires de France, 1954), 251–62; Zinzendorf diary, 11, 12 December 1761, 9 January 1762, 15, 16 January, 16, 17, 19, 22 February, 3, 8, 18, 28 March 1763, and 9, 15, 16 January 1764; Hutchison, *Before Adam Smith*, 225–27; Lebeau, "Ludwig et Karl von Zinzendorf," 213–14.

41. The translations are listed in Hildegard Kremers, "Quellenkritische Analyse des ökonomischen Denkens von Joseph von Sonnenfels: Vermittlung und Anpassung" (Ph.D. diss., University of Graz, 1983), 120–57. Forbonnais's translation of Uztáriz (Paris, 1753) was dedicated to the controller general of finances Machault; a copy is in the Österreichische Nationalbibliothek, Vienna, 37.E.26. Cf. Alexander Wirminghaus, *Zwei spanische Merkantilisten: Gerónimo de Uztáriz und Bernardo de Ulloa: Ein Beitrag zur Geschichte der Nationalökonomie* (Jena: Gustav Fischer, 1886).

42. Franco Venturi, *Settecento riformatore: Da Muratori à Beccaria* (Turin: Giulio Einaudi, 1969), 571–75.

43. Diary, 26, 28, 29 March and 1, 7 April 1762; Peter Hersche, *Der Spätjansenismus in Österreich* (Vienna: Verlag der Österreichischen Akademie der Wissenschaften, 1977), 125–34.

44. On the popularity of Muratori and the translations of his books into German (1758, 1761), see my *Staatsverwaltung und kirchliche Autorität im 18. Jahrhundert* (Vienna: Verlag für Geschichte und Politik, 1970); and Eleonore Zlabinger, *Ludovico Antonio Muratori und Österreich* (Innsbruck: Österreichische Kommissionsbuchhandlung, 1970). Muratori's *Della pubblica felicità* (Lucca/Venice, 1749) is apparently identical with the brief title *Felicité publique*, mentioned in diary, 14, 15 March 1777, a French translation having been published in Lyon in 1772.

45. George Shelton, *Dean Tucker and Eighteenth-Century Economic and Political Thought* (London: Macmillan, 1981), 70–87; Hutchison, *Before Adam Smith*, 228–47.

46. Weullersse, *Mouvement*, 28, 36; Murphy, *Développement*, 523, 535.

47. Nachlaß, vol. 124. Lebeau briefly mentions it, attributing the translation to 1766; see "Ludwig et Karl von Zinzendorf," 212n.56.

48. Diary, 30 January and 23 March 1763.

49. Diary, 20, 25, 27 March 1763. Hume's *Ecrits philosophiques* was subject to group reading in a small society. On luxury and commerce, see diary, 9, 10 July 1763. See Peter Kopf, *David Hume: Philosoph und Wirtschaftstheoretiker, 1711–1776* (Wiesbaden: Franz Steiner, 1987); and Richard Brandt and Heiner Klemme, *David Hume in Deutschland: Literatur zur Hume-Rezeption in Marburger Bibliotheken* (Marburg: Universitätsbibliothek Marburg, 1989).

50. Adam Wandruszka gives the date 1767, as does Liebel; Wandruszka, *Leopold II.* (Vienna: Verlag Herder, 1964), 1:263; Liebel-Weckowicz, "Count Karl Zinzendorf," 70.

51. Lebeau, "Ludwig et Karl von Zinzendorf," 397–400, 417–18, 429–36, and appendix 11, is very explicit on this fact.

52. Diary, 13, 16, 19 October, 19, 21 November 1761, 18 March 1762, and 10 April 1763.

53. Diary, 23 April, 14–16, 25 May, and 8 June 1763; Weulersse, *Mouvement,* 94; this is also covered in greater detail by Kremers, *Quellenkritische Analyse,* 63–70; and *Dictionnaire des journeaux,* nos. 555, 729.

54. For an introduction, see Erhard Dittrich, *Die deutschen und österreichischen Kameralisten* (Darmstadt: Wissenschaftliche Buchgesellschaft, 1974).

55. See Tribe, *Governing Economy,* 35–55.

56. See my "Der Fall Buresch oder Über die Anfänge der Polizey- und Kameralwissenschaften in Graz," in *Siedlung, Macht und Wirtschaft: Festschrift Fritz Posch,* ed. Gerhard Pferschy (Graz: Merkur, 1981), 397–410.

57. Here I follow Lebeau, "Ludwig et Karl von Zinzendorf," 169–72.

58. For valuable material on Justi's position in Vienna, see Haider-Pregler, *Abendschule,* 466–68. Justi deserves a fundamental reappraisal, especially his activities in Vienna. For the foreign-policy implications of his writings, see Klueting, *Die Lehre,* 84–114.

59. Diary, 21 February, 10, 14, 15 March, 7 December 1762, and 28, 29 March 1763.

60. Diary, 21 February and 3, 10, 14, 15 March 1762.

61. Diary, 12 December 1762. The full title of his lecture is *Abhandlung von dem Zusammenhange der Vollkommenheit der Sprache mit dem blühenden Zustand der Wissenschaften wobey zugleich zu Anhörung einer Rede von dem unzertrennlichen Zusammenhang eines blühenden Zustandes der Wissenschaften mit denjenigen Mitteln, welche einen Staat mächtig und glücklich machen, als mit welcher auf dem (16ten) des Winter-Monaths (nach dem 4.) in dem k.k. Collegio Theresiano das öffentliche Lehramt der Teutschen Beredsamkeit angetreten wird . . .* (Vienna: Trattner, 1750), Nationalbibliothek Wien, 134.837-B.

62. Klueting, *Die Lehre,* 114–37 stresses foreign-policy aspects of Bielfeld's activities.

63. *Institutions politiques,* 2 vols. (The Hague, 1760). This edition, located in the Universitätsbibliothek Wien, was originally acquired by the Jesuit College in 1762,

as the inscription on the first page demonstrates. The new, four-volume Parisian edition of 1761 carries the subtitle *Ouvrages, où l'on traite de la Société Civile, des Loix, de la Police, des Finances, du Commerce, des Forces d'un Etat, et en général de tout ce qui a rapport au gouvernement.* Leopold's extracts in Nationalbibliothek S.n.12.200 bear the title "Remarques et commentaires sur les institutions politiques de Monsieur le Baron de Bielfeld," 483 pp., with the inscription "Anno 1765" on the cover. Bielfeld is briefly mentioned by Wandruszka, *Leopold,* 1:89. Wandruszka has no knowledge of the *Remarques* and doubts whether Leopold read the *Institutions,* finding it "wahrscheinlicher" that he read Bielfeld's *Lettres familières* (1763). It is indicative of Bielfeld's reputation among the courtiers that Zinzendorf mentions the fact that Leopold read Bielfeld (diary, 6 January 1764). Wandruszka's citation is based on the Zinzendorf diary.

64. A full assessment of these official papers cannot be given here, only indications as to selected papers, such as a memorandum by Ludwig on the French alliance in diary, 10 October 1761; the papers of *Hofkammer* president Johann Seyfried Herberstein on commerce in diary, 14, 18–20 September 1762 and 4 April 1763; and a memorandum by Philipp Sinzendorf for the Hungarian Chancellery in diary, 12, 27 April 1763.

65. Diary, 24, 28 February, 1, 2, 7, 8, 11, 12, 14, 17, 18, 23, 28, 29 March, 2, 4, 8, 15–17, 27, 28, 30 April, and 2–4, 9 May 1763. See also Anna Hedwig Benna, "Der Kronprinzenunterricht Josefs II. in der inneren Verfassung der Erbländer und die Wiener Zentralstellen," *Mitteilungen des Österreichischen Staatsarchivs* 20 (1967): 115–79.

66. This is the general tenor of Maria Theresa's so-called *Politisches Testament* of 1750–51, edited by Friedrich Walter in *Maria Theresia: Briefe und Aktenstücke in Auswahl* (Darmstadt: Wissenschaftliche Buchgesellschaft, 1968), 63–97.

67. See Derek Beales, *Joseph II,* 29–68, and my critique in *Historical Journal* 33 (1990): 155–67.

68. Lebeau, "Ludwig et Karl von Zinzendorf," 163.

69. Nachlaß Zinzendorf, vol. 156, 991–1064. That Karl studied the *Verfassungen* assiduously and translated *Transylvania* entirely escaped Lebeau's attention, though she briefly (313n.36) mentions the description of Lower and Upper Austria in vol. 156 of the Nachlaß.

70. The *Anmerkungen* is published anonymously; the author is C. F. Meixner, a person so far not identified.

71. Hofkammerarchiv, Niederösterreich Kommerz, rote Nummer 117, Vortrag Andler-Witten, 1, 7 March 1763.

72. Diary, 1, 2 May 1763 concerns a discussion of Meixner's book with Alexander Freiherr von Schell, a colleague of Karl's at the Lower Austrian Commercial Council; Allgemeines Verwaltungsarchiv, Vienna, Studienhofkommission, Faszikel 10, Kameralwissenschaft, fol. 70; Hofkammerarchiv, Niederösterreich Kommerz, rote Nummer 117, Sonnenfels to Studienhofkommission, n.d.; Meixner's tract escaped Lebeau's attention.

73. Hofkammerarchiv, Bergwerks- und Münzkollegium; so far only the indices of 1751 and 1752 have been consulted.

74. Dittrich, *Die deutschen und österreichischen Kameralisten,* 104.

75. See my chapter on the University of Leipzig in *Der Aufstieg des Hauses Kaunitz.*

76. Hofkammerarchiv, Niederösterreich Kommerz, rote Nummer 117, fols. 92–93, extract of Justi's statement of 15 October 1752, published in Leipzig in 1754; see his *Gutachten von dem vernünftigen Zusammenhange,* 40–43.

77. Hofkammerarchiv, Niederösterreich Kommerz, rote Nummer 117, fols. 94–97, Andler-Witten to Maria Theresa, Vortrag, 21 May 1765. Andler's *Vortrag* is identical with the expert opinion of Karl Holler von Doblhof of 21 May 1765.

78. The details in Hofkammerarchiv, Niederösterreich, Kommerz, rote Nummer 117; see the recent evaluations by Karl-Heinz Osterloh, *Joseph von Sonnenfels und die österreichische Reformbewegung im Zeitalter des aufgeklärten Absolutismus* (Lübeck: Matthiesen Verlag, 1970), 31–35; and Kremers, *Quellenkritische Analyse.*

79. See my *Staatsverwaltung und kirchliche Autorität.*

80. See diary, 1761; and Haider-Pregler, *Abendschule,* chap. 4.

81. See note 6 above.

82. I am grateful to Hildegard Kremers for having given me insight into unpublished preliminary material concerning aspects of Sonnenfels's political language. In this context, further investigation is warranted; see Eric A. Blackall, *Die Entwicklung des Deutschen zur Literatursprache 1700–1775* (Stuttgart: J. B. Metzlersche Verlagsbuchhandlung, 1966); and Dieter Kimpel, ed., *Mehrsprachigkeit in der deutschen Aufklärung* (Hamburg: Felix Meiner Verlag, 1985).

83. Karl Dinklage, "Gründung und Aufbau der theresianischen Ackerbaugesellschaften," *Zeitschrift für Agrargeschichte und Agrarsoziologie* 13 (1965): 200–211.

84. Hofkammerarchiv, Niederösterreich Kommerz, rote Nummer 116, Kommerzialreisen: fols. 247–52, Referat Karl Holler von Doblhof, 3 March 1765; and Andler-Witten to Maria Theresa in her *Resolution* on "Commercial Betrachtungen über die Relation des Herrn Grafen Carl von Zinzendorf das Manufacturwesen in Sachsen betr.," n.d. (date of this *Vortrag* given in Hofkammerarchiv Ms. 290, fol. 105v, as 8 January/5 March 1765).

85. Osterloh, *Joseph von Sonnenfels,* 33.

86. Sonnenfels's theses and translations are for the first time discussed by Fritz Redlich and Kenneth E. Carpenter, "Some Eighteenth-Century Bibliographical Oddities Viewed in the Light of Austrian Economic and Educational Policy," in *Wirtschaftskräfte und Wirtschaftswege: Festschrift für Hermann Kellenbenz,* vol. 2: *Wirtschaftskräfte in der europäischen Expansion,* ed. Jürgen Schneider (Stuttgart: Klett-Cotta, 1978), 657–68.

87. A full list of Sonnenfels's lectures has not yet been established.

88. Tribe, *Governing Economy,* 79.

89. Hofkammerarchiv, Niederösterreich Kommerz, rote Nummer 117, fols. 86–87v. See Kaunitz and Blümegen's statement of 1767 in the *Staatsrat,* directed against Cardinal Migazzi, that Sonnenfels only taught "what famous contemporaries and predecessors taught," in Hock and Bidermann, *Staatsrat,* 61.

90. According to Lebeau, "Ludwig et Karl von Zinzendorf," 318, Karl mentions Sonnenfels in his diary on 24 August 1789.

91. Hock and Bidermann, *Staatsrat,* 60.

92. Ibid.; and Kremers, *Quellenkritische Analyse.*

93. See Lebeau, "Ludwig et Karl von Zinzendorf," 187.

94. Hofkammerarchiv, Niederösterreich Kommerz, rote Nummer 117, Sonnenfels petition to Maria Theresa, n.d., fol. 21v, probably mid-June 1763.

95. See Horst Kraemer, *Der deutsche Kleinstaat des 17. Jahrhunderts im Spiegel von Seckendorffs "Teutschem Fürstenstaat"* (1656; reprint, Darmstadt: Wissenschaftliche Buchgesellschaft, 1974).

96. See diary entries of 11, 13, 15, 17, 23 September 1763, which concern visits to manufacturers in Vienna. For the contacts that Zinzendorf established with merchants and bankers in Paris and Spain, see my article "Spanien im Horizont der österreichischen Aufklärung: Zinzendorfs Kommerzialreise im Jahre 1767," in *Geschichtsforschung in Graz,* ed. Herwig Ebner (Graz: Selbstverlag des Instituts für Geschichte, 1990), 115–26.

97. Hofkammerarchiv, Niederösterreich, Kommerz, rote Nummer 117, fols. 91–97. In the light of the Zinzendorf papers, Osterloh's interpretation of Sonnenfels's plea seems deficient (*Joseph von Sonnenfels,* 132–34).

98. Hofkammerarchiv, Niederösterreich, Kommerz, rote Nummer 117, fols. 98–102v, Doblhof's vote of 21 May 1765, which is identical with Andler's *Vortrag* to Maria Theresa of the same day, submitted 1 June 1765.

99. Ibid., fol. 107, extract of the council's protocol of 26 November 1767.

100. Hock and Bidermann, *Staatsrat,* 62.

101. See Osterloh, *Joseph von Sonnenfels,* 133n.57, for an example of the questionnaire.

102. Hofkammerarchiv, Niederösterreich Kommerz, rote Nummer 117, fols. 110–13, the official *Anzeige* by Franz Krick, registrar and taxator, i.e., stamp official.

103. Hofkammerarchiv, Niederösterreich Kommerz, rote Nummer 116, extract of the council's protocol of 5 March 1763, Hofkammer president Johann Seyfried Herberstein to Kommerzienrat, 14 May 1765, and Doblhof's vote. Sonnenfels's petition is not extant, fols. 75–77. Cf. Osterloh, *Joseph von Sonnenfels,* 129–30.

104. Ibid.; and Hock and Bidermann, *Staatsrat,* 60.

105. See note 95 above and my "Spanien im Horizont." For an enumeration of some of Zinzendorf's interlocutors, see Erzsebet Magda Langfelder, *Les séjours en Suisse, en France et en Belgique du comte de Zinzendorf d'après son Journal, 1764–1770* (Szeged, 1933).

106. Osterloh, *Joseph von Sonnenfels,* 195. Cf. Helmut Reinalter, ed., *Joseph von Sonnenfels* (Vienna: Akademie der Wissenschaften, 1988); and Kann, *Kanzel und Katheder.*

Austria and European Economic Development

What Has Been Learned?

John Komlos

In this essay, I would like to emphasize two distinct, but related ideas: first, that quite a few historical insights can be generated by viewing the Habsburg economy as an integral part of the European economic system. By this I mean that the Austrian economy shared much in common with Europe from as early as the Middle Ages onward. This idea leads directly to my second point: since Austria was indeed a part of Europe in more than just a geographic sense, much can be learned about Continental economic development by studying Habsburg economic history. I would like to demonstrate the latter point on the basis of what I have learned about the Industrial Revolution of the eighteenth century from studying Austrian history and formulating what I call the "Austrian model" of the Industrial Revolution.[1] I would first like to outline how I came, in the course of my research, to emphasize Austria's integration into the European economic system.

When I started out as a graduate student, the Habsburg economy was invariably thought of as essentially "backward" and "different."[2] Scholars were preoccupied with attempting to ascertain when and *whether* Austria experienced a take-off into sustained growth.[3] Almost every upswing of the business cycle had its advocates for designation as the take-off point. Alexander Gerschenkron, one of the most prominent thinkers on this issue in the 1960s, put it this way: "Industrialization either comes as a great spurt or does not come at all."[4] This view became his gospel to such an extent that he found it implausible to entertain the notion of an economy growing healthily without such a great spurt. "Leisurely industrialization," Richard Rudolph's description of Austria's path to modernity,[5] was not the way Gerschenkron thought about this matter. Thus Gerschenkron wrote in 1977 that "it is precisely Austria's failure to have had a great spurt of industrialization [and] the sluggishness of its growth . . . that make me believe that, in the last years of the nineteenth century, Austria was ready for a great spurt of industrialization."[6] These lines from the doyen of economic historians of the time appear to me to be a rather curious piece of historical logic. Gerschenkron's assertion amounts to the following propositions: (1) all (European) states can be expected to have a great spurt sooner or later; (2) Austria did not yet have such a spurt by 1900; and consequently, (3) it should have had one soon thereafter. I do not think that such an argument is defensible; I am alluding to it only to show just how confusing the situation was for a graduate student writing on the subject in the middle of the 1970s. At the same time, this very confusion indicates, I think, the shortcomings of the ways in which many historians then conceptualized the process of industrialization in general.

In my dissertation, I therefore set myself the task of understanding better the processes of growth in the Habsburg Monarchy.[7] The picture that presented itself was rather different both from the accepted view of the monarchy and from the paradigms that up to then had characterized thinking on European industrialization in general. It appeared to me that in the nineteenth century, growth was a regular feature of Austrian economic experience until the outbreak of World War I. Though cyclical, its growth was quite respectable in the European context. The cycles of Austrian economic growth corresponded quite well to the cycles of the other economies of Europe. There seemed to be an integrated European economy, and Austria was an essential part of it. Whatever forces were driving the other economies of Europe—be they weather conditions, demographic and trade cycles, political events, innovative activity, financial crises, or whatever—they had analogous effects on the Austrian economy.

When the West was in the midst of the post-Napoleonic depression, for instance, the Austrian economy stagnated also. When the

European economies began to recover in the 1820s, the Austrian economy did so as well. The Austrian ferrous metals and woolen-goods sectors registered a respectable performance of 3- or 4-percent growth per annum in the late 1820s. Its cotton sector grew at a rate of 12 percent per annum in the 1830s and 1840s, not a very different performance from that reached by its American or even Russian counterparts.[8] In America, too, "the period from the mid-1820s to the late 1830s was an ebullient time."[9] Thus, the rhythm of Austria's development was to a large extent independent of local circumstances: the nature of its business cycles was determined primarily by external factors. It was clearly marching to the same drummer as the rest of the Western world.

I thus realized at about the same time as several other scholars that one needed to appreciate the evolutionary nature of growth and continuity much more than had been the case up to then and to cease seeking the beginning of economic or industrial growth in the nineteenth century.[10] In addition, it became clear to me that the Habsburg economy should be seen in a European context. It performed about as well as most other European economies, and it grew in the same cyclical pattern as most of them. To be sure, Austria did not catch up to the West completely until the second half of the twentieth century, and hence it is not incorrect to consider it as having been relatively backward. Yet, if, instead of emphasizing the relative backwardness of the Habsburg lands, one explores the implications of their integration into the larger European market, I think much can be learned.

In the mid to late 1970s, however, this was as far as I was able to go conceptually. I still subscribed to the premise that developments preceding the nineteenth century surely had to have been very different in Austria from what went on in the core economies of Europe. The eighteenth century had to have been different. Great Britain had its Industrial Revolution, and whatever happened on the Continent was less significant and should be seen in a different light.[11]

Two strands of research undermined this paradigm and complemented my findings with regard to the nineteenth century. One was associated with historians who were examining growth from a long-term perspective. Eric Jones, Rondo Cameron, and

Douglass North pointed to the remarkable consistency of growth in Europe ever since the Middle Ages and perhaps even since Roman times.[12] It was cyclical to be sure, and it was interrupted frequently by crises of various duration and intensity, but the European economy became ever more sophisticated over time. Physical capital was gradually being accumulated, and human capital became an ever more powerful instrument in the service of production. Technology evolved and became more complex. Population density and urbanization increased. The standard of living improved for at least some segments of the society. Institutions became more effective in accomplishing their aims. Governments improved their financial position and their ability to project power. In other words, during the millennium before 1800, Europe as a whole built, little by little, the foundations of a modern economy, and Austria, as part of Europe, did not lag far behind.

Ideas traveled with relative ease. The scientific revolution, the Enlightenment, and rationalism found their way to Central Europe as well, and this common culture enhanced communication. Climatic patterns were broadly similar throughout the Continent. The epidemiological environment became unified. With the movement of people, infections were spread about the Continent, which enabled immunities to be built up and resistance to diseases to accumulate until subsequent epidemics became less virulent. All these growth impulses meant that the salient features of Austrian development correlated highly with those of the rest of the Continent. In broad terms, this meant an expansion until the fourteenth century, followed by a collapse in the wake of the Black Plague. The subsequent stagnation, lasting almost two centuries, was overtaken by another upswing in economic activity in the sixteenth century. This upswing also came up against Malthusian ceilings and dissipated itself by the seventeenth century, only to start anew in the eighteenth. Thus the synchronous cycles between Austria and Europe that I found for the nineteenth century had their analogue during the previous millennium.

In the main, the pattern of growth was what Eric Jones calls "growth recurring": cycles of growth followed by reversals and stagnation.[13] However, the trend was generally upward. Each new cycle of economic activity brought the Europeans to a higher level of achievement, to a higher level of per capita income. This pattern was incorporated into the Austrian model of the Industrial Revolution.

I alluded above to two strands of research that merged to provide the basis of the Austrian model: the realization of the shared European experience of long-term development and an independent research program devoted to exploring the quantitative aspects of the Industrial Revolution in England. Historians such as Nick Crafts, Knick Harley, and Jeffrey Williamson asked fundamental questions about the consensus view that had reigned in the 1960s and 1970s.[14] This view had rested on five propositions: (1) that the Industrial Revolution was practically synonymous with technological change, particularly in the textile sector insofar as it was closely associated with the mechanization of spinning and weaving cotton; (2) that the Industrial Revolution was a dramatic break with past developments; and (3) that it meant a change in industrial organization, i.e., firms switched to factory production. From these three propositions it followed (4) that England had been the first industrial nation and (5) that the Continental countries essentially followed in Britain's footsteps.

These tenets were debated and scrutinized in the 1980s and were found wanting. The upshot was that the consensus view was replaced by four counterarguments: (1) that the Industrial Revolution was not revolutionary and proceeded more slowly than had been thought; (2) that technological change was not as broad as hitherto represented: as late as 1841, the "modern sector employed fewer than 20 percent of all workers" in England;[15] (3) that the eighteenth-century expansion was a continuation of a millennium of intermittent growth rather than a sudden break with prior developments; and (4) that capital formation did not increase discontinuously during the eighteenth century.

With this reorientation of our thinking about the English experience in the eighteenth century, it became possible to conceptualize the Austrian, and indeed Continental developments in general, as an integral part of the cyclical upswing of the second half of that century. After all, growth in the eighteenth century was hardly a British monopoly.[16] Although the industrial development of Continental

Europe was previously put into a different category from that of Britain, there were many similarities, and one can argue that it is just as valid to accentuate the similarities as the differences. In fact, in many ways the similarities were more salient. The mainsprings of the eighteenth-century expansion were broadly similar on the Continent. They were based on centuries of accumulation of both human and physical capital. The spread of a scientific (problem-solving) mentality also played a role.[17] Moreover, broadly speaking, the expansions all started at about the same time throughout.[18] The proximate causes were also similar, insofar as practically all economies of Europe experienced a very rapid demographic expansion conducive to urbanization and to sectoral shifts. As in prior centuries, the increases in population densities tended to bring with them the positive effects of rise in demand and decrease in costs of doing business. These were, broadly speaking, widespread European phenomena, and it seems to me valid to point to these parallel developments.

As far as East Central Europe was concerned, the economic expansion was both rapid and broad by the standards of the time. In Austria a number of factories were founded in the early eighteenth century or before: Horní Litvínov (1715), Schwechat, Šaštin (Sassin), Pottendorf, Osek (Ossegg), and in Linz, to mention just a few of the better-known ones. By the 1790s, 126 factories operated in Lower Austria and another 91 in Bohemia, requiring immense amounts of capital.[19] Many of these firms produced for a mass market. The needle factory in Nadelburg, Lower Austria, produced 30 million needles per annum, and there were thirteen other needle factories in Lower Austria.[20]

As far as we can ascertain, aggregate growth was also impressive. For instance, both the industrial labor force and industrial product in Bohemia-Moravia expanded at a rate of 4 percent per annum in the late eighteenth century. Iron production grew at a rate of 2 percent, and textile production at a rate of 3.7 percent per annum. This was the beginning of a new cycle of economic development that lasted, with minor interruptions, in Austria and elsewhere in Europe until World War I. In contrast to Austria, the expansion of the British industrial labor force in the eighteenth century was slower, just 1.4 percent per annum.

Hence, regardless of the indicators one chooses, one finds a multitude of fundamental structural changes in the Habsburg Monarchy of the eighteenth century, fostered by the government's efforts to introduce wide-ranging institutional reform. The thoroughgoing impulse toward modernization did not elude contemporaries. For example, after studying the foreign trade statistics of the monarchy in 1784, Count Zinzendorf, president of the *Hofrechenkammer*, remarked: "How can one still believe that there are no industries in the German hereditary provinces?"[21] Zinzendorf was hardly alone in noticing the momentous changes.[22] The feeling was widespread in Europe that progress was being made in increasing the well-being of the population through the enlightened financial policies of the eighteenth-century monarchs. In previous centuries, "so little consideration was given to the well-being of the subjects and the increase in their sustenance, that our times should be seen as happy indeed."[23]

The eighteenth-century developments were unique insofar as, in stark contrast to earlier episodes of expansion, the European economies were no longer constrained by Malthusian forces. The economies were sufficiently advanced to overcome the basic problem of food procurement. The threat of a subsistence crisis was still evident, but the food shortages that did occur were not as severe as earlier ones, and they could be alleviated. It is possible then to define the Industrial Revolution as *the* eighteenth-century upswing in economic activity or as the escape from the Malthusian demographic regime; and if one thinks of the Industrial Revolution in these terms, then it is no longer difficult to think of it as a widespread European experience. As in the Middle Ages and again in the sixteenth century, economic expansion in the eighteenth and nineteenth centuries was a pan-European phenomenon. Of course, there were great differences in the level of development. Austria was much less urbanized, and its economy was less productive than that of Western Europe. There were, however, as many similarities as well: for example, the rhythm of growth and the fact that textile production played a prominent role in both Austria and in Great Britain during the early phases of the Industrial Revolution.

In essence, there were four ways in which the eighteenth-century expansion was experienced by the European societies: first, in Central Europe, institutional change was an important aspect of the increased productivity of the economy. The monarchs and their cameralist advisors attempted to remove the legal obstacles restraining economic development. Responding to the demographic pressure and increasing misery brought about by a growing population, Maria Theresa and Joseph II worked persistently to overcome the power of the guilds, to limit the privileges of aristocrats, and to foster growth by reforming backward-looking institutions. A number of agricultural reforms during their reigns granted greater mobility to the peasants, thereby fostering their entry into the industrial labor force as a means of defending their standard of living. The government also attempted to raise the peasantry's well-being by redistributing income in its favor at the expense of landlords.

The second type of experience was provided by the British. In contrast to the Austrian "interventionist" approach, the British experience might be considered the autonomous market-expansion model. In Britain, where the private sector was sufficiently advanced to do without active government intervention, autonomous market processes played a more prominent role, and government intervention a less important one, than in Austria.

The third experience, that of France, was less fortunate than either Austria's or England's. Since the French economy was not as well developed as the English, market expansion there could not maintain the living standards of the population. At the same time, government efforts to counter the impoverishment brought about by population pressure were less successful than in Austria. The government vacillated, and when it did intervene, it did so more in keeping with physiocratic principles, which were less appropriate for counteracting the destabilizing effects of population growth than the mercantilistic ones applied in Austria. The crisis in France ultimately could not be avoided, and a political upheaval took place that interrupted economic expansion for a quarter of a century.

The fourth example of the ways in which European economies experienced the Industrial Revolution is provided by the Irish experience. There the British government followed a laissez-faire policy, but the market was not sufficiently developed to grow without government support. Its experience with the Industrial Revolution was among the least successful in Europe.

I have argued that much can be learned from studying the development of the Habsburg economy because much of that history was an integral part of the common European experience. I have also argued that we think very differently about industrialization in general, and about Habsburg economic performance in particular, than we did a generation ago. That is not to say that the ideas I have attempted to develop here have all been assimilated into the mainstream of historical scholarship. There would be no point in discussing them if that were the case. Many of the issues I touch upon are still being discussed, and no doubt refinement and healthy controversy will continue.[24]

Notes

1. John Komlos, *Nutrition and Economic Development in the Eighteenth-Century Habsburg Monarchy: An Anthropometric History* (Princeton, N.J.: Princeton University Press, 1989; German edition, St. Katherina: Scripta Mercaturae, forthcoming).

2. William Otto Henderson, *Britain and Industrial Europe* (Leicester: Leicester University Press, 1972).

3. See, for example, Eduard März, *Österreichische Industrie- und Bankpolitik in der Zeit Franz Joseph I. am Beispiel der k.k. priv. österreichischen Credit-Anstalt für Handel und Gewerbe* (Vienna: Europa, 1968); Nachum Gross, "Economic Growth and the Consumption of Coal in Austria and Hungary, 1831–1913," *Journal of Economic History* 31 (1971): 898–916; and Roman Sandgruber, "Österreich," in *Handbuch der europäischen Wirtschafts- und Sozialgeschichte*, ed. Wolfram Fischer et al. (Stuttgart: Klett-Kotta, 1993), 4:619–87.

4. Alexander Gerschenkron, *Economic Backwardness in Historical Perspective: A Book of Essays* (Cambridge, Mass.: Harvard University Press, 1962), 362.

5. Richard Rudolph, *Banking and Industrialization in Austria-Hungary: The Role of Banks in the Industrialization of the Czech Crownlands, 1873–1914* (Cambridge: Cambridge University Press, 1976).

6. Alexander Gerschenkron, *The Economic Spurt That Failed* (Princeton, N.J.: Princeton University Press, 1977), 54.

7. John Komlos, *The Habsburg Monarchy as a Customs Union: Economic Development in Austria-Hungary in the Nineteenth Century* (Princeton, N.J.: Princeton University Press, 1983; German edition, Vienna: Österreichischer Bundesverlag, 1986).

8. Robert Zevin, "The Growth of Cotton Textile Production after 1815," in *The Reinterpretation of American Economic History*, ed. Robert Fogel and Stanley Engerman (New York: Harper and Row, 1971), 122–47; John Komlos, "Economic

Growth under the Romanovs and Bolsheviks," *Rivista di storia economia,* n.s., 2 (1985): 194–201.

9.   Stanley L. Engerman and Robert E. Gallman, "U.S. Economic Growth, 1783–1960," in *Research in Economic History,* ed. Paul Uselding (Greenwich, Conn.: JAI Press, 1982), 8:1–46.

10.   Richard Rudolph, "The Pattern of Austrian Industrial Growth from the Eighteenth to the Early Twentieth Century," *Austrian History Yearbook* 11 (1975): 3–43; David Good, *The Economic Rise of the Habsburg Empire, 1750–1914* (Berkeley and Los Angeles: University of California Press, 1984).

11.   Phyllis Deane, *The First Industrial Revolution* (Cambridge: Cambridge University Press, 1969); Peter Mathias, *The First Industrial Nation* (New York: Charles Scribner's Sons, 1969).

12.   Eric L. Jones, *The European Miracle: Environments, Economies, and Geopolitics in the History of Europe and Asia* (Cambridge: Cambridge University Press, 1981); Rondo Cameron, "A New View of European Industrialization," *Economic History Review* 2d s., 38 (1985): 1–23; Douglass North, *Structure and Change in Economic History* (New York: Norton, 1981).

13.   Eric L. Jones, *Growth Recurring: Economic Change in World History* (Oxford: Clarendon Press, 1988).

14.   N. F. R. Crafts, *British Economic Growth during the Industrial Revolution* (Oxford: Clarendon Press, 1985); Knick Harley, "British Industrialization before 1841: Evidence of Slower Growth during the Industrial Revolution," *Journal of Economic History* 42 (1982): 267–89; Jeffrey Williamson, "Why Was British Growth So Slow during the Industrial Revolution?" *Journal of Economic History* 44 (1984): 687–712.

15.   Jones, *Growth Recurring,* 14.

16.   François Crouzet, "England and France in the Eighteenth Century: A Comparative Analysis of Two Economic Growths," in *The Causes of the Industrial Revolution in England,* ed. R. Max Hartwell (London: Methuen, 1964), 154; Richard Roehl, "French Industrialization: A Reconsideration," *Explorations in Economic History* 12 (1976): 230–81.

17.   To be sure, major inventions occurred in Western Europe, but the spirit of improvement which brought them about was far more widely distributed. For example, an atmospheric steam engine operated in the mines at Schemnitz (Banská Štiavnica) in northern Hungary in 1738, and new machines were being invented there to improve the lifting of water from the shafts. See Wilhelm Franz Exner, *Beiträge und Erfindungen Österreichs von der Mitte des XVIII. Jahrhunderts bis zur Gegenwart* (Vienna: Wilhelm Braumüller, 1873), 2:4.

18.   This was the case even in Russia; see Arcadius Kahan, *The Plow, the Hammer, and the Knout: An Economic History of Eighteenth-Century Russia* (Chicago, Ill.: University of Chicago Press, 1985).

19.   Gustav Otruba et al., eds., *Österreichische Fabriksprivilegien vom 16. bis ins 18. Jahrhundert* (Vienna: Böhlaus, 1981), 33. The capital stock of the wool-tex-

tile factory in Linz reached one million florin at a time when the daily wage of a female yarn spinner was about 0.08 florin. See Viktor Hofman, "Beiträge zur neueren österreichischen Wirtschaftsgeschichte, I." *Archiv für österreichische Geschichte* 108, no. 2 (1920): 738.

20. Johann Andreas Demian, *Statistik des oesterreichischen Kaiserthums* (Leipzig: im Schwickertschen Verlag, 1820), 124.

21. "Wie darf man nunmehr noch behaupten, in den deutschen Erblanden sey keine Industrie?" Vortrag of Grafen von Zinzendorf to Joseph II, RA Chotek, signatur L5i (carton 77), Státni Oblastni Archiv, Prague, Czechoslovakia. He concluded "daß in diesen deutschen Erblanden wirklich sehr viel Industrie sey, ohngeachtet man so oft das gegentheil behaupten höret."

22. "Die Fabriken und Manufakturen haben in der österreichischen Monarchie große Fortschritte gemacht, und ob sie gleich erst eine Blüthe neuerer Zeiten sind, so giebt es doch keinen Zweig der veredelten Industrie mehr, der nicht jetzt auf österreichischem Boden kultivirt würde. Dieses mächtige Emporsteigen seiner Fabrikengewerbe verdankt Oesterreich größtentheils Joseph II., der den kunstfleiß seiner Völker weckte, ihn durch thätige Aushülfe unterstützte, Privilegien und Freiheiten ertheilte, fremde Arbeiter ins Land zog, und fähige Subjekte ausländische Fabrikplätze bereisen ließ. Im Jahr 1786 verbot er die Einfuhr fremder Manufaktur- und Fabrikwaaren [*sic*]. Der Gewerbfleiß nahm nun mit raschen Schritten zu, eine Fabrik folgte der andern, und man sah die Vornehmsten des Landes, entweder selbst als Unternehmer auftreten oder die Anlagen Anderer durch Vorschüsse zu unterstützen" (Demian, *Statistik des oesterreichischen Kaiserthums,* 85).

23. "Wenn ich die Geschichte der alten Zeiten durchlaufe, und ihre Finanzgrundsätze und Einrichtungen aufmerksam betrachte; so findet man darinnen so wenig Uebereinstimmendes mit dem Endzweck aller bürgerlichen Verfassungen, der gemeinschaftlichen Glückseligkeit, so wenig Betracht vor die Wohlfahrt der Unterthanen und das Aufnehmen des Nahrungsstandes, daß man unsre Zeiten allerdings glücklich preisen muß, in welchen man wenigstens anfängt, die Finanzgrundsätze mit denen wesentlichen Endzwecken der bürgerlichen Verfassungen in ein besseres Verhältniß zu setzen; und wenn man nach diesem Anfange sich unterstehet, einen Blick in die Zukunft zu thun; so werden die künftigen Zeiten nach der Maaße immer glücklicher werden, als das Wachsthum der gesunden Vernunft in denen Regierungen die billige Schaam erregen wird" (Johann Heinrich Gottlob von Justi, *Gesammelte politische und Finanzschriften über wichtige Gegenstände der Staatskunst, der Kriegswissenschaften und des Cameral- und Finanzwesens,* 2d ed. [Copenhagen and Leipzig: Rothenschen Buchhandlung, 1761], introduction).

24. John Komlos, "Vierundzwanzig Lektionen in geschichtswissenschaftlicher Rezension," *Österreichische Zeitschrift für Geschichtswissenschaften,* forthcoming. Joachim Liese and Max-Stephan Schulze, "Geldpolitik und Konjunktur in Österreich: Die 'Plener'sche Stagnation' 1862 bis 1866," *Vierteljahrschrift für Sozial- und Wirtschaftsgeschichte* 80 (1993): 510–30.

Part 4

**Government and the People
during the *Aufklärung***

Introduction

James Van Horn Melton

"Müssige Bettler" (idle beggars); "landesschädliche Vagabunden" (pernicious vagabonds); "herrenlose Gesindel" (masterless rabble)— these formulaic epithets are familiar to anyone who has worked in the field of early modern Austrian social history. They recur repeatedly in the sources, from Habsburg edicts to town sumptuary laws, from cameralist treatises to noble estate records. The sheer frequency with which they appear, and the mixture of revulsion and fear they usually reflect, point to the poor as a chronic problem facing Habsburg government in the early modern period.

Judging from the growing number of edicts aimed at vagabonds and mendicants from the mid-seventeenth century on, the poor were becoming increasingly visible, if not more numerous. Warfare was partly to blame, at least as a short-term precipitant. The Thirty Years' War and its depressing legacy of orphans, widows, deracinated *soldateska,* and pauperized peasants helped to create a large group of propertyless individuals precariously perched on the threshold of starvation and disease. Although the wars of the eighteenth century were less devastating to civilian populations, they did produce temporary surges in mendicancy. These usually occurred after the conclusion of a major peace treaty, as in 1714, 1742, 1744, and 1763, when discharged soldiers flooded the monarchy's towns and cities in search of subsistence.[1]

Adding to the visibility of the poor in the eighteenth century was the rapid growth of Vienna as an urban center following the defeat of the Turks in 1683. The presence of the court, along with the wealthy aristocrats who began to build palaces in the city, was a magnet for those in search of work or alms. Royal officials could not fail to notice the steady stream of beggars who lined the streets or crowded the entrances to churches, and the conspicuous concentration of the poor in the city doubtless did much to inspire the repeated denunciations of mendicancy and idleness that one encounters so often in monarchical edicts of the period: "Now, more than ever, countless foreign and native beggars are to be found throughout the entire territory" (1749); "everywhere [there are] swarms of vagabonds and brigands" (1759); "disorderly public begging is rampant" (1767); "both within the city as well as in the outskirts, evil thieves, plunderers, and robbers disrupt and weaken the public security and order" (1765).[2]

Compounding the problems of poverty and mendicancy was the class of rural poor that was expanding so rapidly in the eighteenth-century countryside. This expansion was both the cause and effect of the dramatic growth of rural commodity production occurring in regions such as Bohemia and Upper and Lower Austria. The expansion of textile manufacturing drew on the labor of a sub-peasant stratum no longer dependent upon land for subsistence. While this development spurred population growth in the countryside, it also created a landless or land-poor class highly vulnerable to unpredictable fluctuations in demand. Many of those whom cameralist treatises condemned as shiftless vagabonds were unemployed spinners and weavers driven by economic need to seek work in towns or throughout the countryside.[3] Owning little or no land in their own villages, they were usually excluded from membership in the peasant *Gemeinde* and were hence cut off from the communal safety net that in times of famine helped to shield the more affluent peasants from economic disaster.[4] Throughout much of the seventeenth and eighteenth centuries, the Habsburg government responded to the expanding class of urban and rural poor with measures that were primarily punitive and exclusionary. The time-honored method in most towns and cities was simply to round up beggars and expel them; this measure was highly ineffective, since it merely shifted the burden of poor relief from one community to another. It also had the effect of driving more hardened vagrants into the countryside, where they banded together and used the threat of arson to extort food and money from the local peasantry. This was the criminal underclass of highwaymen and arsonists described by the Lower Austrian nobleman Wolff Helmhard von Hohberg: "They often join together and through threats, violence, and murder, force the unfortunate peasant to give them what they demand. The peasant does not even dare to complain, out of fear that they will burn down his hut."[5] Another response to the problems of poverty and mendicancy was the workhouse (*Zucht- und Arbeitshaus*), the first of which was established in Breslau in 1668. During the course of the next century or so, other workhouses were established in Vienna (1671), Olmütz (1702), Innsbruck (1725), Prague (1737), Troppau (1753), Klagenfurt and Laibach (1754), Triest (1762), Altbreisach in Further Austria (1769), Ackerghem and Vilvoorde in the Austrian Netherlands (1772), Linz (1775), and Görz (1779).[6] Since workhouses primarily targeted the "nondeserving poor"—able-bodied beggars, petty thieves, and prostitutes—they affected only a tiny proportion of those caught in the cyclical waves of eighteenth-century poverty and unemployment. Under Maria Theresa, efforts to rid the Habsburg territories of vagrants also included forbidding them from marrying (1754), transporting them to the Turkish border (1763), and drafting them into the army (1741 and 1756).[7] To cope with the mass of unemployed veterans who filled the land after the Seven Years' War, Maria Theresa offered free transportation to the Banat, where colonists received plots of land and six years of freedom from taxes. The use of colonization as a safety valve showed some success—unemployed journeymen, soldiers, and others without an occupation flocked to the Banat, 19,000 of them between 1763 and 1770.[8] The government soon found the cost of transporting the colonists too expensive, however, and after 1771 only those who could pay their own way received land and tax exemptions.

Yet as the essays in this section demonstrate, the final decades of the eighteenth century were also marked by more positive and innovative measures addressing the problems of mendicancy and poor relief. Although partly inspired by the enlightened and reform-Catholic ideals that gained currency from the 1750s onward, these innovative policies were more often pragmatic responses to social and political exigency.

Paul Bernard's essay traces the recurrent concern with chronic poverty and its social consequences from the late seventeenth century to the end of the Josephinian period. Bernard links this concern with a general rise in poverty during the eighteenth century and shows how those in authority—from the central government down to the noble estate—searched for new and more effective countermeasures. Their efforts, argues Bernard, signified a transition from the medieval ideal of *caritas,* which venerated poverty and the giving of alms, to the cameralist condemnation of idleness and indigence as a social disease to be eradicated by governmental action.

But, as Bernard shows, it was not until the reign of Joseph II that methods of poor relief fundamentally changed. Here the initiative came not from bureaucratic-Josephinian fiat but from the private efforts of a Bohemian aristocrat, Count Johann Buquoi. This is not as unusual as it might seem: the great aristocratic houses that arose in Bohemia following the defeat of Bohemian Protestantism in 1620 had long administered their vast domains like self-enclosed states. These lords employed large cadres of estate administrators, which in the case of wealthier families, such as the Liechtensteins, were quite on par with the territorial bureaucracies of their princely counterparts in the Holy Roman Empire.[9] They issued police ordinances, administered justice, regulated religious worship, built schools and orphanages, and generally governed in lieu of a state whose institutions did not begin to operate in any kind of efficacious manner until the administrative reforms of the Theresian and Josephinian period. That they could also brutally exploit their peasants must not obscure the extent to which their experience in running their estates at the local level could directly shape absolutist policy. We are generally accustomed to thinking of the Bohemian aristocracy as an impediment to reform during the Theresian and Josephinian era. Here Buquoi, who happened to be one of the more progressive of his breed, is an excellent example of the positive social and political role Bohemian aristocrats sometimes played in the Habsburg Monarchy.

Another feature of the Buquoi system described in Bernard's essay also merits attention. As with the efforts by Maria Theresa and Joseph II on behalf of compulsory schooling, Buquoi made the parish clergy the chief agents of his system of poor relief. In both instances, the use of the parish clergy as the linchpin of reform points to the relative weakness of Habsburg local administration. The ultimate failure of much of the Josephinian program shows that despite some four decades of administrative reorganization, the monarchy still did not possess an effective bureaucratic apparatus at the local level through which it could implement its policies. There did exist the so-called *Kreishauptmänner,* or "circuit captains," the district officials who supervised the execution of governmental policy in the towns and countryside of Austria and Bohemia. But the number of *Kreishauptmänner* was simply too small, and their range of responsibilities too great, for them to serve as effective agents of administration. In the wake of the Theresian administrative reforms of 1751, for example, Bohemia had sixteen circuit captains, whose duties included supervising tax collection, policing local markets, organizing famine relief, enforcing sanitation measures, overseeing the conscription and billeting of soldiers, and quelling riots and popular disturbances.[10] That these duties exceeded their resources and capacities was attested by Carl Egon von Fürstenberg, the royal governor of Bohemia, during the famine of 1771–72. Fürstenberg complained that in a typical Bohemian *Kreis,* comprising ten districts, thirty towns, and hundreds of villages, it was simply impossible for a lone circuit captain to carry out his duties effectively. Fürstenberg grimly concluded that "a ruler and his advisors can issue as many edicts as they desire, but their enforcement depends wholly on a handful of officials scattered throughout the kingdom."[11] Incidentally, a detailed study of the *Kreishauptmänner* in eighteenth-century Austria is long overdue and would greatly illuminate our understanding of the relationship between state and society in the Habsburg Monarchy.[12]

Bernard notes the logic but also the limits of making the parish church the cornerstone for a reformed system of poor relief. Here one might mention another disadvantage, namely, the inability of the parish to bear the weight of governmental and ecclesiastical burdens that had been slowly heaped on it since the sixteenth century. Not only was the parish priest responsible for the spiritual welfare of his flock and the religious life of the community, with its yearly succession of masses, processions, festivals, weddings, baptisms, and funerals. He was also expected to visit the sick, help mediate feuds and conflicts among his parishioners, and supervise the master of the local parish school (usually the sacristan) in accordance with the school reforms of the 1770s. And now, with the reform of poor relief, priests were expected to become poorhouse managers as well—all of this at a time when the population of parishes was expanding rapidly, especially that of the rural poor. The problems stemming from this population growth are what in part led Joseph to attempt to reorganize the monarchy's system of parishes—another topic, I think, that begs further investigation. At any rate, one must wonder whether the parish church and community were any longer capable of fulfilling the kind of financial and administrative responsibilities that an increasingly activist government was assigning it.

The problem of local government is also the theme of Georg Schmidt's essay on the Austrian *Vorlande* during the famine of 1771–72. The effects of the famine were catastrophic throughout Central Europe, but they were especially severe in the territories of the Habsburg Monarchy. This was above all true in Bohemia, where thousands of rural inhabitants died of starvation. But the long-term political effects of the famine were no less dramatic, for it provoked a kind of *crise de conscience* that strengthened the cause of domestic reform across the board. It revealed the inadequacy of existing methods of poor relief; it hastened the process of agrarian reform that culminated in the so-called Raab system, which established a model for the future commutation of peasant labor services;[13] it encouraged the efforts of educational reformers such as Ferdinand Kindermann, whose introduction of spinning classes into Bohemian village schools helped to create the most extensive network of protoindustrial education in all of Europe;[14] it hastened proposals for the liberalization of trade within the monarchy, culminating in the abolition of inland tolls in 1775 and the creation of a customs union that included all of Bohemia and Austria with the exception of the Tyrol;[15] and, as Schmidt's essay shows, it spurred local officials to place greater emphasis on the market as a mechanism for guaranteeing the production and supply of foodstuffs.

Schmidt describes the efforts of Heinrich von Kageneck, a Further Austrian official, to find an alternative to the measures traditionally employed to provision the population in times of dearth. Kageneck's opposition to grain embargoes and his qualified advocacy of free trade bore the unmistakable stamp of physiocracy, whose principles had begun to spill across the borders of the monarchy via Baden-Durlach, Basel, and France. His position ultimately rested on an idea that had become a key tenet of eighteenth-century social theory: the belief that self-interest (*Eigennutz*), far from being antithetical to the public good, was essential to achieving it.[16] Enlightened reformers in the Theresian and Josephinian period articulated a corollary of this principle in their insistence that coercion was a poor guarantor of social and economic discipline, and that civic virtue, social stability, and economic productivity must in the end rest on mainsprings of human action that were internal rather than external.[17]

As Turgot was to soon to learn in France, however, times of dearth were unpropitious times for economic experiments. As elsewhere in Europe, efforts at market liberalization in the *Vorlande* met the entrenched opposition of urban consumers accustomed to the "moral economy" of market regulation. Yet Schmidt also suggests that the famine forced governments throughout the Holy Roman Empire to reconsider the remedies hitherto employed to provision their populations. Viewed in this light, the famine encouraged the transition—in theory if not in practice—to a more integrated market economy in the empire. For the famine laid bare the glaring disjunction between the empire's fragmented political structure on the one hand and its increasingly integrated markets on the other. It was proving more and more difficult for rulers to conduct a coherent territorial policy, especially in regions like the *Vorlande* and southwestern Germany, where the inextricable interdependence of foreign and domestic markets rendered political boundaries progressively more porous and arbitrary. It is a dilemma, one might add, that is quite familiar to us today, when governments struggle in a no less confused and befuddled fashion to formulate national economic policies in a world of globally integrated markets.

Notes

1. See Hannes Stekl, *Österreichs Zucht- und Arbeitshäuser 1671–1920* (Vienna: Oldenbourg, 1978), 23; and Paul Frauenstadt, "Das Bettel- und Vagabundenwesen in Schlesien vom 16.–18. Jahrhundert," *Preussische Jahrbücher* 89 (1897): 497. For a good introduction to the question of poverty in early modern Central Europe, see also Rudolf Endres, "Das Armenproblem im Zeitalter des Absolutismus," in *Aufklärung, Absolutismus, und Bürgertum in Deutschland,* ed. Franklin Kopitzsch (Munich: Nymphenburger Verlagshandlung, 1976).

2. *Codex Austriacus,* 6 vols. (1704–77), 5:449; 6:19; 1046, 685.

3. On the expansion of rural industry and its social consequences in eighteenth-century Austria, see James Van Horn Melton, *Absolutism and the Eighteenth-Century Origins of Compulsory Schooling in Prussia and Austria* (Cambridge: Cambridge University Press, 1988).

4. Ibid., 129.

5. Wolff Helmhard von Hohberg, *Georgica Curiosa, oder Adeliges Landleben,* 3 vols. (Nuremberg, 1716), 1:74–75. Cf. *Codex Austriacus,* 2:474 (1673), which condemns "the wicked rabble . . . who roam the countryside and cause great damage by setting fires, who attack and rob people on the roads, and who at night break into the houses of Our subjects, whom they rob and beat and abuse in an evil and murderous fashion."

6. Stekl, *Österreichs Zucht- und Arbeitshäuser,* 62–63.

7. *Codex Austriacus,* 5:840; 6:405–6; 5:21.

8. *Codex Austriacus,* 6:405–6; Sonja Jordan, *Die kaiserliche Wirtschaftspolitik im Banat im 18. Jahrhundert* (Munich: Oldenbourg, 1967), 92.

9. See the discussion of Liechtenstein estate administration in Thomas Winkelbauer, "Haklich und der Korruption unterworfen: Die Verwaltung der liechtensteinischen Herrschaften und Güter im 17. und 18. Jahrhundert," in *Der ganzen Welt ein Lob und Spiegel: Das Fürstenhaus Liechtenstein in der frühen Neuzeit,* ed. Evelin Oberhammer (Vienna: Verlag für Geschichte und Politik, 1990).

10. The duties of a *Kreishauptmann* are summarized in detail in Johann Mayern, *Einleitung zur kreisämtlichen Wissenschaft im Königreich Böhmen* (Prague, 1776), a manual published for Bohemian circuit captains.

11. Carl Egon von Fürstenberg, "Wohlgemeinte Gedanken über die sich täglich und augenscheinlich verschlimmenden Umstände des Königreichs Böhmen," Haus- Hof- und Staatsarchiv, Vienna: Nachlass Zinzendorf, vol. 158, fol. 124.

12. An excellent analysis of Styrian circuit captains is found in the dissertation by Gernot Peter Obersteiner, "Repräsentation und Kammer im Herzogtum Steiermark 1749–1763" (Ph.D. diss., University of Graz, 1989).

13. Helen Liebel-Weckowicz and Franz Szabo, "Modernization Forces in Maria Theresia's Peasant Policies," *Histoire sociale—Social History* 15 (1982): 320–21.

14. Melton, *Absolutism,* 220–22.

15. Helen Liebel-Weckowicz, "Modernisierungsmotive in der Freihandels-politik Maria Theresias," in *Maria Theresia und ihre Zeit,* ed. Walter Koschatzky (Salzburg: Residenz Verlag, 1979), 157.

16. On this idea, see Albert Hirschman, *The Passions and the Interests: Political Arguments for Capitalism before Its Triumph* (Princeton, N.J.: Princeton University Press, 1977).

17. See Melton, *Absolutism,* xix–xxii.

Poverty and Poor Relief in
the Eighteenth Century

Paul P. Bernard

The poor have always been with us, and in the Judaeo-Christian tradition, charity has long been enjoined as a sacred duty upon believ-
ers. In general, they meet this obligation, well or less well, according
to their lights. Nevertheless, by the fourth quarter of the eighteenth
century, the numbers of the poor in the Habsburg dominions, as
well as in much of the rest of Europe, exceeded what could be dealt
with within the traditional frameworks of private and ecclesiastical
charity. This is not the place for a comprehensive economic history of
the early modern Habsburg Monarchy. Instead, I will confine myself
to identifying some of the reasons for the increasing numbers of
poor, most notably the incomplete and sporadic recovery from the
general economic decline of the seventeenth century, the impover-
ishing effect that the Silesian and Seven Years' wars had on a considerable sector of the population, and the movement of the rural
population into the towns.

By 1770 complaints could be heard everywhere, strident or
despairing, depending on the outlook of the speaker, that beggars
and vagabonds infested the countryside, that the roads were made
unsafe by *vagierendes Volk,* that honest folk found no work, that
foodstuffs were exorbitantly priced so as to be out of reach for those
on the lower end of the economic ladder, that charitable institutions
were overburdened, and that the *Obrigkeiten* had to step in to set
matters right.[1]

Obviously, complaints of this nature tended to intensify in times of economic crisis and to abate during the recoveries that followed. It would surely be mistaken to estimate the overall number of the poor from the number of persons in need of aid in the midst of a major famine: given the still relatively unintegrated aspect of the eighteenth-century economy, famines could be so severe locally that the majority of the population might be affected, and to designate all of them as belonging to the great body of the poor would be stretching the term beyond all serviceability. But what clearly *does* seem to have been going on was that with each crisis and recovery, a varying but significant number of people did not recover their former status but, rather, joined the number of the permanent poor.[2] In addition, there was a problem of perception and definition: in the course of the eighteenth century, perhaps under the prodding of cameralist thinking, the definition of poverty was extended from those who were unable or unwilling to work due to a deficiency of nature or of the spirit, to those people who could not find work in spite of their best efforts, and to those who did not earn enough to support themselves while they worked.[3]

Let us begin, however, by discussing the reasons for the general increase of poverty in this period, since these undoubtedly had something to do with the attempted solutions that eventually emerged. Contemporaries tended, like economic observers in any period, to attribute this evil either to overwhelming catastrophes, in this case the depredations of the Thirty Years', Silesian, and Seven Years' wars or to a decline in morality, in self-imposed standards, and in willingness to work.[4] Later on, Marx and Engels and their followers would attribute this increase in poverty almost exclusively to the effects of the Industrial Revolution, which, for this purpose, they conveniently moved back in time by half a century or so. Nowadays, economic historians tend to place the blame for this on what in our own times is called stagflation. The pressures of a steadily and, by the end of the century, dramatically rising population tended to drive up the price of agricultural goods. However, except in those regions where the independent peasant proprietor predominated—and these were scarce within the Habsburg Monarchy—the resulting increase in profits was not passed on to the agricultural laborers but largely held on to by the landowners. In a related phenomenon, also a consequence of the rather rigidly structured nature of ancien régime society, the influence of the guilds had in most places survived the onslaught of the centralizing state to a sufficient degree to enable them to continue to impose a strict regulation upon wages, which nowhere kept up with prices. The inevitable result was the relative pauperization of significant portions of the population. It has been estimated that, leaving aside the recognized poor, in the towns some 20–25 percent of the population lived at just above the poverty level, and that it took only a relatively modest downward turn of the economy to push them below it. In the countryside, the percentage in many regions was even higher.[5]

It requires only a moment's reflection to conclude that these conditions could not be readily addressed by the ancien régime mentality, which, in this respect basing itself entirely on medieval tradition, regarded poverty as part of God's scheme, implying some necessary discomfort for those afflicted by it but also allowing the righteous to engage in charity and so to contribute toward their salvation. In the Habsburg lands, the poor even constituted a separate estate and were counted in a category of their own in the Theresian census of 1762.[6] This was all very well as long as the number of the poor was kept within bounds, but this system could not cope with the needs of a fifth or a quarter of the entire population. In addition, being poor in the eighteenth century often implied adopting certain essentially medieval behavior patterns, such as breaking loose from one's moorings and swelling the ranks of the beggars and *vagranti*. When the number of beggars began to exceed that of the alms-givers, the former frequently turned to more direct means of raising money, and this created obvious problems of social control. Michel Foucault maintains that poor relief was never anything but a prophylactic device used by the propertied classes to keep the growing numbers of the poor from redistributing worldly goods by violence, which is doubtless an overstatement of the case. Still, this aspect of the question should not be overlooked.[7]

As the number of the poor grew, there was a corresponding attitudinal shift in the methods addressing the problem. In the past, whenever a temporary economic crisis had exacerbated the problem to the point where private and church charities could no longer cope with it effectively, the local authorities—mayors and town councils or noblemen with jurisdiction in their own districts—had stepped in. But from the last quarter of the seventeenth century onward, there is an increasing involvement of the crown through the promulgation of poor acts valid for all the lands of the monarchy. A law of Leopold I's in 1679 seems to have been the first major attempt on the part of the central government to impose some sort of regulatory principle on poor relief. Its emphasis is very largely on control: the preamble states explicitly that the poor had themselves to blame for their condition, and only those among them (the rescript refers to beggars, but it is clear from the text that not only professional beggars were meant) who could establish their right of residence were to be helped; all others were to be expelled. If they returned, they would be subject to beatings and exposure in the stocks.[8]

Eventually the crown concluded that the irreducible number of poor who qualified to receive help under the public-assistance programs should not simply be given their pittance and then allowed to go about their business, which as often as not was begging. In 1704 an imperial *cassa pauperum* was established for the express purpose of coordinating all charitable contributions, whether individual, ecclesiastical, or from public funds, and of making sure that only deserving individuals received aid. More and more, the view prevailed that anyone who remained idle was by definition undeserving and that by far the greater part of the *cassa*'s funds should be distributed only to those persons who performed useful labor in a workhouse, either as permanent inmates or as day laborers.[9]

It should, of course, be pointed out that growing governmental involvement in poor-relief questions was not merely a response to the expanding number of the poor. Undoubtedly, the principle of state absolutism, as it was increasingly translated into practice, would inevitably have led to such a result, even without the urgent pressures of a deteriorating economic situation. But one can surmise that the two factors reinforced one another.

At any rate, the notion that alms should depend upon work performed in return took a firm hold in the monarchy. It received theoretical underpinnings from cameralists such as Justi, who taught that all subjects, even the destitute, had a sacred duty to serve the state in whatever capacity they were able. A somewhat paradoxical consequence of this opinion was the systematic introduction of child labor, inasmuch as the principle that no one should be helped who did not also work was soon extended even to the young. It did not take long for resourceful entrepreneurs to take advantage of this circumstance. Thus a glove manufacturer in Prague, Georg Ludwig Malvieux, was soon relying exclusively on the labor of children, who, needless to say, got rather less than the going wage.[10]

Nevertheless, not all social thinkers who addressed themselves to the problem of poverty took so bleakly pragmatic a view of it. In Germany, a number of Pietists, notably Karl Heinrich Seibt, who took his inspiration partly from *Aufklärer* such as Johann Christoph Gottsched and Christian Fürchtegott Gellert, were of the opinion that only by bringing the mechanisms of the state into agreement with humanity's inner convictions could social problems be solved: it was useless to try to force the idle to work, only education could convince them of work's inherent dignity and necessity.[11] In a number of North German cities, notably Hamburg, Bremen, Lübeck, and Braunschweig, reforms were introduced which represented something of a compromise between the principle that only those willing to work should receive public assistance and the opinion that the needy, including those unable to work for whatever reason, had to be helped. By and large, these experiments combined three elements: a continuation of the practice of concentrating the poor into workhouses as much as possible; home relief for those for whom this was not a practicable solution; and efforts at providing them with an education, both to inculcate them with a work ethic and to teach them a marketable skill.[12]

In the Theresian monarchy, effectively insulated from progressive, particularly German Protestant currents, the emphasis continued to be more on attempting to solve the problem of poverty by getting rid of the poor. Curiously, these draconian methods were, at least in part, inspired by the enlightened opinions of the great Italian reformer Lodovico Muratori, who had insisted that a necessary precondition for coming to grips with the problem of poverty was to rid oneself of all foreign beggars, vagabonds, and general riffraff.[13]

Thus fortified, Maria Theresa issued a series of ordinances, in 1746, 1750, 1753, and 1754, that empowered local authorities to organize the notorious *Bettlerschub,* whereby all those indigent who could not produce proof of citizenship were unceremoniously marched to the Transylvanian border under armed guard and pushed across with kicks and blows.[14]

Yet even in the monarchy, there existed exceptions to the generally harsh treatment accorded the poor. Particularly in Upper Austria, attitudes that attributed the exponential increase in the numbers of beggars not to a corresponding increase in idleness but rather to a generalized economic crisis were voiced.[15] Doubtlessly these atypical sentiments resulted largely from the circumstance that Upper Austria was perhaps the richest of the monarchy's provinces, with both a considerable proportion of peasant proprietors among its landowners and a well-developed textile industry. It was a province that had long been famous for the relative opulence of the common person's life, so that a sudden increase in poverty would appear not as a regularly recurring and inevitable phenomenon but rather as a shocking interruption of normalcy.[16]

Still, a fundamental change in the poor-relief system of the monarchy had to await the generalized bureaucratization of life that was such a prominent feature of the rule of Joseph II. As luck would have it, when it did come, it arose not out of the usual complex of administrative committee work but rather out of a purely private initiative. Two kinds of workhouses had existed in the monarchy since the turn of the century: those—like the great *Armenhaus* in Vienna, which sheltered some five hundred individuals—whose inmates were assigned to it by the authorities, and which were thus in reality not much different from houses of detention; and those where the needy voluntarily performed various types of work in return for a stipend. Neither sort enjoyed much popularity with its clientele. In fact, conditions in both tended to be so unpleasant that the poor, by whatever means at their disposal, avoided them, and so the whole purpose of the system tended to be vitiated.[17] This was, then, in essence the situation at the end of the 1770s, when a still relatively young nobleman, Count Johann Nepomuk Buquoi, decided to do something for the benefit of the poor on his estates in southern

Bohemia.[18] While still a university student, he had come under the influence of Seibt and had, as early as 1772, established what would become the prototype of the Austrian village school on his estate at Kaplitz.[19]

Stunned by the great misery caused by the famine of that year, Buquoi was determined to prevent a repetition of that catastrophe. He saw that the whole economy of the region would have to be diversified. Toward this end, he subsidized numerous peasants on his estates who were willing to take up weaving in their homes. But an affordable means would also have to be found to provide help for those whose needs were immediate and who could not readily find work. It was to accomplish the second of these goals that he founded an *Armeninstitut* on his estate of Gratzen and caused a description thereof to be written, printed, and circulated at his expense.[20]

The guiding principle as well as the characteristic element of Buquoi's institute was that it was an entirely private, ecclesiastical initiative. In contrast to the traditional caritative societies—that is, societies whose main thrust came from whatever monastic order they were associated with—in this system the responsibility for caring for the poor, as well as that of raising the money necessary for this purpose, rested entirely upon the parish priests. They were to determine need, turn over a stipulated fraction of their Sunday collection money to the poor fund, place alms boxes in the homes of all their parishioners, and distribute the proceeds, both *in specie* and *materia,* to the deserving poor. No one was to receive more than the equivalent of a third of a day's wage for a common laborer. Furthermore, all begging was to cease at once, and persons who continued to distribute alms privately were to be reprimanded and, if they continued to do so, fined.[21]

Buquoi's system had some very evident advantages from the point of view of a reforming, centralizing government such as that of Joseph II. First of all, it did not cost the state any money. The entire burden of collecting the necessary funds remained squarely on the church. But this burden was shifted from the monastic orders—which were in part moribund and for which Joseph did not care in the least—to the parochial organization, which the emperor regarded as the core of the church. Secondly, there was at least the prospect that beggary, which had become a common plague, might at least be considerably diminished, if it did not disappear entirely. Third, the stipend distributed to the poor without requiring any work from them in return was sufficiently modest so that it was thought that anyone capable of obtaining work of any sort would clearly prefer to do so. Finally, Buquoi succeeded in getting a papal charter for his institute in which it was clearly recognized that he himself would be in charge of policy making.[22] The principle was unmistakable: private individuals gave, the church bore the costs of collecting the money, and the political authority decided to whom and in what amounts it should go.

This arrangement could easily be extended from the local to the national level, a point not lost upon Joseph, who was very favorably impressed with the reports of Buquoi's institute. Still, the emperor remained somewhat skeptical at first: what seemed to work in rural Bohemia would not necessarily solve the problems of the towns of the monarchy, where poverty seemed most indigenous and ineradicable. Instead, a more traditional solution was initially adopted. In October 1782, the abbot of the *Schottenkloster* in Vienna, one of the few monastic houses that remained in Joseph's good graces, was appointed as director-general of a newly created *Armenwesenabteilung.*[23]

Either the new system did not work at all, or else Joseph had been convinced to sanction it only *à contre coeur*. At any rate, within six months of the creation of the new authority, Buquoi was summoned to Vienna, ostensibly to assist the abbot in his duties but in fact to replace him. In May 1783, it was announced that an institute modeled upon the one in Gratzen had been established in Vienna and would shortly be followed by similar ones in the monarchy's principal population centers. As had been the case in Bohemia, a massive effort to enlist the parish clergy in the cause of poor relief was now launched, with sermons describing the new system and stressing the clergy's duty to participate in it and the parishioners' duty to funnel their alms-giving into it henceforth being preached in all the principal churches of the capital.[24]

Shortly thereafter, Joseph ordered that all the funds belonging to various ecclesiastical caritative societies be merged with those of the institute, including the so-called *Konvertitenfonds,* which had been used to purchase conversions to Catholicism among the poor of other confessions. Various fines for minor transgressions collected by local governments were now to go to the institute as well.[25] When a substantial part of the funds confiscated from the monasteries dissolved by Joseph was added to this, the institute's capitalization ultimately reached half a million florins, a goodly sum. In addition, there were, of course, the proceeds of the weekly collections, of which the alms boxes in private houses, which averaged 20 kreuzer (⅓ fl.) per household per week, supplied the major portion. While this may not sound like a lot, the total from these collections came to fl. 93,000. In the following years, the institute took in, on average, fl. 140,000 yearly, of which it disbursed just under 100,000 to anywhere between 5,000 and 6,000 persons (roughly 2½ percent of the city's population). The amount received varied from a full portion— 8 kr. daily, figured on the basis of ⅓ of a laborer's income—to as little as one quarter of a portion.[26]

As for the percentage of disbursement, roughly five sevenths of the funds it took in, the institute certainly performed extremely well compared to some of its predecessors, which, in some admittedly extreme cases, distributed only about one percent of the funds they received.[27]

Less convincing was the actual distribution to individuals. If one extrapolates from the year 1787, for which the full figures are available, the average size of a stipend was roughly ⅜. Thus one can arrive at a yearly individual income of fl. 7½, in truth a mere pittance and certainly nothing like a third of the fl. 140 or so that a common laborer could expect to earn. Even if one takes into consideration that as many as half of those receiving aid were children, many of whom would not have been working and certainly would not have been paid full salaries, the average support level works out to be, at best, half of what Buquoi had intended.[28]

If the system worked this badly in Vienna (and also in Linz, where a virtual carbon copy of the Viennese *Armeninstitut* was created), how then did it function in the provinces, where it was also meant to operate but where, in the absence of actual institutes, the local authorities were expected to coordinate poor relief on the parochial level? Let us take the example of the commune of Rittenhain in the Pusterthal of south Tyrol. A fairly rich agricultural area specializing even then in the production of fruits and garden vegetables, with land ownership divided approximately equally between noble (mostly absentee) landlords and independent peasants, the district had a population of some 8,000 souls in the 1780s.[29] In the year 1787, the district had to support a total of 278 poor persons, 146 adults and 132 children, or 3½ percent of the total population.[30] Available for this purpose was a total of fl. 311 from the interest on donations and legacies in favor of the poor, plus fl. 506 in voluntary contributions. Taking into consideration the distribution of the needy between adults and children, it would seem reasonable to assign half a portion as the average support figure, or fl. 23 per person per year, in which case one arrives at a total of fl. 6,294, or almost eight times the money available under the terms of the Buquoi system. As the difference had to be made up somehow, the district had no choice but to resort to a nonvoluntary assessment on all persons of means. As was usual in the eighteenth century, this was levied not on income, which was difficult to establish with any exactitude, but on capital and real estate, to which an arbitrary valuation could be assigned.

It will astonish no one that there were many who felt that this was unjust, and some went so far as to refuse payment. There was, for instance, Georg Tutzer, whose personal holdings were assessed at fl. 11,000. He defaulted on his assigned annual payment of fl. 20 in two consecutive years. He was cited before the district court, ordered to pay up, appealed to the provincial government in Innsbruck, and lost his appeal on the grounds that "every district under the law was responsible for the support of its poor and that consequently it was only just that every inhabitant of that district share that burden in accordance to his means."[31] What is of particular interest here is, first, that these records enable us to establish with precision the size of the assessment, two tenths of one percent per annum, a levy that does not appear to be confiscatory; and second, the fact that the proposition that the state, and consequently its citizens, is directly responsible for the support of the needy is here given official expression.

Equally interesting is Tutzer's justification of his refusal to pay, which he stated when he handed over his assessment under protest. Nothing, he maintained, had changed under the new system.

Just as in the past, his farm was overrun with beggars: if he refused them their customary alms, they interfered with his workmen. This being the case, he did not see why he should also have to pay a special assessment. Apprised of this complaint, the provincial government answered that while it sympathized with the appellant's plight, it could grant him no relief beyond issuing instructions to the local authorities to enforce the regulations against begging more effectively; and, in any case, he was himself not blameless in the matter: had he refused outright to give the beggars anything, they would eventually have gone away.[32]

Tutzer's discontent with these special assessments is all the more understandable when one learns that there were frequent one-time levies as well, on the average of one a year in the 1780s, on behalf of the victims of some extraordinary catastrophe, such as a flood or a local famine.[33] But what is crucial for our understanding is not so much the circumstance that there were those who objected to the special levies: some people will always complain about being made to contribute to any cause, no matter how good it can be shown to be. It is rather the fact that the Buquoi system, at least in this instance, fell so far short of its goals. Given the percentage of poor in the population, it was simply not possible to meet their needs with charitable contributions, even when overseen and centralized under state authority. One would either have to continue to sanction widespread beggary (which was often, as Tutzer pointed out, thinly disguised blackmail), or one would eventually have to go from special assessments to a more direct form of state aid to the poor. Semichaotic conditions such as those which seem to have prevailed in the Pusterthal doubtless were not without importance in making up people's minds in this direction.

Notes

1. The phenomenon of expecting relief for the problem of poverty from the political authorities goes back at least into the sixteenth century in the German lands and may be considered an integral part of the politicization of public life that is so prominent a feature of the Reformation. See Rudolf Endres, "Das Armenproblem im Zeitalter des Absolutismus," *Jahrbuch für fränkische Landesforschung* 34/35 (1975): 1003–20.

2. This can be readily seen in the case of the Bohemian famine of 1770–72. See Erika Weinzierl-Fischer, "Die Bekämpfung der Hungersnot in Böhmen 1770–1772 durch Maria Theresia und Joseph II.," *Mitteilungen des österreichischen Staatsarchivs* 7 (1954): 478–513; and Fritz Blaich, "Die wirtschaftspolitische Tätigkeit der Kommission zur Bekämpfung der Hungersnot in Böhmen und Mähren (1771–1772)," *Vierteljahrschrift für Sozial- und Wirtschaftsgeschichte* 56 (1969): 299–331. See also Carsten Küther, *Menschen auf der Straße* (Göttingen: Vandenhoeck & Ruprecht, 1983), 15–17.

3. See Louise Sommer, *Die österreichischen Kameralisten in dogmengeschichtlicher Darstellung,* 2 vols. (Vienna: Scientia, 1920, 1925), 2:348–49; and Alois Brusatti, *Österreichische Wirtschaftspolitik vom Josephinismus zum Ständestaat* (Vienna: Jupiter, 1965), 15–18.

4. Endres, "Armenproblem," 1009. This sort of vituperation against beggars appeared as early as the *Liber vagatorum* of 1510, which came out in numerous editions over the next two centuries. See Christoph Sachße and Florian Tennstedt, *Geschichte der Armenfürsorge in Deutschland* (Stuttgart: Kohlhammer, 1980), 51–80. A useful account of the perseverance of these views in neighboring Switzerland is given by Anne-Marie Dubler, *Armen- und Bettlerwesen in der gemeinen Herrschaft "Freie Ämter" (16. bis 18. Jahrhundert)* (Basel: R. Habelt, 1970).

5. Endres, "Armenproblem," 1007; Wilhelm Abel, *Massenarmut und Hungerkrisen im vorindustriellen Europa* (Hamburg/Berlin: Gesellschaft für westfälische Wirtschaftsgeschichte, 1974), 210–11; idem, *Massenarmut und Hungerkrisen im vorindustriellen Deutschland* (Göttingen: Vandenhoek & Ruprecht, 1972), 5–7, 32–33, 46–48; idem, *Der Pauperismus in Deutschland am Vorabend der industriellen Revolution* (Dortmund: Parey, 1966), 4–15.

6. Wolfgang Zorn, *Handbuch der deutschen Wirtschafts- und Sozialgeschichte* (Stuttgart: Union, 1971), 1:586.

7. Michel Foucault, *Discipline and Punish* (New York: Pantheon, 1977); and Hannes Stekl, "Soziale Sicherung und Soziale Kontrolle: Zur österreichischen Armengesetzgebung des 18. und 19. Jahrhunderts," *Bericht über den 14. österreichischen Historikertag in Wien* (Vienna, 1979), 136–51.

8. Hannes Stekl, *Österreichs Zucht- und Arbeitshäuser 1671–1920* (Munich: Oldenbourg, 1978), 29–31.

9. Imperial rescripts of 1704 and 1724, cited by Stekl, *Österreichs Zucht- und Arbeitshäuser,* 26–29.

10. Catharina Lis and Hugo Soly, *Poverty and Capitalism in Pre-industrial Europe* (London: Harvester, 1980), 211; James Van Horn Melton, *Absolutism and the Eighteenth-Century Origins of Compulsory Schooling in Prussia and Austria* (Cambridge: Cambridge University Press, 1988), 136–40; Gernot Heiß, "Erziehung der Waisen zur Manufakturarbeit: Pädagogische Zielvorstellungen und öko-nomische Interessen der maria-theresianischen Verwaltung," *Mitteilungen des Instituts für österreichische Geschichtsforschung* 85 (1977): 316–31.

11. Melton, *Absolutism*, 136–37.

12. Sachße and Tennstedt, *Geschichte der Armenfürsorge*, 125–30; and Mary Lindemann, *Patriots and Paupers: Hamburg, 1712–1830* (New York/Oxford: Oxford University Press, 1990), 4–13, 100–102.

13. Lodovico Antonio Muratori, *Gedanken über die Abschaffung des Bettelns*, German translation by Peter Obladen (Innsbruck, 1784), 45–49.

14. Eleonore Zlabinger, *Lodovico Antonio Muratori und Österreich* (Innsbruck: Österr. Kommissionsbuchh. in Komm., 1970), 145.

15. Stekl, *Österreichs Zucht- und Arbeitshäuser*, 34.

16. See Roman Sandgruber, "Lebensstandard und Ernährung in Oberösterreich im 18. und 19. Jahrhundert," *Österreich in Geschichte und Literatur* 21 (1977): 273–94; and Alfred Hoffmann, *Wirtschaftsgeschichte des Landes Oberösterreich* (Salzburg: Müller, 1952), 1:248–49, 498–99.

17. Josef Karl Mayr, "Zwei Reformatoren der Wiener Armenfürsorge," part 1, *Jahrbuch des Vereines für Geschichte der Stadt Wien* 8 (1950): 110–35.

18. Buquoi was born in 1741 and was thus the exact contemporary of Joseph II. The family name also appears occasionally as Bouquoi or Buquoy.

19. Melton, *Absolutism*, 137; Eduard Winter, *Der Josefinismus*, 2d. ed. (Berlin: Rutten & Loening, 1972), 179–81; Mayr, "Zwei Reformatoren," 126–27.

20. Bernard Spazierer, *Zuverlässige und ausführliche Nachricht von dem Armeninstitut, welches auf den gräflich Buquoischen Herrschaften in Böhmen im Jahre 1779 errichtet worden* (Prague, 1780).

21. Winter, *Josefinismus*, 180–81; Mayr, "Zwei Reformatoren," 126–27.

22. This is reported in Anon., *Erinnerungen an die Mitglieder der Vereinigung aus Liebe des Nächsten bei der in Böhmisch-Gratzen gehaltenen feierlichen Einführung derselben* (Prague, 1781).

23. The decision to leave matters in the hands of the monastic clergy reflected a report of the *Hofkanzlei* that Joseph had especially requested. Cf. Mayr, "Zwei Reformatoren," 128.

24. See Joseph Schneller, *Predigt von dem Beweggrunde und den Vorzügen des neuen Armeninstitutes . . .* (Vienna, 1783). Schneller was dean of St. Stephen's Cathedral.

25. Winter, *Josefinismus*, 181; Mayr, "Zwei Reformatoren," 131–33.

26. Cf. Anon., *Summarischer Ausweis über das bey dem Armeninstitute der k.k. Residenzstadt Wien seit dem Oktober 1787 bis letzten Dezember 1788, eingebrachte, und zur Vertheilung der in der Versorgung gestandenen Armen verwendete Almosen* (Vienna, 1789).

27. Winter, *Josefinismus*, 182.

28. *Summarischer Ausweis*, 8, 11.

29. Archivio di Stato, Bolzano, Josefinischer Kadaster, Abschrift für den Bezirk Bozen.

30. Archivio di Stato, Bolzano, Politische Regierung (Pol. Reg.) xxxii, Kreisamtsakten 56, Beschreibung des dermahligen Bestandes der Armen Versorgung in Gericht zum Hain auf den Ritten, 19 January 1788.

31. Archivio di Stato, Bolzano, Pol. Reg. xxxii, Kreisamtsakten 56, Governor Count Saurau to District of Rittenhain, 12 April 1788.

32. Archivio di Stato, Bolzano, Pol. Reg. xxxii, Kreisamtsakten 56, Governor Count Saurau to Kreisamt Pusterthal, 6 June 1788.

33. Archivio di Stato, Bolzano, Pol. Reg. xxxii, Kreisamtsakten 54.

"Libertas commerciorum" or
"Moral Economy"?

The Austrian *Vorlande* in the Famine of the 1770s

Georg Schmidt

This essay deals with the great famine caused by two bad harvests in Central Europe from 1770 to 1772.[1] It will not focus on the suffering of the people or their reactions,[2] but on the crisis management of the governments and the local magistrates. In the Austrian *Vorlande,* the famine revealed the total fragility of the established structures and solutions, which were oriented toward the interests of the Austrian state as a whole and were dominated by mercantilist and cameralist ideas. It was in response to this crisis that the concept of *libertas commerciorum* arose as a pragmatic form of economy that transcended all theories and found more and more supporters—even in the governments.[3]

Traditionally, during a famine officials would prevent the export of any surplus foodstuffs, close the borders, subsidize bread prices, and control market and supply. This policy had been practiced with more or less success since the late Middle Ages.[4] It shaped the experience and the expectations of the subjects, but now the policy makers were confronted with a new reality: far-reaching economic relationships and the necessity of providing for a larger population in the central towns, the garrisons, and the protoindustrial regions.[5]

These circumstances implied that the peasants in the *Vorlande* increasingly focused their attention on the market and on a more fluid division of labor that had already reached the *Vorlande.*

Although consisting of only small dominions, the territories of Further Austria (*Vorderösterreich*) were dependent on a certain amount of export and on an exchange of goods. In addition, the farmers badly needed money to pay their taxes. Moreover, there was a lack of dairy products in the grain-exporting regions of Upper Swabia and a lack of grain in the cattle-breeding regions of the Black Forest.

The Austrian *Vorlande* were very closely connected with the Swabian and Upper Rhenish circles.[6] These fragmentary dominions became a coherent province only during the rule of Maria Theresa.[7] Since 1759 the government of the *Vorlande* was united in Freiburg. In spite of all lip service paid to the importance of this possession,[8] situated in one of the central districts of the old *Reich,* the politics of Vienna's Austrian court chancery was nearly exclusively dictated by the interests of a great power. Its objective was to bring unification and standardization to all territories of the Habsburg Monarchy, and it always had less regard for the special requirements and peculiarities of this seemingly archaic world.

The government at Freiburg was, however, anxious to resist centralization. In addition to all the considerations of imperial politics and relations to the smaller Swabian estates, there were two additional factors that arose during times of crisis which could not be ignored. First, there was the possibility that the Swabian estates would be able to blockade the Austrian possessions; second, past experience had demonstrated that the directives of the central government (especially *Polizeiordnungen*) in this politically fragmented region would be ineffective unless they were harmonized in advance with as many neighbors as possible.[9]

The very high price of food at the end of the 1760s had already resulted in massive criticism of the allegedly insufficient *Polizeiwesen* in *Vorderösterreich* and, above all, in the Breisgau. The Viennese court chancery demanded a report on the situation by the Freiburg government. Since 1768 Heinrich von Kageneck had been in charge of the relevant *Generallandespolizeikommission*. In accordance with the prevailing principles of Theresian economic policy—a more or less improvised application of mercantilism in the modern form of cameralism favored by Johann Heinrich Justi or Joseph von

Sonnenfels[10]—the commission had to deal with the promotion of agriculture, mining, and industry as well as with the improvement of the school system.[11] In a memorandum of 8 March 1769,[12] Kageneck criticized the government for directing all economic activities within its borders. His recommendations—made more than one year before the beginning of the famine—were influenced by the prevailing physiocratic ideas,[13] which had already been partly realized in neighboring France, Basel, and especially the Baden-Durlach of Margrave Charles Frederick.[14] Although Kageneck did not dogmatically defend a special theory, he rejected such traditional measures of crisis management as banning the export or fixing the price of meat and grain or other market controls. Instead he advocated a more modern, mixed policy that ranged from some physiocratic ideas to the economic self-reliance of the individual.

At the beginning of his memorandum, Kageneck showed that the rise in prices concerned most of all soldiers and officials receiving a fixed pay. By contrast, day laborers and workers in the manufacBy contrast, day laborers and workers in the manufactories were protected by higher wages and the ability to raise their output. Those who worked too slowly, argued Kageneck, did so at their own expense. There would be no reward for lethargy. If the Breisgau's products had really been too shoddy and too expensive, as some anonymous complaints claimed, they would not have been able to sell anything because everyone would have bought these things in neighboring countries. Kageneck also maintained that prices were high in every region of Germany due neither to usury nor excessive export nor even bad *Polizei*. Rather, the blame lay with a combination of bad harvests, enormous population growth (for which there was "dem lieben frieden zu danken"), the luxury of the rich, and the influx of money from France and England. The development of manufactures in Germany had led not only to population growth but also to an increase in money available, since people no longer had to buy a lot of things in foreign countries. More money necessarily meant a rise in food prices. Even the small peasants in the Black Forest were no longer satisfied with cheese soup. Exports could not be blamed for the comparatively higher food prices in the Breisgau, since exports were only worthwhile if merchants could earn more money on foreign markets. For the state to combat the rising prices that naturally stemmed from prosperity would merely induce poverty. To pay taxes the peasants had to be able to obtain the highest price for their products.

Kageneck maintained that wine and grain had to become more expensive during a dearth. That the Swabians and the region's prelates nevertheless bought this wine was nothing to complain about, since it brought a lot of money into the Breisgau. If prices were fixed, the peasants would not be able to repay their costs and would therefore have to grow less, thereby driving themselves to starvation in times of bad harvests. Moreover, because the margraviate of Baden-Durlach was trying to advance the wealth of its subjects through unregulated trade and self-responsibility, the Durlachers would not assist in establishing blockades and other forms of intervention. Indeed, even the Swabian Circle had refused to impose embargoes during the last few years. In principle—and particularly in this situation—actions such as export prohibitions, additional duties, or tax reductions were "widrig, gewalttätig und untunlich." In any case, the subjects would always find illicit ways around them. In a free market, anything more than the existing prices for meat and bread and the checking of weights would have been outrageous and would only have kept away foreign merchants, from whose customs duties everyone profited. Even keeping stocks of food would have been a mistake because grain could only be kept for about two or three years. In addition, the towns did not have the money for granaries, nor could they be forced to store grain or any other kinds of food.

Kageneck was emphatically against the protection of guild monopolies and the artificial separation of town and country economy. A peasant could not be forced to have a wheel repaired in town, since a craftsman in the country paid trade taxes, too. Moreover, Kageneck was evidently anxious not to accuse the food trade of being usurious and wanted to categorize it instead as a useful business for the *bonum commune:* the larger the supplies, the lower the prices. Kageneck also provided many examples to demonstrate that usurious practices were merely ordinary and desirable economic transactions because the small peasants in the Black Forest could not otherwise bring their products to the market themselves. If someone tried to buy up wine after the harvest and store it in good barrels in order to earn a higher price later, he was not a usurer but a good householder. And since wealthy subjects are the real treasury of a sovereign, no one should do anything against high prices caused by prosperity.

Nor should any attention be given to the lament of soldiers and officials, who represented their own special interests as *bonum com-mune*. In fact, no one should endanger the prosperity of all the 200,000–250,000 inhabitants of the *Vorlande* simply because 2,000 people could buy less with their income than before. The majority was obviously happy with the circumstances, for in spite of rising prices fewer and fewer wanted to emigrate.[15] The only thing the government should have done was spend *"schweres Geld"* on the soldiers, since the officials had already had an increase in their sala-ries. The report concluded by urging the government "den unterthan auf keine art im handel und wandel zu hemmen, sondern selbem alle mögliche freyheit zu gestatten."

Kageneck's position for free trade without any political inter-vention and his use of the singular "freyheit" do not make him a protagonist of economic liberalism.[16] Even if he accentuates in his arguments the efficiency and prosperity of the individual, who must be able to do his job without political tutelage, he appreciates the benefits offered by the state: self-interest serves not only the *bonum commune*[17] but also the government, which would collect higher taxes.[18] While Old Regime society condemned "Eigennutz" as the worst form of social behavior, Kageneck was familiar with the fun-damental change in values that was advocated by men such as Justi or Adam Smith in the second half of the eighteenth century. Winfried Schulze has, in fact, recently shown that there had been many forerunners since the sixteenth century.[19]

To Kageneck and nearly all political economists, cameralists, and physiocrats,[20] the freedom of "Handel und Wandel," the au-tonomy of the economy, did not serve "der Selbstverwirklichung der wirtschaftenden Individuen, sondern ist Mittel zur salus publica oder zur Glückseligkeit als anzustrebende Staatszwecke . . . deren Verwirklichung der Obrigkeit durch 'gute policey' obliegt."[21] Kageneck's report is thus very important because it shows the ideas of a politician who was interested not in establishing or verifying a scientific system but rather in making crisis management more effective. His memorandum shows considerable pragmatism. Most of all, he was in agreement with the mercantilists.[22] But characteristically Kageneck did call for individual industry, without condemning rising aspirations.[23] There is no link in his argument between simplicity or austerity and *bonum commune*. This is a very important point.

Having evolved to cameralism,[24] mercantilism could hold its ground in the old *Reich,* particularly because government administrators needed to lay down rules and stimulate economic development. In spite of all the lip service paid to free trade, societal bliss still had be achieved by the government itself through an effective administration that was able to judge and politically manage the whole situation from above.[25] Therefore it believed that it had the right to suspend old privileges and special rights (such as those of the guilds) if they obstructed the general welfare. The ruler or sovereign conceived of this new form of liberty as a privilege; absolutism and cameralism were now one and the same.

The physiocrats even demanded absolute and unlimited monarchy as a political system because they believed that this was the only way to overcome public opposition to the establishment and maintenance of a laissez-faire economy.[26] Indeed, Johann August Schlettwein, who urgently demanded economic freedom from state regulation, was able to test his physiocratic ideas in Baden-Durlach only when he employed political intervention to uphold mercantilist strategies. The ruler himself had to promote an increase in agrarian productivity; "laissez-faire" itself remained an abstract, long-term goal.[27]

Kageneck's pragmatic report describes the situation in the Breisgau and the *Vorlande* and deals with the profits of free trade. It fully reflects the contemporary theoretical discussion without ignoring reality. There is no sense here of a hopelessly backward Further Austrian government. To show his familiarity with enlightened ideas, Kageneck gratuitously criticizes the large number of pilgrimages because they are not suited to help people in need; for utterly destitute people, it would be better to stay at home and work than to be under this "deck-mantel . . . unterwegs ihre bösen gelüste auszuüben oder hier und da zu stehlen."[28]

Kageneck's memorandum had no effect in Vienna. When the bad harvest of 1770 led to a drastic increase in prices and imminent famine, the court chancery fell back on the traditional measures of crisis management in response to the expectations of those subjects who were most affected in Bohemia and in the *Vorlande*. As early as the summer of 1768, it had issued a decree that forbade the speculative buying and storing of grain during times of dearth by threatening all trespassers with corporal punishment and rewarding informers with one third of the confiscated food.[29]

The high food prices had a profound effect on the population of the *Vorlande*. There was a sense of crisis, even when enough grain was at hand. People knew from their long experience of suffering that a comparatively small shortfall in the harvest could endanger their daily bread. Neither did a general increase in prices necessarily mean the same as a subsistence crisis, since nowhere in Europe was there a full market society.[30] In spite of this, people reacted very sensitively to long and cold winters and to hot and wet summers. They feared starvation and began to hoard grain.[31] Because of the limited supply of grain, prices shot up immediately; the crisis struck everyone and people called for their patriarchal-provident government to apply immediately and rigorously the customary market regulations, price freezes, export bans, and prohibitions on every form of grain speculation.[32] Under these circumstances, every government or magistrate found it hard either to advocate free trade or to implement it.

This was true even for a comparatively large territorial state such as the duchy of Württemberg. It was very difficult for the government to direct scanty and expensive grain from regions with a surplus to Stuttgart or Ludwigsburg.[33] Since the fixed prices in Württemberg were significantly lower than those on the free markets in the neighboring imperial towns or even in Switzerland, the peasants responded to market forces and smuggled their grain successfully across the borders. Thus, on 13 July 1770, Duke Charles Eugene of Württemberg started a new round of embargoes by forbidding the export of grain. Two months later, Maria Theresa extended the embargo that was already in effect for Bohemia[34] to all of her dominions despite all of the Freiburg regime's reservations. Though perhaps still sensible for a large, centralized state, such an embargo spelled economic catastrophe for the *Vorlande* because it cut them off from the rest of Swabia.

Already in August, the contradictions of the first, hastily arranged embargoes became obvious. In Triberg officials asked permission to export cattle and butter because otherwise foreigners would no longer visit their markets and offer grain, which they wanted badly. The Freiburg government had to accept the request but wanted things to be handled carefully.[35] On the other hand, in September the administration of Rottenburg got a stiff reprimand because it had arbitrarily stopped the particularly sensitive grain export to the county of Hohenzollern-Hechingen.[36]

Day by day, it became more evident that an inflexible embargo was unsustainable. For example, a miller had to be given back his confiscated five sacks of grain when he proved that he had bought them for other Austrian subjects living in the Black Forest who did not have any means of transport. Merchants from Durlach were finally permitted to export eight fattened oxen because the government of Baden, which limited the right to export goods very late,[37] had allowed the export of six hundred sheep to the Breisgau.[38]

The Freiburg government dealt with the abbey of St. Georgen far more resolutely. The customs officer of Villingen had stopped their load of grain, which had obviously been heading for Switzerland. The abbot was advised that even if the grain had not been harvested in Austria, he could not be allowed to export grain once it entered its territory, especially since he was a clergyman—for the clergy should primarily be motivated by *Menschenliebe*.[39] Although the government knew that every export permit would open the door to widespread abuse,[40] there was no chance to stop or even to reduce the smuggling of grain.

There were other problems as well: the county of Hohenberg reported an influx of foreign beggars and tramps.[41] The *Oberamt* Schönberg informed the Freiburg government about the small estates' practice of discharging their soldiers. This problem became

even more urgent because of the dismissal of many domestic servants and craftsmen, "welches in der folge die zusammenrottung
allerley gefährlichen gesindels und diebs bande haben wirdet."
Therefore the Hohenberg officials suggested a greater presence of
the military by stationing about thirty soldiers in every district of
the *Vorlande*.[42]

Meanwhile the rapid spread of shortages and some food riots
induced the imperial estates around Lake Constance, including
Austrian Constance and Stockach, to put into effect another traditional measure: a limited embargo over Switzerland.[43] The Swiss
Confederation was the most important customer for surplus
Swabian grain.[44] Even the estates expected that this measure would
quickly drive down prices and appease popular discontent. Nevertheless, the Further Austrian government thought that the weekly
export quota of three hundred *malter* was too high to induce a significant reduction in local grain prices.[45]

In Vienna the court chancery tried to handle the crisis in the
traditional way—with strictly controlled embargoes, internal compensation, and supplemental shipments of Hungarian grain. This
model was practiced more or less successfully in Bohemia.[46] In
Freiburg, however, the officials advocated an absolute embargo over
Switzerland and free trade with the Swabian and other Upper
Rhenish estates. This demand for free trade with neighboring territories did not stem from a particular theory but from recent experience. No one was able to control all the sanctions of traditional crisis
management, which consequently merely led to a change in the
trade routes—to the left side of the river Rhine—and strangled the
exchange of goods nearly completely between neighboring areas.
Further Austria lost considerable tolls and most of its badly needed
foreign goods.

Therefore the Freiburg government wanted the restoration of
free trade, above all with the two neighboring imperial circles.
Count Philipp von Welsperg, *Landvogt* of the margraviate of
Burgau and Austrian minister to the Swabian Circle,[47] was asked to
convince the two princely directors of his circle that a total embargo
against Switzerland was a necessary precondition for free trade in

Swabia.[48] The delegates of some Swabian Austrian *Oberämter* who met near Lake Constance at Mimmenhausen in November 1770 recommended the same things: a limited embargo of the Swiss Confederation and free trade in Swabia. If peasants were forbidden to export their surplus grain, the officials could not see where the peasants would get their money to pay taxes. Moreover, if only the Austrians did so, they would ruin themselves. Consequently, all trade would go to the markets of imperial cities such as Ulm, Biberach, Ravensburg, or Lindau, and to the new markets that every imperial count tried to establish during the crisis.[49]

In the fall, reports from the individual *Oberämter* became more urgent: in spite of the general shortage of food, most of the subjects wanted and needed to export particular products. The climatically determined partial monoculture demanded this exchange in order to prevent a greater food shortage or an imminent famine. While on the one hand the *Oberämter* asked permission for export, on the other hand they prevented the internal circulation of some food products.[50] What appears at first glance to be absolute confusion actually makes sense: the priority of the local market had to be asserted—a basic demand of the common man's "moral economy."[51] The masses would have agreed with Baron Franz Karl Kressel von Gualtenberg, *Hofrat* at the Bohemian-Austrian court chancery, when he demanded the inexorable punishment of speculative buyers. But whether the subjects in the *Vorlande* agreed with the Viennese *Hofrat* concerning the rigorous prohibition of the profitable smuggling was questionable at best. Where enough grain was at hand, people wanted to trade for butter and cheese and, most of all, for money.

Explicit orders from Vienna obliged the Freiburg government to enforce strict market regulations by threatening military service or prison. The fact that younger peasants had resorted to smuggling and neglected their farms put the state at a considerable disadvantage.[52] Yet, ironically it was the prohibition itself that made this kind of grain trade by far the most profitable business, since even the local magistrates in the agrarian exporting regions covered up the smuggling. This was also compatible with the specific rationality of the "moral economy," which was oriented toward local necessity. Where there was enough food, the surplus had to be sold with as much profit as possible.

Baron Kressel, who on 26 October 1770 had repeated the absolute prohibition of grain export from all Austrian dominions,[53] later changed his position and blamed the promotion of special industries and artificially low grain taxes for the Bohemian catastrophe.[54] As early as November 1770, Baron von Ulm, from 1769 to 1781 president of the government at Freiburg, strictly opposed Kressel and his absolute export prohibition because the interruption of tithe shipments would prompt severe conflicts with the Swabian prelates. Therefore he inquired if the blockade was targeted not only against foreign states, such as France, Switzerland, the Palatinate, or Bavaria, but also against the Swabian imperial estates, which had likewise imposed embargoes against Switzerland or were thinking of doing so. A broader regional embargo was, in fact, unnecessary. Since the Swiss were the largest buyers of grain, prices would fall automatically if they alone were kept away from the market. An all-inclusive embargo that restricted trade to within Further Austria would be unworkable because the other imperial estates could block every transport of foodstuffs. Without the Swabian Circle, the Austrian subjects could not be fed. To forbid the export of the tithe would make little economic sense but would damage relations with the most loyal clients of the imperial house.[55] To give one example, the Austrian blockades dealt the abbey of Buchau a severe economic blow. It only ruled a very small area and covered its own considerable expenses mainly through tithes collected beyond its borders. The abbey's solicitor reminded the Freiburg government of former times of dearth when the abbess had helped Austrian subjects like her own. He asked for a relaxation of the blockade.[56] Even in Vienna no one could ignore these counterproposals from the Freiburg government. In other words, how much political capital would be lost in this famine? Austria would no longer be seen as a reliable partner, having abandoned her clients.

Although the central government was troubled by the export to the Swabian Circle, it ultimately allowed the Freiburg government a free hand.[57] Baron von Ulm wanted to assume this responsibility on condition that the entire Swabian Circle and the margraviate of Baden-Durlach would join in the embargo against Switzerland. He indicated to Count Welsperg the importance of coordinated and controlled actions, since the embargo against the Circle could only lead to further price increases in the *Vorlande*.[58] In Freiburg one knew only too well what the Viennese court chancery did not want to acknowledge: the *Vorlande* had to cooperate with the Swabian Circle. Further Austria, which formally belonged to the essentially dormant Austrian Circle, was, in practice, an associate, nonvoting member of the Swabian Circle.

Hence, the limited blockade against Switzerland that the Swabian estates voted on 23 November 1770 also placed the *Vorlande* under an obligation. Most of all, the grain traffic had to be strictly controlled for fear that more than the allowed grain would be exported to Switzerland.[59] In order to supply the poor with food without padding the merchants' profits, only those merchants who were authorized by their government would get permission to buy grain. Because the blockade meant great economic damage to the market towns around Lake Constance and because their "patriotische Bemühungen" helped all estates to get more and cheaper food, they should open the borders now and should no longer hinder grain shipments to these towns.[60]

This opposed the interests of many Swabian estates that did not want to forfeit the enormous profits their subjects were making through Swiss exports. But even when the Circle and the margraviate of Baden had joined in an embargo against Switzerland, not all problems were solved. Swabia was dependent on Swiss butter, cheese, and money at least as much as the Confederation was dependent on Swabian grain. Therefore even a complete blockade of Switzerland would have been hindered by the estates on the Lake Constance frontier. The example of the town of Waldsee shows that cross-country trade was not limited to farm products, since it asked for permission to export sixty *malter* of grain to St. Gallen. Some manufacturers in St. Gallen, upon whom Waldsee's inhabitants were dependent for handicraft contracts, would only maintain economic relations if they could get shipments of grain. Therefore grain export was the town's only chance of escaping an economic catastrophe.

It reflected a rule of human society—so the magistrate told Count Welsperg—to do one favor for another. If this were no longer true, all economies would collapse. If the Waldseers were forbidden to export their grain, it would mean the same as to forbid them to collect wages for handicraft. The petition was granted. This example also shows that in spite of bad harvests in the grain-rich regions of Upper Swabia, there was still enough grain at the height of the famine but simply not enough work and cash.[61]

In 1771 during the height of the crisis, one can detect a general rethinking, thanks to the insight that the problems could not be solved within the territorial framework, that the embargoes became counterproductive, and that the cross-frontier economic integration should not be ruined. The Viennese court chancery, which had been convinced by the many grievances of the Swabian imperial estates and particularly by the imperial city of Augsburg, lifted the embargo against the Swabian Circle on 21 September and further asked the Freiburg government to report under what conditions free trade with Switzerland might be allowed.[62]

But a lot of blockades still existed in Swabia, and the administration was not able to compensate fully for all of them. The surplus did not flow to the regions where it was most badly needed but rather to the towns and markets where smugglers could get the highest prices. Instead of selling grain with less or no profit in Further Austria or in Württemberg, it was smuggled to markets without price freezes, especially to Switzerland or to the imperial cities, often with the tacit approval of the government or local magistrates. At the end of 1771, Baron Ried, the new Austrian minister to the Swabian Circle, concluded that the blockades within the Circle and—despite strict military enforcement—the relative ineffectiveness of the ban on exports to Switzerland were the main causes of Swabia's economic ills and grievances.[63] Meanwhile, the grain blockades served to increase the profits of peasants, merchants, smugglers, and even the many imperial estates that participated in it through local taxes and deliveries. Insofar as they yielded surplus profit for a special estate, private interest and *bonum commune* became identical because there was no *libertas commerciorum,* only a specific variant of mercantilism. Obviously, many governments exploited this opportunity—not only to get precious metals but also to make or keep imperial cities dependent. The fragmentation of the dominions (*Herrschaften*) and estates in the southwest of the old *Reich* was responsible for the fact that there was no overall consistent experience in individual profit making, *bonum commune,* and feeding the hungry. When the governments of the larger estates noticed that this configuration affected the food supply of their towns and the protoindustrial regions, the general blockade policy collapsed, and the triumph of *libertas commerciorum* began at last in Germany. Indeed, the imperial diet debated whether the entire empire should become a unified economic region. The long-standing argument expressed by many theoreticians and imperial cities that export limitations were primarily responsible for price explosions and for the collapse of commerce was slowly making an impact on the governments.[64]

Nevertheless, grain had to be taken away by force from the agrarian regions to resolve even more critical shortages in the growing towns. The people concerned judged these actions as the revocation of a social compact, of a "moral economy." But this was a *conditio sine qua non* for the paternalistic-provident economic policy, which favored the *bonum commune* through fair prices that everyone could pay. If the governments gave up this policy, the consuming towns would regard this as an offense against their duty to promote public welfare and to preserve the traditional order. This was why France, Baden-Durlach, and Basel ultimately had to abandon their physiocratic experiments with a free grain-trade in times of dearth. The increasing revolts demanding behavior in accordance with the principles of the "moral economy" became dangerous for the governments.[65] Thus the people forced them to return to the well-known traditional crisis management.

Yet even in the old *Reich,* with its small territorial estates, the patriarchal-provident policy came into conflict with interdependent economic relationships, the peasants' more sophisticated market connections, and the increasing population. The crisis of the early 1770s showed that the traditional solutions had become more or less ineffective. It had become impossible to solve economic problems within the borders of a single, individual estate; the development of the market demanded a reaction on a larger scale. The interruption of trade and the obstacles to the already existing division of labor only led to greater poverty. Although the supply situation worsened after a second bad harvest in 1771, Joseph II slowly began to turn away from the blockade policy and now favored free trade at least between the *Vorlande* and the Swabian Circle. In Vienna physiocrats and free traders became more influential, though they did not get the chance to reform Austrian economic policy fundamentally.[66]

The dearth of 1770–72 also proved decisive in promoting the idea of *libertas commerciorum* within the *Reich*. After long discussions, the diet at Regensburg decided to put an end to all food blockades in the old *Reich*. Joseph II ratified this imperial memorandum, or *Reichsgutachten,* on 28 February 1772.[67]

But the time was not yet ripe for a comprehensive, "liberal" economic policy that went beyond the estates, circles, or sovereign states. Their subjects remained particularly suspicious. In Germany we thus find the same problems and events that accompanied every dearth in France or England: an increasing number of food riots, with the people demanding a "moral economy."[68] Hilton L. Root has shown that governments that intervened according to this "moral economy" defended a system of access to the scarce grain which was in no way more "moral" than distribution to the markets. It only favored the well-organized consumers in the towns at the expense of the *bonum commune*.[69] But in times of crisis, law and order often could only be maintained if the governments took a politically pragmatic approach by intervening with the help of export prohibitions, price freezes, and market regulations.[70] Even during the revolutions of 1848, food riots played an important role. As Manfred Gailus has shown, the violence on the street could unite with the vestiges of a popular monarchism to become antirevolutionary.[71] In spite of this, it seems that, even for the prenational old *Reich*, the famine crisis of the early 1770s turned out to be a catalyst that marked the beginning of the transition from a regional, paternalistic economic policy to a more nationally oriented market society.

Notes

To Monika and Herbert Effenberger I offer my thanks for their great help with the translation.

1. For a general introduction to the topic, see Wilhelm Abel, *Massenarmut und Hungerkrisen im vorindustriellen Europa: Versuch einer Synopsis* (Hamburg/Berlin: Paul Parey, 1974): 200–257.

2. Ulrich Bräker, *Der Arme Mann im Toggenburg* (1789; reprint, Munich: Winkler, 1965).

3. Judith A. Miller, "The Pragmatic Economy: Liberal Reforms and the Grain Trade in Upper Normandy, 1750–1789" (Ph.D. diss., Duke University, 1987).

4. Wilhelm Naudè, *Die Getreidehandelspolitik der Europäischen Staaten vom 13. bis zum 18. Jahrhundert* (Berlin: Paul Parey, 1896); Ulrich-Christian Pallach, ed., *Hunger: Quellen zu einem Alltagsproblem in Europa und der Dritten Welt* (Munich: Deutscher Taschenbuchverlag, 1986).

5. Steven Laurence Kaplan provides a paradigm of this problem in *Provisioning Paris: Merchants and Millers in the Grain and Flour Trade during the Eighteenth Century* (Ithaca, N.Y.: Cornell University Press, 1984).

6. Most notable among the Habsburg Swabian lands were the margraviate of Burgau, the landgraviate Nellenburg, the Swabian *Landvogtei*, the counties of Hohenberg, Vorarlberg, the former imperial city of Constance, and the Breisgau. See Friedrich Metz, ed., *Vorderösterreich: Eine geschichtliche Landeskunde* (Freiburg: Rombach,1967); Hans Maier and Volker Press, eds., *Vorderösterreich in der frühen Neuzeit* (Sigmaringen: Thorbecke, 1989).

7. Franz Quarthal et al., *Die Behördenorganisation Vorderösterreichs von 1753 bis 1805* (Bühl: Konkordia, 1977), 59.

8. Eberhard Gothein, *Der Breisgau unter Maria Theresia und Joseph II.* (Heidelberg: Winter, 1907), 2.

9. Johann Jakob Moser defines *Polizei* as "diejenige(n) landesherrliche(n) Rechte und Pflichten, auch daraus fließende(n) Anstalten, welche Absicht haben, der Untertanen äusserliches Betragen im gemeinen Leben in Ordnung zu bringen und zu erhalten, wie auch ihre zeitliche Glückseligkeit zu befördern" (*Von der Landes-Hoheit in Policey-Sachen . . .* [Frankfurt/Leipzig, 1773], 2). See Hans Maier, *Die ältere deutsche Staats- und Verwaltungslehre* (Munich: C. H. Beck, 1980); Franz Ludwig Knemeyer, "Polizei," *Geschichtliche Grundbegriffe*, 4:875–97.

10. Gustav Otruba, *Die Wirtschaftspolitik Maria Theresias* (Vienna: Bergland, 1963), 29; Fritz Blaich, "Die wirtschaftspolitische Tätigkeit der Kommission zur Bekämpfung der Hungersnot in Böhmen und Mähren (1771–1772)," *Vierteljahrschrift für Sozial- und Wirtschaftsgeschichte* 56 (1969): 330–31; idem, *Die Epoche des Merkantilismus* (Wiesbaden: Steiner, 1973), 60–76, 158–69.

11. Quarthal et al., *Behördenorganisation*, 68–69, 182, 214–16. Kageneck became a count on 8 January 1771 (Vienna), and after 1779 he belonged to the "Reichsgrafenstand."

12. Memorandum Kageneck, Hauptstaatsarchiv (HStA) Stuttgart, B 17, Bü. 218.

13. Elizabeth Fox-Genovese, *The Origins of Physiocracy: Economic Revolution and Social Order in Eighteenth-Century France* (Ithaca, N.Y.: Cornell University Press, 1976).

14. Helen P. Liebel, *Enlightened Bureaucracy versus Enlightened Despotism in Baden, 1750–1792, Transactions of the American Philosophical Society*, n.s., 55 (1965); Markus Mattmüller, "Die Hungersnot der Jahre 1770/71 in der Basler Landschaft," in *Gesellschaft und Gesellschaften: Festschrift zum 65. Geburtstag von Professor Dr. Ulrich Im Hof*, ed. Nicolai Bernard and Quirinus Reichau (Bern: Wyss, 1982), 271–91.

15. Werner Hacker, *Auswanderungen aus Baden und dem Breisgau* (Stuttgart: Theiss, 1980).

16. Diethelm Klippel, "Der Einfluß der Physiokraten auf die Entwicklung der liberalen politischen Theorie in Deutschland," *Der Staat* 23 (1984): 205–26.

17. Even Justi argued in this way: "glücklicher Weise stimmet das eigene Interesse eines jeden Menschen, wenn es auf Einsicht und Vernunft gegründet ist, auch allemal mit dem gemeinschaftlichen Besten vollkommen überein" (Johann Heinrich Gottlob von Justi, *Die Grundfeste zu der Macht und Glückseligkeit der Staaten* . . . [1760; reprint, Aalen: Scientia, 1965]: 1:557).

18. Scharnweber was in favor of liberating the grain trade, but most of all he sees advantages for the state (Johann Ludwig Friedrich Scharnweber, *Beurtheilung der wichtigen Fragen, ob es für einem Ackerbau treibenden Staat geratener sey, einen gesezlichen Korn-Preiß für ein oder mehrere Jahre einzuführen oder ob* . . . [Göttingen, 1771], A3). Cf. Winfried Schulze, "Ständische Gesellschaft und Individualrechte," in *Grund- und Freiheitsrechte von der ständischen zur spätbürgerlichen Gesellschaft*, ed. Günter Birtsch (Göttingen: Vandenhoeck & Ruprecht, 1987), 161–79.

19. Winfried Schulze, "Vom Gemeinnutz zum Eigennutz: Über den Normenwandel in der ständischen Gesellschaft der frühen Neuzeit," *Historische Zeitschrift* 243 (1986): 591–626.

20. Ulrich Muhlack, "Physiokratie und Absolutismus in Frankreich und Deutschland," *Zeitschrift für historische Forschung* 9 (1982): 20–21.

21. Diethelm Klippel, "'Libertas commerciorum' und 'Vermögens-Gesellschaft': Zur Geschichte ökonomischer Freiheitsrechte in Deutschland im 18. Jahrhundert," in *Grund und Freiheitsrechte im Wandel von Gesellschaft und Geschichte*, ed. Günter Birtsch (Göttingen: Vandenhoeck & Ruprecht, 1981), 318. Franz Joseph Bob (1733–1802), since 1768 the first professor for "Kameral- und Polizeiwissenschaften," taught that the government had to take care that private interest and *bonum commune* became identical. See Friedhelm Biesenbach, *Die Entwicklung der Nationalökonomie an der Universität Freiburg i. Br. 1768–1896* (Freiburg: E. Albert, 1969), 27. Since 1772–73, Kageneck and Bob were members of the Further Austrian *Studienkommission*. See Quarthal et al., *Behördenorganisation*, 215–16.

22. See Reinhold Zech, "Die Merkantilisten," in *Pipers Handbuch der politischen Ideen*, ed. Iring Fetscher and Herfried Münkler (Munich/Zurich: Piper, 1985), 562.

23. Paul Münch, *Ordnung, Fleiß und Sparsamkeit: Texte und Dokumente zur Entstehung der 'bürgerlichen Tugenden'* (Munich: Deutscher Taschenbuch Verlag, 1984); idem, "Grundwerte der Ständegesellschaft? Aufriß einer vernachlässigten

Thematik," in *Ständische Gesellschaft und soziale Mobilität,* ed. Winfried Schulze (Munich: Oldenbourg, 1988), 53–72; Rudolf Schenda, "Fleissige Deutsche, fleissige Schweizer: Bemerkungen zur Produktion eines Tugendsyndroms seit der Aufklärung," in *Ethische Perspektiven: "Wandel der Tugenden,"* ed. Hans-Jürg Braun (Zurich: Verlag der Fachvereine an den schweizerischen Hochschulen und Techniken, 1989), 189–210.

24. Eli Filip Heckscher, *Mercantilism* (London: G. Allen & Unwin, 1935); Erhard Dittrich, *Die deutschen und österreichischen Kameralisten* (Darmstadt: Wissenschaftliche Buchgesellschaft, 1974); Keith Tribe, *Governing Economy: The Reformation of German Economic Discourse 1750–1840* (Cambridge: Cambridge University Press, 1988).

25. Anton Tautscher, *Staatswirtschaftslehre des Kameralismus* (Bern: Francke, 1947), 9; Herbert Hassinger, "Politische Kräfte und Wirtschaft 1350–1800," *Handbuch der Deutschen Wirtschafts- und Sozialgeschichte* (Stuttgart: Union, 1971), 1:612–14.

26. Heinz Holldack, "Der Physiokratismus und die absolute Monarchie," *Historische Zeitschrift* 145 (1932): 517–49; Irene Oswalt, "Das Laissez-faire der Physiokraten" (Ph.D. diss., University of Freiburg, 1961), 143–53; Folkert Hensmann, "Staat und Absolutismus im Denken der Physiokraten: Ein Beitrag zur physiokratischen Staatsauffassung von Quesnay bis Turgot" (Ph.D. diss., University of Frankfurt/Main, 1975); Thomas Nieding, "Physiokratie und Revolution: Ansichten einer facettenreichen Interdependenz," in *Aufklärung, Politisierung und Revolution,* ed. Winfried Schulze (Pfaffenweiler: Centaurus, 1991), 51–84.

27. Clemens Zimmermann, *Reformen in der bäuerlichen Gesellschaft: Studien zum aufgeklärten Absolutismus in der Markgrafschaft Baden 1750–1790* (Ostfildern: Scripta Mercaturae, 1983), 60; Muhlack, *Physiokratie,* 43–44.

28. On the popular reactions after restrictions of pilgrimages, see Rebekka Habermas, *Wallfahrt und Aufruhr: Zur Geschichte des Wunderglaubens in der frühen Neuzeit* (Frankfurt/New York: Campus, 1991).

29. *Sammlung aller k.k. Verordnungen und Gesetze vom Jahre 1740 bis 1780 . . .* (Vienna, 1786), 5:359–60.

30. John Walter, "The Social Economy of Dearth in Early Modern England," in *Famine, Disease and the Social Order in Early Modern Society,* ed. John Walter and Roger Schofield (Cambridge: Cambridge University Press, 1989), 75–128.

31. Jean Delumeau, *Angst im Abendland: Die Geschichte der kollektiven Ängste im Europa des 14. bis 18. Jahrhunderts* (Reinbek: Rowohlt, 1985), 228–34.

32. Edward P. Thompson, "The 'Moral Economy' of the English Crowd in the Eighteenth Century," *Past & Present* 50 (1971): 71–136; John Stevenson, "The 'Moral Economy' of the English Crowd, Myth and Reality," in *Order and Disorder in Early Modern England,* ed. Anthony Fletcher and John Stevenson (Cambridge: Cambridge University Press, 1985), 215–38.

33. Cf. Georg Schmidt, "Die frühneuzeitlichen Hungerrevolten: Soziale Konflikte und Wirtschaftspolitik im Alten Reich," *Zeitschrift für historische Forschung* 18 (1991): 269–74.

34. Alfred Ritter von Arneth, *Maria Theresia's letzte Regierungszeit 1763–1780* (Vienna: Wilhelm Braumüller, 1879), 4:41–80; Erika Weinzierl-Fischer, "Die Bekämpfung der Hungersnot in Böhmen 1770–1772 durch Maria Theresia und Joseph II.," *Mitteilungen des Österreichischen Staatsarchivs* 7 (1954): 481; Derek Beales, *Joseph II,* vol. 1: *In the Shadow of Maria Theresia 1741–1780* (Cambridge: Cambridge University Press, 1987), 340–43.

35. 22 Aug. 1770 Conclusion, HStA Stuttgart, B 17, Reg. Prot., vol. 244.

36. 12 Sept. 1770 Conclusion, HStA Stuttgart, B 17, Reg. Prot., vol. 245.

37. Rolf Walter, "Merkantilpolitische Handelshemmnisse (im territorialen Vergleich) am Beispiel eines territorial relativ zersplitterten Gebietes," in *Die Auswirkungen von Zöllen und anderen Handelshemmnissen auf Wirtschaft und Gesellschaft vom Mittelalter bis zur Gegenwart,* ed. Hans Pohl (Stuttgart: Steiner, 1987), 103f.

38. 18 Sept. 1770, HStA Stuttgart, B 17, Reg. Prot., vol. 245.

39. 29 Sept. 1770, HStA Stuttgart, B 17, Reg. Prot., vol. 245. Cf. also the intervention against the abbey of Säckingen, 16 Oct. 1770. HStA Stuttgart, B 17, Reg. Prot., vol. 246.

40. 13 Oct. 1770, HStA Stuttgart, B 17, Reg. Prot., vol. 246.

41. 19 Sept. 1770, HStA Stuttgart, B 17, Reg. Prot., vol. 245.

42. Oberamt Schönberg, Sept. 1770, HStA Stuttgart, B 17, Bü. 218.

43. Mersburg, 13 Oct. 1770 Conclusion, Haus- Hof- und Staatsarchiv (HHStA) Wien, Reichskanzlei, Schwäbische Kreisakten, D 2a.

44. Frank Göttmann, *Getreidemarkt am Bodensee* (St. Katharina: Scripta Mercaturae, 1991); idem, "Aspekte der Tragfähigkeit in der Ostschweiz um 1700: Nahrungsmittelversorgung, Bevölkerung, Heimarbeit," in *Gewerbe und Handel vor der Industrialisierung,* ed. Joachim Jahn and Wolfgang Hartung (Sigmaringendorf: Glock & Lutz, 1991), 152–82. As a result of negative experiences during the famine of 1770–72, the magistrate of Zurich decided to control the grain market very strictly. See Peter Giger, "Verwaltung der Ernährung: Obrigkeitliche Kontrolle des Zürcher Kornmarktes im 18. Jahrhundert," in *Schweiz im Wandel: Festschrift für Rudolf Braun zum 60. Geburtstag,* ed. Sebastian Brändli et al. (Basel/ Frankfurt/M: Helbing & Lichtenhahn, 1990), 317–29.

45. Letter to the bishop of Constance, Oct. 1770, HHStA Wien, Reichskanzlei, Schwäbische Kreisakten, D 2a.

46. Blaich, "Wirtschaftspolitische Tätigkeit"; Weinzierl-Fischer, "Bekämpfung."

47. Quarthal et al., *Behördenorganisation,* 346.

48. Thaddäus von Brandenstein, assessor of the Generallandespolizeikommission, to Count Welsperg, 20 Oct. 1770, HHStA Wien, Reichskanzlei, Schwäbische Kreisakten, D 2a.

49. Mimmenhausen, Nov. 1770 Conclusion, HStA Stuttgart, B 17, Bü. 218.

50. On 6 October 1770, for example, the Triberg officials complained about the *Vogt* of Horb, who had stopped all grain trade with Triberg (HStA Stuttgart, B 17, Reg. Prot., vol. 246). In the summer of 1771, Constance was not allowed to take food

or wood from the county of Nellenburg, which belonged to Austria, too. HStA Stuttgart, B 17, Reg. Prot., vol. 254.

51. Thompson, "Moral Economy."

52. 31 Oct. 1770 Decree, HHStA Wien, Reichskanzlei, Schwäbische Kreisakten, D 2a.

53. Letter from Baron Kressel, 26 Oct. 1770, HHStA Wien, Reichskanzlei, Schwäbische Kreisakten, D 2a.

54. Blaich, "Wirtschaftspolitische Tätigkeit," 310–13.

55. Baron Ulm to Baron Kressel, 20 Nov. 1770, HStA Stuttgart, B 17, Bü. 218.

56. Letter to the government at Freiburg, HStA Stuttgart, B 17, Bü. 218.

57. Aulic Council, 24 Nov. 1770, HStA Stuttgart, B 17, Bü. 218.

58. Baron Ulm to Count Welsperg, 21 Dec. 1770, HHStA Wien, Reichskanzlei, Schwäbische Kreisakten, D 2a.

59. Frank Göttmann, "Kreuzschiffe auf dem Bodensee: Die grenzpolizeiliche Überwachung des Getreidehandels im 18. Jahrhundert," *Schriften des Vereins für Geschichte des Bodensees und seiner Umgebung* 106 (1988): 145–82.

60. Meersburg, 23 Nov. 1770 Conclusion, HHStA Wien, Reichskanzlei, Schwäbische Kreisakten, D 2a. Cf. Frank Göttmann, "Die Versorgungslage in Überlingen zur Zeit der Hungerkrise 1770/71," *Vermischtes zur neueren Sozial-Bevölkerungs- und Wirtschaftsgeschichte des Bodenseeraumes: Horst Rabe zum Sechzigsten,* ed. Frank Göttmann and Jörn Sieglerschmidt (Constance: Hartung-Gorre, 1992), 75–134.

61. Schmidt, "Frühneuzeitliche Hungerrevolten," 275.

62. Decree, HStA Stuttgart, B 17, Reg. Prot., vol. 255.

63. Baron Ried to Count Lacy, 5 Dec. 1771, HStA Stuttgart, B 17, Bü. 218.

64. Even Justus Möser, publicist and prime minister of Osnabrück, interceded emphatically for a free grain trade: "Das beste Mittel, einer Theuerung des Korns vorzubeugen oder sich bei einer anscheinenden theuren Zeit zu helfen, scheint mir dieses zu sein, daß man die Preise steigen lasse, wie sie wollen und dem Handel seinen Lauf gönne, ohne sich von obrigkeitlichen Amtswegen im geringsten darum zu bekümmern oder Ausfuhr und Branntweinbrennen zu verbieten" ("Patriotische Phantasie," *Sämtliche Werke* [Oldenburg/Berlin: Gerhard Stalling, n.d.], 5:27).

65. Clemens Zimmermann, "'Noth' und 'Theuerung' im badischen Unterland: Reformkurs und Krisenmanagement unter dem aufgeklärten Absolutismus," *Aufklärung* 2 (1987): 95–119; Louise A. Tilly, "The Food Riot as a Form of Political Conflict in France," *The Journal of Interdisciplinary History* 2 (1971): 33.

66. Blaich, *Epoche,* 168; idem, "Physiokratie," *Handwörterbuch der Wirtschaftswissenschaften,* 6:88; Karl-Heinz Osterloh, *Joseph von Sonnenfels und die österreichische Reformbewegung im Zeitalter des aufgeklärten Absolutismus* (Lübeck/Hamburg: Matthiesen, 1970).

67. Fritz Blaich, *Die Wirtschaftspolitik des Reichstags im Heiligen Römischen Reich: Ein Beitrag zur Problemgeschichte wirtschaftlichen Gestaltens* (Stuttgart: G. Fischer, 1970), 204–8.

68. Andrew Charlesworth, ed., *An Atlas of Rural Protest in Britain 1548–1900* (London/Canberra: Croom Helm, 1983); George Rudé, *The Crowd in History: A Study of Popular Disturbances in France and England 1730–1848* (New York: Wiley, 1964); Tilly, "Food Riot"; Heinz-Dietrich Löwe, "Teuerungsrevolten, Teuerungspolitik und Marktregulierung im 18. Jahrhundert in England, Frankreich und Deutschland," *Saeculum* 37 (1986): 291–312; Schmidt, "Frühneuzeitliche Hungerrevolten."

69. Hilton L. Root, "Politiques frumentaires et violence collective en Europe au XVIIIᵉ siècle," *Annales: Economies, sociétés, civilisations* 45 (1990): 167–89.

70. Abel, *Massenarmut,* 326–43; Arno Herzig, *Unterschichtenprotest in Deutschland 1790–1870* (Göttingen: Vandenhoeck & Ruprecht, 1988).

71. Manfred Gailus, *Straße und Brot: Sozialer Protest in den deutschen Staaten unter besonderer Berücksichtigung Preußens, 1847–1849* (Göttingen: Vandenhoeck & Ruprecht, 1990).

Part 5

Foreign Policy

Introduction

Charles W. Ingrao

Few observers would dispute that foreign policy was the first concern of the Austrian Habsburgs. Their dynastic diplomacy had created their East Central European patrimony—together with the even larger empire of their Spanish cousins. Moreover, with its formation, they never forgot that maintaining the monarchy involved defending its interests and security on the international stage. For that reason, foreign policy remained their first concern in policy making throughout the early modern period. Foreign affairs were the primary concern of the monarchy's highest bodies, the Privy Conference and (after 1742) the State Chancery, which not only determined foreign affairs but also informed the duties and direction of other state offices, such as the *Hofkammer, Hofkriegsrat,* and *Reichshofrat.* Even the Austrian Chancery owed its meteoric rise to prominence ahead of its imperial, Bohemian, and Hungarian counterparts to the key role it played in dispatching foreign policy formulated by the Privy Conference. Only with the creation of a Council of State (1761) did the Habsburgs finally establish a single, domestic policy-making body that claimed competence for all of their dominions—and then primarily because State Chancellor Kaunitz realized that it was indispensable in meeting the monarchy's military and foreign-policy objectives.[1]

This focus on foreign affairs has helped sustain the sense among scholars that the Habsburg Monarchy was a uniquely personal, "dynastic enterprise." Certainly its career depended heavily on the ideas, policies, and talent of its rulers and their advisors—individuals who gave unity and purpose to an otherwise diverse realm that had no ethnic, economic, demographic, cultural, or social continuity of its own. This helps explain the rather traditional tendency to discuss Austrian history from the perspective of those who governed it and to rely for our evidence on what monarchs, ministers, and diplomats said to each other—and what they collectively *did* to the country.

If there was one unifying structure in the monarchy's history that transcended the work of individuals, it was geography. Unlike its Spanish counterpart, the realm of the Austrian Habsburgs was largely contiguous for most of its history. Even during the eighteenth century, when it held remote outposts in Italy and Belgium, its leaders' perspectives were governed almost exclusively by the security and welfare of the monarchy's core lands. An even more crucial geographical structure was the monarchy's location in the heart of Europe, a reality that obliged it to confront a number of prospective attackers from every direction of the compass. It was this multiplicity of foreign threats that determined the rather conservative, consensual nature of Austrian policy, both at home and abroad. Indeed, a cautious approach to domestic reform that preserved vested interests and social inequities had the virtue of minimizing the threat of internal revolts by privileged elites that might also prompt outside intervention; meanwhile, an essentially defensive diplomacy based on norms of international behavior greatly facilitated the enlistment of foreign allies and domestic support for increased taxation.[2]

It also encouraged the adoption of an essentially radial foreign policy that aimed at maintaining strategic buffers in Germany, Italy, Poland, and the Balkans. Each of these four flanks demanded a discrete set of allies: to defend its German interests against France and Sweden, the monarchy's statesmen sought the assistance of Habsburg Spain (until 1700) and the Maritime Powers (until 1756), together with a continuously changing constellation of loyal German princes. The German states also helped fend off the Turks through a succession of Balkan coalitions that also embraced the papacy,

Venice, Poland, and Russia. Until 1740 Saxony, Brandenburg-Prussia, and Russia cooperated closely with the monarchy in combating Swedish and French influence in Poland. In Italy the monarchy's circle of potential allies was much smaller, though no less effective. During the seventeenth century, it simply relied on the more powerful Spanish Habsburgs to fend off any threat from France; with their extinction in 1700, it assumed that responsibility, either alone or with occasional assistance from the house of Savoy.

Once security had been attained, the monarchy's statesmen were usually content to preserve the status quo, not only during the early modern period but right up until 1918. Of course, each region underwent dynamic changes during the monarchy's last three centuries. By 1720 the decline of Poland and Turkey and the perpetuation of Habsburg hegemony over the small German and Italian states afforded the monarchy unprecedented security all along its frontiers. For this reason it essentially became a status quo power, with no master plan for territorial aggrandizement. Instead, its statesmen attempted to preserve the integrity of the Ottoman Empire and the German princes, often by restraining the greed of their own allies. When they were unable to forestall Prussia and Russia from partitioning Poland, they reluctantly cooperated with them in promoting an enduring settlement among the conquering powers. Similarly, having failed to prevent the emergence of a united Germany and Italy, they opted to secure both flanks by engaging both countries in a Triple Alliance (1882). Austria-Hungary's eventual dismemberment can been explained in terms of the collapse of these buffer zones and of its efforts to maintain lasting alliances with four of the five countries that had taken control of them (Italy, Russia, Serbia, and Romania).

Whereas hindsight makes it possible for us to visualize how such overarching geopolitical structures predetermined Austrian foreign policy, they were much less evident at the time. Only on one occasion—during the War of the Spanish Succession—were the monarchy's statesmen actually obliged to counter simultaneous strategic threats on its German, Italian, Balkan, and Polish flanks. More typically, their concerns involved setting priorities that anticipated hostilities on just two fronts. Thus, during the Thirty Years'

War, the emperors Ferdinand repeatedly appeased Transylvania and the Turks in Hungary in order to pursue more important objectives within Germany; in 1684 Leopold I signed the so-called Twenty Years' Truce with Louis XIV that tacitly accepted French annexations on the Rhine so that he would be free to reconquer Hungary from the Turks; a half century later, Charles VI sacrificed Lorraine to France so that he could prevent a French client from becoming king of Poland; after the death of Joseph II in 1790, Leopold II relinquished his brother's extensive Balkan conquests in order to forestall a Prussian invasion of Bohemia; Francis Joseph forfeited Russia's goodwill during the Crimean War in the vain hope of protecting his possessions in Italy; and, with the outbreak of World War I, he and his successor forbore Conrad von Hötzendorf's fumbling attempts to shift priorities between the Balkans and Poland (1914–15), and then between Italy and Poland (1916–17).

Early modern diplomatic historians have also tended to visualize a bipolar grand strategy that focused on Germany and the Balkans at the expense of the relatively more secure Polish and Italian flanks. The monarchy's breakup has likewise encouraged the persistence of our focus on the familiar East-West dilemma that confronted the monarchy in combating the Turks in the Balkans and France (followed by Prussia) in Central Europe. Whereas Anglo-American diplomatic historians have assumed a more global perspective of early modern Habsburg foreign policy, scholars from the various successor states have tended to focus on those aspects of Habsburg foreign policy that concern their own countries. Magyar historians, such as Kálmán Benda, Béla Köpeczi, and Domokos Kosáry, have concentrated on Hungary's relations with its immediate Balkan neighbors, or with its sometime French ally. Their Polish counterparts have focused on Austro-Polish cooperation in John Sobieski's celebrated relief of Vienna and the subsequent Holy League against the Turks. German scholars, such as Karl Otmar von Aretin, have investigated the Habsburgs' relations with Germany, primarily in their capacity as Holy Roman emperors. Meanwhile, Austria's emergence as a nonaligned nation has encouraged its current generation of scholars to focus its attention on nondiplomatic themes and newer methodologies, such as those covered in this volume.[3]

All three of the essays in this section deal with these latter two regions. Those by Heinz Duchhardt and Volker Press illustrate the contemporary German focus on the imperial princes' interaction with the Habsburgs in their capacity as Holy Roman emperors. They also examine the Habsburgs' *Reichspolitik* at a time when they were redefining their relationship with the Holy Roman Empire. Having at last accepted the impossibility of establishing effective Habsburg dominion over Germany, Ferdinand III and his successors pursued the less ambitious goal of maintaining the empire as a loose confederation in which they alone would exercise decisive leadership. Rather than impose their will over the more significant armed estates, such as Bavaria, Brandenburg, and Saxony, they enlisted their support by offering—or threatening to withhold—those rights of patronage that the imperial office still enjoyed under the imperial constitution. In effect, the Habsburgs politicized the application of imperial laws and institutions by using them either to favor any vassal who served Austrian interests or to oppose those whose agendas ran contrary to them. Despite the absence of a truly sovereign authority, such an approach permitted the emperor to enjoy hegemony within Germany as long as he could prevent any state or group of states from becoming independent of his patronage.

This goal underlies the paradox behind Heinz Duchhardt's essay on electoral diplomacy immediately after the Peace of Westphalia. By emphasizing the imperial electors' intensive activities, he contributes to the considerable school of British, American, and German historians who stress the continued resilience and vitality of imperial institutions after the Peace of Westphalia. He also reaffirms the conventional picture of the prince-bishops and the empire's *Kleinstaaterei* as advocates of the rule of law against the practice of *Realpolitik*. At the same time, however, Duchhardt demonstrates that both the French king and Habsburg emperor were instrumental in frustrating the electors' peace initiatives. Indeed, an independent force of German princes threatened to limit France's freedom of action within Europe as well as the emperor's within Germany itself.

If the emperor was finally able to rein in the independent-minded electors, it was because both French and Turkish aggression awakened them to the need for close cooperation with Vienna. The resulting Indian summer of *Reichspatriotismus* may have inspired a generation of political thinkers and the smaller principalities, whose survival depended on their acceptance of imperial and international law, but it did little to temper the separate dynastic agendas of Germany's larger states. Nor did it sway Emperor Leopold I (1658–1705) and his two sons from exploiting their imperial prerogatives to serve Austrian state and Habsburg dynastic interests. Thus Leopold I and Joseph I (1705–11) completed the progressive emasculation of the Imperial Chancery, while Joseph I used both the imperial army and the Imperial Aulic Court to establish Austrian hegemony over Italy. Not unlike his predecessors, Joseph I rejected the Catholic electors' offer to mediate during his short war with Pope Clement XI (1708–9), just as he excluded them from the process by which the Imperial Aulic Court banned the pro-French duke of Mantua. As the War of the Spanish Succession drew to a close, both he and his brother, Charles VI (1711–40), also prevented the six imperial circles of the *Nördlinger Assoziation* from concluding an alliance with the Dutch or participating in the subsequent peace conferences.[4] These actions provide yet additional evidence in support of Duchhardt's judgment that "great-power pretensions and emperorship were fundamentally incompatible."

The question arises whether there could have been any other outcome to the electors' forlorn attempts to strengthen multilateral adherence to international law. Or were they, as Duchhardt suggests, simply naive? It was certainly a well-developed sense of their true self-interest that led them to promote adherence to both imperial and international conventions; indeed, international law will always be the first refuge of satiated powers and the last refuge of the weak. The electors were, however, doomed from the start, if only because the emperor's failure to mold the empire into a vehicle for Habsburg *Realpolitik* forced him into a more exclusive identity with his own hereditary dominions. With the final repulse of Louis XIV during the War of the Spanish Succession, the larger German states matched their Habsburg overlord in their willingness to utilize—or circumvent—imperial law and institutions in quest of their own dynastic goals. By 1720, the rulers of Saxony, Prussia, Hanover, and Hesse-Kassel all wore royal crowns. Among the lay electors, only the Wittelsbachs of Bavaria and the Palatinate lacked such a dignity, partly because they had sought their crowns *within* Germany at the expense of the Habsburgs' own pretensions as rulers of Bohemia (1619, 1741), Belgium (1701, 1777, 1785), and the empire itself (1618, 1702, 1742).

Although the Wittelsbachs failed where the Hohenzollerns, Wettins, and Guelphs succeeded, the Habsburg emperors opposed the dynastic ambitions of all of their more powerful vassals at one point or another. They assisted them only when there was a *quid pro quo* to be gained but never when their vassals' gains threatened Habsburg hegemony within the empire. The story of Habsburg-Hohenzollern relations is, in fact, one of constant stress between the advantage of enlisting Brandenburg-Prussia's military assistance versus the disadvantage of promoting its pretensions as Germany's second-greatest power. Austro-Prussian competition did not begin in 1740. At the beginning of his essay, Volker Press alludes to the two states' earlier territorial expansion into Eastern Europe. Once again, geopolitical structures predetermined the parallel development of the two states' *Drang nach Osten:* As Central European powers, the Habsburg and Hohenzollern monarchies initially needed to strengthen their military and fiscal systems in order to defend their German lands against the prospects of Franco-Swedish aggression. Having better marshaled their resources against these western juggernauts, both German powers were subsequently able to redirect their military eastward to overpower the more primitive political and military systems of Poland and Turkey.

Press's contribution focuses on developments within the empire. He mentions Elector Joachim II's (1535–71) adherence to Protestantism. This was not only a religious but also a political conversion, since the takeover of church wealth and responsibilities increased government authority in the emerging cameralist welfare state. He also suggests that a northward shift away from

Habsburg-dominated southern Germany further facilitated the Hohenzollerns' rise to European prominence. Both dynasties had been expanding northward for some time: the Hohenzollerns into Brandenburg and its environs, the Habsburgs into the Low Countries (1477) and Bohemia (1526). During the seventeenth century, the Habsburg emperors actually seized the Silesian fiefs of Beuthen (1617), Jägerndorf (1623), Liegnitz, Brieg, and Wohlau (1675), all at the Hohenzollerns' expense. Yet Brandenburg's electors counterbalanced these losses by establishing themselves farther north along the banks of the Rhine and the shores of the Baltic. Moreover, whereas the early eighteenth century brought virtually no increase in the Habsburgs' northern German patrimony, Brandenburg-Prussia added numerous appendages, including parts of Guelders, Pomerania, and Frisia.

In a sense, these gains came at the expense of the other imperial electorates, all of which declined relative to Brandenburg-Prussia. As Press points out, the emperor actually assisted in the process because he badly needed its military assistance against France. Emperor Leopold I's decision to elevate Elector Frederick III (1688–1713) to the rank of king in Prussia in 1701 represents the high-water mark in Habsburg patronage of its Hohenzollern vassal. Yet the emperor was not blind to the changing balance of power both among the German electors and between himself and his Hohenzollern vassal. Hence his recognition of the Prussian royal crown also represents the beginning of Habsburg resistance to further Prussian expansion. The emperor was so reluctant to encourage Frederick's pretensions to equal status that he recognized him only as *König* in *Preußen,* but not within the empire or anyplace else. Two years later, he declined the Prussian king's offer of generous reinforcements for the pivotal Blenheim campaign against Bavaria in order to avoid making further concessions to him. Of course, 'twas a famous allied victory at Blenheim, but the imperial army failed miserably in subsequent campaigns largely because Emperor Joseph I's opposition to Frederick's numerous desiderata cost it the assistance of Brandenburg's sizeable *Reichskontingent.* Similarly, Emperor Charles VI purposely slighted Prussia in adjudicating constitutional disputes in Mecklenburg and East Frisia, fighting the

War of Polish Succession, and deciding the succession in Jülich-Berg.[5] At no point did the emperors' policies foreshadow territorial designs of their own. Their focus was on maintenance of Habsburg leadership—and thus security—within the empire. Hence Joseph I never seriously contemplated annexing Bavaria, even after Blenheim had placed it at his disposal. Nor did Charles VI intend to escheat Jülich-Berg for his dynasty, as had Emperor Rudolph II a century before. Nevertheless, by blocking further Prussian expansion within the empire, the Habsburgs made inevitable yet another confrontation between the emperor and one of its great vassals. Unfortunately for them, Mollwitz would not be another Mühlberg, White Mountain, or Blenheim.

With Frederick II's surprising triumph in the War of the Austrian Succession, the reality of Austro-Prussian dualism superseded all of the empire's constitutional norms and institutional relationships. Simply put, dualism doomed the Holy Roman Empire to a stultifying paralysis that would ultimately result in its dissolution. The degenerative process was, however, not irreversible. Had Maria Theresa succeeded in regaining Silesia—as she nearly did in the Seven Years' War—Habsburg hegemony would have been reestablished within the empire; Joseph II's abortive attempt to swap Belgium for Bavaria might have also sufficed to restore Habsburg leadership. Yet once they failed, there were no other credible prospects for compensating for the loss of Silesia. Notwithstanding some idle speculation by Joseph II, the monarchy's statesmen never seriously contemplated any annexations in Italy, where the monarchy was well protected by control of Lombardy, its Tuscan secundogeniture, and dynastic compacts with the Bourbons.[6]

Nor did they view expansion into the Balkans as a likely source of new military strength. Surely there was no need to add to the monarchy's already formidable Hungarian glacis against the Turks. By midcentury, it was clear to everyone that the sultan was far preferable as a neighbor than the far more powerful and aggressive Russian tsar. Of course, the monarchy continuously cultivated close ties with Russia. Yet, as Karl Roider has shown, the monarchy's leaders were far more interested in using such an alliance to slow Russia's entry into the Balkans than to assist it in partitioning the Ottoman

Empire; if they prized the Russians as allies, it was as a defensive weapon against the French, the Turks, and especially the Prussians.[7] Roider's essay points out that the monarchy's leaders could see no compelling economic argument for additional Balkan conquests. The region had a small, impoverished, and technologically ignorant population whose peacetime contributions to Western civilization had been limited to the periodic export of smallpox and plague. Roider suggests that the monarchy's leaders reached this conclusion after years of painful firsthand experience colonizing the Banat and, perhaps, its other Balkan winnings in Croatia-Slavonia, the Vojvodina, and Transylvania. In short, by the eighteenth century, the Habsburgs had become the first great power to appreciate the wisdom of modern statesmen from Bismarck to Bush that involvement in the Balkans addressed no identifiable national interest.

Hence the monarchy entered the modern era as an essentially satiated power. In those instances when it contemplated acts of aggression, such as in the Seven Years' War, the Napoleonic Wars, the seizure of Bosnia-Hercegovina, or the projected Third Balkan War of 1914, it did so either to regain lost territory or to retain what it already possessed. Rarely, if ever, did it contemplate new conquests for their own sake. Such a conservative application of *Realpolitik* may be compatible with international law, but it is not without negative consequences. In the case of the Balkans, the monarchy's leaders decided that territorial expansion was not worth the effort at a time when the tsar was helping create a half dozen grateful client states. At the same time, however, they concluded that the monarchy could not tolerate losing the arc of Balkan dominions in southern Hungary that they had already acquired during the early modern period. Unfortunately, Balkan demography dictated that the monarchy needed to expand into regions such as Moldavia, Wallachia, Serbia, and Bosnia if it was going to retain firm control over all of greater Hungary. Perhaps the Habsburgs should have paid closer heed to the Hohenzollern dictum that states which cease to expand must eventually contract.

Notes

1. Even then, its competence in Hungarian affairs was challenged by that country's diet. P. G. M. Dickson, *Finance and Government under Maria Theresa 1740–1780* (Oxford: Oxford University Press, 1987), 2:228, 234.

2. Charles W. Ingrao, *The Habsburg Monarchy,* 1618–1815 (Cambridge: Cambridge University Press, 1994), 2–6, 18–20.

3. I cite this suggestion by Grete Klingenstein in Charles W. Ingrao, "From the Reconquest to the Revolutionary Wars: Recent Trends in Austrian Diplomatic History, 1683–1800," *The Austrian History Yearbook* 23 (1993): 201.

4. Roger Wines, "The Imperial Circles, Princely Diplomacy and Imperial Reform 1681–1714," *The Journal of Modern History* 39 (1967): 22–25.

5. For Charles's use of the *Reichshofrat* vis-à-vis Prussia, see Michael Hughes, *Law and Politics in Eighteenth-Century Germany: The Imperial Aulic Council in the Reign of Charles VI* (Wolfeboro, N.H.: Boydell, 1988).

6. Derek Beales, *Joseph II,* vol. 1, *In the Shadow of Maria Theresa* (Cambridge: Cambridge University Press, 1987), 277, 437.

7. Karl A. Roider, Jr., *The Reluctant Ally: Austria's Policy in the Austro-Turkish War, 1737–1739* (Baton Rouge: Louisiana State University Press, 1972); and idem, *Austria's Eastern Question* (Princeton, N.J.: Princeton University Press, 1982).

International Relations, the Law of Nations, and the Germanies

Structures and Changes in the Second Half of the Seventeenth Century

Heinz Duchhardt

The past two decades have witnessed a steady increase in scholarly interest in the political system of the Holy Roman Empire. Among the trove of new publications, special attention has been paid to the reevaluation of the Habsburg emperorship and its incorporation into international politics in the second half of the early modern period. For a long time, historians adhered to the rather undifferentiated view that the eight emperors who reigned between the Peace of Westphalia and the end of the Holy Roman Empire were generally weak, disinterested, and hopelessly overmatched by the more powerful German princes. Beginning in the 1970s, however, a new approach has emerged that is more sensitive to the Hofburg's tendency to use those means at its disposal to make the empire a pillar of its own political agenda, whether by employing its remaining feudal prerogatives that were still operative, exercising its control of the Imperial Aulic Court, building up a more or less efficient diplomatic service, or exploiting its leadership of Catholic and other traditionally loyal client princes, especially in the southern and southwestern reaches of the empire. Recent scholarship is now more aware than ever before that, with the Westphalian settlement, there was a built-in tension in all Habsburg policy in and toward the empire between Austrian great-power politics and the imperial idea. It was no longer helpful to seek acceptance of the abstract but somehow outdated idea of a *Sacrum Imperium;* instead, Habsburg *Realpolitik* simply made use of this idea in order to promote Austria's rise as a great power. After 1648 the Hofburg was almost certainly aware that if it was ever to realize the contemporary political ideal of a close and strictly organized central state, it could no longer be attained within the empire itself but only within the Habsburg patrimonial lands.

This tension between the imperial idea and great-power politics has been intensively researched and analyzed as far as the last two Habsburg emperors, Joseph I and Charles VI, are concerned.[1] On the other hand, except for a few more recent biographical studies,[2] very little attention has been paid to their father, the somewhat colorless but often underestimated Leopold I. This is all the more regrettable because it was the period of Leopold's reign that largely determined whether it would still be possible for the Habsburgs to continue along the path toward *Reichsabsolutismus*[3] and dominate their imperial vassals as they had intended at the climax of the Thirty Years' War.

This decision essentially depended on the states' ability to build up their own networks within and outside the empire and thus to seek support against any possible Habsburg pressure. Karl Otmar Freiherr von Aretin has recently analyzed the degree to which the empire was integrated into international relations during the period 1648–1740,[4] and particularly the political options that the Habsburg emperor and the states of the empire had at their disposal during the Age of Louis XIV. I intend to examine one aspect of the empire's incorporation into international politics that the French and Swedish architects of the Westphalian settlement had explicitly sought to bring about, namely, its projected role in the contemporary notion of the law of nations. More specifically, I will consider to what extent the German states could—and did—make use of the international political opportunities inherent in the peace treaties of 1648. Indeed, to a great extent the treaty provisions were nothing but programmatic designs and statements of intent whose transformation into practical politics depended on princes' and statesmen's skill, power, and determination. Such an examination will also shed some light on the changing understanding of politics in the empire during the second half of the seventeenth century.

The famous Article VIII of the Treaty of Osnabrück that granted the German princes the *ius foederis*[5]—the right to conclude alliances even with foreign crowns—should not be overrated. It is certainly true that the article represents the end of the Hofburg's eleventh-hour attempts to transform the empire into a kind of absolutist state, which had culminated in the Edict of Restitution (1629). Yet, far from being revolutionary, the *ius foederis* merely gave constitutional form to what had long since been the actual state of affairs in the empire. One can certainly agree with Aretin's judgment that this article and its consequences have been greatly exaggerated by previous historical research, since only very few states and princes were actually in the position to follow a really active and independent foreign policy. But in any case, Article VIII did grant the German states a certain measure of equality in international law. The question arises, however, whether they could realistically expect to become fully enfranchised members of the international community. Would they be able to assume the responsibilities and participate in the diplomatic networks that the law of nations accorded other states, or would they eventually decide—or be forced—to forfeit their newly won legal position?

The years immediately after the Peace of Westphalia were hardly propitious for the conduct of an active foreign policy. Having incurred the severe economic and fiscal consequences of a long war, states such as the Palatinate, Württemberg, Saxony, and even Brandenburg were obliged to confront pressing domestic problems. Nevertheless, there is no question that many smaller states sustained a rather pretentious foreign policy, either individually or, more typically, in alliance with other states. Within the empire, this took the form of associations of princes who, in most cases, shared the same rank or religion or who belonged to the same imperial circle. No one was more active during the international conflicts of the 1650s and 1660s than the three ecclesiastical electors and the other members of the electoral college—which is not totally surprising, since they ranked first in the hierarchy of the empire.[6] In both instances, they were led by the archbishop-elector of Mainz, Johann Philipp von Schönborn. Schönborn was not only the most senior of this small and most exclusive group of German princes but was also one of the most energetic statesmen of the postwar generation. Just as he had helped effect a swift conclusion to the peace treaties in 1648,[7] he now led his fellow electors in their efforts to effect peace negotiations between Central Europe's remaining belligerent powers.

Their record of unabashed political activism speaks for itself. In the early summer of 1658, the electors of Mainz and Cologne secured France's permission to intervene together with the Roman Curia and Venice in the continuing Franco-Spanish War. In fact, the diplomats of the two archbishop-electors participated in the peace negotiations in Frankfurt. From the very beginning, however, their activities were so restricted that the belligerent powers eventually arrived at a final agreement by themselves, without any help from outside. Although they were not allowed to perform any official function, the delegates from Mainz and Cologne were admitted as observers and were afforded the diplomatic courtesy of attending the signing ceremony of the treaty in the Pyrenees. Their mediatory efforts, together with those of the two Italian states, were mentioned only in general terms, but not explicitly, in the preamble of the treaty.[8]

Almost at the same time, the archbishop-elector of Mainz accepted a second request from King Sigismund of Poland and Archduke Leopold, the Habsburg successor-designate to the imperial throne, to enlist the electoral college's help in trying to mediate an end to the First Northern War (1655–60).[9] Once again, the electors' efforts came to nothing. Nevertheless, they were hardly discouraged by this latest failure; on the contrary, they were quite ready and eager to resume international duties at the first opportunity.

Shortly thereafter they received another request, this time from the Curia, which had anticipated a serious military conflict with France as early as 1662.[10] In addition to several other states and individuals, it now asked the ecclesiastical electors for *"consilium et assistentia"*—whatever this formula, originating in the sphere of feudalism, was meant to say. The three archbishop-electors were, in fact, already allied with France by the *Rheinbund* and, in many respects, also dependent on the Curia. After careful examination of the various risks and perspectives, Mainz and the other two electorates decided to undertake a mediation, doubtless also considering the fact that such a mediation could prevent them from having to support one or the other side in a conflict that stirred up the whole of Christianity. In the end, this latest attempt at mediation was also displaced by other activities and failed to achieve any success. The ecclesiastical electors had, however, not only stood their ground in this delicate and politically explosive situation but had undertaken measures and projects that had definitely mitigated tensions and positively influenced the subsequent Franco-Papal settlement.

The same pattern of activities soon unfolded in a number of other brewing conflicts. Led once again by Schönborn, the electors responded to a Spanish request to help prevent the outbreak of what eventually came to be known as the War of Devolution (1667–68).[11] They even initiated a congress at Cologne in order to include other states in their peace efforts. But it was always the same old story: they failed both to reestablish harmonious relations between Madrid and Paris and to find the means and support to settle the conflict once it had broken out. As a courtesy, a delegation from the Congress of Cologne attended the negotiations as observers and signed the Treaty of Aix-la-Chapelle (1668).[12] Yet the peace stemmed not from the electors' mediation but from political pressure applied by the Triple Alliance. It should thus hardly come as a surprise that Schönborn and his fellow electors unsuccessfully endeavored to forestall the outbreak and spread of the Franco-Dutch War (1672–79), which had indeed been foreseeable for a long time.

None of these various attempts to assume international duties was crowned with success. Not only had the electors been unable to prevent or settle conflicts; they had also failed to establish themselves as equal partners in the application of international law and thus to achieve the typical status of a corpus that was above material political ambition and capable of acting as a Catholic or ecumenical peacemaking body, depending on the situation. This is not to say, however, that these activities could be neglected as a *quantité négligeable,* especially since modern research shows a significant tendency to draw more attention to historical projects that were not crowned with success. The fact remains that, during times of crisis, several European states—Spain, Poland, the Roman Curia—definitely enlisted the electoral college or its ecclesiastical members to employ the instruments of international law in establishing diplomatic contacts and offering their good offices and mediation. Mediation of peace was (and is) always a highly spectacular act of exercising international duties. Hence the electors saw their great opportunity as the most prominent group of German princes to enhance their political prestige and become accepted as discrete entities in international law. As has been shown, the electors did not necessarily wait for requests from one warring party or another but also sent out definite political signals of their willingness to offer their services. Moreover, since there were no "born" mediators once the Curia had isolated itself, and since both political practice and theory clearly preferred "weak" mediators, the relatively impotent and undynamic German electors envisioned a real opportunity to attain a prominent position within international law. At the same time, however, it became equally evident that the French, in particular, had many reservations against allowing the German electors to acquire such a key political position. Because of these many failures and the subsequent death of Schönborn, it was the French position that finally prevailed. But it would be too shortsighted to look at the electors' numerous attempts to play a role on the European stage as a mere episode. The electors really did try to breathe life into the *ius foederis* that had been accorded them by the Peace of Westphalia. Nor were they deterred or doomed to failure from the very beginning. Some, though not all, European states also appear to have shared their vision of an electoral college that would be capable of meeting the actual demands of international law, especially since its membership had an ecumenical character and did not evince any particular interest in the dynamics of power politics.

There are, of course, many other examples of diplomatic negotiations and alliances among the German states and the various imperial circles. This brief survey has, however, illustrated some of the numerous activities of a select group of German princes who buttressed their pretensions as legitimate international entities by undertaking responsibilities as members of the international community. It also shows how France and other leading members of the society of European states aborted these efforts, primarily because they did not want the German princes, either individually or collectively, to bring about an international peace. As a result, these efforts to participate in international affairs had virtually ended by the late 1660s, both because France had made clear its steadfast opposition to future electoral diplomacy and because the electors themselves realized the fruitlessness of their endeavors. Indeed, nobody wants to live with nothing but failures, especially not in the long run.

The German states' failure to assert themselves on the international stage and gain acceptance as legitimate international entities by the European powers was hastened by the Habsburg emperor's total indifference to their attempts. To Vienna it was simply inconceivable that the empire or a corpus of states could act as an equal partner in international affairs. The emperors demonstrated this diffidence on more than one occasion, most notably during the great European peace congresses that punctuated the wars of Louis XIV. The empire as a political body enjoyed at least a moral right to participate as a political body at Nijmegen, even though the Regensburg diet had not officially declared war during the Dutch War;[13] but it enjoyed a clear legal imperative at both Ryswick and Utrecht, since the diet had formally declared war on France and her allies. Actually, the imperial diet had made more or less intensive efforts to represent the empire's interests at all three congresses by dispatching its own delegations, instead of relying solely on the Habsburg emperor's goodwill. In the end, however, the court of Vienna counteracted and dodged all these efforts and was awarded, tacitly or explicitly, with the exclusive right to negotiate for the empire as a whole.[14] It would hardly be an exaggeration to conclude that, despite the enormous differences between them, the European crowns formed a kind of grand alliance that was determined to keep the empire in a subordinate position from the standpoint of international law. In this sense, the empire and the European states always remained essentially antithetical. And as far as Vienna was concerned, that position was immutable. Leopold I and Joseph I thwarted

all attempts made by the *Kreisassoziationen*—the league of the most
threatened and most active circles in the southern and western
parts of the empire—to sign agreements with the Netherlands and
other neighboring countries, thereby preventing them from gaining
freedom of action in foreign affairs.[15] This consistency reflects once
more the Hofburg's firm determination to prevent its vassals from
gaining any individual or collective independence with respect to
international law and foreign affairs. It is not difficult to discern the
basis for its opposition: since both the ecclesiastical electors and the
Kreisassoziationen comprised traditional Habsburg clients, such
freedom of action would have threatened a collapse of imperial
power and prestige in those western and southern reaches of the
empire that were still oriented toward Vienna.

From Vienna's point of view, it was bad enough that the northern German princes had progressively withdrawn from imperial
control by instrumentalizing their new right of *ius foederis,* but the
monarchical tendencies of the states was an even greater concern.
Saxony and Hanover were just two of several German states whose
rulers acquired foreign royal crowns either by election or by reason
of dynastic succession. It was much more of a problem for Vienna
that Brandenburg pushed itself more and more into the foreground
of European politics by intensively employing its military power
and *ius foederis;* in a particularly critical situation, on the eve of the
War of the Spanish Succession, it had become so indispensable to
Leopold I that the emperor was obliged to conclude the Crown
Treaty of 1700, which finally satisfied the Hohenzollern quest for a
royal crown based on the duchy of Prussia.[16] While Brandenburg's
interests had still been treated with characteristic brusqueness at
Ryswick (1697), Brandenburg-Prussia had the satisfaction of being
readily admitted to full participation at the Congress of Utrecht
(1712–13), where its new crown was acknowledged without delay or
difficulty by most of the European powers. Thus it was the Habsburg emperor himself who helped introduce this north German new-
comer as an entity in international law and a fully accepted member
of the community of European states. The irony becomes more acute
in view of the fact that, in the course of the decades to follow,
Brandenburg-Prussia not always turned out to be a stabilizing

factor in the law of nations before earning a position as an equal
member of the European great-power system, whose first aim was
the preservation of the social and political status quo.

The majority of the German states could make no use of the opportunities that the *ius foederis* theoretically offered them; they never
achieved equality within the law of nations. The reason was not so
much their own inability and lack of interest but the fact that the
European crowns, including the court of Vienna, erected a dense
barrier in order to keep the group of international-law entities as
small as possible. It did not matter whether the German states were
equal to such activities on the international stage or lacked the necessary physical resources, highly qualified statesmen, patience, and
staying power. What the German states also lacked, however, was a
realistic, modern understanding of politics. For them politics was
first and foremost the equivalent to law, especially the protection
that law afforded. A political body such as the empire—which had a
nearly immeasurable multitude of minor states, relatively few compact territories, and an emperor who "ruled" principally in the role of
primus inter pares—needed one thing in particular: the strict maintenance of the law, of the status quo, of privileges, properties, and
frontiers whose disposition could be maintained or adjusted only
through legal processes. Indeed, no brief definition of the empire
as a political organism is complete without the terms "multitude,"
"status quo," and "imperial courts." Characteristically enough, after
the Peace of Westphalia the electors in particular were convinced
that they could prevent any political cooperation between Vienna
and Madrid—which they regarded as detrimental to internal and
external peace—by prosecuting a claim based solely on law, namely,
an article of Leopold I's electoral contract (*Wahlkapitulation*) of
1658.[17] In the political culture of the empire, there was, in principle,
no room left for political dynamics, for the will to change things.
Consequently, for the rest of the seventeenth century right up until
the time of Samuel Pufendorf, no political theory was conceived in
Germany that went beyond descriptions of the constitution and reflections on the state of *majestas* (sovereignty) within the empire. It
was symptomatic that authors such as Machiavelli or Hobbes met

with intense disapproval within the empire, and that only very few political theories dealing with categories such as power or political practicability were conceived there.[18] The notion that a monarch such as Louis XIV could unilaterally change things for his own selfish advantage was wholly foreign to the German states and diametrically contradicted their understanding of politics and their interpretation of a body politic.

Given this perspective, it is understandable how the states of the old empire would ultimately turn away from a French king who was obviously not interested in respecting law and who had become an unpredictable factor by the end of the 1660s. Once again, the German princes gravitated toward the Habsburg emperor, who more than anyone else was expected to protect the law of the empire and safeguard the status quo. Yet the imperial court quickly jumped to conclusions about the change in the European political climate and began to question the immutability of existing structures. Because of its deficient inner development, seventeenth-century Austria could not yet be classified as a great power, even if its sovereign wore the most prominent crown of Christianity. With the defeat of the Turks in 1683, however, the Hofburg suddenly adopted a new political ideology:[19] its leaders were no longer satisfied with the reestablishment of the *status quo ante bellum* but wanted to proceed offensively against the Ottomans in order to gain not only territories in the southeast but also the political prestige that was apparently unattainable against Louis XIV in the west. Whether the Spanish inheritance would simply be handed to the Austrian Habsburgs on a silver platter was still an open question. Indeed, the decision in favor of southeastern expansion did not mean that Austria would become a thoroughly "political" state overnight. It did, however, enable it to achieve European great-power status under Leopold I because it demanded an impulse to modernize the state that finally resulted in military success.[20] This great-power status was independent of the imperial crown. On the contrary, the gap between Austrian and imperial politics widened considerably in the decades to come. But it was only after 1740 that Vienna, disappointed by the empire's rejection of the Pragmatic Sanction and of the candidacy of Maria Theresa's husband, definitely chose to assume the position of a European great power. Even then it was handicapped again and again by its obligations toward the empire. The simple fact was that great-power pretensions and emperorship were fundamentally incompatible.

Notes

1. Charles W. Ingrao, *In Quest and Crisis: Emperor Joseph I and the Habsburg Monarchy* (West Lafayette, Ind.: Purdue University Press, 1979; German translation 1982); Karl Otmar Frhr. von Aretin, "Kaiser Joseph I. zwischen Kaisertradition und österreichischer Großmachtpolitik," *Historische Zeitschrift* 215 (1972): 529–606, revised version in idem, *Das Reich: Friedensgarantie und europäisches Gleichgewicht 1648–1806* (Stuttgart: Klett Cotta, 1986), 255–322; Volker Press, "Josef I. (1705–1711): Kaiserpolitik zwischen Erblanden, Reich und Dynastie," in *Deutschland und Europa in der Neuzeit (Festschrift für Karl Otmar Frhr. von Aretin)* (Stuttgart: Steiner, 1988) 1:277–97; Franz Matsche, *Die Kunst im Dienste der Staatsidee Kaiser Karls VI.*, 2 vols. (Berlin/New York: de Gruyter, 1981).

2. John P. Spielman, *Leopold I of Austria* (London: Thames and Hudson, 1977; German translation 1981); Anton Schindling, "Leopold I.," in *Die Kaiser der Neuzeit 1519–1918,* ed. Anton Schindling and Walter Ziegler (Munich: Beck, 1990), 169–85.

3. Adam Wandruszka, *Reichspatriotismus und Reichspolitik zur Zeit des Prager Friedens von 1635* (Graz/Cologne: Böhlau, 1955).

4. Karl Otmar Frhr. von Aretin, "Das Heilige Römische Reich im Konzert der europäischen Mächte im 17. und 18. Jahrhundert," in *Stände und Gesellschaft im Alten Reich,* ed Georg Schmidt (Stuttgart: Steiner, 1989), 81–91.

5. See Ernst-Wolfgang Böckenförde, "Der Westfälische Friede und das Bündnisrecht der Reichsstände," *Der Staat* 8 (1969): 449–78; for a critical comment on Böckenförde's viewpoint, see also Karl Otmar Frhr. von Aretin, *Das Reich,* 169–70.

6. Heinz Duchhardt, "Der Kurfürst von Mainz als europäischer Vermittler: Projekte und Aktivitäten Johann Philipps von Schönborn in den Jahrzehnten nach dem Westfälischen Frieden," in idem, *Studien zur Friedensvermittlung in der frühen Neuzeit* (Wiesbaden: Steiner, 1979), 1–22.

7. Fritz Dickmann, *Der Westfälische Frieden,* 5th ed. (Münster: Aschendorff, 1985), 430, 458; Friedhelm Jürgensmeier, *Johann Philipp von Schönborn (1605–1673) und die Römische Kurie* (Mainz: Selbstverlag der Gesellschaft für mittelrheinische Kirchengeschichte, 1977), 119–20.

8. Peace Treaty 7 November 1659 (Jean DuMont, *Corps universel diplomatique du Droit des Gens . . .*, vol. 7/2 [Amsterdam/The Hague, 1728], 165: ". . . Et bien qu'en d'autres temps, & par diverses voyes, (les deux rois) auroient esté introduites des ouvertures & negociations, d'accomodement, aucune neanmoins pour les mysterieux secrets de la divine Providence, n'auroit pû produire l'effet que leurs Majestez desiroient tres-ardemment . . ."

9. Briefly mentioned by Bernhard Erdmannsdörffer, *Deutsche Geschichte vom Westfälischen Frieden bis zum Regierungsantritt Friedrichs des Großen 1648–1740,* (1932; reprint, Darmstadt: Wissenschaftliche Buchgesellschaft, 1962), 1:329–30. This mediation has not yet been dealt with on the basis of primary material.

10. See Duchhardt, "Der Kurfürst von Mainz."

11. Ibid., 20–21. For further considerations, see Leopold Auer, "Konfliktverhütung und Sicherheit: Versuche zwischenstaatlicher Friedenswahrung in Europa zwischen den Friedensschlüssen von Oliva und Aachen 1660–1668," in *Zwischenstaatliche Friedenswahrung in Mittelalter und Früher Neuzeit,* ed. Heinz Duchhardt (Cologne/Vienna: Böhlau, 1991), 153–83.

12. The treaty of Aix-la-Chapelle was signed by, among others, the Mainz and Cologne diplomats Schönborn and Franz Egon von Fürstenberg; see Jean DuMont, *Corps universel diplomatique du Droit des Gens . . .* , vol. 7/1 (Amsterdam/The Hague, 1731), 90.

13. Klaus Müller, "Zur Reichskriegserklärung im 17. und 18. Jahrhundert," *Zeitschrift der Savigny-Stiftung für Rechtsgeschichte, Germ. Abt.* 90 (1973): 246–59.

14. See Heinz Duchhardt, *Gleichgewicht der Kräfte, Convenance, Europäisches Konzert: Friedenskongresse und Friedensschlüsse vom Zeitalter Ludwigs XIV. bis zum Wiener Kongreß* (Darmstadt: Wissenschaftliche Buchgesellschaft, 1976), chap. 1/4, 34–40.

15. See Aretin, *Das Reich,* 194–201.

16. See Heinz Duchhardt, "Das preußische Königtum von 1701 und der Kaiser," in *Festschrift für Eberhard Kessel zum 75. Geburtstag,* ed. Heinz Duchhardt and Manfred Schlenke (Munich: Fink, 1982), 89–101.

17. Cf. Erdmannsdörffer, *Deutsche Geschichte vom Westfälischen Frieden,* 1:297–98.

18. See Heinz Duchhardt, *Deutsche Verfassungsgeschichte 1495–1806* (Stuttgart: Kohlhammer, 1991), 176–79.

19. The turning point of 1683 has been emphasized by, among others, Bernhard R. Kroener, "Prinz Eugen und die Türken," in *Prinz von Savoyen und seine Zeit,* ed. Johannes Kunisch (Freiburg: Ploetz, 1986), 113–25, especially 113–14; and Heinz Duchhardt, *Altes Reich und europäische Staatenwelt 1648–1806* (Munich: Oldenbourg, 1990), 20–21, 69–70.

20. For Austria's expansion in the Balkans and its problems, see Karl A. Roider, Jr., *Austria's Eastern Question, 1700–1790* (Princeton, N.J.: Princeton University Press, 1982).

Translated by Evelyn Bernholt and Marianne Hopmann

Austria and the Rise of Brandenburg-Prussia

Volker Press

Previous scholarship has maintained that the emergence of German dualism between Austria and Prussia is largely due to their possession of quasi-colonial territories in the East. Brandenburg-Prussia's dependence on developments in the Baltic area has, in fact, been very ably researched.[1] Its role in the *Reich* has also been viewed without the blinkers of a small-German perspective. In this essay, I would like to enquire into the relationship between the rise of Austria and Prussia that took place in the context of the *Reich*.

Brandenburg-Prussia had double roots, the electorate Brandenburg and the *Deutschordens-Land,* since 1525 the principality of Prussia.[2] The margraves of Brandenburg owed the rank of elector to their close association with the late medieval king Louis the Bavarian, who had already attempted to take possession of Brandenburg. Emperor Charles IV made it a dependency of Bohemia, while the feudal primacy of Brandenburg over Mecklenburg and Pomerania opened further opportunities in northern Germany. When the Hungarian crown under the last of the Luxemburg dynasty became over-extended, its king sold Brandenburg to the Zollern dynasty in 1415–17. Although originally from Swabia, the Zollerns were firmly rooted in the center of the *Reich,* where they were also burgraves of Nuremberg and lords in Franconia.[3] While the immediate demise of the Luxemburgs laid the groundwork for the rise of the Austrian Habsburgs, it also gave their future Hohenzollern rivals considerable freedom to maneuver. At the same time, however, it placed the latter in an awkward position by investing them with a special electoral dignity geographically removed from the rest of their patrimony. Elector Albert Achilles (1470–86) established both the indivisibility of Brandenburg and its separation from the Franconian territories in the so-called *dispositio Achillea* of 1473.[4] At the same time, he and his heirs endeavored to preserve the dynasty's unity. One by-product of this strategy was a marriage alliance with the Polish royal family, by which Margrave Frederick V (1486/95–1536) wed the king's daughter Sophie in 1479,[5] while his son Margrave Albert acceded to the office of grand master of Prussia in 1512.[6]

By contrast, the politics of the electorate of Brandenburg in the sixteenth century remained strongly regional, focusing on the politics of northern Germany and East Central Europe. As a result, Brandenburg stayed in Saxony's shadow, regardless of whether it was cooperating or competing with it.[7] Even after Saxony's division in 1485, Brandenburg remained the junior partner in the Hohenzollern-Wettin relationship. One success that was assisted by Saxony's dynastic divisions was the Hohenzollerns' bold advance into the imperial church, which brought Margrave Albert of Brandenburg the archbishopric of Magdeburg (1513), the bishopric of Halberstadt (1513), and the electorship of Mainz (1514).[8] This appears to have strengthened their position vis-à-vis Saxony, virtually guaranteeing their acquisition of the key city of Magdeburg and affording the Hohenzollern brothers Joachim I of Brandenburg (1499–1535) and Albert of Mainz (1514–45) a pivotal role in the competition between Habsburg and Valois in the imperial election of 1519. Yet it soon became clear how difficult it would be to sustain a common policy. Both men adhered to the old church, while the electorate of Saxony quickly assumed the leading role in the Reformation within northern Germany. Saxony also asserted its intellectual primacy over Brandenburg in 1506 when its elector founded a new university.

The Habsburgs entered the North German game when they acquired the crown of Bohemia, with its adjoining lands of Moravia, Silesia, and Lusatia, in 1526. Thus Archduke (later King) Ferdinand became the neighbor and overlord of several fiefs within the electorate of Saxony, which now had to take a more serious look at its southern neighbor. This concern intensified after 1547, when the Saxon electoral office was transferred from the Ernestine to the Albertine branch of the dynasty. Fear of Ernestinian revisionism drove the electors into the arms of the Habsburgs.[9] In its new role as a junior partner to the emperor in northern Germany, its power and influence declined accordingly.

Meanwhile, Brandenburg had become Protestant under the cautious Elector Joachim II (1535–71). Consequently, it was able to follow a more independent policy and to maintain control over Magdeburg, which was now governed by Protestant administrators. At the same time, however, Habsburg and Hohenzollern interests directly conflicted with one another in Silesia. The margraves George (1527–43) and George Frederick (1543/56–1603) of Brandenburg-Ansbach had established themselves there and ruled in the principalities of Jägerndorf, Oderberg, and Beuthen, in addition to the strongholds of Oppeln and Ratibor.[10] Brandenburg also had pretensions to the succession of certain principalities to which the Habsburgs had laid claim as reversionary loans. Finally, the contrast of religious confession also lurked in the background as yet another cause for conflict. For the time being, however, the Hohenzollerns did not dare to challenge the house of Austria.

Toward the end of the century, the rulers of Brandenburg went on a campaign to pillage the churches of the empire. They emerged from their confined territory partly voluntarily, partly under compulsion. Prince John George became the Protestant bishop of Strasbourg (1592–1604). At the same time, however, his religious policies in Magdeburg came under attack from the Catholic majority in the *Reichstag,* and ultimately from the Habsburg emperor. The Hohenzollerns' position was further strengthened when the childless Franconian margrave George Frederick, who already ruled Ansbach, Kulmbach, and the Silesian principality of Jägerndorf, crafted an expansive dynastic project for control of Prussia and northwestern Germany.[11] In the domestic Treaty of Gera (1598), he formally separated Brandenburg from the Franconian margraviates Ansbach und Kulmbach, which lay nearer to the emperor's interests, thereby directing the attention of Brandenburg's policy makers to northern Germany. George Frederick's strategy extended not only outside the empire into Prussia but also to the lower Rhine, where his involvement with the Dutch war of independence brought him into conflict with the Spanish Habsburgs and, therefore, their Austrian cousins. A few years later, Elector John Sigismund (1608– 19) successfully thwarted the designs of Emperor Rudolph II and his commissar, Archduke Leopold, by laying claim to the lower Rhenish principalities of Cleves, Mark, and Ravensberg.[12] It was during this contest that the electorate of Brandenburg first attached itself to the empire's Protestant party and then, after 1614, permanently to the reformed confession. In 1608 it joined the Palatinate in making a dramatic break in the *Reichstag*. By 1618 it was clearly in an unusually exposed position.

When the Bohemian rebellion broke out in that year, Brandenburg followed the lead of Saxony and reaffirmed its loyalty to the emperor. Only Duke John George of Jägerndorf took part in the Bohemian revolt by commanding the Silesian regional force and attempting to assist the rebellious estates in Troppau in wresting control from its ruling Catholic prince, Charles of Liechtenstein. Yet with the rebellion's defeat, the Hohenzollern lost the duchy of Jägerndorf and were driven out of Silesia.

Under the direction of his Catholic chief minister, Adam Count of Schwarzenberg, the new elector George William (1619–40) took no measures to prevent this dynastic catastrophe.[13] Nor could he prevent the victorious emperor from making increasing demands on him. George William responded by seeking support from the elector of Saxony, which was still the senior partner in territorial policy, despite individual rivalries and the constantly recurring tensions between Lutherans and Calvinists. Historians have strongly criticized George William's conduct, but his timidity is wholly understandable, given the dynasty's shaky legal position in the crisis. Moreover, the elector had to take into account Mark Brandenburg's close proximity to Habsburg Silesia, a presence that was constantly brought home by the billeting of imperial soldiers.

Unfortunately, imperial policy showed little appreciation for Brandenburg's restraint. Imperial troops toppled the Protestant administrator of Magdeburg, Christian William, and presented

Archduke Leopold as the future archbishop, with the result that the Protestant forces in the archbishopric eventually turned to the apparently more powerful land of Saxony for support. Prussian historians have generally despised Christian William, who subsequently played the part of a convert and married into Viennese court society; the status of his second and third wives symbolized the Hohenzollerns' loss of status. The Edict of Restitution of 1629 also threatened the foundations of the electorate of Brandenburg. Together with the elector of Saxony, Prince George William repeatedly sought to secure concessions for the Protestant cause. When this did not succeed, he switched to the Swedish side. But King Gustavus Adolphus treated the Hohenzollerns no better than Ferdinand II did.[14] Plans to join the pro-Swedish Heilbronn League did not succeed. Meanwhile, Sweden's defeat at Nördlingen (1634) brought the electorate of Brandenburg back into an alliance with the emperor; George Frederick became a partner in the Prague Peace (1635), which was chiefly directed against foreign powers, a decision that helped Brandenburg little against the billeting and plundering of Swedish troops.

Problematic though Brandenburg's role in the Thirty Years' War may have been, it was precisely then that the roots of Brandenburg's rise can be found—even though its statesmen did little to lay the groundwork for it. Up to that point, the electorate of Saxony had been the hegemonic power in northern Germany since 1547–48, generally as the junior partner of the emperor. But Saxony had come under ever increasing pressure from the emperor, who was rapidly consolidating his position in Bohemia. Meanwhile, the Palatinate was already on the verge of being eliminated, and Bavaria was quickly falling under the shadow of a resurgent Austria. All of this had become evident in the immediate aftermath of the war. It was, however, equally apparent that Brandenburg's new prince-elector Frederick William (1640–88) was in a more powerful position to exploit the situation.[15] He emerged as a ruthless tactician, a prince who acted without scruple, whose only standards were provided by territorial interests and the rules of the European system of power. In 1640 he withdrew from the war, while the electorate of Saxony maneuvered among all positions. But after a short breathing space, Frederick William became an important participant in the Peace Conference of Westphalia, at which point France in particular promoted Brandenburg as a counterweight against Sweden, the great power in the Baltic.[16] The "Great Elector" aimed at building up a position of power in northern Germany in order to provide better protection for his widely scattered possessions.

To be sure, he had to give up western Pomerania, which he keenly desired, especially for its valuable seaports; but he acquired considerable compensation in return, above all the prospect of the permanent acquisition of Magdeburg, which reverted to his possession after the death of the last Wettiner administrator in 1680. Saxony had, at long last, been pushed out of the north German lowlands. Moreover, by moving into yet another area that was far removed from the center of Habsburg power, Brandenburg was able to establish control at the emperor's expense. Frederick William also made skillful use of Saxony's weakness and the Palatinate's defeat in the Thirty Years' War by assuming the latter's leadership of German Protestantism. Shortly after 1648, Brandenburg was visibly aiming at hegemony in the north. The wily Hohenzollern also moved south by reviving his contacts with his Frankish and even his Swabian cousins.

At first, Frederick William sought the emperor's support, just as his father had, in order to assure his position in northern Germany; an ill-considered and unsuccessful plundering expedition against his opponents on the lower Rhine, the dukes of Pfalz-Neuburg, made him dependent on the emperor's goodwill, an important precondition if Ferdinand IV was to be elected king of the Romans.[17] But subsequently Brandenburg, under the direction of the reform-minded Count George Frederick of Waldeck,[18] again took an anti-imperial line and placed itself at the head of a predominantly Protestant opposition against the Habsburgs. The entire period of the Great Elector's rule is, in fact, characterized by a consciously variable policy, whereby he cleverly exploited the advantages to be gained from acquiring western Pomerania and hegemony in northern Germany.

With time, Brandenburg-Prussia's lead over the other electoral princes—which was the result of its maximum freedom of maneuver vis-à-vis Austria's growing imperial power—became more and more clear. With it came a growing mutual distrust between the two parties. The court in Vienna could barely tolerate Frederick William's attempts to play a fundamentally equal role on the international stage.[19] It was also troubled by his efforts to solidify his position in northern Germany by playing France and the emperor off against one another. At the same time, Brandenburg and the other states of northern Germany resented the priority that Vienna gave to its policy in its hereditary lands, preferring the defense of the southeast border against the Turks to meeting the French threat in the west. Despite these conflicts, Emperor Leopold won ever greater influence with his imperial vassals, including Brandenburg.[20] He remained especially influential with the electoral princes, since they relied on him to oppose the rival claims of the smaller imperial princes. The emperor's growing strength made clear the structural advantages that the *Reich* offered the Catholics after 1648, and Brandenburg exploited the resulting anxiety of the Protestant princes by positioning itself to take over effective leadership of the *Corpus Evangelicorum* from electoral Saxony.[21]

Although Frederick William was an electoral prince, Vienna realized that he now had a substantial political base outside the *Reich* in Prussia (which had become a sovereign duchy in 1660). He made deals with the great powers to an unprecedented extent and was beyond imperial control; Leopold's Austrian chancellor Johann Paul Hocher reputedly even spoke of there being a "new king of the Vandals" on the Baltic. And yet, by reducing the power of the electorates of the Palatinate, Saxony, and Bavaria, the Habsburgs themselves had helped to build the stage on which the Great Elector operated. Vienna employed countermeasures by promoting the elector of Saxony in the Polish royal election of 1697, in return for which Augustus the Strong converted and became an imperial client;[22] it also created an electoral office for Hanover,[23] more for imperial objectives than confessional ones. Meanwhile, the emperor continued to burden Habsburg-Hohenzollern relations by arrogantly refusing to reconsider Frederick William's persistent claims to compensation for his lost Silesian patrimony; although Leopold temporarily ceded the enclave of Schwiebus to Frederick William, he eventually compelled the elector's son and successor, Frederick III (1688–1713), to return it to Habsburg control.

And yet this state of the *Reich* could not escape imperial influence. To be sure, Hohenzollern hegemony in northern Germany remained undisputed. Yet it was precisely this which prompted the Great Elector and his successors to pursue accommodation with the emperor throughout the period 1684–1740. Of course, different interests lurked behind this symbiosis. Brandenburg-Prussia wished to protect its soft underbelly on the lower Rhine and retain its freedom of action both within the *Reich* and on the Baltic. For his part, the emperor needed peace in the *Reich* as well as maximum support for his policy against the Turks and the French. Here their interests converged, but their aims remained different. The Great Elector still supported Leopold I in his struggle against the Turks. Frederick III (I) and Frederick William I (1713–40) remained the emperor's allies in the War of the Spanish Succession. In the "royal treaties" of 1700, Vienna did indeed confirm Elector Frederick III's plans to become king in Prussia,[24] while attempting to limit his objectives in the coming war against France.[25]

Indeed, Vienna turned a deaf ear to the Prussian king's annoying demands and was ready to make concessions only in exceptional situations, such as in recognizing the elector of Brandenburg's right of succession in East Frisia. Its promotion of the electorates of Hanover and Saxony was, however, only partially successful: Saxony became increasingly burdened by its link with Poland; Hanover's union with England limited its ability to fill its role as junior partner to the emperor within northwestern Germany. Both of these developments favored Prussia, particularly given the dynamic changes in the Baltic, namely, the rise of Russia and the corresponding declines of Sweden, Poland, and Denmark. In 1720 Frederick William I's belated intervention in the Great Northern War finally realized the long-sought-after goal of the mouth of the Oder, together with the port of Stettin. Moreover, like his predecessors, Frederick William I was able to expand Brandenburg's role as patron of the German Protestants because of the Catholic orientation of imperial policy.

But the soldier-king Frederick William I also attached importance to loyalty to the emperor and to the legitimacy of the empire.[26] Nor should it be forgotten that this was also an important precondition for internal reform of the state. In addition, the king sought the emperor's close support in assuring the acquisition of Jülich and Berg after the main line of the house of Neuburg had died out.[27] With its recent acquisition of the former Spanish Netherlands, Vienna had also reentered northwestern Germany, where it once again found itself confronted by the competing interests of the great regional powers of the lower Rhine and Westphalia, including the Dutch Estates General, the Hanoverian Guelfs, and, above all, Brandenburg-Prussia. For the balance of his reign, Frederick William I maintained a quietist-legitimist imperial policy in order to strengthen his state internally, albeit at the expense of substantive territorial gains. For its part, Vienna thought the situation out very rationally, but the question arises whether its Machiavellian attempt to play Prussia and the Palatinate off against each other on the Lower Rhine was all that constructive, considering its own need to secure their support in settling its own looming succession question. Its policy clearly demonstrated to Frederick William I that Vienna continued to act out of a feeling of superiority and was less willing to treat Prussia as an equal than it was to hold it in check.

From this situation emerged Frederick II's (1740–86) decision to bring the increased power of Prussia into play.[28] That his attack was aimed at Silesia and not Jülich-Berg shows that his purpose was to establish Prussia as the second great power in the *Reich* and to degrade Austria's position in central Germany at the same time. The coup succeeded and was defended by Frederick in three wars. Thus he completed Brandenburg-Prussia's rise from the weakest and last of the emperor's electoral principalities, first to hegemony over northern Germany, and then to the second major power in the *Reich*. It was a career that had been played out in the shadow of the Austrians and had been decisively promoted both by the dynamic situation in the Baltic and by a resurgent Austria's success in reducing the relative power of each of the other three lay electors. Prussia finally filled the vacuum that had been created by the emperor's remoteness from northern Germany, becoming at the same time head of the German Protestants in place of Saxony and the Palatinate. The long-term consequence of Austria's orientation toward the southeast was the rise of an "anti-emperor" in the North.[29]

Notes

1. Erich Hassinger, *Brandenburg-Preußen, Schweden und Rußland 1700–1713* (Munich: Isar, 1953); Klaus Zernack, "Negative Polenpolitik als Grundlage deutsch-russischer Diplomatie in der Mächtepolitik des 18. Jahrhunderts," in *Rußland und Deutschland: Festschrift Georg von Rauch,* ed. Uwe Liszkowski (Stuttgart: E. Klett, 1974), 144–59; Hassinger, "Das preußische Königtum und die polnische Republik im europäischen Mächtesystem des 18. Jahrhunderts (1701–1762)," *Jahrbuch für Geschichte Mittel- und Ostdeutschland* 30 (1981): 4–20.

2. Conrad Bornhak, *Preußische Staats- und Rechtsgeschichte* (Berlin: Carl Heymanns, 1903); Max Braubach, *Der Aufstieg Brandenburg-Preußens 1640–1815* (Freiburg/Br.: Herder, 1933); Otto Büsch and Wolfgang Neugebauer, eds., *Moderne preußische Geschichte 1648–1947,* 3 vols. (Berlin and New York: de Gruyter, 1981); Francis L. Carsten, *The Origins of Prussia* (Oxford: Clarendon Press, 1954); Richard Dietrich, *Preußen: Epochen und Probleme seiner Geschichte* (Berlin: de Gruyter, 1964); idem, *Kleine Geschichte Preußens* (Berlin: Haude und Spernersche Verlagsbuchhandlung, 1966); Johann Gustav Droysen, *Geschichte der preußischen Politik,* 10 vols. (Berlin/Leipzig: Veit, 1866–86); Gerd Heinrich, *Geschichte Preußens: Staat und Dynastie* (Frankfurt/M: Propyläen, 1981); Otto Hintze, *Die Hohenzollern und ihr Werk: Fünfhundert Jahre vaterländischer Geschichte,* 9th ed. (Berlin: P. Parey, 1916); Reinhold Koser, *Geschichte der brandenburgischen Politik bis zum Westfälischen Frieden von 1648* (Stuttgart/Berlin: J. G. Cotta, 1913); Ingrid Mittenzwei and Erika Herzfeld, *Brandenburg-Preußen 1648–1789: Das Zeitalter des Absolutismus in Text und Bild* (East Berlin: Paul-Rugenstein, 1987); Leopold von Ranke, *Zwölf Bücher preußischer Geschichte,* ed. Georg Küntzel, 3 vols. (Munich: Drei Masken, 1930); Johannes Schultze, *Die Mark Brandenburg,* 2d ed. (Berlin: Duncker & Humblot, 1989); Günter Vogler and Klaus Vetter, *Preußen: Von den Anfängen bis zur Reichsgründung,* 4th ed. (Berlin: Deutscher Verlag der Wissenschaften, 1975).

3. Koser, *Geschichte der brandenburgischen Politik,* 77–88; Droysen, *Geschichte der preußischen Politik,* vol. 1, 2d ed. (1868).

4. Günther Schuhmann, *Die Markgrafen von Brandenburg-Ansbach: Eine Bilddokumentation zur Geschichte der Hohenzollern in Franken: Festschrift des Historischen Vereins für Mittelfranken zur Feier seines einhundertfünfzigjährigen Bestehens 1830–1980* (Ansbach: Selbstverlag des Historischen Vereins für Mittelfranken, 1980).

5. Reinhard Seyboth, *Die Markgraftümer Ansbach und Kulmbach unter der Regierung Markgraf Friedrichs des Älteren (1486–1515)* (Göttingen: Vandenhoeck & Ruprecht, 1985).

6. Walther Hubatsch, *Albrecht von Brandenburg-Ansbach: Deutschordens-Hochmeister und Herzog in Preußen 1490–1568* (Heidelberg: Quelle & Meyer, 1960). See also Antjekathrin Graßmann, *Preußen und Habsburg im 16. Jahrhundert* (Cologne/Berlin: Grote, 1968).

7. Paul Haake, *Kursachsen oder Brandenburg-Preußen? Geschichte eines Wett-streits* (Berlin: Ebering, 1939). See also Dietrich, *Kleine Geschichte Preußens.*

8. Friedhelm Jürgensmeier, ed., *Erzbischof Albrecht von Brandenburg (1490–1545): Ein Kirchen- und Reichsfürst der frühen Neuzeit* (Frankfurt/M: J. Knecht, 1991).

9. Gustav Wolf, "Die Anfänge der Regierung des Kurfürsten August von Sachsen," *Neues Archiv für sächsische Geschichte* 17 (1896): 304–57; Otto Fürsen, *Ein wichtiges Jahrzehnt kursächsischer Reichspolitik 1576–1586* (Sonderburg: Druckerei der Sonderburger Zeitung, 1909); Moriz Ritter, *Deutsche Geschichte im Zeitalter der Gegenreformation und des Dreißigjährigen Krieges 1555–1648*, 3 vols. (Stuttgart: Cotta, 1886–1908), passim; and Axel Gotthardt, "'Politice seind wir bäbstisch': Kursachsen und der deutsche Protestantismus im frühen 17. Jahrhundert," *Zeitschrift für historische Forschung* 20 (1993): 275–319.

10. Ludwig Petry and Josef Joachim Menzel, *Geschichte Schlesiens*, vol. 2: *Die Habsburgerzeit 1526–1740*, 2d ed. (Sigmaringen: Thorbecke, 1988); Georg Friedrich Preuß, "Das Erbe der schlesischen Fürsten," *Zeitschrift des Vereins für Geschichte Schlesiens* 49 (1915): 1–40.

11. Reinhard Seyboth, "Markgraf Georg Friedrich der Ältere von Brandenburg-Ansbach-Kulmbach (1556–1603) als Reichsfürst," *Zeitschrift für bayerische Landesgeschichte* 53 (1990): 659–79; Jürgen Petersohn, *Fürstenmacht und Stände-tum in Preußen während der Regierung Herzog Georg Friedrichs 1578–1603* (Würzburg: Holzner, 1963).

12. Hermann Josef Roggendorf, "Die Politik der Pfalzgrafen von Neuburg im Jülich-Klevischen Erbfolgestreit," *Düsseldorfer Jahrbuch* 53 (1968): 1–211; Burkard Rohberg, "Zur Quellenlage und Historiographie des Jülich-Klevischen Erbfolgestreits," *Annalen des Historischen Vereins für den Niederrhein* 179 (1977): 114–35.

13. Significantly, no biography of George William exists. For a summary, see Thomas Klein, "Georg Wilhelm, Kurfürst von Brandenburg," *Neue deutsche Biographie* (Berlin: Duncker & Humblot, 1964), 6:203–4.

14. Johannes Paul, *Gustaf Adolf*, vols. 1–3 (Leipzig: Quelle & Meyer, 1927–32); Michael Roberts, *Gustavus Adolphus: A History of Sweden 1611–1632*, vol. 2.: *1626–1632* (London: Longmans, 1958), 426–90; Günter Barudio, *Gustav Adolf der Große: Eine politische Biographie* (Frankfurt/M: S. Fischer, 1982).

15. Barbara Beuys, *Der Große Kurfürst: Der Mann, der Preußen schuf* (Reinbeck: Rohwolt, 1979); Ludwig Hüttl, *Friedrich Wilhelm von Brandenburg der Große Kurfürst 1620–1688: Eine politische Biographie* (Munich: Süddeutscher Verlag, 1981); Gerhard Oestreich, *Friedrich Wilhelm der Große Kurfürst* (Göttingen: Musterschmidt, 1971); Ernst Opgenoorth, *Friedrich Wilhelm, der Große Kurfürst von Brandenburg*, 2 vols. (Göttingen: Musterschmidt, 1971–78); Martin Philippson, *Der Große Kurfürst*, 3 vols. (Berlin: Siegfried Cronbach, 1897–1903); Albert Waddington, *Le Grand Electeur Frédéric Guillaume de Branden-*

bourg: Sa politique extérieure 1640–1688, 2 vols. (Paris: Plon-Nourrit et Cie, 1905–8).

16. Fritz Dickmann, *Der Westfälische Frieden,* 5th ed. (Münster: Aschendorff, 1985).

17. Walter Isaacson, "Geschichte des niederrheinisch-westfälischen Kreises von 1648–1667" (Ph.D. diss., University of Bonn, 1933); Ernst Opgenoorth, "Der Große Kurfürst, das Reich und die europäischen Mächte," in *Preußen, Europa und das Reich,* ed. Oswald Hauser (Cologne/Vienna: Böhlau, 1987), 19–31; Anton Schindling, "Kurbrandenburg im System des Reiches während der zweiten Hälfte des 17. Jahrhunderts," in *Preußen,* ed. Hauser, 33–46; Anton Schindling, *Die Anfänge des Immerwährenden Reichstags zu Regensburg: Ständevertretung und Staatskunst nach dem Westfälischen Frieden* (Mainz: Steiner, 1991); Hans Schmidt, *Philipp Wilhelm von Pfalz-Neuburg (1615–1690) als Gestalt der deutschen und europäischen Politik des 17. Jahrhunderts,* vol. 1: *1615–1658* (Düsseldorf: Pädagogischer Verlag Schwann, 1973), 40–53.

18. Bernhard Erdmannsdörffer, *Graf Georg Friedrich von Waldeck: Ein preußischer Staatsmann im 17. Jahrhundert* (Berlin, 1869); Gerhard Menk, *Georg Friedrich von Waldeck 1620–1692: Eine biographische Skizze* (Arolsen: Waldeckischer Geschichtsverein, 1992).

19. Opgenoorth, *Friedrich Wilhelm,* 284–413.

20. Volker Press, "Die kaiserliche Stellung im Reich nach 1648: Versuch einer Neubewertung, in *Stände und Gesellschaft im alten Reich,* ed. Georg Schmidt (Stuttgart: Franz Steiner Verlag Wiesbaden, 1989), 31–80; Volker Press, "Österreichische Großmachtbildung und Reichsverfassung: Zur kaiserlichen Stellung nach 1648," *Mitteilungen des Instituts für österreichische Geschichtsforschung* 98 (1990): 131–54.

21. Gabriele Haug-Moritz, "Kaisertum und Parität: Reichspolitik und Konfessionen nach dem Westfälischen Frieden," *Zeitschrift für historische Forschung* 19 (1992): 445–82.

22. Karl Czok, *August der Starke und Kursachsen,* 2d ed. (Leipzig/Munich: Beck, 1989); Cornelius Gurlitt, *August der Starke: Ein Fürstenleben aus der Zeit des deutschen Barock,* 2 vols. (Dresden: Sibyllen Verlag, 1924); Paul Haake, *August der Starke* (Berlin/Leipzig: Gebrüder Paetel, 1926); idem., "Die Wahl Augusts des Starken zum König von Polen," *Historische Vierteljahresschrift* 9 (1906): 31–84; Herbert Poenicke, *August der Starke: Ein Fürst des Barock* (Göttingen: Musterschmidt, 1972); Jacek Staszewski, *August II* (Warsaw: Zamek Królewski, 1986).

23. Volker Press, "Kurhannover im System des alten Reichs 1692–1803," in *England und Hannover = England and Hanover,* ed. Adolf M. Birke and Kurt Kluxen, Prinz-Albert-Studien, vol. 4 (Munich/New York: Saur, 1986), 53–79.

24. Walther Koch, *Hof- und Regierungsverfassung König Friedrichs I. von Preußen 1697–1710* (Breslau: M. & H. Marcus, 1926); Marsha and Linda Frey, *Friedrich I.: Preußens erster König* (Graz: Styria, 1984).

25. Peter Baumgart, "Epochen der preußischen Monarchie im 18. Jahrhundert," in *Das Preußenbild in der Geschichte,* ed. Otto Büsch (Berlin/New York: de Gruyter, 1981), 65–96; Peter Baumgart, "Die preußische Königskrönung von 1701, das Reich und die europäische Politik," in *Preußen,* ed. Hauser, 65–86; Arnold Berney, *König Friedrich I. und das Haus Habsburg (1701–1707)* (Munich/Berlin: R. Oldenbourg, 1927); Heinz Duchhardt, "Die preußische Königskrönung von 1701: Ein europäisches Modell?" in *Herrscherweihe und Königskrönung im frühneuzeitlichen Europa,* ed. Heinz Duchhardt (Wiesbaden: Steiner, 1983), 822–95; idem, "Das preußische Königtum von 1701 und der Kaiser," in *Festschrift Eberhard Kessel zum 75. Geburtstag,* ed. Heinz Duchhardt und Manfred Schlenke (Munich: Fink, 1982), 89–101; Klaus-Ludwig Feckl, *Preußen im Spanischen Erbfolgekrieg* (Frankfurt/M: Lang, 1979); Alfred Francis Pribram, *Österreich und Brandenburg 1688–1700* (Prague/Leipzig: F. Tempskey, 1918); Theodor Schieder, "Die preußische Königskrönung von 1701 in der politischen Ideengeschichte," in *Begegnungen mit der Geschichte,* ed. Theodor Schieder (Göttingen: Vandenhoeck & Ruprecht, 1962), 183–209; Albert Waddington, *L'acquisition de la couronne royale de Prusse par les Hohenzollern* (Paris: E. Leroux, 1888).

26. Otto Büsch, *Militärsystem und Sozialleben im alten Preußen 1713–1807: Die Anfänge der sozialen Militarisierung der preußisch-deutschen Gesellschaft,* 2d ed. (Frankfurt/M: Ullstein, 1981); Klaus Deppermann, *Der hallesche Pietismus und der preußische Staat unter Friedrich Wilhelm III. (I.)* (Göttingen: Vandenhoeck & Ruprecht, 1961); Fritz Hartung, "Friedrich Wilhelm I. von Preußen," in idem., *Staatsbildende Kräfte der Neuzeit: Gesammelte Aufsätze* (Berlin: Duncker & Humblot, 1961), 123–48; Carl Hinrichs, *Preußentum und Pietismus: Der Pietismus in Brandenburg-Preußen als religiös-soziale Reformbewegung* (Göttingen: Vandenhoeck & Ruprecht, 1971); idem, *Friedrich Wilhelm I., König in Preußen: Eine Biographie,* vol. 1, 4th ed. (Darmstadt: Wissenschaftliche Buchgesellschaft, 1974); Heinz Kathe, *Der "Soldatenkönig" Friedrich Wilhelm I. 1678–1740, König in Preußen* (East Berlin: Akademie-Verlag, 1978); Gerhard Oestreich, *Friedrich Wilhelm I.: Preußischer Absolutismus, Merkantilismus, Militarismus* (Göttingen: Musterschmidt, 1977).

27. Hans Schmidt, *Kurfürst Karl Philipp von der Pfalz als Reichsfürst* (Mannheim: Bibliographisches Institut, 1963), passim.

28. Arnold Berney, *Friedrich der Große: Entwicklungsgeschichte eines Staatsmanns (bis 1756)* (Tübingen: Mohr, 1934); Pierre Gaxotte, *Friedrich der Große* (Frankfurt/Berlin: Propyläen, 1974); George P. Gooch, *Frederick the Great: The Ruler, the Writer, the Man* (London: Longmans Green & Co., 1947); Gerd Heinrich, "Friedrich der Große und die deutsche Geschichte," in *Actio tomans: Festschrift für Walter Heistermann,* ed. Gerd Heinrich et al. (Berlin: Colloquium Verlag, 1978), 155–84; Walter Hubatsch, *Das Problem der Staatsräson bei Friedrich dem Großen* (Göttingen: Musterschmidt, 1956); Reinhold Koser, *Geschichte Friedrichs des Großen,* 6th–7th eds., 4 vols. (Stuttgart/Berlin: J. G. Cotta'sche Buchhandlung Nachfolger, 1921); Ingrid Mittenzwei, *Friedrich II. von Preußen: Eine Biographie,*

2d ed. (East Berlin: Paul-Rugenstein, 1980); Gerhard Ritter, *Friedrich der Große: Ein historisches Profil,* 3d ed. (Heidelberg: Quelle & Meyer, 1954); Theodor Schieder, *Friedrich der Große: Ein Königtum der Widersprüche* (Frankfurt/M: Propyläen Verlag, 1983).

29. Karl Otmar Freiherr von Aretin, *Heiliges Römisches Reich 1776–1806: Reichsverfassung und Staatssouveränität* (Wiesbaden: F. Steiner, 1967), 1:19–23.

Reform and Diplomacy in
the Eighteenth-Century Habsburg Monarchy

Karl A. Roider, Jr.

One of the great issues surrounding the debate regarding the origins of World War I is the influence of domestic concerns upon foreign policy. The argument, put forth most vigorously by Fritz Fischer and Arno Mayer, is that foreign policy became in the Victorian period a device to satisfy internal interest groups or to placate unhappy elements of the population by focusing their attention on foreign problems.[1] This argument contends that policy makers welcomed war as an opportunity to take the minds of their troublesome and now in most cases voting populations off the various domestic crises that seemed to plague all of their countries and place those minds on affairs that would inspire patriotism, stability, and, above all, support for the government.

Since domestic matters played such a significantly lesser role in the international politics of the eighteenth century—at least prior to the outbreak of the French Revolution—scholars often approach international relations of that time in what one might call their purest form, assuming that those making policy did so almost exclusively on the basis of the foreign-policy interests of their states, generally within the system—or at least the understanding—known as the balance of power. As we all know, this understanding by no means meant peace. It was, after all, based not upon any actual balance of power but upon a perceived balance of power; therefore, almost any change, even of the slightest consequence, could be interpreted by a statesman as a threat to the balance, most particularly the balance as he saw it affecting his state, and thus worthy of either resistance or a corresponding advantage in order to restore the balance. Another power might see such a change as an act not of advantage but of restitution to preserve the perceived balance. In other words, in the name of stability and balance, states fought wars and expended resources almost without respite throughout much of the century.

Another common assumption at the time was that the addition of territory equaled the addition of strength. If a state annexed a piece of land, that state became measurably stronger. It was measurably stronger in terms of revenue because it had added taxpayers to its rolls; it was measurably stronger militarily because those same taxpayers had sons who could be enlisted into the armed forces; and it was measurably stronger strategically because it now possessed a new territory that, while it would have to be defended, presumably provided a better defense for the old lands that were now less at risk themselves. At the same time, however—and this is particularly true of the Habsburgs—strength was often associated with buffer zones, areas that a state did not want to see conquered by other powers but also did not want to conquer itself. As Charles W. Ingrao so clearly explains in his article on Habsburg geopolitics at this time, the monarchy's policy throughout the century was to have buffer zones on its borders, lands ruled either by small and nonthreatening states or by large but weak ones.[2] The Holy Roman Empire in the German lands, the fragmented political system in Italy, and feeble Poland all served that function through much of the century, and the monarchy's policy was to make certain that those areas were undamaged, a policy that yielded—as we all know—mixed success.

In the southeast, however, Habsburg policy faced somewhat of a dilemma. The area was a natural one for Habsburg expansion. In that time of growing concern about trade and manufacturing, it offered commercial expansion of considerable promise. The route down the Danube to the Black Sea provided great potential for the Habsburgs to take part in the rapidly expanding commercial ventures not only in the Levant but also along the northern coast of the

Black Sea, where Catherine the Great was interested in establishing entrepôts for the export of goods from southern Russia. Likewise, the western Balkans could provide a market for the goods coming to and from Trieste, a port that the Habsburgs were developing throughout most of the century.

In addition to the possibilities of increased revenue through trade, the area also offered a population that one might regard as at least willing to try Habsburg sovereignty. This area was, after all, mostly Christian—Orthodox Christian by and large, but at least Christian—and had been living for centuries under the hated Turks. The experiences of the Habsburg forces in that area in the wars of the late seventeenth and early eighteenth centuries indicated that the local people would willingly join the monarchy in large numbers to rid themselves of an alien and oppressive rule.

Finally, the Ottoman government itself—the hated archenemy of Christendom against which the Habsburgs had fought so many wars—seemed on the brink of collapse. Administrative rot at the center and increasingly independent warlords on the periphery meant that the Ottomans could scarcely threaten the monarchy as they had in the past and indeed, with the right combination of diplomatic finesse and military force, could be made to give up certain of their lands. The one caveat here, of course, was that the Ottoman state was also attractive as one of those buffer zones that Vienna found useful and hoped to keep out of the hands of undesirable predators—i.e., Russia.

All in all, then, the Balkans looked like a ready place for Austrian expansion, if, of course, it could be arranged without the other great powers demanding that the monarchy offer too much in terms of sacrifice to get it. But the monarchy did not want it. One reason was the strategic one just mentioned: the Ottoman Empire served just as well as a buffer in the southeast; after all, if the monarchy added any of its lands, then other powers would seek corresponding acquisitions elsewhere that might be to Austria's disadvantage.

There were, however, other reasons, and these are the ones on which I wish to focus in this essay. While avoiding a serious plunge into definitions of enlightened absolutism, most students of the monarchy would agree that the eighteenth century was a period of reform. Much was changed, sometimes successfully and sometimes not, in an effort to make the monarchy strong and rich but also to make it a modern state that would provide a reasonably pleasant life for many of its inhabitants. And the Habsburg government tried these policies of reform in its Balkan lands as well for the same reasons. There, however, the Austrians encountered not just disappointing results but results that made them wonder if that part of the world might not be beyond the realm of economic, political, and administrative salvation. And that influenced their foreign policy.

In terms of reform, the place the Austrians chose for their experiment in applied enlightenment (or at least cameralism) was the Banat, the area between the Danube, Tisza, and Maroş rivers, whose major city was Temesvár (Timişoara). In the treaty signed at Carlowitz (Sremski Carlovci) in 1699, the Turks ceded all of the Hungarian lands to the Austrians except the Banat. Following the war of 1716–18, the Treaty of Passarowitz (Pozeravac) granted even that province to Emperor Charles VI, who proclaimed it not restored to the Kingdom of Hungary but *neoacquisita,* newly acquired, and therefore under the direct rule of Vienna. The purpose of the declaration was not only to give Vienna an unrestricted strategic base but to prevent the Banat from falling back into the hands of what Vienna regarded as the exploitative Hungarian nobility.[3] Whatever its purpose, it provided Vienna with an administrative *tabula rasa* for whatever reforms and innovations it wished to implement. After all, the Banat had no formal diet, no institutionalized judicial system, and not even a recognized church with which Vienna had to negotiate. It had a significant population—300,000 living in an area of 11,150 square miles—but they were Romanians, who, the central government believed, needed reinforcements from other parts of Europe not only to add to the population but to civilize it as well.[4]

Much has been written about the Habsburg efforts to bring reform to the Banat, especially because the relevant documents are abundant and located in Vienna and because the issue of German colonization there raised considerable interest during the interwar period.[5] Suffice it to say that there were two periods of extensive reform, one in the 1720s and the other in the 1760s. In the first, the Banat's governor, Count Florimund Mercy-Argenteau, represented a joint effort by the War Ministry (*Hofkriegsrat*) and Finance Ministry (*Hofkammer*) to improve the country, and his efforts reflected the prevailing cameralism at the time. He recruited settlers from various parts of Europe, especially Germans from the Rhineland, not only because they possessed in his mind the skills that would make the Banat bloom but also because that was at the time a source of colonists for many parts of Europe and America.[6] In the interests of improving the economy, he launched road- and canal-building enterprises and forbade guilds on the grounds that they restricted manufacturing and would likely discourage more artisans from coming.

Contrary to Habsburg practice in that part of the world, Mercy did not create a military border, contending that the tax-free status of the frontiersmen would hamper revenue enhancement and that border regiments tended to attract rogues and villains, who would prey on the local peasants and artisans.[7] He established the Temesvár Commercial Society to trade the Banat's produce (honey and cattle) with the Turks, but it was apparently unable to break into the Balkan trade and wound up selling most of its products to the army and to other parts of the monarchy instead.[8]

The reforms introduced by Mercy did not last. In the 1730s, the central government reduced its investment in the Banat, and the authorities there did not have the resources to overcome many of nature's obstacles to settlement, notably the springtime flooding of the rivers and the pervasive marshlands. Then came a Romanian rising against Habsburg rule in 1736, the Austro-Turkish War of 1737–39, and, in their wake, an epidemic. In response, those settlers who survived fled to other parts of Hungary. By 1740 the effort expended in the 1720s appeared wasted, and the central government by then had on its mind problems other than reform in the Banat.[9]

In the 1760s, Vienna resurrected its reform effort, although the office in charge (the *Ministerialbancohofdeputation,* created when the head of the bank became head of the *Hofkammer*) changed the focus somewhat. Although it resumed efforts to import colonists (11,000 families arrived in the Banat and Bachka[10]), it sought through educational and religious reforms and closer administrative supervision to improve agriculture as well as the discipline, morals, and work habits of both the new colonists and the native population.

After a few years of implementing these improved methods of government, the administration in the Banat came under the critical eye of the figure most closely associated with enlightened rule in Austria, Emperor Joseph II. In 1768 Joseph made one of his famous visits to the Banat and while there engaged in his customary investigatory whirlwind of visits, interrogations, petition receiving, and all the rest. When he returned to Vienna, he reported to Maria Theresa that he had found the efforts to modernize the Banat utter failures. Everything had failed: transportation, health care, education, and colonization. "Never had 900,000 florin been spent worse, more uselessly, or unwisely as in this colonization business."[11] In fact, he summed up what he had found in a phrase that no Austrian bureaucrat could stomach: "The government might as well still be Turkish."[12] He recommended that the special status of the Banat be abandoned and its government be made like those in the other provinces of the monarchy. The report made quite an impact on Maria Theresa and Kaunitz, but no changes were made as the administration continued to try to introduce improvements. In 1773 Joseph visited the Banat again, found the same problems, and made the same recommendations. In 1778 Maria Theresa annexed it to Hungary, a step that Joseph approved.[13]

The experiment in transforming the Banat did not reap benefits in the eighteenth century. It would in the nineteenth, but of course eighteenth-century Austrian officials could not know that. What they saw as the failed experiment in the Banat made Habsburg policy makers—whether concerned primarily with domestic or foreign policy—wonder about the wisdom of annexing any more Balkan territory. After all, if an area as small as the Banat required so great an investment over such a long time and offered so little return, what would the expanses of Serbia, Albania, Macedonia, and Bulgaria devour? If annexed, they would be no more than enormous drains on Habsburg resources for some time to come.

But what about commercial advantages? What about the access to the growing Levantine markets as well as the developing Russian market in the Black Sea, which control of the Balkans would provide? Indeed, early in the century, Emperor Charles VI believed that his army's victories in 1717 and 1718 opened the way to a trade bonanza for the monarchy in the East. In the negotiations leading to the Treaty of Passarowitz, Charles insisted upon a separate commercial treaty that would give his merchants advantages in the overland trade with the Ottoman Empire.[14] Likewise, since the Austrians in this war had saved Venice from considerable harm, Charles insisted that the republic endorse his declaration of the Adriatic Sea as a free trading area and recognize his cities of Fiume and Trieste as free ports. As the capstone of his efforts to improve commerce to the East, in 1719 Charles granted a charter to the Imperial Privileged Oriental Company (*Kaiserliche privilegierte orientalische Kompagnie*) to carry the banner of Habsburg commerce to the Balkans. The charter, modeled after the French society that the famous John Law was trying at the time to revive, granted the company the exclusive right to trade in the lands of the sultan either along the Danube or through the Adriatic ports. It also allowed the firm to build factories, warehouses, and magazines wherever it wished and guaranteed that it alone could manufacture certain goods in the monarchy.[15] Finally, it enjoyed the "direct protection" of the sovereign, which meant that he would not only defend its property against molestations by foreign powers but also forbid any local estates from interfering in its affairs.[16]

Despite the privileges, monopolies, imperial protection, and investment, the Oriental Company failed. From the beginning, it suffered from liabilities that it could not overcome. For one, owing to various production problems, it could not produce goods of sufficient quality and quantity at a low enough price to be competitive. Likewise, it faced unending difficulties in transporting goods. Despite Trieste and Fiume being free ports, the transportation costs of reaching those cities via overland routes from the manufacturing areas of Bohemia, Lower Austria, and even Inner Austria were prohibitive. For example, when the company took over the sale of Inner Austrian iron and steel, the cost of carrying it over the mountains to Trieste proved so great that by the time it reached its customers, the price was much higher than that of superior Swedish iron and steel brought in the holds of Dutch and British ships.[17] Meanwhile, the Danube, which provided the main river route for goods on the way to Turkey, was still open only so far as the Iron Gates. Wares had to be unloaded from boats at Belgrade and proceed by wagon to

Constantinople, a most expensive operation compared with French and British vessels plying the Mediterranean.

These problems were all compounded by risky financial speculations on the part of the directors. Because they were short of funds, in 1721 the directors introduced a lottery to raise operating capital. Even though they invented a variety of gimmicks to keep from paying off winners, by 1731 the company was so deep in debt that it could not continue. It could not simply dissolve itself, however, for it was obligated to pay its debts, an obligation guaranteed by the emperor. But the emperor's government itself had contributed to the bankruptcy by demanding loans from the company that became larger and larger as time passed. Ultimately, most of the company's assets were in government bonds that it could not redeem. In any case, after 1731 the firm continued a shadow existence as it sold its assets to satisfy its creditors. Commenting on the company's dissolution, one scholar remarked, "It was unable even to establish a time to die, which was around 1741."[18]

The collapse of the Oriental Company virtually ended any Austrian-sponsored trade in the Balkans for the time being. There was plenty of trade, but it was in the hands of Ottoman citizens—the famous Balkan merchants about whom Traian Stoianovich has written so well.[19] The absence of commerce and the apparent lack of entrepreneurial initiative among his countrymen in mid-century prompted the Austrian representative at the Porte to report in 1751 that "there exists no specifically German commerce [in Constantinople]; it consists of only a few Bohemian glass sellers and a Tyrolean canary store. . . . In the whole Levant there is not a single German merchant."[20]

Warnings implicit in this complaint and other reports prompted some measures on Vienna's part to improve trade, but they consisted mostly of efforts to restrict the enterprises of Ottoman citizens rather than to promote Austrian commerce. Then in the 1770s, a revival of interest in Ottoman trade occurred due to a rediscovery of the Danube. In 1771 a merchant-adventurer named Nikolaus Ernst Kleeman published an account of his effort to navigate the Danube from Vienna to the Black Sea, including the passage through the Iron Gates.[21] In this work, Kleeman showed that the Danube was navigable, but also that the journey was by no means serene. The Iron Gates could be only overcome when the river was swollen, and even then they offered a frightening experience: "I heard during this whole time nothing except the crashing of waves and [from his Turkish boatmen] an inarticulate 'Allah, Allah.'" After passing the gorge, he climbed a hill to look at it: "Since I could now see the whole stream, I could scarcely believe that our boat had come through that narrow and dangerous waterway."[22]

Kleeman's book inspired the Austrian government to look once again at ways to improve Austrian commerce via the Danube. In fact, this effort received an added boost when the Russians and the Turks signed the Treaty of Kuchuk-Kainarji in 1774, which now opened the Black Sea to Christian vessels. Not as enamored with monopolies as before, the government relied on pronouncements and encouragement to generate private trade on the Danube, but it still failed to generate much interest among Austrian merchants. After all, Kleeman's book had shown that trade on the Danube was possible but also that it took a hearty merchant indeed to engage in it. The Iron Gates were just one obstacle; there were also river pirates, Ottoman officials who demanded baksheesh as well as duties, a population whose tastes were essentially unknown, and the Danube itself, which, as late as the 1780s, was still uncharted past the Iron Gates.

In 1782 a publicist on the government payroll named Johann Schweighofer published a short book to promote Danubian commerce by assuring Habsburg merchants that they need not fear a journey to the Black Sea. It narrated an imaginary trip down the river in glowing terms, portraying the scenery as lush and beautiful and the towns—Ottoman and Habsburg alike—as friendly and inviting. The detail of the narrative dropped off sharply, however, after it passed the last Habsburg outpost, and it did not even mention the Iron Gates. Schweighofer was probably not trying to minimize the dangers of the lower Danube; he just knew practically nothing about them.[23] One scholar has noted that before 1790 the lower Danube was "less known to Austrians than the mountains of Mexico and India."[24]

A few efforts were made to initiate commerce down the river in the 1780s, but none amounted to much. In 1786 two Italians proposed to Joseph II to start a company if they could have a monopoly on the Danube trade. Although Joseph opposed monopolies in principle, the reluctance of Austrian merchants to make the gamble persuaded him in this case to grant one. He wrote to his brother: "Navigation on the Danube to the Levant and to the Crimea grows daily. . . . There is a company that, at its own expense, has armed twelve vessels in order to reach the mouth of the Danube and transport goods and merchants who arrive there."[25] The Italian company had just begun operations when the last Austro-Turkish war broke out, and, with trade on the Danube disrupted, it collapsed.[26]

What does all of this information tell us? Essentially that when Austrian policy makers spoke of annexing or not annexing portions of the Balkans in the eighteenth century, far more than geopolitical or strategic concerns affected their thinking. The disappointing experiment in the Banat and the repeated failure to develop satisfactory commerce enhanced the perception that the Balkans were just not worth having. Based on the government's experience, transforming that area into a prosperous and modern society that would provide rewards and benefits for the monarchy would demand an investment in time and resources that no one at that time could see paying off in the future. All of the reasons for not advancing farther to the southeast—geopolitical, strategic, political, economic, and even religious—were summed up in a famous passage of Maria Theresa when she wrote at the time of the great debates in 1772 regarding the partition of the Ottoman Empire:

Of all the enterprises, the most hazardous and most dangerous will be the partition of the Ottoman Empire, whose consequences we have the most to fear. What can we gain from such conquests, even to the gates of Constantinople? Provinces unhealthy, depopulated, or inhabited by treacherous and ill-intentioned Greeks [Orthodox]—they would not strengthen the Monarchy but weaken it. . . . Without a fatal combination of unfortunate circumstances, I will never prepare myself for the partition of the Ottoman Empire, and I hope that our descendants will never see it expelled from Europe.[27]

Notes

1. Fritz Fischer, *Krieg der Illusionen* (Düsseldorf: Droste Verlag, 1969); Arno J. Mayer, "Domestic Causes of the First World War," in *The Responsibility of Power: Historical Essays in Honor of Hajo Holborn,* ed. Leonard Krieger and Fritz Stern (Garden City, N.Y.: Doubleday, 1967).

2. Charles W. Ingrao, "Habsburg Strategy and Geopolitics," in *War and Society in East Central Europe,* ed. Béla Kiraly et al., Brooklyn College Studies, vol. 11 (New York: Brooklyn College, 1982), 2:49–66.

3. Josef Kallbrunner, *Das kaiserliche Banat: Einrichtung und Entwicklung des Banats bis 1739* (Munich: Verlag für Südostdeutschen Kulturwerks, 1958), 15.

4. Aurel Tinta, *Colonizarile habsburgice in Banat, 1716–1740* (Timisoara: Facla, 1972), 7–16. By 1760 the population was 400,000, but the Banat was still the least populated of the Habsburg lands per square mile except for Croatia-Slavonia. Konrad Schünemann, *Österreichs Bevölkerungspolitik unter Maria Theresia* (Berlin: Deutsche Rundschau, 1935), 73.

5. See especially Colin Thomas, "The Anatomy of a Colonization Frontier: The Banat of Temesvar," *Austrian History Yearbook* 19–20 (1983–1984), part 2, 3–22. For a discussion of published books on the Banat to 1970, see Tinta, *Colonizarile habsburgice,* 7–16. A list of dissertations on the Banat can be found in Alexander Krischan, "Dissertationen über das Banat (1897–1967)," *Südostdeutsches Archiv* 13 (1970): 203–21.

6. Schünemann, *Österreichs Bevölkerungspolitik,* 234–39.

7. Sonja Jordan, *Die kaiserliche Wirtschaftspolitik im Banat im 18. Jahrhundert* (Munich: Oldenbourg, 1967), 45–48; Kurt Wessely, "The Development of the Hungarian Military Frontier until the Middle of the Eighteenth Century." *Austrian History Yearbook* 9–10 (1973–74): 70.

8. Kallbrunner, *Das kaiserliche Banat,* 60, 67–69.

9. Peter Gänger, "Graf Mercy als Gouverneur des Temescher Banats," *Österreichische Begegnung* 6 (1966): 53–55.

10. P. G. M. Dickson, *Finance and Government under Maria Theresia, 1740–1780* (Oxford: Oxford University Press, 1987), 1:36; Ernst Schimscha, *Technik und Methoden der Theresianischen Besiedlung des Banats* (Baden bei Wien: Rohrer Verlag, 1939), 172.

11. Quoted in Schimscha, *Technik und Methoden,* 167.

12. Quoted in Derek Beales, *Joseph II,* volume 1: *In the Shadow of Maria Theresia, 1741–1780* (Cambridge: Cambridge University Press, 1987), 248.

13. Ibid., 242–51.

14. For the text of this treaty, see *Feldzüge des Prinzen Eugen von Savoyen* (Vienna: Verlag des k.k. Generalstabes, 1891), 17:477–83.

15. Josef Dullinger, "Die Handelskompagnien Österreichs nach der Orient and nach Ostindien in der 1. Hälfte des 18. Jahrhunderts," *Zeitschrift für Sozial- und Wirtschaftsgeschichte* 7 (1900): 47.

16. Victor-L. Tapié, *L'europe centrale et orientale de 1689–1796* (Paris: Centre de documentation universitaire, 1969), 1:124–25.

17. Heinrich Benedikt, *Das Königreich Neapel unter Kaiser Karl VI* (Vienna/Leipzig: Manz Verlag, 1927), 357. Ships in the Atlantic trade used Swedish iron and steel as ballast.

18. Giovanni Bussolin, *Della imperiale privilegiata Compagnia Orientale nel secolo scorso e del Lloyd Austro-Ungarico nel secolo presente* (Triest: Herrmanstorfer, 1882), 164. Even this date cannot be accepted as final, for the company did not sell its famous cotton factory in Schwechat until 1742 or the woolen mill in Linz until 1754. [I. De Luca], "Nachricht von der k.k. Wollenzeug Fabrik in Linz," in *Briefwechsel meist historischen und politischen Inhalts,* ed. August Ludwig Schlözer 10 (1782): 202.

19. Traian Stoianovich, "The Conquering Balkan Orthodox Merchant," *Journal of Economic History* 20 (1960): 234–313.

20. Quoted in Marianne von Herzfeld, "Zur Orienthandelspolitik Österreichs unter Maria Theresia in der Zeit von 1740–71," *Archiv für österreichische Geschichtsforschung* 108 (1919–20): 223.

21. Nikolaus Ernst Kleeman, *Reisen von Wien über Belgrad bis Kilianova, durch die Nogew-Tartarey in die Crim, dann von Kassa nach Konstantinopel, nach Smirna und durch den Archipelagum nach Triest und Wien in den Jahren 1768, 1769 und 1770* (Vienna, 1771). A second edition appeared in Leipzig in 1772, a Dutch translation in 1774, a French translation in 1780, and Russian, English, and Italian translations in 1783.

22. Ibid., 17.

23. Johann Michael Schweighofer, *Grösse der Handlung unter Josef II. Nebst meinen Gedanken von der neuen Handlung auf dem schwarzen Meer* (Vienna, 1782).

24. Hans Halm, *Habsburgischer Osthandel im 18. Jahrhundert* (Munich: Isar Verlag, 1954), 36.

25. Joseph to Leopold, 14 May 1786, in *Joseph II und Leopold von Toscana: Ihre Briefwechsel von 1781 bis 1790,* ed. Alfred von Arneth (Vienna: Wilhelm Braumüller, 1872), 2:17.

26. Hans Halm, *Österreich und Neurussland* (Breslau: Thiel & Hintermeier, 1943), 178–80.

27. Quoted in Karl A. Roider, Jr., *Austria's Eastern Question, 1700–1790* (Princeton, N.J.: Princeton University Press, 1982), 156–57.

Contributors

Paul P. Bernard is a professor of history at the University of Illinois at Champaign-Urbana. His numerous studies of the reign of Emperor Joseph II include *Joseph II and Bavaria* (1965), *Joseph II* (1968), *Jesuits and Jacobins: Enlightenment and Enlightened Despotism in Austria* (1971), *The Limits of Enlightenment: Joseph II and the Law* (1979), and *From the Enlightenment to the Police State: The Public Life of Johann Anton Pergen* (1991).

Robert Bireley, S.J., is a professor of history at Loyola University of Chicago. His books include *Religion and Politics in the Age of the Counter-Reformation: Emperor Ferdinand II, William Lamormaini, S.J., and the Formation of Imperial Policy* (1981) and *The Counter-Reformation Prince: Antimachiavellianism or Catholic Statecraft in Early Modern Europe* (1990).

Heinz Duchhardt is a professor at the University of Münster. He has edited eleven books and written thirteen others, together with more than eighty articles, in the fields of diplomatic and constitutional history. His most recent books include *Das Zeitalter des Absolutismus* (1989) and *Deutsche Verfassungsgeschichte 1495–1806* (1991).

R. J. W. Evans is a reader in modern history at Brasenose College, Oxford. He has written principally on the Habsburg Monarchy's cultural and religious history, most notably in *Rudolf II and His World: A Study in Intellectual History, 1576–1612* (1973) and *The Making of the Habsburg Monarchy 1550–1700: An Interpretation* (1979).

Paula Sutter Fichtner is a professor of history at Brooklyn College and the Graduate Center of the City University of New York. She is the author of *Ferdinand I of Austria: The Politics of Dynasticism in the Age of the Reformation* (1982) and *Protestantism and Primogeniture in Early Modern Germany* (1989), which was awarded a prize by the American Academy of Religion.

Herman Freudenberger is a professor emeritus at Tulane University. He has written three books and more than twenty articles on industrialization in the Bohemian crownlands, most notably *The Industrialization of a Central European City: Brno and the Fine Woollen Industry in the Eighteenth Century* (1977).

R. Po-chia Hsia, a professor of European history at New York University, is the author of several books on early modern German history, including *Trent 1475: Stories of a Ritual Murder Trial* (1992), *The Myth of a Ritual Murder: Jews and Magic in Reformation Germany* (1988), and *Society and Religion in Münster, 1535–1618* (1984).

Charles W. Ingrao is a professor of history at Purdue University. He has written three books, *In Quest and Crisis: Emperor Joseph I and the Habsburg Monarchy* (1979), *The Hessian Mercenary State: Ideas, Institutions, and Reform under Frederick II, 1760–1785* (1987), and *The Habsburg Monarchy, 1618–1815* (1994). His present research focuses on the molding of mass political culture and the dynamics of legitimation in the Age of Revolution.

Grete Klingenstein holds the chair of modern history at the University of Graz. Her books include *Staatsverwaltung und kirchliche Autorität im 18. Jahrhundert: Das Problem der Zensur in der theresianischen Reform* (1970) and *Der Aufstieg des Hauses Kaunitz* (1975) and numerous edited collections. Her wide-ranging research interests include the interrelations of political structures and institutions, international relations, culture, and society. She is currently working on a history of the Habsburg Monarchy from 1699 to 1806.

Herbert Knittler is a professor at the Institut für Wirtschafts- und Sozialgeschichte at the University of Vienna. His work is principally concerned with Austrian economic and social history, urban history, and the relationship between society and architecture.

John Komlos is chair and professor of economic history at the University of Munich. He has written two books on the Habsburg economy, *The Habsburg Monarchy as a Customs Union* (1983), and *Nutrition and Economic Development in the 18th-Century Habsburg Monarchy* (1989), which was the recipient of two book prizes.

Hellmut Lorenz is a professor of art history at the University of Berlin, where he specializes in Renaissance and Baroque art and architecture. He is the author of *Domenico Martinelli und die österreichische Barockarchitektur* (1991) and *Johann Bernhard Fischer von Erlach* (1992).

James Van Horn Melton is an associate professor of history at Emory University. A specialist in cultural and social history, he is the author of the award-winning *Absolutism and the Eighteenth-Century Origins of Compulsory Schooling in Prussia and Austria* (1988).

Nicolette Mout is a reader in Dutch history and professor of Central European studies at the University of Leiden. A member of the Royal Netherlands Academy of Arts and Sciences, she publishes on early modern cultural and intellectual history and on the historiography of the twentieth century. She has published three books, including *Bohemen en de Nederlanden in de zestiende eeuw* (1975).

The late **Volker Press** was chair for medieval and early modern European history at Eberhard-Karls-Universität, Tübingen. His publications include *Calvinismus und Territorialstaat: Regierung und Zentralbehörden der Kurpflaz 1559–1619* (1970), *Kriege und Krisen: Deutschland 1600–1715* (1991), two hundred articles, and numerous collections.

Karl A. Roider, Jr., is a professor of history and dean of the College of Arts and Sciences at Louisiana State University. His principal publications include *The Reluctant Ally: Austria's Policy in the Austro-Turkish War, 1737–1739* (1972), *Austria's Eastern Question, 1700–1790* (1982), and *Baron Thugut and Austria's Response to the French Revolution* (1987).

Anton Schindling is a professor of early modern history at the University of Osnabrück. His main fields of research are the history of the Holy Roman Empire and its territories, the history of the Reformation and the confessions after the Reformation, as well as the history of the universities and schools from the Renaissance to the Enlightenment. His most recent book is *Anfänge des immerwährenden Reichstags zu Regensburg* (1991).

Georg Schmidt is a professor of early modern history at the Friedrich Schiller University at Jena. He has done extensive research on the college of imperial cities and on the nobility of the Wetterau.

John P. Spielman is a professor of history at Haverford College. He has published several books, including *Cristóbal de Rojas y Spínola* (1962), *Leopold I of Austria* (1977), and, most recently, *The City and the Crown: Vienna and the Imperial Court, 1600–1740* (1993).

Karl Vocelka is on the faculty of the Institut für Österreichische Geschichtsforschung of the University of Vienna. He has also taught at Stanford University and at the Summer University of Vienna in Strobl, and is currently president of the Institut für die Erforschung der frühen Neuzeit (IEFN). He has written several books on the interplay of court display and social control, most notably *Die politische Propaganda Kaiser Rudolfs II. (1576–1612)* (1981).

Index

Aix-La-Chapelle, treaties of, 147
(1748), 290 (1668)
Albert, archbishop-elector of Mainz
(1514–45), 299
Albert, margrave of Brandenburg, 299
Albert Achilles, Elector (1470–86), 299
Albrecht, Konrad Adloph von, 100
Allgemeines Landrecht, 64–65
Alsace, 58
Ampringen, Johann Caspar, 111, 114
André, Christian Carl, 149
Ansbach, margraviate of, 300
Aristocracy, Habsburg, 37, 42–43, 222,
232; and estate capitalism, 145,
147, 149–51, 162; and patronage,
89–90, 94
Árpád dynasty, 28–29
Augsburg: Peace of (1555), 31–32, 39,
41, 55, 58, 63; Confession, 54–55
Augustus II ("the Strong"), king of
Poland (1697–1733), 106, 108, 304
Austrian Lands, Protestantism in, 86.
See also individual crownlands
Austrian Succession, War of (1740–
48), 277, 283
Ayrer, Max, 112

Babenberg dynasty, 28, 31
Bachka, colonization of the, 316
Baden-Durlach, margraviate of, 257;
Habsburg commercial relations
with, 235, 254–55, 259, 263, 265
Balance of power, 282, 312–13
Balkans, strategic value of, 276–78,
283–84, 313–14, 321
Banat (of Temesvár), 231, 284;
colonization of, 315–17, 321–22
Bartenstein, Johann Christoph, Privy
Conference secretary, 194
Basel, 235, 254, 265
Bavaria, electorate of: Habsburg
relations with, 279, 281–83, 302,
304
Becher, Johann Joachim (1635–82),
141, 144, 191
Belgium (Austrian Netherlands), 16–
17, 231, 306; exchange projects for,
17, 281, 283
Belgrade, 318
Benedictine religious order, 57–58
Beuthen, principality of, 300
Bielfeld, Jakob Friedrich (1717–70),
political economist, 193, 200, 208

Black Forest, economic conditions in, 253–55, 259

Blenheim, Battle of (1704), 282–83

Bob, Franz Joseph (1733–1802), cameralist, 268

Bohemia: aristocracy of, 232; and Brandenburg, 298–99; Commercial College in, 144; cottage industry in, 151, 230, 234; Counter-Reformation in, 41, 44, 46, 62; and ecclesiastical policy, 29; estates of, 42, 51; famine of 1770–72 in, 233, 244, 249, 258–62; foreign threats to, 278, 281; the poor in, 230, 243–44; manorial conditions in, 155–61, 165, 171; manufacturing in, 146–50, 220; Protestantism in, 30, 86; religious revolt in, 4, 33, 301

Borié, Egid Valentin (1719–93), 142, 183, 196–98

Bosnia-Hercegovina, 284

Botero, Giovanni, 42, 51

Brandenburg-Prussia: acquires royal crown, 293, 305; after Thirty Years' War, 288; Protestantism in, 62–64; Habsburg relations with, 277–79, 282–84, 298–306; rise of, 15, 112, 281–83, 293–94, 302–6

Breisgau, 253–55, 257, 259. See also Further Austria

Brieg, principality of, 282

Brixen, bishopric of, 28

Brno (Brünn), 142, 146–47, 148, 149, 150

Bruck, Pacification of (1578), 32, 39–41

Brunswick-Lüneburg: acquires English crown, 281, 293, 305; becomes electorate, 112, 304–5

Buchau, abbey, 262

Bukovina, 16

Buquoi, Johann Nepomuk, 11, 232–33, 243–48, 250

Bureaucracy, Habsburg, 8–9, 38, 204; circuit captains, 197, 233

Cameralism, 148, 182, 187, 202, 222; and agriculture, 142–43, 152; in the Banat, 315–16; and the poor, 229–30, 232, 239, 241, 252–53, 281; and Polizei, 10, 191–92, 197, 200, 256–57

Capuchin religious order, 57, 61

Carinthia: founds economic society, 198; manufacturing in, 148; Protestantism in, 30. See also Inner Austria

Carlowitz (Sremski Carlovci), Treaty of (1699), 315

Carmelite religious order, 57

Catherine II, tsarina of Russia ("the Great") (1762–96), 314

Český Krumlov (Krumau), 150

Chanceries, 8, 38, 144; Austrian, 3, 5, 100, 253, 275; imperial, 100, 280; state (Staatskanzlei), 275; United (Austro-Bohemian), 258, 260–61, 263–64

Charles, Archduke, of Inner Austria, 32–33, 37, 39

Charles IV, Emperor (1346–78), 298

Charles V, Emperor (1519–56), 3, 27, 31; and the Jews, 74–75

Charles VI, Emperor (1711–40): as builder, 7, 100–106; and court display, 88, 90; German policy of, 280, 282–83, 287, 306; and Hungary, 315; and the Jews, 78; mercantile policy of, 8, 317–19; and the poor, 145; sacrifices Lorraine, 278

Charles Eugene, duke of Württemberg (1744–93), 258

Charles Frederick, margrave of Baden-Durlach (1738–1811), 254

Charles Joseph, Archduke, 114

Child, Josiah, mercantilist, 142

Christian William, Magdeburg governor, 301–2

Christoff, duke of Württemberg, 77

Chur, bishopric of, 28

Clement VII, Pope, 27

Clement XI, Pope, 280

Cobenzl, Johann Karl Philipp (1712–70), 183

Colbert, Jean-Baptiste, 141, 184

Cologne, electorate of, as peace mediator, 289–90

Conrad von Hötzendorf, Franz, field marshal, 278

Constance, 260, 271; Council of, 29

Constantinople, 319, 321

Corpus Evangelicorum, 304

Council of State (*Staatsrat*): and economic planning, 183–84, 196, 199, 201–2; established, 8, 275, 285

Counter-Reformation, 4, 7, 13, 33, 37–41, 44, 56–60, 84–86, 124, 132; Marian devotion, 90, 99

Crimean War (1854–56), 278

Croatia-Slavonia, kingdom of, 322; colonization of, 284; manorial conditions in, 156, 171

Czernin Palace, 96

Dangeul, Louis Joseph Plumard de (1722–77), physiocrat, 186, 189, 200, 202

Daniel, archbishop of Mainz, 76–77

Danube River, as trade route, 313, 318–21

Darjes, Johann Joachim Georg (1714–91), cameralist, 192, 200

Decker, Paul, architect, 106–7

Denmark, decline of, 305

Devolution, War of (1667–68), 290

Dietrichstein, Franz von, cardinal, 38

Directorium in Publicis et Camera-libus, 195–96, 203

Dithmar, Julius Christoph, camera-list, 200

Doblhof, Karl Holler von, councillor, 199, 201–2

Dordrecht, Synod of, 54

Dortmund, expels Jews, 76

Dutch War (1672–79), 290, 292

Ecclesiastical Reservation, 31, 58

Eggenberg, Hans Ulrich von, 38, 43

Elbe, river valley, 156; East Elbia, 155–56, 159

Engels, Friedrich, 156, 239

England. *See* Great Britain

Enlightened absolutism, 10, 64, 121, 181, 221, 231–32, 314–15

Enlightenment, 4, 6–7, 13, 34, 63, 182, 218, 242

Ernest, Archduke, 95

Esslingen, imperial city, expels Jews, 76

Eugene, Prince, of Savoy, 99, 143–44

Eugene IV, Pope, 28

Ferdinand, Archduke, of Tyrol, 33

Ferdinand I, Emperor (1556–64), 3, 8, 28; acquires Bohemia, 299–300; Declaration of, 58; and ecclesiastical policy, 28; and the Jews, 75–77; and Protestantism, 31–32

Ferdinand II, Emperor (1619–1637), 36–47 passim, 84; Balkan policy of, 278; and Brandenburg, 302; political reforms of, 5, 37–44, 51; religious policy of, 13, 33–34, 39–40, 44–47, 50, 60–61, 64; as ruler in Inner Austria, 3–5, 8, 39–41; testament of, 40

Ferdinand III, Emperor (1637–57), 36–37, 43; Balkan policy of, 278; creates standing army, 38; and ecclesiastical policy, 28, 45; German policy of, 279; religious policy of, 44–47

Ferdinand IV, Roman king (1653–54), 303

Fettmilch, Vincent, uprising of, 77–78

Firmian, Karl Count, Milanese minister, 207

Fischer von Erlach, Johann Bernard, court architect, 97, 99–100

Fischer von Erlach, Joseph Emanuel, 100, 103

Fiume (Rijeka), 318

Forbonnais, François Véron de (1722–1800), physiocrat, 11, 186, 189, 193, 200, 202

Formula of Concord, 55, 62

France: and electoral mediations, 289–92; Enlightenment ideas from, 182–84, 186–89, 194, 200, 209, 235, 254, 265; and German princes, 279–80, 303–4; rivalry with Habsburgs, 87, 277–83, 304–5

Francis I Stephen, Emperor (1745–65): as entrepreneur, 146; and imperial election, 8, 295

Francis II, Holy Roman Emperor (1792–1806), 16, 148

Francis Joseph I, Emperor (1848–1916), 278

Franciscan religious order, 57

Franconia, Jews of, 76

Frankenburg (Upper Austria), 61

Frankfurt, 289; Jews of, 78–79

Frederick I, king of Prussia (1688/1701–13), 282, 304–5

Frederick II ("the Great"), king of Prussia (1740–1786): as builder, 103, 106; seizes Silesia, 283, 306; as reformer, 64, 181

Frederick III, Elector. See Frederick I, king of Prussia

Frederick III, Emperor (1440–93), 27–28; and the Jews, 74

Frederick V, margrave of Brandenburg (1486/95–1536), 299

Frederick, Count Palatine, 77

Frederick William (the "Great Elector") (1640–88), 64, 302–5

Frederick William I, king of Prussia (1713–40), 305–6

Freiburg im Breisgau, 253; university of, 58

Fridau (Lower Austria), 147

Fries, Johann, entrepreneur, 147

Frisia, East, 282, 305

Fürstenberg, Carl Egon von, Bohemian governor, 233

Further Austria (Vorlande or Vorderösterreich), 9, 37, 231, 252–72; famine in, 11, 234–35, 252–54, 258–64, 266; Jews of, 74

Galesius, Augustinus, essayist, 127

Galiani, Ferdinando, economist 202

Galicia, 16; Jews of, 13

Gasser, Simon Peter, cameralist, 200

Gellert, Christian Fürchtegott, Aufklärer, 242

George, margrave of Brandenburg-Ansbach (1527–43), 300

George Frederick, count of Waldeck, 303

George Frederick, margrave of Brandenburg-Ansbach (1543/56–1603), 300–302

George William, elector of Brandenburg (1619–40), 301–2

Golden Fleece, Order of, 7, 115

Gottsched, Johann Christoph, 242

Gournay, Jean Claude Marie Vincent de (1715–59), intendant, 186, 191

Gran, Daniel, 100

Gratzen (Nové Hrady), 11

Graz, Counter-Reformation in, 40, 44

Great Britain: alliances with, 276; industrialization compared, 219–22; influences Austrian cameralists, 187, 190, 207

Guelders, Prussian, 282
Güttinger, Martin, court provost, 117
Guilds, opposition to, 148, 222, 240,
    255, 257, 316
Guntersdorf, Andreas Teufel, 126
Gurk, bishopric of, 28
Gustavus Adolphus, king of Sweden
    (1611–32), 64, 302

Halberstadt, bishopric of, 299
Hanover. See Brunswick-Lüneburg
Harrach, Ferdinand (1708–78), Aulic
    Court president, 190
Hauck, Ferdinand Anton, preacher,
    131
Haugwitz, Friedrich Wilhelm (1700–
    1765), 11, 148; and economic
    reform, 184, 203–4; sponsors Justi,
    192, 195–96; restructures offices,
    144, 194
Heidelberg Catechism, 55
Heilbronn League, 302
Helvetic Confession, Second, 55
Helvétius, Claude Adrien, 202
Heraeus, Carl Gustav, 100
Herberstorff, Count, Bavarian
    governor, 61
Herbert, Claude Jacques, physiocrat,
    187
Hesse-Kassel, landgraviate of, 281
Hildebrandt, Johann Lucas, 100
Hobbes, Thomas, 294–95
Hocher, Johann Paul, Austrian
    chancellor, 114, 304
Höller, Anton, 106
Hörnigk, Philipp Wilhelm von (1640–
    1714), cameralist, 142–43, 191
Hofburg, palace, 7, 89, 94–107 passim
Hofkammer (Court Chamber), 3, 87,
    275; in the Banat, 316
Hofkriegsrat (War Council), 3, 38, 87,
    275; in the Banat, 316
Hofrechenkammer, 183–84, 188, 190

Hohberg, Wolff Helmhard, 230, 236
Hohenberg, county of, 259–60
Hohenzollern-Hechingen, principality
    of, 259
Holič (Hollitsch), 146
Holy Roman Empire: diets: 265–66,
    292 (Regensburg), 300–301; effect
    of dualism on, 283; electoral
    associations, 288–92; Habsburgs'
    relationship with, 7, 14–17, 277–
    83, 286–87, 294–96; Kreisassozia-
    tionen, 280, 293
Horní Litvínov (Oberleutensdorf), 146,
    220
Hume, David, 190–91, 200, 202
Hungary: and absolutism, 15, 29, 285;
    manorial conditions in, 155–57,
    160, 171; reconquest of, 278, 315;
    resists Catholicism, 6, 86, role of, 8,
    16–17; strategic value of, 283–84

Imperial Aulic Court (Reichshofrat),
    72–73, 78, 87, 280, 286
Imperial Chamber Court (Reichs-
    kammergericht), 77
Inner Austria: Counter-Reformation
    in, 33–34, 40, 44–46; estates of, 41,
    50; Protestantism in, 30, 39–40
Innsbruck, 231, 247
Iron Gates, 318–20
Italy: Habsburg hegemony over, 280,
    283; strategic value of, 276–78, 313

Jägerndorf, duchy of, 282, 300–301
Jesus, Society of (Jesuits), 6; activities
    of, 57–58, 84, in education, 58, 61,
    124, 192, 195; under Ferdinand II,
    39
Jews, 13–14, 31, 123, 133; the emper-
    ors and Judenschutz, 71–79
Jihlava (Iglau), 146
Joachim I, elector of Brandenburg
    (1499–1535), 299

Joachim II, elector of Brandenburg
(1535–71): conversion of, 281, 300
Jörger, Johann Quintin, Lower
Austrian governor, 133
John George, bishop of Strasbourg
(1592–1604), 300
John George, duke of Jägerndorf, 301
John Sigismund, elector of Brandenburg (1608–19), 62, 301
John Sobieski, king of Poland, 278
Joseph I, Emperor (1705–11): as
builder, 100, 107; and Germany,
280, 282–83, 287, 292–93; and the
Jews, 78
Joseph II, Emperor (1765–90):
agrarian reforms of, 152, 222; and
the Banat, 317; education of, 183,
193–94; foreign policy of, 15–17,
283; mercantile policy of, 208, 222,
225, 266, 321; and the poor, 232–
34, 243–46, 250; as reformer, 9–11,
181, 184, 194; religious policy of,
12–13, 57; resistance to, 64
Josephinism (or "Josephism"), 10–12,
17, 44, 234
Jülich-Berg, duchies of, 283, 305–6
Julius, bishop of Würzburg, 76–77
Justi, Johann Heinrich Gottlob (1717–
71), cameralist, 143, 183, 192–99,
201, 203–4, 225, 253, 255, 268; and
the poor, 241–42

Kageneck, Heinrich, 235, 253–58, 268
Kaunitz, Wenzel Anton (1711–94), 11;
and internal reform, 183–89, 197,
199, 203, 208, 275, 317
Kettenhof (Lower Austria), 147
Kindermann, Ferdinand, educator,
234
Kircher, Athanasius, philosopher, 85,
90
Kleeman, Nikolaus Ernst, 319–20
Klosterneuburg monastery, 7, 90
Krauss-Elislago, Anton, 145

Kressel von Gualtenberg, Franz Karl,
261–62
Kuchuk-Kainarji (1774), Treaty of, 320
Kulmbach, margraviate of, 300

Laibach (Ljubljana), bishopric of, 28,
231
Lambeck, Peter, court librarian, 89
Lamormaini, William, Jesuit confes-
sor, 42, 44, 84
Law, John, financier, 318
Laxenburg, palace, 93–95
Leibniz, Gottfried Wilhelm, 100
Leipzig, 186; university of, 185
Leitenberger (Bohemia), 148
Leitha River valley, 156
Leopold, Archduke, of Tyrol, 37, 58,
301–2
Leopold I, Emperor (1658–1705), 36;
court patronage and pretensions of,
87–89, 95–100, 107, 110–11, 114,
117; and ecclesiastical policy, 28;
foreign policy of, 278; German
policy of, 280, 287, 292–93, 295,
304; and the Jews, 78, 133;
mercantile policy of, 141; and
Northern War, 289; and the poor,
134, 241; and Prussian crown, 282,
305; religious policy of, 46, 86; and
sumptuary edicts, 116; and the
Turkish wars, 34; *Wahlkapitulation* of (1658), 294
Leopold II, Emperor (1790–92): as
reformer, 181, 183, 193, 211; yields
Balkan conquests, 278
Letter of Majesty (1609), 31
Liechtenstein family, 149, 232;
Charles, 301; estates of, 161; Karl
Eusebius, 86; Johann Adam, 99
Liegnitz, principality of, 282
Linz: poor relief in, 231, 246; textile
industry in, 145, 220, 224–25, 323
Lipsius, Justus, 43, 51, 90
Locke, John, 200

Lombardy (Milan & Mantua), 16–17, 283

Lorraine, duchy of, 278

Louis XIV, king of France (1643–1715), 87, 93–94, 278, 280, 292, 295

Lower Austria: after Thirty Years' War, 167; and Bohemian revolt, 60; Council of Commerce (*Kommerzienrat*), 187, 189, 195–96, 198–99, 201–2, 208; Counter-Reformation in, 46–47, 60–62; estates of, 41–42, 60, 155; poor in, 230; Jews of, 73, 78; manorial conditions in, 9, 155–62, 164–71, 175–76, 179; manufacturing in, 145, 146–49, 220; population of, 167; Protestantism in, 30, 32–33

Lucchese, Filiberto, architect, 96

Luther, Martin, 30, 55, 124, 127, 129

Luxemburg (Luxembourg), dynasty, 298

Machiavelli, Niccolò, 42, 294–95

Magdeburg, archbishopric of, 299–300, 301, 303

Mainz, electorate of, 299; as peace mediator, 289–90

Malvieux, Georg Ludwig, manufacturer, 242

Mantua, duchy of, 280. *See also* Lombardy

Maria, Archduchess, 39

Maria Theresa, queen of Hungary and Bohemia (1740–80): agrarian reforms of, 152, 222; and the Balkans, 321; and the Banat, 317; customs union, 234; educational reforms of, 234; and famine of 1770–72, 258–59; fiscal and administrative reforms of, 253; German policy of, 16–17; mercantile policy of, 143–44, 148, 194, 196, 198–99, 208, 222; and the poor,

231–33, 242–43; and Prussia, 283; as reformer, 10, 181; religious policy of, 12–13, 57; succession of, 7

Maritime Powers. *See* Great Britain; Netherlands, United

Marly, palace, 93–94

Matthias Corvinus, king of Hungary (1458–90), 29

Maximilian, duke/elector of Bavaria, 33, 38, 60–61

Maximilian I, Emperor (1493–1519): and the Jews, 73–74

Maximilian II, Emperor (1564–76), 3, 31–32, 95; and the Jews, 71–73, 75–76

Mecklenburg, duchy of, 282, 298

Melk monastery, 90

Melon, Jean-François, economist, 193, 200

Mendel, Gregor, 150

Mercantilism, 8, 142, 189, 222, 252–54, 257, 264

Mercy-Argenteau, Florimund, Banat governor, 315–16

Milan, duchy of. *See* Lombardy

Military Border, 15

Mimmenhausen, 260

Ministerialbancohofdeputation, 316

Mirabeau, Victor Riqueti Marquis de, 191, 202

Mödling (Lower Austria), 147

Möser, Justus, publicist, 271

Mollwitz, Battle of (1741), 283

Monceau, Henri Louis Duhamel de, physiocrat, 187

Montesquieu, 184, 193, 200

Moravia: Counter-Reformation in, 46, 62; manorial conditions in, 155–56, 158–61; manufacturing in, 146–49, 220

Moser, Johann Jakob, cameralist, 200, 267

Mühlberg, Battle of (1547), 283

Müller, Ignaz, abbott, 190

Münster, bishopric of, 59
Mun, Thomas, mercantilist, 142
Muratori, Lodovico Antonio (1672–
1750), 190, 242

Nadelburg (Lower Austria), 220
Náměšt (Namiest), 148
Napp, Franz Cyrill, abbott, 150
Neffzer, Baron, 147
Nellenburg, county of, 271
Netherlands, United, 277, 305; and
Kreisassoziationen, 280, 293
Neubeck, Caspar, bishop of Vienna,
127–28
Neuburg, Pfalz-, dukes of, 303, 306
Neumann, Balthasar, architect, 102
Nijmegen, Treaty of (1678), 292
Nördlingen: Association, 280; Battle
of, 302
Northern War, First (1655–60), 289,
305

Oderberg, principality of, 300
Ofen, conquest of (1686), 126
Offermann, manufacturer, 148
Olivares, Count-Duke of, 36
Oppeln, duchy of, 300
Oriental Company, 141, 145, 318–19,
323
Osek (Ossegg), 146, 220
Osnabrück: bishopric of, 59, 271;
Treaty of. *See* Westphalia
Ottoman Empire: image of the Turk,
121, 126, 129–31; as strategic
buffer, 314, 321; trade with, 145,
316–20; wars against, 7, 14, 27, 39,
130, 143, 276–79, 281, 283–84, 295,
304–5, 316, 321

Paar, Counts, imperial postmasters, 88
Paderborn, bishopric of, 59
Palatinate, electorate of, 281, 306; and
Thirty Years' War, 288, 301–4

Papacy: and electoral mediations,
289–91; and Turkish wars, 277
Pardubice (Pardubitz), 146
Paris: and the Enlightenment, 186,
190, 201
Passarowitz (Pozeravac), Treaty of
(1718), 145, 315, 318
Passau: bishopric of, 28, 47; Contract
of, 63
Petri, Barnhard, 149
Pfefferkorn Affair (1508), 73
Philip II, king of Spain (1556–98), 31
Philip IV, king of Spain (1621–1665),
36
Physiocracy: in the monarchy, 11, 182,
191, 222, 235, 254, 256–57, 266
Piarist religious order, 57, 124
Pietism, 242
Poland: and electoral mediation, 291;
manorial services in, 156, 160;
Saxon succession in, 304–5;
strategic value of, 276–78, 313;
vulnerability of, 281
Polish Succession, War of (1733–38),
283
Polizei, 10, 12, 79, 84, 191–92, 195–
201, 256, 267. *See also* Cameralism
Pomerania, duchy of, 282, 298, 303
Poor relief, 8–11, 229–51 passim.
Pottendorf (Lower Austria), 148, 150,
220
Pragmatic Sanction (1713), 8, 295
Prague: archbishopric of, 29, 231;
defenestration of, 4; Jews of, 73,
79; Peace of (1635), 37, 302
Privy Conference, 275
Protestantism, in the monarchy, 4,
12–13, 30, 32–33, 39, 45–46, 57,
60, 86
Prussia, duchy of, 293, 298, 300–301,
304; kingdom of. *See* Brandenburg-
Prussia
Puchberg, Johann Matthias, 188

Pufendorf, Samuel, 294
Pyrenees, Peace of (1659), 289

Quesnay, François (1694–1774),
    physiocrat, 191

Raab, Franz Anton, 144–45, 152, 234
Rájec (Raiz), 150
Ratibor, duchy of, 300
Reformation Commissions, 44–46, 53,
    61
Regensburg, expels Jews, 76
Restitution, Edict of (1629), 34, 59, 64,
    288, 302
Rheinbund, 290 (1658)
Ried, Baron, diplomat, 264
Rinck, Gottlieb, 110
Rittenhain (Pusterthal), poor relief in
    246–48
Robot (or *Frondienst*), 43, 151–52,
    155–70, 175–78, 234
Römheld, Ferdinand, industrialist,
    146
Romania, 277; Banat Romanians,
    315–16
Rosthorn, Matthew, entrepreneur, 148
Rottenburg (Further Austria), 259
Rudolph II, Emperor (1576–1612), 3,
    28, 87, 123, 130, 283, 301; and the
    Jews, 73, 76; and Protestantism,
    31, 33, 40
Russia: alliances with, 277–78, 283–
    84; and the Balkans, 314, 317; and
    Polish partitions, 277
Ryswick, Treaty of (1697), 292

Salm-Reifferscheidt, Hugo Altgraf zu,
    150
Salzburg: archbishopric of, 28, 57;
    university of, 57
Sancta Clara, Abraham à, court
    preacher, 87, 129–30
St. Florian, monastery, 90;

St. Gallen, monastery, 263
St. Georgen, monastery, 259
St. John of Nepomuk, 90
Šaštin (Sassin), 146, 220
Savoy, duchy of, 277
Saxony, electorate of: acquires royal
    crown, 28 1, 293, 305; after Thirty
    Years' War, 288; and Austrian
    cameralists, 185, 187, 192, 198;
    Austrian relations with, 277, 279;
    relationship with Brandenburg,
    299–304, 306
Scharnweber, Johann Ludwig
    Friedrich, economist, 268
Schemnitz (Banská Štiavnica), 224
Schillig, Florentinus, preacher, 132
Schlettwein, Johann August,
    physiocrat, 257
Schönborn, Johann Philipp, arch-
    bishop-elector of Mainz, 289–91
Schönbrunn, palace, 97
Schröder, Wilhelm von (1640–88),
    cameralist, 142, 191
Schwarzenberg family, 142, 151;
    Adam, 301; Joseph II, 150–51
Schwechat (Lower Austria), 145, 218, 322
Schweighofer, Johann, publicist, 320
Schweitzer, David, preacher, 126–27
Schwiebus, Silesian enclave, 304
Seckau, Martin Brenner, bishop of, 45
Seibt, Karl Heinrich, pietist, 242, 244
Serbia, 277, 284, 317
Seven Years' War (1756–63), 283–84;
    impact of, 238–39
Sigismund, king of Poland, 289
Sigismund of Luxemburg, Emperor, 29
Silesia, duchy of: Counter-Reformation
    in, 6, 46; Habsburg consolidation
    of, 282, 300–301, 304; manufactur-
    ing in, 149; Protestantism in, 86;
    seizure of, by Prussia, 306
Silesian Wars (1740–45), impact of,
    238–39

Simon of Trent, 73

Sind, Christian, merchant, 145

Sinzendorf, Georg Ludwig, *Hof-kammer* president, 141

Sinzendorf, Philipp Joseph (1726–88), 183, 187, 189–90, 199, 208

Slavkov (Austerlitz), 146

Slovakia (or Upper Hungary), 146, 224; manorial conditions in, 155–56, 178

Smith, Adam, 190, 255

Sonnenfels, Joseph (1733–1817), 10–11, 143–44, 181–82, 188–89, 253–54; and German language, 181, 197–98; limitations on, 195–202, 204

Sozialdisziplinierung, 66, 119–34

Spain: Habsburg, 275–77; influences Austrian cameralists, 186–87, 189–90; seeks electoral mediation, 290–91

Spanish Succession, War of (1701–14), 280–81, 293, 305

Speyer, diet of (1526), 31

Sporck, Count, 6

Stettin (Szczecin), 305

Stockach (Further Austria), 260

Stormont, Lord, British ambassador, 151

Strasbourg (Strassburg), bishopric of, 58

Styria, duchy of: manorial conditions in, 158–60, 171; Protestantism in, 4, 30, 40. *See also* Inner Austria

Sumptuary laws, 116, 123–24, 229

Swabia, imperial circle, 253, 255, 260, 261, 262–64, 266; principalities of, 253–55, 258–60, 262–64. *See also* Further Austria

Sweden: decline of, 305; rivalry with, 277, 281; and the Thirty Years' War, 61, 287, 301–3

Switzerland, trade with, 258–64

Temesvár (Timişoara), 315; Commercial Society, 316

Theresianum, 193, 195, 197, 203

Thomasius, Christian, 5

Thornton, John, entrepreneur, 150

Toleration, Edict of (1781), 57

Transylvania, principality of: colonization of, 284; during Thirty Years' War, 278; poor expelled to, 243

Trattner, Johann Thomas, publisher, 188

Trent: bishopric of, 28; Council of, 32, 54–56, 58

Triberg (Breisgau), 259, 271

Trier, electorate of, as peace mediator, 289–90

Trieste, 13, 208, 231; as commercial gateway, 186, 314, 318

Triple Alliance, 277 (1882), 290 (1668)

Troppau, duchy of, 231, 301

Tschoffen, Bernhard von, entrepreneur, 147–48

Tucker, Joshua, economist, 190

Tull, Jethro, entrepreneur, 187

Turgot, Anne Robert Jacques (1727–81), physiocrat, 187, 190, 202, 235

Turkey. *See* Ottoman Empire

Tuscany, grand duchy of, 283

Tutzer, Georg, 247–48

Twenty Years' Truce (1684), 278

Tyrol, county of: and customs union, 234–35; Jews of, 74; poor relief in, 247–48

Ulloa, Bernardo de (1690–1750), mercantilist, 189, 200

Ulm, Baron von, 262

Upper Austria, archduchy of: Counter-Reformation in, 41, 44, 46, 60–62; estates, 42, 51, 60; the poor in, 230, 243; manorial conditions in, 155–59, 161–65; Protestantism in, 30

Upper Rhenish Circle, 253; principalities of, 260
Ursuline religious order, 57
Utraquists, 29
Utrecht, Treaty of (1713), 292–93
Uztáriz, Gerónimo de (1670–1732), mercantilist, 189–90, 200

Venice, republic of, 16, 277, 289, 318
Verneuerte Landesordnung (1627), 42
Victor Amadeus II, duke of Savoy (1675–1730), 112
Vienna, bishopric of, 28, 38; Armeninstitut of, 245–47; banks, 142, 145, 150–51; Enlightenment currents in, 188, 193, 199, 266; expels Jews, 78; grain supply for, 166, 168; as Habsburg capital, 38, 87, 95; and the high baroque, 94; and the poor, 145, 229–31, 243; manufacturing in, 141, 147–48; siege of, 89, 97, 278; university of, 61, 195, 197, 204
Villingen (Further Austria), 259
Vladislav II, king of Bohemia and Hungary (1491–1516), 29
Vojvodina, colonization of, 284
Volmarius, Markus, pamphleteer, 128
Vorlande. See Further Austria

Waldsee (Further Austria), 263–64
Waldstein, Count, entrepreneur, 146

Wallenstein, Albrecht von, 38, 116
Wasener, Ignaz, envoy to London, 207
Welsperg, Philipp, Landvogt, 260, 263, 264
Werow (Galicia), 147
Westphalia, Peace of (1648), 59, 61, 289, 303; impact of, 15–16, 63–64, 279, 286–88, 294; and ius foederis, 288, 291–94
White Mountain, Battle of (1620), 4, 283; aftermath of, 41, 60
Wiener Neustadt, 147; bishopric of, 28
Wohlau, principality of, 282
Workhouses, 133–34, 231, 241–43
Worms, imperial city, persecutes Jews, 75–78
Württemberg, duchy of, 258, 264; after Thirty Years' War, 288
Würzburg, bishopric of, persecutes Jews, 75

Zincke, Georg Heinrich, cameralist, 200
Zinzendorf, Karl (1739–1813), 11, 144, 183, 185, 187–95, 197– 200, 203, 208; at university of Jena, 187, 192
Zinzendorf, Ludwig (1720–80), 11, 144, 183–89, 192–93, 199–200, 203, 208, 221;
Zwiespalten (Upper Austria), 61